Cambridge Papers has maintained a consistently high standard of Christian reflection on contemporary issues.

JOHN STOTT

What a brilliant idea ... the spirit of the Inklings lives on.

ANNE ATKINS, novelist, columnist and broadcaster

They never fail to make connections between biblical principles and current affairs.

THE RT REV JAMES JONES, Bishop of Liverpool

Sometimes provocative, always stimulating, invariably worth reading.

ELIZABETH CATHERWOOD, publisher and editor

The Cambridge Papers are multidisciplinary in scope and I would recommend them to all those interested in applying Christian principles to contemporary social, political, economic and scientific issues.

PROFESSOR BRIAN HEAP, Master of St Edmund's College, University of Cambridge

CHRISTIANITY IN A CHANGING WORLD

BIBLICAL INSIGHT ON CONTEMPORARY ISSUES

Michael Schluter

and the Cambridge Papers Group

Marshall Pickering
An Imprint of HarperCollins*Publishers*

Marshall Pickering is an imprint of
HarperCollins*Religious*
part of HarperCollins*Publishers*
77–85 Fulham Palace Road, London W6 8JB
www.christian-publishing.com

First published in Great Britain in 2000
by Marshall Pickering

1 3 5 7 9 10 8 6 4 2

A catalogue record for this book
is available from the British Library.

ISBN 0 551 03241 3

Printed and bound in Great Britain by
Creative Print and Design (Wales), Ebbw Vale

CONTENTS

Part IV Economics and Finance

Part V Science and Medicine

Part VI History and Providence

Part VII Postmodernism and Culture

Acknowledgements

We wish to thank Roy Clements, who contributed so much to our discussions and to these papers over the first ten years of our meetings, and Gill Smith who undertook all the administration for seven years of publication. We are deeply indebted to them both. We are also grateful to a large number of friends and supporters, including Ian Garrett who for a time was a member of the Writing Group, who have helped to refine our thinking and encouraged us in our endeavours.

Cambridge Papers Writing Group
Cambridge, November 1999

FOREWORD

DAVID JACKMAN

For several years in the 1980s I faced the challenge and opportunity of giving the 'Morning Thought' on a local radio station, sandwiched between the sports results and the weather forecast. Ninety seconds was all I had, but I came to realize that one Christian concept or reaction could be got across, reasonably coherently, if the time was used well. Fifteen years on, I suspect that the sound-bite now rules the airwaves, and that is an even more demanding exercise. Christian comment is required instantly, with a focus and an immediacy many of us find difficult.

The problem is often that our own thinking on particular issues is fuzzy at the edges and muddled in the middle, so that we find it hard to articulate a Christian position, of whatever length or level of detail, with clarity and penetration. In our hectic lives, where reading time, let alone in-depth study time, is increasingly difficult to carve out, Christians are being asked a bewildering array of questions on a wide variety of social, political and ethical issues. We know that there must be biblical principles which are relevant, but we are not always sure of their location or, once found, the validity of our interpretative processes. Thoughtful Christians are also acutely aware of the complexity of specialist knowledge in every field of study today and naturally feel reticent about launching into issues in which a little learning is indeed a dangerous thing.

The tragic result is all too often the muzzling of the biblical voice, so that the opinion-shapers in our culture are able increasingly to brand the Christian position as antiquarian and irrelevant. The danger is that any comments Christians may offer sound naive and simplistic. They become, in effect, a dumbing-down of the profundity of thought and application which is biblical wisdom, and join the file of yesterday's discarded sound-bites.

All of this explains why I thank God for the Cambridge Papers, and why I am delighted that they have been brought together in the present volume. Ever since they first appeared, I have read them with great profit and found them to be an excellent source of biblical insight and practical application. The issues they deal with are contemporary and urgent. The base-line convictions from which they build are thoroughly biblical. The specialist knowledge they contribute and the discussions that follow are well-researched, rigorous and stimulating. They not only make you think, they enable you to do so more biblically, and with greater confidence. Of course, you will not agree with all the positions taken, or be convinced by all the arguments expounded, but that is the whole point of the exercise. What you will find is that your framework is always challenged and often changed, on issue after issue, so that in the end you are much more confident in bringing a distinctively Christian contribution to the debates of our culture, in whatever context you have opportunity to participate.

I warmly commend this collection, with great thanks to the team who, under God, have made a unique contribution both to the thinking and subsequent activity of many Christians over the past decade. And I look forward to the continuation and development of the process of informed debate, which this book represents, on into the new century, with all the challenges, seen and as yet unseen, which it will undoubtedly produce.

David Jackman
Director
The Cornhill Training Course, London

INTRODUCTION

The Fullest Context

MICHAEL OVEY

There is no longer a Christian mind. The Christian mind has suc-
cumbed to the secular drift with a degree of weakness and nerveless-
ness unmatched in Christian history. It is difficult to do justice in words
to the complete loss of intellectual morale in the twentieth-century
Church.[1]

Harry Blamires

Origins

Originally things were very impromptu. We would meet at Michael
Schluter's house (he was our convenor) and one of us would bring
in an idea which the others would run with, develop and test as
best we could, but always aiming to think Christianly. That was
prompted in part because we each felt the force of Blamires' challenge about the 'Christian mind'. We were all Christians from various denominations and academic disciplines, yet our nagging
suspicion was that Christian thinking was not being brought to
bear on our particular fields. Certainly Christians were working
and thinking very hard in those fields. But we were not aware of distinctively Christian contributions arising from a biblically formed
mind-set. This could almost suggest that Jesus was not the Lord of
all creation, or if he was, then in many modern disciplines he was
sadly dependent on secular help.

Another troubling feature was that secular 'help' seemed increasingly feeble anyway, because of a growing inability to locate our
wealth of information in a viable context or framework, to put a

piece of information in its appropriate 'place'. Modernism had once claimed – vociferously – to provide just such a context for our knowledge: the overarching power of objective human reason to find truth, not with external help from God, but by dispassionate inquiry. Yet this 'objective' human-centred context proved unsustainable when the work of thinkers like Michael Polanyi[2] showed the irreducibly personal, subjective element in human knowing.

Yet post-modern thinking itself fares little better. For its mood is one where a complete account of our condition (a meta-narrative in the jargon), seems implausible, so that any context for our knowing seems fractured and partial, unable to account for why we know what we know or what the real significance of our knowledge is. This loss of context or framework presents a real difficulty for us: how can we rightly value and use what we know without a full context within which to see and understand our knowledge? For a piece of information without its full context threatens to become information without full significance. Our current culture has an ocean of facts, but is finding navigation increasingly difficult.

We perceived a genuine need here for a distinctive, biblically-based contribution from Christians. Before us, of course, was the example of John Stott's book *Issues Facing Christians Today*,[3] and as time went on, we became more structured in our meetings, with a paper being presented to spark reflection. Later we came across others wanting to consider the kinds of questions which concerned us (even if differing from our conclusions). That encouraged us to publish our writing under the title *Cambridge Papers*. We happened to be in Cambridge and were aware of a concern in Cambridge, dating back to the Puritans and before, to relate the Bible to all of life's issues rather than only some. We adopted more self-disciplined procedures, so that each paper went through several drafts and rounds of uninhibited discussion before publication. To that extent any paper really is collaborative, even though the fundamental view comes from an individual mind, and indeed may not command unanimous support. That individuality is reflected in the choice of topic, ranging from law to economics to the philosophy of science as well as more traditional theological questions such as providence or the Trinity. But always attempting to think Christianly – if you like, trying to think God's thoughts after him on a far broader range of issues than just the physical sciences to which that dictum was originally applied.

Thinking God's Thoughts...?

But what does it mean 'to think Christianly' on these highly contemporary topics? Two very different groups are uneasy here: avowedly secularizing thinkers and Christians themselves. For many secularists, Christianity seems to have no contribution to make, either because bringing Christian belief to bear puts the search for truth in danger by biasing dispassionate inquiry, or because it is oppressive to use what is only one perspective amongst many in a 'totalizing' way.

Christian Misgivings about Christian Engagement

Christians too can fight shy of this kind of engagement, and not merely because of other-worldly blindness. Some weighty theological arguments are at stake. In fact, they are weightier than is sometimes thought, and so deserve a detailed rehearsal. It is argued, quite rightly, that Romans 1:18–23 describes how sin affects the mind, as well as other features of the human person. Everyone, Jesus excepted, sins (Romans 3:23), and hence suffers from a corruption of the mind. It is the work of the Holy Spirit to overcome this, at any rate in relation to knowing the truth about Jesus (1 Corinthians 12:1–3). To insist, therefore, on the need for rational argument on secular topics with secular people, even from a Christian position, seems dubious. Why? For at least three reasons.

First, because of the impact on the doctrine of God's revelation. Such purely 'rational', or rather rationalist, argument can open the door to mere rational discourse, on its own, without the aid of God's Spirit, conveying God's truth. This suggests that we can do theology viably and responsibly independent of God's revelation – in other words, a 'natural' theology.

Secondly, this approach affects the doctrine of salvation by God's grace alone. For, if mere rational discourse, on its own, can convey God's truth, then sin seems not to be genuinely enslaving. If one can, without God's grace, think with purity, then why can one not ultimately act with purity? And if so, this argument suggests, then we have forgotten that salvation has to be by grace and not by works.

Thirdly, and perhaps most obviously, there is what one might call the fear of drinking foreign water. Here the thought is that if we start meeting secular thought in this kind of way, we may take on much that is harmless and even useful, but eventually we end up imbibing some idea that is genuinely wrong and dangerous. Moreover, because secular ideas are not located in their proper theological framework, it is harder to deal with such foreign bodies. Thus basic theological hygiene requires minimal traffic between theology and secularized disciplines. For these reasons, then, some suggest that Christian belief should not contribute in the way *Cambridge Papers* attempts.

This is all somewhat ironic. Theology was once called the queen of the sciences. But the sciences have long been republican, while even some faithful theologians advocate abdication.

A Christian Knowledge of God and the World

So how can we as Christians contribute? Much of the Christian argument outlined above carries conviction, but still needs supplementing with further biblical considerations, which nuance the picture considerably. In fact, Romans 1:18–23 is predominantly concerned with the knowledge of God, and is not a general account of all human knowledge. This contextual limitation appears in v. 19 – '…what can be known about *God*' [my italics]. And the discussion then proceeds on the basis of a sinful ignorance, or ignoring, of God, not sinful ignorance more generally. This prompts the thought that Romans 1 does not expressly state that sin equally devastates all our knowledge, including knowledge of things other than God, although its effects may go beyond God.

Other biblical material suggests humans can genuinely know things other than God quite naturally. Job 28:1–11[4] brings this out. It uses the example of mining, and the human ability to uncover and use the resources of the natural world. Humans can come to know their world and therefore direct it. This lies very close to the Creation mandate of Genesis 1:28–30, and clearly knowledge helps humans exercise dominion in God's world. It is noteworthy too that this position of responsible dominion is retained even after the Fall (Genesis 9:1ff.). If the dominion is retained, it is no surprise that the knowledge is too.

However, part of the fascination of Job 28 is that after the celebration of human ability and knowledge with respect to created things, vv. 12–28 speak of human inability, the inability by ourselves to discern wisdom. Now wisdom in the Old Testament is certainly complex, but it does include the idea of an overarching framework within which to view life in God's creation. It is, so to speak, knowing creation in its fullest context.[5] Unfortunately for creaturely knowledge, that kind of ultimate context is only available to the Creator. Hence for the creature, the only route to knowing creation in its fullest context is to turn to the God who created. This is indeed the perspective of Job 28: God alone knows wisdom in this sense (v. 23), but in his mercy communicates it (v. 28).

This, then, suggests a nuanced account of the effect of sin on knowledge. Much depends on the object of knowledge. We do not know God our Creator (Romans 1:18–23), but we may know objects within his creation and know them usefully (Job 28:1–11). The Bible gives an integrated account of us as knowers, the objects of our knowledge, and even why there is something that we do not naturally know. However, even our knowledge of creation is shorn of its ultimate purpose and meaning, for it is removed from its final, fullest context: it is decontextualized knowledge, although still valuable.

Workable Secular Knowledge in a Christian Framework

Where does this leave secular knowledge? Three things follow. First, secular knowledge is possible, but decontextualized, because it is ignorant of our triune Creator. The problem with any decontextualisation is that while it may be harmless, it can also be highly misleading. Theology the queen of the sciences? Yes, for only so can the sciences find their fullest meaning: she is a benevolent monarch.

Secondly, secular knowledge works with borrowed capital. The borrowed capital is the capacity for knowledge that relates to our position as holders of dominion over God's creation and the knowability of a cosmos created for that dominion. Secular knowledge works – without acknowledgement – because of a Christian creation. Indeed, secular knowledge can work very well and may therefore have much to teach on many levels. One can use a gift without recognizing the giver. Conversely, the more explicit and consistent its denial of a Christian creation, the less knowledge coheres, for the gift itself is then being denied. Jettisoning any working capital, even borrowed capital, can lead to bankruptcy. The queen of the sciences, though, to extend the metaphor, is a benevolent monarch providing viable working capital for knowledge, whether her subjects acknowledge it or not.

Thirdly, this suggests something about the relationship between secular knowledge and Christian thought. Secular thought 'works' through its unacknowledged borrowed capital from a Christian creation. This, though, suggests that common rational discourse between Christian and secularist is not taking place on the secularist's territory, nor on some 'neutral' meeting-ground, but on Christian territory, on which the secularist is unconsciously standing. For a Christian, meeting secular thought on the basis of common rational discourse is a match played at home. But the Christian must also recall that secular knowledge is to be set in its fullest context, its theological context. When the Christian does this, she or he is most able to evaluate that secular contribution effectively and constructively, winnowing out what is falsified, but gratefully and humbly accepting what the fullest context endorses.

An 'In-house' Answer?

Now, it will be objected that this is a Christian answer to a Christian objection. Let us turn then to secularists, whether modernist or post-modernist. For the modernists, one naturally sympathizes with their defence of rationality. Naturally, for a Christian account of Creation stresses this too. But modernist rationalism is indefensible. Scientists, to take the paradigm profession of modernism, also have inescapable personal perspectives, even at work. Yet they still attain knowledge. Clearly, then, perspective does not in itself exclude knowledge. The point has often been made but bears repetition: it is not so much having a perspective which is the problem, but which perspective one has. And there are good reasons for accepting that Christianity does provide the right perspective, the fullest context.

For the post-modernists, one appreciates both their emphasis that human knowers are not 'neutral' and their stress on what relativizes knowledge. However, our problem is worse than they think. A nostalgic aroma of modernism clings to some post-modern thinking, for it has not grasped the full depth of what relativizes and skews our knowledge; not just time, place, race, gender, class, amongst others, but the problem of our rebellion against our Creator. And it is that supremely relativizing factor that makes one sceptical of dismissing the Christian context as 'totalizing'. The dismissal is too self-interested. And the question is not simply, is Christian discourse 'totalizing', but rather, is it true?[6] For a Christian, without that understanding of the sinful relativity of our knowledge, it is difficult either to demonstrate the validity of post-modern contributions, or to challenge and supplement their views where that is necessary.

So, to Christian and secularist alike, we find ourselves committed to offering analyses on various issues which try to set them in the fullest possible context, that of our Creator and Redeemer, and we reproduce some of those analyses here[7]. This is a distinctively Christian contribution, since it is Christians who are committed to God's self-revelation in Jesus Christ through the pages of the Bible. We think the contribution helpful and, we find in our own discussions, deeply explanatory of the world we meet. We also think it necessary and hope readers will see the principle as valid, even where we ourselves have applied it imperfectly.

1   Harry Blamires, *The Christian Mind* (SPCK, 1963), p. 3.
2   E.g Michael Polanyi, *Personal Knowledge: Towards a Post-Critical Philosophy* (Routledge & Kegan Paul, corrected edition, 1962).
3   John Stott, *Issues Facing Christians Today* (Marshall Pickering, revised edition, 1990).
4   I take it that Job 28 is in fact an editorial reflection inserted between Job's speeches in chs 26–27 and 29–31.
5   Cf. L.G. Perdue, *Wisdom and Creation: the Theology of Wisdom Literature* (Abingdon Press, 1994) p. 341.
6   To dismiss all truth questions as irrelevant is itself a form of tyrannical 'totalizing' discourse.
7   The papers span a period of eight years. Particular allusions may reflect the circumstances of original composition some years ago. We have, however, largely kept their original form since particular examples were used to illustrate more general points and much of their argument is deliberately at the level of principle rather than based on, say, the latest statistical data.

PART I

HUMAN IDENTITY AND SEXUALITY

Chapter 1

THE HUMAN IDENTITY CRISIS

Can We Do without the Trinity?

MICHAEL OVEY

Summary

This chapter examines contemporary problems surrounding human identity and discusses their causes and consequences. It analyses the claim that Trinitarian doctrine is now redundant and argues that, far from being a mere parlour game, it alone allows the perfect personal characteristics of the God revealed in the Bible to be fully expressed. The doctrine also confronts the tendencies both to individualism and uniformity which characterize Western societies, thereby providing an essential justification for the identity and value of humanity.

Preface

'Mirror, mirror, on the wall, who is the fairest of them all?' The Stepmother from *Snow White and the Seven Dwarfs* is an unlikely place to start a discussion of the Trinity, but there is something fascinating about her question. It is not enough for her to have her own opinion about her beauty. Above all she craves objective knowledge of herself, something which only someone other than she herself can provide. The mirror in the tale witnesses truthfully to who she really is, and accordingly she needs it to know her place in the world. On her own, she lacks, so to speak, definition.

The Problem of Who We Are

Perhaps unflatteringly, we share this question with the Stepmother. Of course, this is a perennial question since it deals with a permanent human problem. Yet the end of the twentieth century poses it exceptionally acutely. It is worth reflecting which features today make this so. Two are of particular interest here:

Individualism

One of the most striking aspects of modern life is the place of the individual. The individual is often increasingly isolated as communitarian dimensions to life become more difficult to protect.

Naturally, this has its attractions, since the burden of responsibility is often lessened as the social bond dissolves. This offers very considerable freedom of action, but what we observe goes beyond the simple fact or phenomenon that late twentieth-century life is individual: it is also individualist. The fact is ideologically justified – individualism is a creed.

In practice, this creed means I am ultimately answerable to myself, not others. My first duty is to my own self, an attitude resonating with a market-oriented culture. But there is a price: others too owe a duty to themselves in the first instance; they are not primarily accountable to me. In that sense individualism is a lonely creed.

Uniformity

Paradoxically, a trend to uniformity coexists with individualism. Modern lifestyles have tended to create a global, mass culture in which differences are gradually eliminated. You can have McDonald's fries in New York, Moscow and Bangkok. Even languages, those badges of human cultural diversity, are becoming extinct as a global culture puts a premium on relatively few languages.

However, in such a climate it becomes increasingly difficult to see what makes any given human individual unique. He/she has so much in common with such huge numbers of others that they seem interchangeable. Indeed, twentieth-century culture, with its drive for efficiency and convenience, has a vested interest in uniformity. Interchangeability among the workforce can seem highly desirable to an employer, and having the 'standard' customer makes for streamlining.

The Causes of Our Problem

Of course, no factor is solely responsible for these features of life. It is only possible to scratch the surface of what has contributed to our present situation. But a number of different factors require comment.

Modern Lifestyle

A combination of trends and developments makes modern life distinctive and contributes to both our individualism and our uniformity. Whatever the original intention, our patterns of work and leisure in large, fluid and anonymous cities can make us remote from extended family. Close friendships can become temporary. This tends to create isolated and atomized individuals.

Moreover, family breakdown and a careerist ethic can so focus attention on identity as a function of work that broader questions about the individual are submerged. As work emerges as the central function for an individual's life, and since that work is often far from unique, the differences between individuals can sink from view. It is no surprise to see the individual him/herself becoming merely one of many in a mass, global culture. Personal relationships tend to become dispensable and the individual can become insulated from others and, indeed, insular.

Reductionism

Our understanding of the mechanics of our universe has increased and we are more and more able to 'reduce' events by providing explanations in terms of more and more basic scientific laws. This type of reduction is, of course, a perfectly proper part of the scientific method. Yet with this has also come a different type of reductionism, an ideological tendency to say that philosophically 'all' we are is nothing but a collection of organs, or a collection of atoms: our existence has no transcendent or metaphysical dimension. This type of reductionism is the ideology of 'nothing buttery'.

This reductionism takes many forms. At a popular level psychology has been seen as reducing human beings to a bundle of instincts, conditioned reflexes and neuroses, a crude behaviourism, in which it is redundant to talk of a coherent 'self'. More radically, others argue that we are simply biological machines for propagating our genes. Going still further, we could be analysed as conglomerations of subatomic particles whose activity is governed by the fundamental laws of physics.

Reductionism of this type could be criticized on several grounds, but for present purposes it is worth noting that it 'levels' humanity out: there is nothing intrinsically different between different members of the human race. Indeed, there is no intrinsic difference between us and the rest of the universe.

The significance of this for twentieth-century attitudes is profound. It provides a reason, in fact something like a moral justification, for treating individual human beings as essentially interchangeable. One is very much the same as another, since all can be reduced to the same basic constituents. It legitimates the uniformity of our culture.

Western Philosophical Tradition

Some aspects of mainstream Western philosophy can also prove less than beneficial. There has been a tendency to seek answers to human identity by looking at individuals as individuals, self-contained and self-existent, with no necessary contact or communion with others.

This is deeply rooted. Boethius is an example, with his assertion that a person is an individual substance of a rational nature. This stresses the individual both as self-contained and also as purely rational. Descartes continues this approach in stating: 'I think, therefore I am.' This is clearly ego-centred since all inquiry starts with me, the thinker, and that inquiry needs no external input.

A successor in this tradition of the self-existent 'I' is Kant. Kant was attempting to meet David Hume's scepticism about our knowledge of the physical world. To do this, he investigated the faculty of human reason, which involved looking at how 'I' perceive the world and my abilities and my limitations in doing that. But in starting there, Kant finds it difficult to verify that the human mind can indeed scrutinize its abilities and limitations correctly. If this were verifiable then, of course, the Stepmother in *Snow White* would not require the external aid of her mirror: she would know herself. If only she had read her Kant …

Disconcertingly, this philosophical tradition provides an ideological underpinning for both individualism and uniformity.

Thus, if the self is approached in terms of a self-contained, self-explaining entity, then others are in some ways irrelevant to that self. Indeed, verifying the existence of other 'selves' is problematic. I know that I am rational since I can observe my own mental processes (following Boethius) but I cannot observe others in the same way.

This tends to justify me in holding myself accountable only to myself: after all, I can only speak for myself as definitely being an individual. Tragically, though, this has a corollary: as an ideological individualist I can have no call on others; I have conceded they are unaccountable to me.

However, this philosophical tradition can also legitimate uniformity when developed slightly differently. If I assume that what makes me 'human' is my rationality and that others actually do exercise rationality, then what makes me different from all of them? One Apple Mac computer is very like another. Others share my 'human' faculty almost indistinguishably.

What is so potent about these three influences is not their individual impact. Rather, they form a cocktail of influences, in which social facts and ideology combine together and reinforce each other to produce a culture in which individual definition becomes extremely problematic and in which human identity becomes, in practice, epiphenomenal: something that, if there, is secondary and not an essential part of the basic model.

The Results

Civic Relationships: Fragility of Human Rights

Given these twin features of individualism and uniformity, the basis for human rights to be enjoyed by all starts to become fragile. After all, on an individualist level, if I am a self-contained, self-existent ego, why should I bother with your rights at all? My world is complete without you, and respecting your rights or invading your rights are equal options, dependent on my personal sovereign choice alone. What is more, on a uniformity basis, there is nothing in you which cannot be replaced by another creature from the global community: your value is undercut.

We naturally resist such conclusions, and historically have attempted to ground rights pragmatically: I demand and assert certain rights but am willing to accord reciprocal rights to others in exchange for those rights so that society can function. The difficulty here is our inclination to freeload, to demand our 'rights' while trying to withhold the 'rights' of others. And pragmatism cannot ultimately provide a moral framework to say this is wrong.

Transcendent Relationships: the Exclusion of God

Naturally, a society that has bought heavily into ideological individualism puts the self at the centre of the universe. This means that God cannot be treated 'as God' (Romans 1:21), because to treat God as God must include seeing him as the centre of existence rather than ourselves. Moreover, reductionism tends to deny either the existence of God or the necessity of relationship with him: if I am truly 'nothing but' atoms and molecules, it seems farcical to demand that it is necessary for me to know God and enjoy him for ever.

Dispensing with the Trinity?

At first glance the doctrine of the Trinity appears to deal with a completely different area of thought, the nature and person of God rather than the character of being human. The only thing in common, some would argue, is that Trinitarian doctrine is equally an 'add-on', a non-essential: an epiphenomenal dogma.

In recent years several considerations, even though hardly Christian orthodoxy, push us in this direction.

First, there is the sheer difficulty of explanation. The old joke is that in mathematics one plus one plus one is three, while in theology one plus one plus one is one. And it is argued that something so difficult to believe and comprehend makes evangelism more difficult. Moreover, it may make us dishonest as we insist on something that we do not clearly comprehend ourselves.

Second, there are the demands of interfaith dialogue. The Trinity is such a distinctively Christian doctrine that it prevents co-operation with the monotheistic religions of Islam and Judaism, and with monist streams in Hinduism and Buddhism too. And, the argument runs, we could happily jettison the Trinity as a non-essential, or refrain from mentioning it in polite interfaith company.

Third, the doctrine stems from a view of Jesus as fully and uniquely divine, which can only separate us from a secular world which would like to embrace Christian ethics, and from other faiths which, like us, want to oppose the materialism and inhumanity of modern life.

Fourth, it is said that the doctrine is a post-biblical development, only one of a number of theological 'options' available on the biblical material.

Nevertheless, dispensing with the Trinitarian doctrine of God has a very high price tag.

The Personhood of God

If God is not Trinitarian, but is still the sole God who is uncreated and eternal, and therefore without any existing personal relationships within his own being, then we end up having to say some very odd things about his nature. One of two things must be true:

On the one hand we could say that he simply does not have personal relationships. He did not have them before creation and creation has not altered this: whatever his relationship is with creation, it would not be personal. He is in fact incapable of personal relationships. Rather, his relationship with creation resembles that of a giant supercomputer towards the objects of its thought or that of electricity towards the object it affects.

However, this creates unpalatable consequences. If we are capable of personal relationships, this means we have a capacity, not inherently immoral, which God does not, a bizarre result for an omnipotent God. Or we could conclude that, since we are in God's image, our own claims to personal relationships are in fact as illusory as his.

On the other hand, we could say that God is only potentially personal. Before creation he had no personal relationships and only started to have them when he embarked on creation. On this view God is having to find out about relationships as he goes along (scarcely an encouraging thought). But this view leaves us with an acute dilemma:

if God was self-sufficient before creation (as the major monotheistic traditions maintain) then personal relationship is not essential for him; he does not need it: it is epiphenomenal, and at rock bottom God is impersonal, which leaves us with a picture which differs little from the first option above.

if God was not self-sufficient before creation, but was essentially personal, and had to create the universe in order to complete himself, then our relationship with him is obviously not what, for example, Paul depicts in Acts 17:24–7, where Paul insists on God's complete independence of creation. He becomes a God who needs us and depends on us in order to fulfil himself. That would put us in a position to bargain (we will love him if he drops the adultery clause from the Decalogue).

Whichever non-Trinitarian course one takes here, we are left with a lesser God, because we are left with a God for whom personhood is unsatisfied in his essential being before creation.

That in turn creates other tensions. John (one of the most explicitly 'Trinitarian' of the New Testament writers) speaks of God as love (1 John 4:8). And in this he is speaking of God's essential being. But it is hard to see how this could be true if God is either impersonal or not essentially personal. Moreover, the love of the biblical God towards us is free and gracious. Indeed, our salvation depends on that very quality (Romans 5:6–8), and it is one we are called to imitate. Yet the character of God's love, if there at all, changes if God is not Trinitarian: it becomes self-seeking and conditional, because God needs our love in order to complete himself.

However, it is not just God's loving character that is affected. Other fundamental aspects of God's character become problematic, too. For instance, the Bible stresses God's faithfulness. But faithfulness is possible only within an existing personal relationship. The same arguments apply to faithfulness as do to love. A non-Trinitarian God means a God for whom faithfulness is either irrelevant, since he is not personal, or else a God who is finding out about faithfulness as he experiences personal relationships with his creation for the first time. This is devastating since it means we do not actually know now that God is permanently faithful – he might turn out not to be. That doubt eats away at the assurance of our destiny with him.

Similarly, Broughton Knox remarks in *The Everlasting God* (Lancer, 1988) that God's character as just also becomes questionable under a straightforward non-Trinitarian monotheism. To be just, Knox argues, requires that there be someone to whom to be just. It certainly is hard to see how a self-existent, not essentially personal being can be properly described as 'just'.

A Diminution of Humanity

If God is not essentially personal, then we too are affected by that. The biblical claim is that we were made in God's image. But as we have seen above, a non-Trinitarian God is at best only potentially personal. In that case, personhood ought only to be potential and non-essential for us too. On that basis, personhood really is only epiphenomenal for us, just as it is with God.

That again would have implications for the values of personal identity: they cannot be as fundamental as all that. Rather, it would be more accurate to say that God has created a universe that is sublimely indifferent to these things. That is scarcely desirable since it undermines the importance of maintaining both the rights of individuals and the dignity of the race as a whole. These things we are so keen to protect would be merely interesting accidents of creation, but nothing more.

The Relevance of the Trinity

In fact, the Bible presents a picture of God which inevitably pushes us in a Trinitarian direction. God is consistently portrayed as personal (to love and to be faithful are personal qualities). But he is also portrayed as complete in himself, needing nothing from creation, us included. For this to be true his nature must be such as to enable those personal attributes to be actual before creation and not merely potential.

This is indicated in passages like John 1:1ff., Hebrews 1:1ff. and Colossians 1:15–20, which speak of the *eternal* co-existence of the Son with the Father. The existence of the other person enables these personal qualities to be actual: following Augustine, love requires an object, and the different persons of the Trinity fulfil that. Moreover, as Richard of Saint Victor noted, the fact that there are three and not two persons in the Trinity gives an extra dimension to the personal relationships involved: the Son and Spirit *join* in loving the Father and doing his will. The Spirit and Father *join* in loving the Son, and so on.

As regards God, therefore, the Trinity underlines the *personal* perfection of God: we need this as a guarantee of the perfection of his personal characteristics and of our own security with him.

However, we also need the doctrine to underwrite our own

identities and value. For we are made in the image of God, and therefore an essentially personal God indicates both that we too are created to be personal beings, and also that this aspect of our existence is not epiphenomenal and dispensable. We are given a vital basis for our claims to personhood, and this helps us answer the individualism and uniformity of our own time.

Individualism

In terms of God himself, Father, Son and Spirit, the Trinity means that we do not have a monist or 'individualist' God. For God, personal identity is found in relationships rather than in the kind of self-contained, undifferentiated unity that tends to underlie Boethius, Descartes and Kant. We 'locate' the Father by reference to his relationships with the Son and the Spirit: he himself as Father is, in a way, defined by where he stands with respect to the other persons of the Trinity (Calvin raises this in his *Institutes of the Christian Religion*, Book 1, Chapter 13, section 6). In that way, personal relationships are essential and not optional extras. And this implies for humans made in his image that we know ourselves truly in relationship, not in isolation.

Trinitarian doctrine provides a rationale defending individuality without degenerating into individualism. We can justify the common value of each member of the human race without depending on the notion of the self-contained ego, with the problems that entails.

Uniformity

This Trinitarian understanding also guarantees diversity rather than uniformity. The Son and the Spirit have distinct roles within the Godhead, mirrored, for instance, by the way the Spirit acts as a pointer to the achievements of the Father and the Son (Acts 2:1–11) or the way the Son supremely obeys the will of the Father (e.g. John 17:4). Although equally divine, there is a diversity between the persons: they are not mere clones, nor simply interchangeable. Equality of value does not mean symmetry of role.

It is for this reason that some recent developments of Trinitarian doctrine seem rash. It has been suggested that there is a symmetrical, mutual submission between the persons of the Trinity. This makes the Father completely interchangeable with the Son and the

Spirit in their relationships. That in turn starts to eliminate the individuality of the persons of the Trinity since they are a common coin. Obviously that is not the way the persons appear in salvation history. (Biblically, the Father does not submit to the Son: in fact, 1 Corinthians 15:24 makes it clear that the Father is the final monarch after the general resurrection and the conquest of evil.)

This suggestion is disastrous, both for our doctrine of God, because it tends to make the persons of God contingent and not essential, and also for our doctrine of humanity, because we would be persons in the image of a clone-type God who could not guarantee our unique value as human individuals. (As it happens, this argument emerged during the ordination discussions in order to safeguard the value of women. Ironically, it undercuts their value as human beings.)

However, orthodox Trinitarian doctrine gives a rationale for seeing ourselves as unique individuals rather than as essentially uniform, interchangeable clones. With God, we find that relationships are, as it were, constitutive of us as persons, and our very diversity of relationships indicates a diversity of persons enjoying them. Accordingly, I am not simply substitutable by any other member of the human race in my relationships: someone else could not straightforwardly replace me as friend or parent or spouse or child. Rather, they would form different constitutive relationships in their own right.

In this way the Trinity gives an account of human uniqueness which tends to compel respect for the dignity of each individual. This in turn implies an objectivity to human rights and responsibilities, and the significance of that in a world so often lukewarm to both is obvious.

Conclusion

This means that the Trinitarian account of God is necessary for us. We need it to understand and value both our relationship with him and also our relationships with one another. The Trinity is a uniquely Christian doctrine and underlines what Christian belief contributes to understanding ourselves, our God and our place in his world. In fact, in a world struggling to validate human values, it could be presented as one of the most attractive features of our faith to those outside, a tool for evangelism and a feature of our apologetics, not a disability for which we apologize.

Chapter 2

WOMEN, MEN AND THE NATURE OF GOD

Equality But Not Symmetry

MICHAEL OVEY

Feminists of the Jewish and Christian faiths are faced with a basic dilemma. Are they to be faithful to the teachings of the Hebrew scriptures and the Christian scriptures, or are they to be faithful to their own integrity as whole human beings?[1]

Letty M. Russell, *Feminist Interpretation of the Bible*

Summary

Presuppositions matter in any debate. This chapter looks at a pre-supposition sometimes held in the debate over women's ordination, that God could not by his nature restrict certain roles in churches to men. In the light of the relationship between God the Father and God the Son, it will argue that this presupposition is mistaken.

The full humanity of women is a heart-cry of feminist theology today, and rightly so. But as this quotation indicates, this legitimate concern has sometimes been perceived as hopelessly inconsistent with commonly held biblical interpretations of women's roles. It is suggested, for example, that we must choose between accepting restrictions on women's teaching authority and accepting the full humanity of women. The two are mutually exclusive, it might be said, because to exclude a person from a particular function amounts to denying that person's full humanity.

Humanity in the Image of God

The idea of 'full humanity' is obviously central to this position and has far-reaching consequences. Thus, Margaret Farley remarks that the full humanity of women implies two principles: first, equality (women and men are to be treated as equally human and valued as such) and second, mutuality (humans are relational as well as autonomous and free).[2] Biblically, full humanity is rooted in the creation narrative of Genesis 1 and 2 in which both women and men, uniquely in creation, are made in the image of God (see especially Genesis 1:27). This truth is vital because our own uniqueness in creation as humans is bound up with the image of God: to understand ourselves fully as humans we must understand what it means to be made in the image of God. Only then can we answer the question 'What does it mean to be fully human?' Without answering that question it is extremely difficult to see how to evaluate any distribution of authority, whether between the sexes or otherwise.

This chapter, therefore, takes the widely held starting point that women share full humanity in the light of Genesis 1:27 and must be valued as such. The next step is to look at what the image of God involves. The Bible teaches that God has revealed himself to us not only in the Word of God written but also within creation. To a limited extent the image can be seen in human experience. However, as a result of the Fall of Genesis 3, sin mars that image. Just looking at ourselves, or meditating on what we find within, does not give us an authenticated picture of what the image of God means. Our own experience, therefore, cannot safely be used either as a source or as an absolute criterion of religious truth. Christians of whatever persuasion face this predicament.

The Image of God in Jesus

Instead, we have to look at Jesus. For the biblical teaching is that he is the image of God. He is the image both in his divinity and in his perfect humanity. Seeing him, we do not need to ask to see the Father, for we have seen him in Jesus (John 14:9) who reveals him to us since he is equally divine. Jesus is uniquely the image, for he is divine. At the same time he is the image in that he is the perfect human, for he is sinless, the Adam who did not fall. As such he shows us what it means to be fully human, human as God intended. In him the image of Genesis 1 and 2 remains intact and unmarred. Jesus' humanity is normative humanity: he teaches us, both men and women, how to be fully human.

All this is important for the debate over women's roles due to the implications it may have for traditional interpretations of biblical texts relating specifically to women, such as Ephesians 5 or 1 Timothy 2. Of course, many committed to the supremacy of Scripture have concluded that those traditional interpretations are incorrect: the texts simply do not say what these interpretations suggest. Others accept the interpretations as accurate, but feel that the texts themselves simply cannot be of God because they say something inconsistent with the nature of God. God, so it is said, simply could not say these things, because he is not like that. This chapter is concerned with examining this latter position. To assess its strength we must find out what God is like from elsewhere in the biblical witness, in order to see what could be in accord with the divine nature. The significance of Jesus in this is that he reveals to us both the nature of God and the nature of full humanity. In this way, looking at the nature of God may illuminate what could or could not be conceivable for a humanity made in his image.

These two aspects of Jesus as the revealed image of God are the concern of what follows: first the divine nature of Jesus in relation to God the Father, which is a question of the eternal character of the triune God, and second the perfect humanity of Jesus in relation to other humans.

Jesus and God the Father

It is bedrock orthodoxy to see Jesus as fully divine: as divine as the Father is. Nevertheless, Jesus and God the Father remain distinct persons. This is particularly clear in one aspect of their relationship: the obedience of Jesus. John's gospel, which has such striking incidents as Thomas' confession ('My Lord and my God'), also stresses the sonship of Jesus: he is the obedient Son of God, the one who does his Father's will. This is poignantly clear in his prayers in Gethsemane, ' … not my will but yours …' This father/son language points to distinct persons in the Godhead, as the church fathers observed. Moreover, because it is language of submission to another's will it points to a 'subordination' between Father and Son, yet without derogating from the full equal divinity of Jesus. As the church fathers also found, it is difficult to capture in words this relationship between Father and Son. The word chosen here is subordination, which must be understood, following the fathers, as pointing to a subordination of function and not a subordination of being. Further, the father/son language appears to capture the eternal dynamics of this Trinitarian relationship. The primacy of the Father neither derives from the Father enjoying a higher order of being than the Son nor confers such a superiority. The Word always has been and is equally divine.

This means there can be a permanent relationship between beings who have equal value but asymmetrical roles, for the Son obeys the Father's will and the Father glorifies the Son. There is equality but not symmetry. Reference was made earlier to Margaret Farley's remark that full humanity involved equality and mutuality. So here with full divinity: there is the equal value and mutuality of two persons but their roles are not symmetrical. Yet since the triune God is a perfect being, this must be a perfect relationship. It is, moreover, not incompatible with a relationship of love: the love of God the Father for the Son and the Son for the Father is a continual biblical theme. It is worth stressing that in the biblical view the Father's relationship with Jesus is one of both primacy and love. The Godhead, therefore, shows us that relationships can exist between equals involving subordination but without being necessarily immoral or unloving.

The Relevance of 1 Corinthians 11:3 – Headship as 'Source'?

For many, a central text to support this view comes in 1 Corinthians 11:3.

> The head of every man is Christ, the head of a woman is her husband, and the head of Christ is God.
>
> RSV

A crucial question in construing this passage is whether or not the word for head, *kephale*, imports a note of authority or whether it should simply be taken as meaning 'source'. Some scholars, including some evangelicals, take the view that source is the appropriate sense in that passage.

However, the source translation is not taken here, for a number of reasons. It is certainly true that in extra-biblical literature *kephale* can simply mean source, but when the Old Testament was translated into Greek *kephale* was used at times to import authority. The frequency of this usage is disputed, but the word can have that sense. The question, then, is whether it bears that (some would say unusual) sense in this instance.

The most obvious area of misgiving comes in the implications which the source idea has for the person of Christ. In what sense would Christ be equally divine if the Father was his source? In the other two relationships mentioned in 1 Corinthians 11:3, the head is the source in a temporal sense. There was a time when men were not, and when women were not, but there came a point when their existence was derived from their 'heads'. But to use headship in this way with respect to the Father and the Son makes the Son into a lesser derived being – it would mean that, once, the Son was not, rather similar to Arian thought. This is at odds with other elements of the biblical witness which endorse the idea of the Son's obedience and submission to the Father.

Some would say, perhaps, that Paul is referring to the Son being eternally begotten of the Father, but this has been understood to refer not to an inferiority of being between the two but to the Son's eternally existing relationship with the Father, one of eternal willing submission to the Father in which the authority notion is clearly present. Others would say, possibly, that the words of 1 Corinthians 11:3 refer to the sending of the Son in the Incarnation. But the authority idea certainly is present in the Incarnation. The Son on earth does the Father's will and it is not orthodoxy to believe that the Son ceased to be divine during the Incarnation. If he did, it would suggest that divinity is not an essential attribute but is rather like a snake's skin, something which can be sloughed off leaving the same essential being behind. This would create the paradox that the incarnate Jesus was rightly executed for blasphemy. For he was claiming to be divine during the Incarnation, when he had ceased to be.

Moreover, in Ephesians 5:21–4 Paul uses the head idea in the context of the church's submission to Christ – this seems particularly clear in v. 24 (again, this interpretation is disputed). This text suggests *kephale* as importing authority would not be unparalleled in the Pauline corpus.

Furthermore, in terms of the headship relationship between the man and Christ, a note of authority would by no means be out of place. It does not follow from this that authority would therefore have to be the sense, but it does show that *kephale* as importing authority fits two out of the three pairs of relationships well, whereas in at least one of the pairs (God–Christ) to take *kephale* as source is definitely inappropriate.

For these reasons the traditional interpretation of *kephale* in 1 Corinthians 11:3 is preferred here, so that the headship relationship between God the Father and Jesus the Son, and therefore also between husband and wife, is seen in terms of authority rather than simply source.

Father and Son Are Equals in an Asymmetrical Relationship

Looking at the relationship of Father and Son within the Trinity shows that having different roles in a relationship does not imply necessarily an inferiority of being, even where that difference relates to authority and submission. To say that it necessarily does would logically falsify the eternal Trinitarian relationship of Father and Son. That in turn would suggest that Jesus cannot give us accurate information about God and therefore casts doubt on him as the incarnate God.

In addition, relationships between equal beings without symmetry of function exist elsewhere than between women and men. Complementarity underlies Paul's discussion of the church as a body with different parts, yet there is no hint that one part is inferior to others. For Paul, different roles do not entail diminished value. Moreover, Paul enjoins obedience to church leaders and those in civil authority. In neither case is it suggested that leadership derives from or confers a superiority of being; rather what is at stake is God's right to delegate a degree of authority to others, and his delegates are not chosen because they are higher beings. We do not obey them because they are intrinsically higher beings (although their qualities may make obedience easier) but because of our quite independent obedience to a third party, God.

Is this simply endorsing 'hierarchy'? The Father/Son relationship within the Godhead does indicate a 'hierarchy' of sorts but, crucially, not a hierarchy of being, rather of voluntary submission by an equal to an equal. Nor is it a hierarchy of exploitation but of perfection. It shows there can be 'hierarchies' involving authority where the authority is not intrinsically evil. It is to the question of the nature of authority that we now turn, and it will be examined within the framework of Jesus' relationships with other humans.

Jesus' Exercise of Authority

The gospels show Jesus as a person of authority, able to command nature, demons and, of course, people. His relationships with others are certainly 'mutual' in that they are personal. They involve responsiveness and care, but also authority. However, this is not a domineering authority. Jesus does not lord it as Gentile rulers do, and he instructs his followers that their pattern of authority is to be similarly distinctive too. The model for the exercise of authority is that of a humble servant, strikingly illustrated when he washes his disciples' feet. Christians are in a relationship of submission to Jesus, and yet his promise is that in this relationship we enjoy not a stunted life but life in all its fullness. In that sense, being subordinate, far from diminishing human experience, actually fulfils it. Authority as normatively revealed by Jesus is a relationship not of exploitation but of benefit, since authority is given for serving others, not aggrandizing self.

At this point men, and indeed the church, must recognize that the texts on submission of wives have often been cited to justify authority which has been sinfully perverted from its servant purpose to enforce service on others. This is something that cries out for repentance. If men want to be biblical then they must live out John 13 rather than simply expecting their wives to observe those parts of Ephesians 5 that they as husbands find most congenial. That in itself forces a re-evaluation of stereotypical roles: part of the thrust of the footwashing in John is that Jesus assumes tasks which are genuinely menial. His authority is not used to try and make sure someone else does them. In terms of our present social structures, this servant ideal is no doubt as unwelcome to men as the authority idea is to women: it forces them to look again at things like distribution of domestic labour, or the proper place for their career ambitions ('Do I genuinely want that promotion for the sake of my family?'). Furthermore, if one accepts the principle of 'equality but not symmetry', then that equality must be recognized and defended in, for example, the workplace.

The general failure by men to use authority as God intended calls for repentance and change. But is this not one feature of the general human tendency to pervert authority, a tendency also found in the way men treat men or women treat women? This does not mean that every authority relationship is intrinsically evil or sinful and should be abolished. Rather, we should strive to purify those relationships which involve or require authority.

Concluding Remarks

This chapter has not dealt with all the usual texts discussed in connection with the role of women. It has, therefore, not dealt with the question 'Has God actually established equality but asymmetry between the sexes?' Rather, it has looked at the question 'Could God conceivably establish equality but asymmetry between the sexes?' Given his eternal nature as the Trinitarian God, and given humanity in his image as shown to us by Jesus, it is clear that God could indeed establish asymmetry without denying the equality of the sexes. Indeed, since we are made in the image of this Trinitarian God, equality and asymmetry in our relationships need not be surprising. (Galatians 3:28 is not a bar to this, since its context is not church order or the wider social order but the universal availability of salvation through Christ, and we know that Paul did envisage sexual distinctives being preserved after salvation: marriage, for instance, continues.)

This is obviously relevant for the debate over women's ordination. Space precludes discussing all the relevant texts and issues – for example, what exactly ordination involves, or whether the same considerations apply to 'sacramental' and pastor/teacher ministries. But it is clear that we cannot assume that God, by his very nature, must inevitably be in favour of ordination for both sexes in order to maintain their equal value, as some seem to assume. This means that in answering the question of ordination of women we cannot say, for example, that the traditional interpretation of 1 Timothy 2, confining ultimate responsibility for teaching in the church to men, is so wildly out of character with other parts of the biblical witness that we can safely disregard it. Whether that interpretation is in fact correct is, of course, a separate question. The fear is that in the present climate an erroneous presupposition controlling what God 'must' say about ordination obscures what he actually has said.

It should also be stressed at this point that the traditional interpretation of 1 Timothy 2 is not a blanket ban on women's ministry. It deals with only one aspect of ministerial work. The contribution of women already made and to be made in the future in ministry should not be allowed to disappear from view in the present debate, nor be devalued. On this point, again, men need to reconsider and repent.

We all agree that women and men are made 'in God's image', but our understanding of this phrase must be controlled by God's self-revelation. At this point, far from being trivial the ordination debate touches on the most fundamental ideas about God's nature. Further, taking the image of God as the starting point throws into sharp relief the question 'What is the kind of God you believe in?' Perhaps one of the dangers in this debate is that inadvertently we create our own image of God which conforms to our own cultural presuppositions, rather than ensuring that our image of God is conformed to what Jesus reveals.

1 Letty M. Russell (ed.), *Feminist Interpretation of the Bible* (Blackwell, 1985).

2 Margaret Farley, 'Feminist Consciousness and Scripture' in Letty M. Russell (ed.), *Feminist Interpretation of the Bible* (Blackwell, 1985), p. 45.

Chapter 3

HOMOSEXUALITY

Finding the Way of Truth and Love

CHRISTOPHER TOWNSEND

Biblical judgements against homosexuality are not relevant to today's debate.[1]

Robin Scroggs, *The New Testament and Homosexuality*

Summary

Christians today hold divergent views on homosexuality. This chapter reviews the key biblical material on homosexual practice and considers scientific and theological explanations of the origin of homophile attraction. Finally, an indication is given of the multifaceted response of the gospel to the needs of the homosexual person and the importance of Christian churches being communities of acceptance and friendship.

The Church and Homosexuality

In society at large, recent legal changes have tended to increase 'gay rights'. Parliament has reduced the age of consent for male homosexual intercourse to 18 years and a further reduction to 16 years is on the cards. The European Court of Human Rights has ruled that the armed forces may no longer exclude homosexuals. The House of Lords has decided, in a case concerning inheritance of a tenancy, that a homosexual couple in a stable relationship can be regarded as a family; indeed, in certain parts of the world, 'homosexual marriage' has been recognized in law. The repeal of section 28 of the Local Government Act 1988 (which prohibits the promotion of homosexuality by local authorities) is firmly on the political agenda and, generally, continuing change is expected.

In the churches, homosexuality is debated with increasing intensity and growing divisions of opinion. Until the post-war period, in the long history of the church there were few, if any, dissenting voices to the view that Scripture and nature teach us that homosexual behaviour is, without exception, immoral. The last few decades have seen a reappraisal by academic theologians, heated discussions in denominational bodies, and the emergence of organizations such as the Lesbian and Gay Christian Movement promoting an active homosexual lifestyle as consistent with Christian teaching. Four approaches now represent the wide spectrum of views and attitudes within Christian circles to homosexual behaviour and orientation: 'rejecting–punitive', 'rejecting–compassionate', 'qualified acceptance' and 'full acceptance'.

A 'rejecting–punitive' stance rejects homosexual behaviour and orientation as incompatible with Christianity and, often buttressed by cultural stereotypes, is hostile towards people who are homosexual.

A 'rejecting–compassionate' approach regards homosexual behaviour as contrary to God's creative intent and never permissible for Christians. However, actions and orientation are distinguished and the church is to welcome into the community of forgiven sinners all who will follow Christ – irrespective of sexual orientation.

The position 'qualified acceptance' amounts to saying: the homosexual person is rarely, if ever, responsible for his sexual orientation; the prospects of developing a heterosexual orientation are minimal; celibacy is not always possible; stable homosexual unions may offer the prospect of human fulfilment and are obviously better than homosexual promiscuity. Homosexuality is never ideal because God's intention in creation is heterosexuality; attempts to develop heterosexual desires must be made, but, occasionally and reluctantly, one may accept a homosexual partnership as the only way for some people to achieve a measure of humanity in their lives.

'Full acceptance' stresses the 'unitive purpose' of sexuality as central in God's sight and regards the 'procreative purpose' as, by comparison, incidental. Same-sex relationships can fully express the central purpose for sexuality, so homophile attraction may be affirmed. All sexual acts should be evaluated by their relational qualities: what matters is whether or not a particular relationship or action will enhance human fulfilment, faithfulness between persons, genuine intimacy and mutuality. The gender of the persons concerned is immaterial.

The view reached by Christians on the morality of homosexual behaviour impinges directly on church life, pastoral care and evangelism. The overall contours of theological belief not only shape, but may also be shaped by, the conclusions reached. Much is at stake when we discuss this subject. However, we must speak with care. Much unnecessary pain has been caused by divisive and insensitive remarks. The moral, intellectual and pastoral issues must be considered in the light of all that unites us. Homophile or heterophile, we share a common situation as human beings, sexual beings and sinful beings.

Homosexual Behaviour: Some Key Biblical Texts

There are, in fact, relatively few texts that address directly the issue of homosexual behaviour. The main passages are:

Genesis 19:1–29

Our word 'sodomy' owes its origin to this incident – perhaps inappropriately. The men of Sodom demand that Lot bring out his guests (two angels who look like men) so that they may 'know them' (v. 5, AV). In 1955 D. Sherwin Bailey in *Homosexuality and the Western Christian Tradition* argued that 'know' has no sexual connotation here.[2] His views have been influential – despite the fact that students of the text have on the whole dismissed Bailey's arguments. The word 'know' is, statistically speaking, most often used in a nonsexual sense. However, in several places it refers to sexual relations. The context here all but demands that we understand such an intention – Lot certainly did (vv. 6–8). Nonetheless, disapproval of all homosexual acts cannot be inferred from this passage. The men of Sodom intend homosexual rape. Sexual violence is a key characteristic of Sodom's sexual sin. When 2 Peter 2:7–8 speaks of the 'lawless deeds' of the people of Sodom, the sins condemned are not identified precisely and may or may not include all homosexual behaviour. Jude 7 says that the people of Sodom 'gave themselves up to … perversion' (more literally, 'went after other/strange flesh'). However, Jude may well be referring to Sodom's lusting after the bodies of angels, trying to transgress the boundary between the earthly and heavenly realms.

Leviticus 18:22; 20:13

These verses prohibit sexual intercourse between two men and describe such behaviour as 'detestable'. These prohibitions appear without exception but their scope and intent have been debated. Some maintain that here, as in some other Old Testament passages, the word 'detestable' has cultic connotations. On this view, Leviticus condemns homosexual acts in the setting of idolatrous worship, practices mimicking the pagan worship of the Egyptians and Canaanites. However, both Leviticus 18 and 20 deal with sexual taboos: intercourse with blood relations (e.g. Leviticus 20:17) and adultery (e.g. Leviticus 20:10) are also condemned. This context, and the fact that nowhere else in Leviticus does 'detestable' have cultic overtones, indicates that a general moral proscription is intended.

1 and 2 Samuel

The friendship of David and Jonathan is recorded in language that strikes the modern Western ear as intensely emotional. After David's triumph over Goliath 'Jonathan became one in spirit with David, and he loved him as himself' (1 Samuel 18:1) and the two men bound themselves together in a formal bond of friendship. On hearing of Jonathan's death David laments: 'I grieve for you, Jonathan my brother; you were very dear to me. Your love was wonderful, more wonderful than that of women' (2 Samuel 1:26). Some have concluded that David and Jonathan had a homosexual relationship. Did not their relationship bring 'shame' upon Jonathan's mother (1 Samuel 20:30)? It cannot be denied that David led an active heterosexual life but it is possible he was bisexual. However, this view relies upon extra-biblical parallels, textual emendations and conjecture. There is no hint of erotic behaviour in the biblical text. Jonathan's shame is not linked to his sexuality but to his lack of loyalty to his father and his family line in the dispute between Saul and David. David and Jonathan should be seen as a model of devoted male friendship, intimate and affectionate but not erotic.

Romans 1:18–32

These verses speak of homosexual acts as contrary to nature (vv. 26–7) and one consequence now of God's judgement on human idolatry and rejection of God. The passage does not set out to provide ethical instruction for Christians but has implications for Christian sexual ethics, many of which hinge on the meaning of 'nature' *(phusis)*. Jonathan Boswell in *Christianity, Social Tolerance and Homosexuality* claimed that this 'passage strongly implies that he [i.e. Paul] was not discussing persons who were by inclination gay' and the 'persons Paul condemns are manifestly not homosexual: what he derogates are homosexual acts committed by apparently heterosexual persons'. That is, he disapproves when people act against their own individual 'nature'.[3] But the idea that some individuals have an inherent homosexual disposition and are constitutionally 'gay' is essentially a modern one which took root only in the nineteenth century. Boswell is not leading us to the text's original meaning but imposing anachronistic ideas on it, allowing the concepts of psychology to take precedence over those of theology.

The word *phusis* does not bear a uniform meaning in either the New Testament or extra-biblical literature. At times it means custom, convention or human moral reflection. On this view, Romans 1 would be saying that rebellion against God results in rejection of human moral standards. The implication would be that Christian attitudes today to homosexuality should depend not on views held in Paul's day but on twentieth-century human moral standards. However, a satisfactory interpretation of Romans 1 must recognize that Paul drew on the attitudes and language of Hellenistic Judaism. Hellenistic Jewish thinkers not only viewed homosexual behaviour with abhorrence but tended to link the philosophical category of 'nature' with God's law and creative purpose. This leads us on to the decisive factor in Paul's use of *phusis*, namely his biblical doctrine of creation. In C.E.B. Cranfield's words, by 'natural' and 'unnatural', 'Paul clearly means "in accordance with the intention of the Creator" and "contrary to the intention of the Creator" respectively'.[4] The Creator's intention, unlike human conventions and scientific understanding, does not alter with changes in era or culture.

1 Corinthians 6:9–11; 1 Timothy 1:9-10

Here we read that *arsenokoitai* are among the wicked who will not inherit the kingdom of God (1 Corinthians 6:9–11) and are lawbreakers and rebels, ungodly and sinful (1 Timothy 1:9–10). The meaning of *arsenokoitai* is debated. Some argue that its meaning is restricted, for example, to male prostitutes or pederasts. The linguistic evidence for these views is not strong. The word *arsenokoitai* is a compound of the words for 'male' and 'bed'; it reflects closely the language in the Greek Septuagint version of Leviticus 18:22; accordingly, it appears to refer to anyone who has homosexual intercourse. Had Paul, for example, wished to condemn only pederasty he could have used one of a number of Greek words with this more restricted meaning. The words *arsenokoitai* and *malakoi*, both found in 1 Corinthians 6:9–11, may be intended as complementary terms denoting the whole range of homosexual behaviour, *malakoi* having connotations of passivity and receptivity to homosexual advance and *arsenkoitai* more active connotations.

Conclusion

This review of key passages reveals a consistent antipathy towards homosexual behaviour in both Old and New Testaments. It is striking that the immediate theological context for the New Testament texts involves God's creation (Romans 1:26–7), God's law (1 Timothy 1:9–10) and God's kingdom (1 Corinthians 6:9–11). Love is often championed as the one principle by which sexual conduct should be guided. But biblical ethics has more than one ingredient. The love felt by a man for another man, a woman for another woman, can be as passionate, sensitive and committed as that known by a heterosexual couple. But love, however tender, however faithful, cannot be its own guide. Love, seeking the highest welfare of others, must be informed and shaped by God's purposes for his creation and his kingdom. Nonetheless, some of the key texts are not as straightforward as one might imagine. They must be read in the light of the fundamental principles of a biblical perspective on sexuality. Doing this reinforces the conclusion that biblical judgements, far from relating solely to homosexual practices found in the ancient world, remain indispensable to today's debate.

Human Sexuality: Biblical Foundations

Sexuality, sexual differentiation, sexual intercourse and human procreation are woven into the divine plan for humanity (Genesis 1:26–9). However, the relationship between the first man and woman is given by God for another reason: 'It is not good for the man to be alone' (Genesis 2:18). Marriage, given for companionship, involves leaving, cleaving and becoming 'one flesh' (Genesis 2:24). 'One flesh' refers to the personal union of a man and woman, at all levels of their lives, expressed and deepened through their sexual relationship. The permanent, exclusive relationship of husband and wife is given as the one proper context for sexual intimacy.

In *Church Dogmatics* Barth argued that the image of God in humankind is found in the fellowship of man and woman. To be human is to be 'male or female, male and female'. Scripture nowhere defines the image of God, and Barth probably places too much emphasis on gender and sexuality as integral to the *imago Dei*. Nonetheless, there are important analogies between the differentiation-in-unity of the Trinity and the differentiation of humankind into male and female who find their unity in coming together as one flesh. The marriage of a man and a woman, a bond of fellowship open to procreation, reflects, even symbolizes, the triune, Creator God. To contend that the unitive function of sexual intimacy can be fulfilled in a homosexual relationship is to isolate one aspect of a complex symbol – putting asunder what God has joined together.

The life of Christ shows us that neither a committed, exclusive partnership nor sexual experience is essential to personal fulfilment. Jesus, who lived the only perfect human life, was single and celibate. The need not to be 'alone' may be met through friendships without sexual intimacy. Indeed, while human sexuality is affirmed by the Bible, its significance is also qualified. Our true humanity does not ultimately rest in our sexuality but in fulfilling our capacity for personal communion with God.

Understanding the Origin of Homosexuality

In the 1940s Dr A.C. Kinsey conducted a famous investigation into human sexuality and identified everyone as falling somewhere on a continuum from 0 (an exclusively homosexual bias) to 6 (an exclusively heterosexual bias). Between these poles, people are found with dual, indeterminate or fluctuating sexual orientation. He concluded that 4 per cent of (white American) men are exclusively homosexual throughout their lives, and 10 per cent for up to three years. His research methods have, however, been criticized. The table below presents some findings from a survey funded by the Wellcome Trust.

	Men (%)	Women (%)
Any homosexual contact	6.1	3.4
Includes:		
Any genital contact	3.6	1.7
At least one homosexual partner in last 5 years	1.4	0.6

Source: A. Johnson *et al.*, *Sexual Attitudes and Lifestyle* (Blackwell Scientific Publications, 1994), Chapter 7

Over 90 per cent of men and over 95 per cent of women who had had a partner of the same sex had also had a partner of the opposite sex. Exclusively homosexual behaviour is rare.

Suggested explanations of the origin of homosexual orientation fall into two broad categories: biological and environmental. 'Biological' theories point to genetic and hormonal factors. Some recent studies appear to support such theories. However, the reliability of the studies and the explanatory power of such theories are still under investigation, and disputed, within the scientific community.

'Environmental' theories point to psychological and social factors. Many psychoanalytic theories identify disturbances in parent–child relationships as crucial: a perceived rejection by a child's same-sex parent may, depending on the child's reaction, result in emotional needs. The sense of rejection by and loss of the parent may occur, for example, because of divorce, prolonged absence, illness or ill-treatment, and the child becomes a 'psychological orphan'. The seeds of longing for closeness with another man (or, as the case may be, woman) may be sown, and alleviation of those emotional needs may be sought in sexual encounters. Dr Elizabeth Moberly, a research psychologist, argued along these lines in *Homosexuality: A New Christian Ethic.*[5] Learning theories claim that homoerotic experiences in infancy or adolescence may increase the likelihood of subsequent selection of homosexual interactions.

Notwithstanding recent developments, scientific knowledge regarding homosexuality is incomplete and we may sum up by saying:

There is a general if informal consensus today that no one theory of homosexuality can explain such a diverse phenomenon. There is no completely determinative cause … there appears to be a variety of facilitating influences … while homosexuality can develop without genetic or hormonal factors being operative, it generally does not develop without the influence of learning and socialisation.[6]

A theological account of the origin of homophile attraction complements and undergirds a scientific account. It does not explain the presence of such attraction in particular individuals but explains, at a spiritual level, why there are some people of homophile orientation. The rejection of God by the human race has led to 'every kind of wickedness' (Romans 1:29), but in Romans 1 there is, in particular, a link between idolatry and homosexuality. Rejection of the Creator *by all* humanity results in, and is made manifest by, rejection of the creation pattern for sexual relations *by some*. Henri Blocher observes that creatures who worship the Creator are in relationship with a being who in a profound sense is 'Other' and suggests that rejection of the 'Other' is aptly mirrored in the sexual realm by rejection of those 'other' in gender.[7]

Sin's impact is multi-faceted and its relation to homophile attraction complex. Sin is sometimes understood in terms of choice alone: a deliberate decision to disobey God. When this is done (subject to any element of choice that may be present in some people in the formative processes which determine sexual orientation) links between sin and homophile attraction are difficult to sustain. However, since the Fall, sin has been the root cause of a deep state of disorder within human nature. What is found innate in men and women is not necessarily good. As the Book of Common Prayer puts it, 'there is no health in us': pride, greed, heterosexual lust, homosexual orientation may all be 'natural' to a person and yet wrong. Further, sin is a power which dominates people and deceives us that we are free. We are all 'slaves to sin' (John 8:34), filled with compelling desires leading us into disobedient actions, living out involuntary but culpable rebellion (see, e.g., Romans 7:13–25). Those compelling desires are different for different people; for some they are homosexual desires. Moreover, 'environmental' theories accord with the fact that people are affected by the sins of others (rejection by parents does occur) and some inward effects of sin (making one's own needs paramount, distorting perceptions, possibly leading to imagined rejection).

The Church, the Gospel and the Homosexual Person

The meeting of Jesus and the woman caught in adultery (John 7:53–8:11) has much to teach Christians as we reflect on how to act towards homosexual people. First, Jesus reminds the Pharisees of their sin and does not tolerate hypocrisy (v. 7, cf. Matthew 23). None of us is without sexual sin and we must not throw stones. Paul, after speaking of unnatural relations, went on to say that the one who condemns others has 'no excuse' himself (Romans 2:1). Richard Lovelace has written: 'Most of the repenting that needs to be done on this issue of homosexuality needs to be done by straight people, including straight Christians. By far the greater sin in our church is the sin of neglect, fear, hatred, just wanting to brush these people under the rug.'[8] Second, Jesus does not condemn the woman, but neither does he condone her sin (vv. 10–11, cf. Luke 7:36–50). The challenge is for the church to find ways in which to express a similar balance. Third, Jesus acts as the woman's friend before he confronts her sin. She is friendless, an outcast in a hostile society, in danger even of her life, and Jesus is the one person on her side.

The gospel is God's answer to the problems caused by human sin. Full forgiveness for the past, the love of a new heavenly Father, membership of a new family, new resources for living as God intends and a new future are available. These, over time, dismiss the spectres of guilt, fear, loneliness and lack of self-respect some homosexual people feel keenly. Sin is present in a homosexual lifestyle and in some form ultimately lies behind homophile attraction. The gospel offers 'gay liberation' by breaking the power of sin. We now consider three aspects of the outworking of the gospel.

Identity

In *The Church and the Homosexual*, J.J. McNeill writes:

> No person with heterosexual tendencies would be inclined to answer the question, Who are you? with the response: I am a heterosexual. But if they felt free to do so, this would be the response of homosexuals ... people with a homosexual orientation tend to accept their homosexuality as their deepest self-identity image, the most important single fact about themselves.[9]

Everyone who hears Christ's call to follow him is confronted with the need for radical repentance: to deny himself and take up his cross. For many who turn to Christ the depth of repentance to which we are called may dawn slowly over the years; for the homosexual his or her whole identity, as he or she sees it, is on the line from the outset. Our evangelism must be sensitive to this. We must preach grace – Christ receives us as we are – but not cheap grace – none of us may remain as we are. Our true identity is ultimately to be found not in our sexuality but in taking up a new identity in Christ. Jesus 'calls his own sheep by name' (John 10:3), knowing us intimately and addressing us personally. Yet he purposes to give each believer 'a new name ... known only to him who receives it' (Revelation 2:17), a new, unique and eternal identity.

Holiness

For all unmarried Christians, a holy life involves celibacy. We should not underestimate the struggles sometimes involved. One homophile man, having begun to abstain, told a Christian counsellor:

> Since then I've felt more lonely and depressed than ever. It doesn't seem fair that I've given up something that's wrong but still feel all these conflicts. It just makes me want to go back. I don't really want to do it with a man again, I just want the pain to stop.[10]

As God works within, however, the Christian battling with homosexuality can normally expect homosexual attractions to grow less frequent, less intense, less of a preoccupation. Nonetheless, he or she may feel that the situation is frustrating and unfair. The heterosexual person, by contrast, may have chosen singleness or believe marriage is likely in the future. Coming to see singleness as God's gift, bringing advantages unavailable to the married person (1 Corinthians 7) is part of the answer. So is an awareness that the gospel promises a new wholeness, including an end to homophile attraction, one day. In this life, progress may be only partial. Nonetheless, academic and anecdotal evidence reveals that some people, through Christian experience and/or psychotherapy, undergo a change from homophile to heterophile attraction. Specialist input is sometimes appropriate. Dr Elizabeth Moberly recommends a twin-track strategy involving targeted prayer and regular meetings with a same-sex counsellor. Therapy focuses on meeting legitimate same-sex needs for love and resolving same-sex hurts and difficulties.

Community

Many people of homosexual orientation experience a sense of alienation from the church. Yet the church is called to be a 'new community' where people may know and be known, love and be loved. We need to review the life of our churches at congregational level, small group level and one-to-one level to see if it matches this ideal. Do homophile people know that the church is fully committed to accepting and supporting them? Patterns of church life are often designed with married couples and their children uppermost in mind. Our churches need to be communities of friendship in which the single person may find deep fellowship. Friendship can be the answer to 'aloneness', a therapeutic experience, a source of support and human enrichment. Barnabas, befriending Paul when he first turned to Christ and was viewed with suspicion, is an example to us; David and Jonathan in their intimate and loyal friendship are another.

Concluding Remarks: Love and Truth

The Christian community must respond to the issue of homosexuality and to homophile people in a way that combines love and truth, compassion and biblical integrity. There are homosexual people outside our churches or struggling within them because as Christians we have not yet learned to love as we should. Meanwhile, the debate among Christians about homosexuality is, implicitly, a debate about how to do theology. Homosexual behaviour can only be affirmed by Christians if the following are accepted: the repudiation of a created moral order, a shift from an objective to a subjective morality, and a new centre of gravity in theology whereby human insights and 'pastoral concern' can take precedence over divine revelation. But love and truth are not in the end isolated from, or opposed to, one another. The church will only be able to love homosexual people to the full if we have, along with more tender hearts, a firm grasp on the searching insights and transforming power of Christian truth.

1 R. Scroggs, *The New Testament and Homosexuality* (Fortress Press, 1983), p. 127.
2 D. Sherwin Bailey, *Homosexuality and the Western Christian Tradition* (Longmans, 1955).
3 J. Boswell, *Christianity, Social Tolerance and Homosexuality* (Chicago University Press, 1980).
4 C.E.B. Cranfield, *The Epistle to the Romans,* International Critical Commentary, vol. 1 (T & T Clark, 1975), p. 125.
5 E. Moberly, *Homosexuality: A New Christian Ethic* (James Clark & Co. Ltd, 1983).
6 S.L. Jones and D.E. Workman, 'Homosexuality: the Behavioural Sciences and the Church', *Journal of Psychology and Theology*, 1989, vol. 17, no. 3, p. 221.
7 H. Blocher, *In the Beginning* (IVP, 1984).
8 Cf. Richard F. Lovelace, *Homosexuality and the Church* (The Lamp Press, 1979).
9 J.J. McNeill, *The Church and the Homosexual* (Beacon Press, 1976, 4th edition), p. 157.
10 J. Dallas, *Desires in Conflict* (Harvest House, 1991), p. 120.

PART II

CHRISTIANITY AND SOCIETY

Chapter 4

THE GREAT COMMISSIONS

RANALD MACAULAY

We need not doubt that the Evangelical movement had a powerful effect in waking up 18th century England ... Where it failed was in its long-term effects ... You floated, safely enough on the little raft of your own faith, eagerly throwing out the lifeline to such drowning neighbours as were ready to catch it; meanwhile the ship was foundering.

Ronald Knox, *Enthusiasm* (Oxford, 1950), p. 589

Summary

Failure properly to relate the Gospel Commission of the New Testament to the Commission of Genesis (the Creation Mandate) lies behind much of evangelicalism's current weaknesses and internal conflicts. The New Testament, when clarifying the radical nature of the gospel, appears at times to disparage the created order within which we now live. But this is to misunderstand it. The gospel must in fact be understood in terms of Christ's restoration of creation, the supreme evidence of which is the resurrection of the body, rather than the immortality of the soul.

Introduction

Evangelism has always been one of the defining characteristics of evangelicalism, so much so that the two expressions are often used interchangeably. Though an awkward confusion, it does at least reflect a measure of authenticity, for clearly evangelism ought to be normative in the Christian Church. Despite this proper emphasis on outreach, however, evangelicalism has been marginalized in the

West. Why? Why, in particular during the past century and a half when evangelism was given such prominence, has it produced such limited results in our culture?

Evangelism and Social Involvement – an Evangelical Dilemma

The varying attempts to come to terms with this marginalization explain in large measure the history of evangelicalism during the past half-century. Carl Henry's *The Uneasy Conscience of Modern Fundamentalism* (Eerdmans, 1947) shows, even by its title, the discomfort felt by many younger evangelicals towards their own tradition. They agreed with the stand taken against liberal theology and the 'social gospel', but knew that its intellectual defensiveness and neglect of social action were both biblically untenable and pragmatically disastrous. Hence Henry and others in North America, and their equivalents a little later in the UK, pioneered a different vision which, among other things, sought to combine evangelism with a proper engagement socially and intellectually. It was a necessary change and later received international endorsement in the Lausanne Covenant of 1974.

Despite its remarkable achievements, however, Lausanne also produced a rift between differing views of gospel and mission. Centring on the meaning of the phrase 'the kingdom of God', a heated debate developed. Many felt that social action was distracting the church from its central task of evangelism. The concerns of Scripture, they argued, were being overshadowed by the concerns of society, and evangelicalism's doctrinal distinctives were suffering as a result. As one writer put it, 'The Evangelicals joined the Liberals in a concern for social issues, but it was the world and not the church which set the agenda.'[1]

Not surprisingly a conservative 'reaction' followed which emphasized the centrality of the Scriptures in both theology and practice, highlighting their importance by means of careful Bible study and expository preaching. In the process, however, it ran the danger of overreaction, particularly in its tendency to place an exclusive emphasis on evangelism. A little while ago, for example, the Australian-based bi-monthly magazine *The Briefing* published an article on work which resulted in an unprecedented reader response. To quote a later editor, 'In the ensuing debate, it became clear that many people were deeply hurt by the implication that paid secular work was anything less than valuable. A number wrote to complain of being made to feel like "second-class citizens" because they weren't in full-time ministry.[2] In similar vein, others have been made to feel that the sole value and significance of secular work is to provide for one's immediate physical needs and the support of 'gospel work'. Though not entirely wrong, is this in fact biblical? Is the value of work indeed merely functional? For that matter, does the value of *anything* we do as Christians lie solely, or even primarily, in its evangelistic implications?

In *Your Work Matters to God*, Sherman and Hendriks identify four unwarranted assumptions lying behind the belief that evangelism is the only priority Christians should have: that God is more interested in the soul than the body; that the things of eternity are more important than the things of time; that life divides into two categories, the sacred and the secular; and that because of the nature of their work, ministers and other clergy are more important to God's programme than the laity.[3] These are, of course, views informed as much by Platonic dualism as by the biblical text, and unrepresentative of orthodox Christianity. Yet they often issue from an affirmation of Scripture and a reaction against liberal evangelicalism which we share. One way to overcome this particular dualistic mindset, while preserving the appropriate emphasis on Scripture and evangelism, is to re-examine the theology behind the two great commissions of creation and salvation (the Creation Mandate of Genesis 1:28 and the Great Commission of Matthew 28:18ff.) as well as some of the ostensibly biblical arguments used to redress the recent imbalances.

Not that theological reflection by itself is sufficient, given the subtlety and complexity of the practical outworking of the biblical teaching in this area. The church has always struggled to find and then maintain the right expression of its two-sided calling, to be fully engaged in the world yet with priorities transformed by its own eternal perspective. Like a boat at anchor, the conflicting currents of creation and salvation, of this world and the next, have pulled the church in different directions: first to recognize the importance of the 'natural order' and then to disparage it.

The Need for a Biblical Framework

The question is, does a biblical framework exist within which to understand the relationship between the two? For without one it becomes difficult to moderate the imbalances which easily arise. When Jesus urges his disciples not to lay up treasure on earth but rather in heaven, or to hate themselves, or, like grains of wheat, to fall into the ground and die, how is he to be understood? Likewise, when Paul exhorts believers to 'set their minds on things above' or to 'beware of vain philosophy', is he suggesting that Christians should neglect temporal concerns and disparage the mind? Some sort of 'organizing principle' is needed if biblical texts like these are not to be distorted. For, superficially at least, they appear to set creation and salvation in opposition to one another, the physical against the spiritual, the temporal against the eternal. The abiding attraction of Greek dualism is just this, that it resembles biblical Christianity.[4]

Yet the differences between them could not be more profound. For the biblical narrative derives its very meaning from the coherence of these two central themes: creation and salvation – whether viewed from the beginning, especially in the creation of the image of God, or from the events which introduced the end – the death, resurrection and ascension of the 'new man', Jesus. As in the famous text John 3:16, it is because 'God so loved the world' (which he had created) that he gave his only Son (that all might eventually be restored). Those who would otherwise 'perish' through judgement and death he enables to live eternally because of Christ's salvation, not as disembodied spirits but as restored human beings with resurrected bodies. For the resurrection of Christ, as Oliver O'Donovan puts it, 'directs our attention back to the creation which it vindicates', it constitutes a 'proclamation that the very thing which God has made will continue and flourish', and demonstrates 'that the God who rules the world is the same as the God who made it, and that the outcome of history will affirm and not deny the order of its making'.[5]

This is the framework defended and elaborated here, specifically the resurrection of the image of God.

The Renewal of Creation

An immediate problem with the idea of the renewal of creation, however, is that it seems to imply less radical distinctions than Scripture allows, whether between Old and New Testaments, between old and new natures, or between this world and the next. For Jesus insists that everyone must be 'born again', and Paul likewise emphasizes the need for a 'new creation'. The old cannot simply be tinkered with like a malfunctioning engine; it has to be replaced. 'The old has gone, the new has come!' (2 Corinthians 5:17). Nothing is clearer in fact than this biblical theme of the failure and incapacity of the original which is weak, transient, distorted, corrupt, demonic even. Doomed to destruction, it will be burned up at the Last Day. So the New Testament exhorts us to 'live as aliens and strangers' in this life, to look beyond this world to a city with lasting foundations.[6]

Superficially, these and similar passages make it seem as if the New Testament takes a negative view of human experience and culture. But this is to misread it. Humanity is corrupt and powerless – left to itself. But, like polluted water or a damaged work of art, the fault lies not with the water or the picture but with what has become of them. The water remains good in essence; so does the picture. Both need to be restored to purity and beauty.

So with human nature. I am helpless to save or change myself unaided; only Christ can redeem me. But what he rescues me from is not my 'self' in the sense of my created being. I am saved, rather, from the guilt and power of sin. I am gradually restored to the sort of experience for which I was made. The humanity ruined in Adam is rescued in Christ, it is delivered even from death and as such becomes a new creation. But all in continuity with what exists now, as Paul stresses in his analogy of a seed and its resultant 'body' – different yet the same.[7]

Thus the ordinary categories of human experience are affirmed by God. By definition they enable me to be his image. I accept all my experience as 'spiritual'. The more 'ordinary' I am, the more Christian my experience becomes – ordinary in the sense of the original self as made by God, the self without sin, the self as defined by God which thinks, acts, feels; which is able to enter into social relationships and enjoy and create beauty; which is humble, pure, patient, kind, self-controlled, and so on. In a word, Christ's *image*.

But a virtuous image not merely in a private sense, as if individual and social experience can be disengaged from one another. The heart of human experience is social, since it reflects the relationship between the members of the Trinity. Therefore Christian compassion and creativity have to be expressed publicly as well as privately – in politics, education, commerce, recreation and so on.

The Two Universal Commissions

Another important element in the biblical framework of the two great commissions is that, while profoundly different, they are equally important. This is not to say that the interests appropriate to creation are never to be subordinated to the exigencies of salvation. Christians are called to a life of sacrifice. Jesus says, 'Whoever serves me must follow me; and where I am my servant also will be' (John 12:26). As he laid aside what was his by right and made himself a servant, so must we. Yet still, as O'Donovan cautions in relation to the debate between kingdom ethics and creation ethics, we must not be 'tempted to overthrow or deny either in the name of the other'.[8]

The two commissions are equally important, first because they are equally *divine and universal commands*. As Adam and Eve and their descendants were sent to exercise dominion over *all* the earth, so the apostles and their followers were sent to preach to *all* peoples. The first was a universal command to exercise righteous and beneficent dominion in keeping with their nature and status as 'the image of God', a command they could no longer fulfil adequately after the fall of Genesis 3, yet binding still. Though limited and corporeal 'creatures', and to that extent similar to their natural surroundings, nevertheless as 'persons' they were distinct. As Bavinck puts it, 'If now we comprehend the force of this "subduing" [dominion] under the term culture ... we can say that culture in the broadest sense is the purpose for which God created man after his image ... [which] includes not only the most ancient callings of ... hunting and fishing, agriculture and stock-raising, but also trade and commerce ... and science and art.'[9] None of this is altered by mankind's fall into sin: the New Testament, reflecting the view taken throughout Scripture, refers explicitly to sinful human beings as the image of God (James 3:9).

The Great Commission is a universal command also, though somewhat differently. The Creation Mandate is inherent in the way men and women are made, so in that sense unavoidable. The latter involves human choice and divine grace. Only those who have received Christ can pass on the good news. Nevertheless, since the gospel represents the epitome of God's love and reflects his desire that none should be lost, what is true of him must become true of those who are his image. From God's view – that is, from the way reality actually is – the idea of love is inconceivable without the proclamation of the gospel. Therefore, following Christ and sharing his love means being completely committed, like him, as an 'evangelist'.

Problems and Disagreements

Yet, if Christians are supposed to take the Creation Mandate this seriously, why does the New Testament contain few, if any, unequivocal references to public and social action, or to art and culture? Why, if these are legitimate and necessary concerns, are they not spelled out more clearly? Why too, using the familiar illustration of the *Titanic*, should we spend time rearranging the deckchairs on a doomed ship? Surely other concerns have to be subordinated to evangelism, for this is all that really matters into eternity, the destiny of the lost?

Silence of the New Testament

This first argument overlooks the background of the Old Testament, the only scripture used by the apostolic church and presupposed by the New Testament. Like the warp and woof of a tapestry, the threads of which are so fundamental to the fabric that the whole cannot be 'seen' (let alone exist) apart from them, the Old is present in the New. Sexuality, for example, can be understood only in reference to the biblical creation. This is the force of Jesus' reply when questioned by the Pharisees about divorce. Though divorce is allowed, the norm remains 'as at the beginning', life-long monogamy (Mark 10:1–12). The same is true of other aspects of human experience less clearly expressed in the New Testament, such as beauty and creativity. They are important because God is concerned about them and we are made like him. Yet they find little mention in the New Testament. Is it then legitimate to encourage Christian believers in the arts? Certainly. For beauty is intrinsic to mankind, explicit in creation, and illustrated within the Old

Testament (as in the design and building of the tabernacle). And though Jesus' encouragement to his disciples to 'consider the lilies of the field' is addressed primarily to the need for trust, its aesthetic significance surely cannot be denied. 'Solomon in all his *glory* was not arrayed like one of these' (Matthew 6:28, KJV).

In respect to social action not only do we find an intrinsic logic in Scripture (the fact that every human being has been made for society), but the Old Testament is full of God's instructions concerning the well-being of Israel. And if the Pentateuchal laws may not now be applied *simpliciter,* as if laws designed for all nations just as they stand, at the very least they indicate the seriousness with which God views the larger social relationships of nationhood. Likewise, since political justice is so important, the Psalmist draws a parallel between human rule and God's rule (Psalm 82). Yet the New Testament nowhere encourages believers to become involved, say, in law. Similarly in relation to the education of children in schools, the development of science in universities, the practice of medicine in hospitals, etc. – in all these the New Testament is silent. Yet within Western culture all are in large measure the product of Christian civilization. Why? Because they are rooted in the distinctive understanding of reality provided by the doctrine of creation. They do not need specific endorsement in the New Testament, for they are implicit.

This argument is strengthened, of course, by the way Jesus reinforces the Old Testament principle of national or state authority. His simple directive to give Caesar what is Caesar's reflects the continuing relevance of government, even when unjust – not simply as a social order his disciples should acknowledge, but one they should actively engage in.[10]

Gospel Priority

While the expression 'gospel priority' is not itself scriptural, it helps reinforce the urgency of the Great Commission, and in that sense is entirely appropriate. When Scripture speaks of the need of the world – including nature's groaning – it posits one solution only: rescue by the only Saviour. Christians concerned to see political and social improvements in society need to keep this prominent in their thinking and doing. Legislation is powerless to reform sinners. Material aid alone cannot bring lasting amelioration to stricken communities. Idolatry and sin remain the root causes of social distress and only the gospel of Christ has power to deal with them adequately. Yet, in the light of the 'resurrection framework', it is important to remember that the gospel priority is one of efficacy, not replacement. The efficacy of the gospel in bringing sinners to salvation does not preclude the significance of the creation order, especially our need to care for a broken world. The two must not be separated. Concern to communicate the gospel is not a concern for 'souls' but for flesh-and-blood people with all their needs. Nor should our being-in-the-world be treated as if only a vehicle from which to rescue the drowning. Life in all its variety has value in and of itself.

Careers and Ministry

What then of the importance of 'ministry'? If the Word of God is central in Christian life, does it not follow that those called to its teaching have a more important role than others? Again, yes and no. For while it is essential for the church to encourage many towards ministry, whether at home or abroad, and to honour them highly through prayer and financial support, this must not be confused with clericalism – as if 'Word-based ministry' is first-class and everything else secondary. Paul's encouragement to 'eagerly desire spiritual gifts, especially the gift of prophecy' (1 Corinthians 14:1) is a call addressed to all believers. All are exhorted to a deepening understanding and experience of God's revealed truth so that they can communicate the gospel's significance authoritatively to Christian and non-Christian alike. It is emphatically not a call to leave secular employment to be 'ordained for the ministry' – though some will. Rather, the concepts of ministry and mission have to be enlarged so that the specific 'gift' of teaching as exercised within the ecclesia is understood to be for the sake of the world. '[God] ... gave some to be ... pastors and teachers, to prepare [his] people for works of service' (Ephesians 4:11, 12). The purpose of Word-based ministry in the church is, in part, to enable Word-based ministry (service as well as evangelism, prophecy as well as proclamation) within the world. And the degree to which this broader work of the gospel is successful indicates the success of 'ministry'.

Therefore, the notion that one type of ministry is better than any other needs consciously to be avoided. When Jesus summons his disciples to leave all and follow him, or when he urges us to pray for 'labourers in the harvest', he is not expecting the answer to be simply an increase in the number of clergy, important as they are. For 'harvesting' by means of the gospel is the responsibility not primarily of those we call 'ministers' or 'missionaries', but of all believers equally. By insisting that the Great Commission is a universal responsibility and by enabling Christians, whatever their spheres of work and life, to develop a Christian mind and a Christ-like attitude of service, those who teach and preach in church enable the gospel to penetrate the whole of society. What such teaching should be is an important concern, but falls outside the scope of this brief survey. However, if secular employment is described simply in terms of 'feeding your face', it cannot help but limit the possibility of the gospel's penetration of society. The biblical alternative is to make Christians aware of the breadth of their calling and responsibility: as Paul puts it, 'we take captive every thought to make us obedient to Christ' (2 Corinthians 10:5).

Gospel and Community

But in what sense *should* we be concerned for 'the whole of society'? Part of the answer lies in a better understanding of the New Testament's emphasis on community. Interestingly, community is a more prominent practical concern of the New Testament letters than mission. Community is not just an adjunct of mission, but an essential part of the purposes of God. As well as benefiting those within, it constitutes the supreme reflection of the being and nature of God, the loving unity and diversity of the Trinity from 'before the world began' (John 17:21; 13:35). Indeed, to affirm the diversity of God's world and to demonstrate the dignity and glory of a humanity in process of being redeemed by Christ, is to provide the most effective (not to mention indispensable) platform for evangelism. The importance and attractiveness of Christian community, particularly in its ordinariness, cannot be overstated within the context of an increasingly fragmented postmodern society. But community requires constant nurturing and necessitates the affirmation of all types of human experience for its fullness to be revealed (1 Corinthians 12:14ff.).

However, the New Testament's 'church' focus indicates no lack of concern for secular society. The Bible never isolates itself from the larger context of society. In fact the opposite is the case. Jesus'

Parable of the Good Samaritan is aimed specifically at ecclesiastical parochialism in the area of human need. The Christian is responsible for his or her 'neighbour', and a neighbour is everyone he or she meets. As Jesus healed all and fed all, so Christians are to show compassion to all in need. Likewise, he tells us to let our light shine before men so that they may see our good deeds and glorify our Father in heaven, clearly indicating the need for a concern beyond the limits of Christian community, as well as an ultimate evangelistic objective. One wonders how this overarching compassion towards human need and suffering in Scripture comes to be limited to individual philanthropy. For that is how some interpret the alleged 'silence' of the New Testament. Quite unnecessarily, they choose private social responsibility (in which they often excel) to the detriment of public. But why?

The Transience of This World

The fact that Scripture encourages an eschatological perspective and warns against an improper focus upon the present leaves the principle of creation unchanged. Mortality surrounds us on every hand. The world awaits a judgement in which all will be burned by fire (2 Peter 3:10). But in both cases human action derives value not from its permanence but from its provenance. Though it springs immediately from human thought and energy, it derives value and meaning from God. Hence we are exhorted to glorify him in all we do, morally and physically, for the two cannot be separated. Love's profoundest expression is a body nailed to a cross. The judgement of 'sheep and goats' rests upon tangible material kindnesses – cups of water, clothing and prison visiting (Matthew 25:31–46). On Christ's authority, what endures beyond the final judgement includes the physical and temporal. 'Whatever you did to one of the least of these … you did to me,' he says. In addition, the New Testament heralds the restoration of all things; even the non-personal creation will be 'liberated from its bondage to decay', and 'the kings of the earth will bring their splendour into it [the Holy City, the New Jerusalem]' (Romans 8:21; Revelation 21:24). Human society and culture are important to God and retain their value *in him* even though transient. Hence Luther's famous remark: 'If I knew Jesus would return tomorrow I would plant a tree today.' This is Reformation Christianity. This is biblical Christianity.

Conclusion

The competing tensions between Scripture's two 'great' commissions, the tides of creation and gospel, help to explain some of our current difficulties as evangelicals. Simultaneously, the culture's intellectual and moral bankruptcy presents us with unprecedented opportunities, which sadly are being squandered. Partly this is because evangelicalism has yet to discover and maintain a proper coherence between the two commissions. Either social activism has been promoted at the expense of the 'gospel priority', or the Creation Mandate has been neglected. The fact that on one side the vital evangelical distinctives of the past (biblical doctrine, expository preaching and evangelism) are being recovered and emphasized gives hope of improvement. But, in the absence of a proper recovery of the significance of the Creation Mandate for evangelism, the long-term effects of such reforms will be limited. Though superficially more 'orthodox' they threaten to return us, ironically, to the very ineffectiveness from which our leaders in the 1940s sought to rescue us.[11]

1   Sir Fred Catherwood, quoted in M. Tinker (ed.), *Evangelical Social Action Today* (Christian Focus, 1995), see pp. 189, 191. See also p. 54 on liberal scholarship.
2   *The Briefing*, St Matthias Press, nos 178/9; cf. no. 176.
3   NavPress, Colorado, 1990, p. 46, quoted in *The Briefing* as footnote 2.
4   For further treatment of Platonism see R. Macaulay and J. Barrs, *Being Human* (Solway, 1996), pp. 29ff.
5   Oliver O'Donovan, *Resurrection and Moral Order* (Apollos, 1994), pp. 31, 53; see too C.E. Hummel, *The Galileo Connection* (IVP, Downers Grove, 1986), p. 218.
6   Hebrews 11:13; 1 Peter 2:11; 2 Peter 3:7.
7   See 1 Corinthians 15:37. O'Donovan (*ibid.*) all of Chapter 3, 'Eschatology and History', is helpful.
8   *Ibid.*, p. 15.
9   Herman Bavinck, *Our Reasonable Faith* (Baker, 1977), pp. 206, 207.
10 Matthew 22:21; cf. Matthew 21:12; Acts 16:37.
11 See also John Stott, *The Contemporary Christian* (IVP, Leicester, 1992), Chapter 3, 'Holistic Mission'.

Chapter 5

RELATIONISM

Pursuing a Biblical Vision for Society

MICHAEL SCHLUTER

It is now axiomatic that the big idea is an anachronistic concept. The central theme the think tanks share is that society has become too diverse and fragmented to be reduced to simple organising concepts such as the market or socialism.

Richard Cockett, *The Times*, 8 August 1994

Summary

This chapter tells the story of my search over the last twenty years to find an alternative social paradigm which is closer to biblical norms than democratic capitalism or market socialism. Biblical teaching on this issue is found in Old Testament law, where God provides a normative framework for Israelite society. Jesus says that biblical law hangs on the twin commands to love God and love neighbour. Love is not a term of economics or finance, but the language of relationships. Hence the term Relationism. The principles of biblical law, interpreted in relational terms, provide a coherent basis for public policy and personal lifestyle decisions. So Relationism holds great promise for broad-based reform of society, provided it is not severed from its roots in biblical revelation.

Do We Still Need the 'Big Idea'?

The fall of the Berlin Wall marked a watershed. The day of high principle in politics is now over. What is good is what works. Policy should be assessed only on pragmatic criteria – if it works, use it; if it doesn't, dump it. This is a period of single-issue politics, when a plural society must live with multiple visions of what is socially desirable.

However, the pragmatic approach has problems. It takes a long time to observe the full effects of policy, so even by its own criteria pragmatism is experimentally hazardous. More fundamentally, policies are seldom if ever value-neutral. Pension provision, for example, involves a choice between individual, family and state responsibility. The tax and benefit system may support marriage, or make cohabitation more financially attractive. A policy platform built on a case-by-case approach is likely to be full of internal contradictions.

Since Margaret Thatcher's commitment to market economics, there have been few attempts to outline a coherent social vision. The Communitarian movement demands greater attention be given to issues of citizenship and community, but fails to address the causes of growing individualism. The Green movement has gained a place on the national agenda, but is peripheral to many central political concerns such as urban unemployment and the future of the NHS.

Some look back with nostalgia to the utopian dreams of the Christian past. The Reformation vision of the 'Christian commonwealth' might appeal, but how do we first restore widespread belief in God strong enough to shape personal behaviour? Likewise, the Christian Socialist ideal looks fatally flawed when state control of the economy is reduced to an occasional nervous tug at a corporate sleeve.

Seeking an Alternative to Capitalism, Marxism and Socialism

My search for an alternative social vision built on biblical foundations stretches back over twenty years. The story begins in East Africa in the 1970s. Kenya was then at the centre of ideological debate. In neighbouring Tanzania, Nyerere was implementing '*ujamaa* socialism', which included forcibly removing peasants from traditional homesteads into villages. To the north, the autarchic rule of Hailé Selassie was about to be replaced by a repressive Marxist regime. In Kenya itself, barely restrained capitalism was introducing extreme income inequalities. African Christian leaders were seeking a biblical response to these regimes.

Contemporary Christian reflection in Britain centred on identifying biblical principles to critique public policy. The Left stressed justice; the Right stressed stewardship. However, such general principles were inadequate to evaluate compulsory villagization in Tanzania. The story circulated that the bishops in Tanzania had been asked by Nyerere to critique his policies. When they had nothing to say, he asked for their public support. Was there really no biblical basis for critical evaluation?

My discussions with Roy Clements, then pastor at Nairobi Baptist Church, pointed towards a fresh look at Old Testament law as an ethical foundation for public life. New Testament ethics were given largely to Christians; they assume the indwelling power of the Holy Spirit and were given to guide individuals and the church rather than societal behaviour. So the command by Jesus to 'turn the other cheek' is not an appropriate basis for sentencing armed robbers in a law court. Jesus himself points to OT law as the God-given source of ethical teaching when urging his disciples to act as salt and light in society, in the tradition of the prophets (Matthew 5:11–20). He underlines that biblical law continues to be God's standard for unregenerate society (Matthew 5:17–19), given in part as an accommodation to the hardness of the human heart (Matthew 19:8).

From the summer of 1975 we undertook a careful and system-atic study of the political, economic and social system contained in the Law of Moses. This proved a rich and rewarding enterprise. Although the laws appeared at first sight to be a random collection, closer study revealed remarkable internal consistency. The inter-locking themes which emerged are considered later. Suffice to say, here was a coherent pattern of political economy which had self-evident relevance to the questions we had been seeking to answer in East Africa.

Overcoming the Objections

Having 'discovered' biblical law, we were confronted with a host of reasons why we should not seek to apply it to life today. Each had to be worked through. Four of the more important objections were:

'Biblical Law Has No Continuing Role in the New Testament'

A superficial reading of the New Testament makes it appear that OT law has been abolished by the coming of Jesus. Paul, for example, says that 'Christ is the end [or goal] of the Law' (Romans 10:4). But Jesus insists that he has not come to abolish the Law (Matthew 5:17) and Paul elsewhere says that 'the Law is good if one uses it properly' (1 Timothy 1:8). Fortunately, Chris Wright's doctoral thesis helped to clarify the role of OT law for the Christian. He found three levels of fulfilment or application: typological, eschatological and paradigmatic.[1] The last of these, that Israel's distinctive social organization was part of its calling to be 'a light to the Gentiles' (Isaiah 42:6), had immediate relevance for our work.

'There Is No Mandate for Christians to Promote Biblical Law in Society Today'

The immediate answer lies in the incentive offered by Jesus, 'anyone who practises and teaches these commands will be great in the kingdom' (Matthew 5:19). There is some intrinsic link between law and kingdom. As Paul says, the law was put in charge to bring us to Christ (Galatians 3:24). However, if the kingdom is only where the rule of Christ is acknowledged in people's hearts, what is Christ's relationship with the rest of humanity? The New Testament claims that Christ's *reign* is over all humanity, both as creator and as redeemer, whether people recognize it or not (Matthew 28:20). So Christians have the God-given authority to address society with both law and gospel.

'Biblical Law Upholds a Society Based on Patriarchy and Slavery'

The gender issue in OT law is complex and some allowance must be made for cultural context. However, agricultural societies cannot allow land inheritance to pass down through both sons and daughters or plots become even more quickly subdivided and scattered. This was clearly an issue in Israel (Numbers chapters 27 and 36). The law chooses the patriarchal route, consistent with the Genesis account. With respect to slavery, Israel's institution was a far cry from life in ancient Greece or Rome. Slaves in Israel were allowed to run away (Deuteronomy 23:15–16), and were released every seventh year (Deuteronomy 15:12–15). Indeed, OT slavery is more like a domestic service contract, albeit giving considerable power to the householder. It was in effect punishment in the community for a thief or a person in debt (Exodus 22:3), and was probably more humane than the social exclusion and enforced inactivity of a modern prison.

'It Is Not Clear Which Parts of Biblical Law Should Be Applied Today'

While many of the laws and their penalties are part of Israel's ceremonial law, and thus are fulfilled in Christ and no longer binding on
the Christian (e.g. the food laws), Jesus insists no part of the Law
can be entirely dismissed on grounds of cultural irrelevance
(Matthew 5:17). The reformers' categories of moral, civil and ceremonial law are helpful if seen to describe different purposes rather
than different types of law. One specific command, to keep the
Sabbath holy, for example, may be regarded simultaneously as
having moral, civil and ceremonial functions. It is the moral–civil
function of the Law, not its role as a sign of the OT covenant (Exodus 31:13), which is relevant to the ordering of society today.

There were many other objections we faced in the early years of
pursuing this approach. It seemed that Christians had found many
reasons over the last 300 years not to study the application of biblical law to contemporary society.

What Principles for Political Economy?

The next step was to ascertain which principles of biblical law could
be applied today, in a largely secular context. We identified, among
others, these:

- The foundation of the state should be a covenant or promise
  between regions or sections of society which binds the parties
  together for good or ill, as in a marriage, so that there is
  commitment to resolving disputes rather than resorting to force
  or withdrawal.
- The Family (extended family) should be given as great a role as
  possible to ensure its long-term cohesion. This should include
  economic and welfare functions as well as provision of
  emotional support, and nurture and education of children.
- All Families should have geographic roots in a physical location
  and some permanent stake in property. This helps to ensure
  proximity in Families and stable local communities, and also
  some equality in social relationships while allowing differences
  of wealth.[2]
- Surplus money should be channelled as far as possible within
  Families and communities where returns are non-pecuniary, or

provided as equity capital to business so that risk is shared fairly
between suppliers and users of capital.[3]

■ Crime should be regarded not as the individual breaking the
rules of the state, but as a breakdown of relationship between
offender and victim, and between offender and local/national
community.

■ The power of central government should be restrained to
ensure participation of people in decisions governing their lives.
'Subsidiarity' encourages direct political involvement and helps
develop relationships within the local community.

■ National unity is to be built not on military or executive centralization, but on a national system of law, education and medicine
informed by shared values and aspirations.

These principles were found to be mutually reinforcing; they form
a pattern of political and economic organization.

Identifying the 'Big Idea' of Biblical Law

By 1981 much of the groundwork had been completed. We had
studied the economic and social implications of the Jubilee laws for
land; implications of the interest ban, and why it did not extend
to foreigners; political structures; the role of the Levites; welfare
arrangements and military organization. But one issue still trou-
bled us: what held all these laws together? In brief, capitalism was
concerned primarily with the deployment and growth of capital,
while socialism focused on the role and organization of the collective, and advocated community ownership and control of the
means of production. What was the central theme of the pattern
found in biblical law?

The answer was found to be as simple as it was profound. After
replying to a slightly different question from a lawyer, Jesus went on
to address directly the question I was asking:

'Teacher, which is the greatest commandment in the Law?'
　　Jesus replied: ' "Love the Lord your God with all your heart and
with all your soul and with all your mind." This is the first and greatest
commandment. And the second is like it: "Love your neighbour as
yourself." All the Law and the Prophets hang on these two commandments.'

Matthew 22:36–40

Love, of course, is not the language of finance or economics: it is the language of relationships. God measures a society, Jesus says, not by the size of its GNP or by the efficiency of its markets, but by the quality of its relationships.

Such a finding is hardly surprising. Christianity is a relational religion. John points out that God is not an isolated individual living in a silent universe. Rather, 'In the beginning was the Word, and the Word was with God, and the Word was God' (John 1:1). As John Zizioulas has observed:

> The chief lesson is that if God is essentially relational, then all being shares in relation: there is, that is to say, a relational content built into the nature of being. To be is to exist in relation to other beings.[4]

Other aspects of Christian doctrine are equally focused on relationships. The central term 'covenant' is a promise which establishes and shapes a relationship. The atonement is explained by Paul as bringing about reconciliation (2 Corinthians 5:18–19), the restoration of a broken relationship. Eternal life is a developing relationship (John 17:3). Paul teaches that spiritual gifts, knowledge and generosity to the poor are worth nothing without the right quality of relationships (1 Corinthians 13:1–3). From the moment of conversion, the individual is called to become part of a new community and not to live or act in isolation (e.g. Ephesians 2:19). The language of relationships is pervasive in Christian doctrine and experience.

Relationships: What Relevance to Public Policy?

After the insight in 1981 that relationships were the key to interpreting and applying biblical law today, there was a gap of ten years before the next steps were taken towards applying this insight consistently into public life. It was not immediately obvious how the focus on relationships could be used to develop new approaches to diverse areas such as economic policy, financial services, the NHS and the prison system.

In the meantime, in 1985, I was drawn into running the Keep Sunday Special Campaign. To have any chance of winning, a wide coalition of retailers and unions had to be brought together to work with the churches. As the spokesman for such a coalition, it was not possible to use explicitly Christian arguments. The case had to rest on family life, protection of low-paid shopworkers from pressure to work unsocial hours, and environmental factors. These are hinted at in Scripture as reasons for the Sabbath institution (e.g. Deuteronomy 5:15; Exodus 20:11). The approach was consistent with Christian teaching without being labelled Christian. This was to provide a model for the future in how to balance the need to involve the wider world in seeking social reform while remaining faithful to biblical ideals.

In 1991 David Lee began to work with me on a book to examine systematically the impact of public policy on people's relationships.[5] We developed the concept of 'relational proximity', incorporating five facets or dimensions of interpersonal relationship. The factors influencing the closeness of a relationship could be assessed in terms of:

- quality of communication (directness)
- frequency, regularity and amount of contact, and length of relationship (continuity)
- variety of context of meetings (multiplexity)
- mutual respect and fairness in the relationship (parity)
- shared goals, values and experience (commonality).

The opportunity to work with the Scottish Prison Service to assess the quality of relationships between prison officers and prisoners led to the development of a formal measurement tool based on relational proximity. This tool has since been applied in companies and homes for the elderly, and between organizations in the NHS. Although without explicit biblical foundation, relational proximity grew out of reflection on the reasons behind many biblical laws; the concept helped to identify the impact of much biblical law on the structure of neighbour relationships.

Many features of Western society today undermine relational proximity. High levels of mobility make it difficult for people to develop close relationships with neighbours. Modern communications have had the effect of dividing our time among more and more people, so that each contact tends to become more superficial; television and the music culture often inhibit conversation; urban planning norms and high-rise buildings have lessened opportunities for people to have frequent contact; the large size of companies, schools and hospitals today reduces frequency of interaction between colleagues.

The relational approach can be used to critique legislation and the structures and working practices of organizations. It offers an alternative ethos for sectors of public policy, for example 'relational justice' for the criminal justice system and 'relational healthcare' for the NHS. In these and other ways the relational approach, informed by biblical principles, can provide a reform agenda for public life.

Relational Lifestyle

The relationships theme overcomes the artificial divide in much liberal thought between justice in public life and virtue in private life. Christians wishing to think and act relationally in their lives at work and at home will study the life of Jesus, who shows us how to relate to God and to other people perfectly, both by his life and in his teaching. This covers every area of life. '*Agape* love', which does not love 'because of' but 'in spite of', is the ultimate goal for the Christian (1 John 4:7–12).

The primary requirement of a relational lifestyle is the need for long-term, deep, committed relationships. These will generally be focused within the Family but also reach outside it. To achieve such relationships, roots are critical; this is why teaching about the Jubilee, which is primarily concerned with maintaining roots, is foundational to the social structure of OT law.[6]

Time is the currency of relationships. In society today, technology facilitates contact with greater numbers than ever before, but such wider contact is generally characterized by greater superficiality. To have a few close and deep friends, inside and outside the extended family, it is essential to prioritize relationships. Jesus sets relational priorities in his ministry after much prayer (e.g. Mark 3:13–17; 5:37). His relationship with his Father in heaven always takes priority over all other relationships (e.g. Mark 1:35–7).

Close friendship, however, is more than a commitment to roots and prioritizing of relationships. It involves sacrificial (*agape*) love, a willingness always to forgive, and an ability to expose one's innermost thoughts and feelings to another person. Such self-exposure is often painful, always risky. The experience of deep and painful relationships has enriched much of the greatest literature and art, including Goethe's poetry, Solzhenitsyn's novels and Rossetti's painting.

Relationism: Secular Ideology or Christian Strategy?

Does Relationism have the ideological ambitions of capitalism and socialism? Such a suggestion immediately rings alarm bells for Christians. Ideologies smack of idolatry, solutions apart from salvation, and frameworks of political thought and action which do not acknowledge the Lordship of Christ. While Relationism could perhaps be regarded as an ideology in the sense of flowing from a worldview which is not shared by everybody, it should certainly not be regarded as an autonomous body of human thought.

Some would prefer to regard Relationism potentially as the basis for a Christian political party. This route presents serious difficulties. The Christian Democratic parties of continental Europe have demonstrated the dangers of baptizing the politics of the Right (Germany) or the Left (Holland) with the name of Christ. While the *values* of political life can be drawn from the Bible, and as moral absolutes can be appropriately termed 'Christian', it is dangerous to attach the same label to the socio-economic means chosen for their implementation. In South Africa, for example, failure to distinguish between principled rejection of apartheid, and the specific policy of sanctions as a way of combating apartheid, unnecessarily alienated some from the church.

The Relationships Foundation (RF), which I helped to establish in 1993 as a catalyst to help make Britain into a more relational society, is based on Christian values, while not requiring any theological beliefs of its supporters.[7] Following the earlier model of the Keep Sunday Special Campaign, the RF simply states that it is founded on the ethical values of the Judaeo-Christian tradition. Thus its framework can be endorsed by any who recognize the central importance of good relationships for human well-being, and who are persuaded by rational argument or intuition that the underlying principles are sound, regardless of their source.

So Relationism is less than a fully Christian framework of thinking. By focusing on love for neighbour exclusively, it fails to require the first commandment: to love God. The absence of the vertical dimension of relationships means that the essential motivation for building strong social bonds and restoring broken relationships, even at personal cost, is missing. However, in seeking to influence a society where Christians are a minority, Christians cannot appeal to the first commandment, to love God, in the way that the OT prophets did. Such an appeal today is the task of evangelism. The most Christians can hope for in a pluralist society is to persuade people of the benefits of biblical social teaching, and thus to have national law based on Christian rather than secular values.

In addition, by focusing public policy and personal lifestyle on the issue of relationships, Relationism is speaking in the categories and language of Christianity. It has been termed a 'translation strategy', helping to express in contemporary terms many of the core concerns of biblical teaching.[8] If biblical law plays the role of a schoolmaster to bring people to Christ (Galatians 3:24), Relationism must occupy the middle ground between on the one hand setting out ethical standards which do not assume that people are already in a relationship with Christ, while on the other hand affirming the relational nature of all reality.

Promoting Relationism into the New Millennium

For those who are convinced that it is possible to derive a biblically based agenda for political, economic and social reform using the relational approach, it is essential not just to analyse what is wrong in society but also to try and change it. Jesus called us not to be passive onlookers, but to be active as salt and light. The task is immense. Western societies are locked into an individualistic and materialistic worldview which is reinforced by the priorities of the mass media, especially commercial advertising, and by the preoccupation of political parties with economics and human rights. The centralization of state power and individualization of financial services (e.g. pensions, insurance, savings) provide further reinforcement. How can this stranglehold be broken?

The day of the think tanks is passing away; it is no longer sufficient simply to promote ideas at an intellectual level. Policy is made increasingly after practical experiment, pilot schemes and regional initiatives. If Relationism is accepted as a strategy for Christian political and personal engagement, we can expect widespread reform initiatives at national, regional and local levels based on relational thinking. Those in national and local politics, in business and financial services, in the professions and in caring roles will work to a fresh agenda.

Whether Relationism has a long-term impact on Western society will depend, I believe, primarily on whether it stays in touch with its biblical roots. Divorced from biblical teaching, it will lack the coherence and cutting edge derived from the wisdom of God's revelation in Scripture. It will also fail to attract and sustain the support of Christians who recognize explicitly or intuitively the truth and wisdom of its approach. If constantly renewed with the insights of biblical reflection, it may challenge successfully the dominant Western ideologies of global capitalism and market socialism.[9]

1 See Christopher J.H. Wright, *Living as the People of God* (IVP, Leicester, 1983).
2 See Chapter 6.
3 See Chapter 13.
4 Report of the BCC Study Commission on Trinitarian Doctrine Today, *The Forgotten Trinity* (British Council of Churches, London, 1989), p. 16.
5 Michael Schluter and David Lee, *The R Factor* (Hodder & Stoughton, London, 1993).
6 See Chapter 6.
7 The Relationships Foundation, 3 Hooper Street, Cambridge, CB1 2NZ. E-mail: rf@clara.net
8 John Ashcroft and Christopher Townsend, *Political Christians in a Plural Society* (Jubilee Centre, Cambridge, 1994), p. 81.
9 The Jubilee Centre, a sister charity of the Relationships Foundation, is based in the same building as the Relationships Foundation and is intended to provide an ongoing stream of biblical research and reflection to help develop Relationships Foundation initiatives and policy perspectives.

Chapter 6

DISESTABLISHMENT AND THE CHURCH OF ENGLAND

JULIAN RIVERS

Summary

Any discussion of religious establishment raises fundamental questions about the nature and relationship of church and state. Before addressing specific issues within the establishment debate, this chapter seeks to identify the Christian understanding of these two institutions and discusses various models for their interrelationship. It concludes that while some reforms are desirable, the principle of Christian establishment is correct.

Introduction

Religious disestablishment is on the cards. From within the Church of England there are signs of increasing dissatisfaction with the role of the government in church affairs.[1] The Labour Government's zeal for reforming the constitution may in time turn to the Church of England. Recent comments by the Prince of Wales question the nature of church–state relations. Wherever the impetus for change lies, we must be prepared to see the relationship of the state to religion generally and Christianity in particular radically challenged in the near future.

Establishment is a word of no certain meaning. In a sense which no longer has currency in this country, it can mean the unity of the state and the church, as in medieval Christendom. On this account, the church was disestablished by the Toleration Act 1689. Most commonly, a religion is established where there is some degree of organizational overlap between church and state. This is the sense in which the Church of England is established, and it will be adopted in this chapter. Again, a religion is established when the state, in its institutions and laws, tends to reflect the values of that religion. Finally, there is the social fact of establishment, which occurs when a majority of individuals in a state is committed to a religion.

Much recent debate about religious establishment has been driven by a false understanding of the nature of both the church and the state. The church is perceived as one interest group among many, not significantly different from a football club. The state is perceived as that body which in a neutral fashion regulates the activity of all these different interest groups ensuring that each is as free as possible. It must not be biased towards any one group, or the worldview that group represents.

The Christian Vision of Church and State[2]

The Christian message is the proclamation of the kingdom of God: that is, the authority of the Lord Jesus Christ over all people and all areas of life. God gave public demonstration of this through the death and resurrection of Christ, it is proclaimed and partly seen by the power of the Holy Spirit today, and it will be fulfilled and acknowledged by all on Christ's return in judgement. This authority applies to every aspect of life, both individual and institutional. Christ's authority over the visible church and the state flows both from his authority over the individuals who constitute these institutions and from the fact that they have been specifically ordained for the extension of his kingdom. But the two are not identical, and the issue of religious establishment raises the question of the correct relationship between them. What is the nature, function and mode of action of church and state?

The Church

Within the Protestant tradition, the church is regarded primarily as the invisible body of the elect. The church becomes visible in Christian profession and conduct, in the ministry of the Word and the sacraments, and in external organization, government and discipline. While one recognizes the inevitable presence of unbelievers and the periodic rise of false teachers within the visible church, its essence and hope is still the invisible church. The purpose of the church is clear: it is to be a witness to the saving power of Christ in both word and deed, calling all people to a life of repentance and faith in him. Its mode of action is limited by its nature: through loving persuasion and, if ultimately necessary, exclusion from its corporate life.

The Nature and Function of the State

The state is not the church, but neither is it fundamentally in opposition to the church. We are able in principle to give to Caesar what is Caesar's and to God what is God's (Matthew 22:21) since the state is an authority established by God (Romans 13:1; Titus 3:1). While it is capable of great evil, its purpose is to be subjected to the highest authority of Christ (Ephesians 1:20; 1 Peter 3:22). It is the fear of Christ as Lord of lords (Psalm 2) that leads us to submit to this authority.

There is less certainty about the correct function or purpose of the state. Some aspects are, however, plain. 1 Timothy 2:1–7 is a key passage here. Prayers are to be offered for all those in authority 'that we may live peaceful and quiet lives in all godliness and holiness. This is good, and pleases God our Saviour, who wants all men to be saved and to come to a knowledge of the truth.' One function of the state is therefore to preserve peace and good order that the church may be free to proclaim the gospel. But is the state limited in its function to the maintenance of defence and the protection of life, liberty and property through the criminal law? The task of civil authorities is expressed in the New Testament (1 Peter 2:14) both negatively (to punish the wrongdoer) and positively (to commend those who do what is right), and Calvin was in no doubt that the state could not effectively maintain the second table of the Ten Commandments without a concern for the first (*Institutes* IV.xx.9). Calvinist and Thomist alike can agree that at a fundamental level the state should be concerned that all people love God, do his will and believe on the one he sent. The Christian can be wholeheartedly a servant of the state, precisely because basic objectives are shared. But where then is religious toleration?

Three Limits to the State's Power

Even granting that the state is fundamentally concerned to bring all people into a right relationship with Christ, there are three limits to the state's power. First, it is limited by the means available to achieve its ends. It can only discourage by the deprivation of external goods (life, liberty and property, represented by the sword in Romans 13:4 and taxation in Romans 13:6) and encourage by the redistribution of wealth. But the gospel cannot be proclaimed in this way. Jesus eschewed physical retribution on those who refused to believe (Luke 9:51–6), and Paul proceeded by 'taking captive every thought to make it obedient to Christ' (2 Corinthians 10:5). Put positively, the way that the state fulfils its duty to extend the kingdom of God is by leaving the church free to proclaim the gospel. Religious freedom is a fundamental principle of the state simply because the attempt to promote Christianity through the deprivation of external goods distorts the gospel and is counter-productive. This defence of religious liberty is rooted in the Reformation, was developed by seventeenth-century English puritans, most notably John Owen, popularized by Locke and Milton, and thus passed into the common heritage of Western civilization. Although it depends on a highly contentious understanding of truth and religious commitment, it still provides the most resilient defence of religious liberty.

Second, the state is limited by the structures that must be put in place to guard against corruption. The state is capable of great evil, and part of bringing it under the rule of Christ involves putting structures in place, such as those of democratic or judicial accountability, that prevent the slide to tyranny. But those structures may themselves prevent the enforcement of desirable policies in the short term.

Finally, the state is limited by rule of law principles, among which the most significant are that laws must be capable of being obeyed and enforced. This means that legal obligations cannot be too far out of step with society's moral standards, otherwise the failure of the law will bring the whole system into disrepute. A society may simply not be good enough for certain laws.

Duties of Church and State to Each Other

The duty of the state is thus to preserve the freedom of the church to be the visible body of Christ, and to promote the gospel by the means at its disposal, remembering always that Christ's kingdom 'is not of this world'. But it may in principle have laws that promote at least external obedience to the law of God and act as the schoolmaster, leading its citizens to Christ. The church also has duties to the state to teach good citizenship, to intercede on its behalf and then to act, as Canon Max Warren[3] put it, by prophesying to the nation, by purifying it and by preparing it for the return of Christ and the consummated kingdom of God into which the kings of the world will bring all their wealth (Revelation 21:24).

Models of Church–State Relations

It is possible to identify a spectrum of models for the right relationship between church and state ranging from total separation to complete unity. Five basic models are identified here, and all have had exponents within the Christian tradition.

Complete Separation

Under this model, the state must be completely independent of religious organizations. Religious freedom is maintained by a 'wall of separation' between church and state, for to do otherwise would corrupt the church and affect the free commitment of the individual in matters of faith. The best-known example of this approach is the First Amendment (1791) to the US constitution: 'Congress shall make no law respecting an establishment of religion, or the free exercise thereof …' Originally, this was intended to protect individual state establishments from interference by the federal organs of government. But the last establishment was dismantled in 1833, and by the Fourteenth Amendment (1868) the principles of the First Amendment were extended to cover individual states as well. On the Christian understanding of this model, the church is free to be the church and justice is maintained by campaigning for individual just laws. One would want to maintain the *organizational* neutrality of the state, while affirming the *ideological* commitment to a Christian worldview. And no-one can deny the potential vitality of the church in such a system.

The problem with the model of separation is that organizational neutrality tends to collapse into religious neutrality, which itself can become state-sponsored atheism. The Supreme Court interprets the no-establishment clause as requiring no support by the state of any particular religious worldview, and this disproportionately benefits non-theistic worldviews. For example, it is a breach of the no-establishment clause to make rooms available during school hours for students to pray, let alone to have official school prayers, even when students are permitted to opt out. The category of 'religion' masks the fact that when the state refuses to promote a religious worldview, it ends up promoting an irreligious one.

The degree to which this is a problem depends on the scope of the public sphere. Where the state is a minimal one, merely concerned with defence and basic criminal law, ideological 'neutrality' is largely unproblematic, simply because most worldviews concur in what is desirable in these fields. But as the role of the state expands, so atheistic ideology becomes more pervasive. The problem is most severe in Marxist countries, where no distinction between public and private spheres is maintained. The state cares for everything and everybody, including those deluded into disagreeing with it. To witness to your faith is thus a breach of state neutrality on matters of religious belief. In Western countries, as the role of the state expands to cover health, education, employment and social security, the space left to those of any religious convictions to mould their lives according to their faith is correspondingly reduced.

Neutral Co-operation

The first model strives for religious neutrality by exclusion. In practice it turns out to be biased towards atheism, and intolerant. The second model strives for religious neutrality, but by even-handed co-operation. It recognizes the ultimate significance of faith in people's lives, and where functions of the state and religious concerns overlap the state seeks to work together with the organizations or religions in question. The best example of this approach is in the law of marriage. It is possible to get married according to the rites of the Church of England, by secular ceremony in the Registrar's office, according to the usage of Quakers or Jews, and according to any other ceremony which takes place in a building certified as a place of public religious worship and registered as a place for the solemnization of marriage. Thus in theory the whole gamut of religious convictions is covered.

Some would like to apply this model to the issue of religious representation in the House of Lords. Lord Hailsham has argued that the second chamber functions best as a House of 'experts' from all walks of life.[4] This model would require representation by the leaders of religious groups according to their share of allegiance; thus, the present situation where 26 bishops of the Church of England sit by right and a few others, notably the Chief Rabbi, by the whim of Prime Ministerial patronage is imbalanced. Of course, one might reject this quasi-democratic understanding of the House of Lords in favour of one which sees it as a guardian of fundamental rights against unjustified incursions by the Commons. This would justify a disproportionate representation of those committed to the ideological foundations of the state.

There is no doubt that the approach of neutral co-operation can work in individual instances, but is it appropriate as an overall strategy? In one case, it may well be the outcome of a principled refusal to persuade others of the truth of Christianity in any way other than by rational debate. In another, it may be dictated by the need for structures that preserve the justice of state action. However, total neutrality on religious questions is impossible to achieve, and the drive to achieve it leads inexorably back to the first model of intolerance. The state cannot avoid taking 'religious' decisions, as is well illustrated by a closer look at the example of marriage above. On the surface, all faiths are treated equally, but in practice various groups cannot be registered: the Scientologists because they do not worship, the Exclusive Brethren because they do not worship in public. Only a tiny proportion of Sikh and Hindu temples and Muslim mosques are registered, arguably because of the requirement to use English marriage vows, and one writer rounds off by suggesting that atheists might find offensive the questionable definition of legal marriage as lifelong.[5] But why stop there? What about homosexuals and polygamists and those advocating total sexual licence? A choice must be made between one legal institution of marriage, a range of legal forms, or no legal institution of marriage. But none of these choices is a position of neutrality; at least one conflicting religion/ worldview must be excluded from public life.

This is just one example of the fact that while ideological separation is intolerant, ideological co-operation is incoherent. States must be conceived of as persons or at least consistent systems, and every attempt to interpret the state results in favouring some particular worldview on basic questions such as human nature, the definition of the good and the value of religious commitment. Modern liberalism's search for the ideologically neutral state is doomed to failure, for in practice the formal and informal structures of any society will make some worldviews easier to live out and some harder. The key question is which worldview is to be the central one?

Symbolic Commitment

The discussion of the first two models demonstrates that the state must be constructed around a coherent conception of what it means to live a good life. Further, if the state is to do justice to all members of society it must be built on a Christian worldview, with all that this entails for religious toleration. That worldview is rendered vulnerable by the type of separation that one saw in Communist Europe and is seeing increasingly in the capitalist United States. In what ways, then, may the state legitimately mark out Christianity as its foundational worldview? At what point does the state become unjust, or compromise the freedom of the church?

Perhaps the least obtrusive way to acknowledge the authority of God over the state is by symbolic commitment. Those countries that have a foundational constitutional document sometimes do just this. For example, the Canadian constitution (1982) starts: 'Whereas Canada is founded upon principles that recognize the supremacy of God and the rule of law ...', the Australian (1900) starts: 'Whereas the people ... humbly relying on the blessing of Almighty God ...', and the German constitution (1949) opens: 'Conscious of their responsibility before God and people ...' The United States also seems to have made such a commitment when in 1956 it sanctioned the motto 'In God we trust.' Such statements perform a valuable function in reminding governments that the will of the people is not the ultimate arbiter, but of course in practice they are not allowed to have an impact on public life. Their effect is intangible. Furthermore, the concept of God is open to interpretation in a way that that of Jesus Christ is not. If it is correct that Christ is King of kings, there can be no reason why that should not be symbolically recognized as well.

The symbolic recognition of Christ as ultimate ruler can be found in both the Irish and the British constitutions. The Irish constitution (1937) commences: 'In the name of the most Holy Trinity, from whom is all authority and to whom, as our final end, all actions both of men and states must be referred, We, the people of Eire, humbly acknowledging all our obligations to our Divine Lord Jesus Christ ...' In fact, in Eire, this statement is of more than symbolic significance since it has been used in the legal interpretation of the constitution. Within the United Kingdom, in the absence of a written constitution, this symbolic function is represented by the coronation of the monarch. The Queen, while entering into office by hereditary right, is crowned by the Archbishop, and the service of accession makes the submission of the Queen to the rule of the Trinitarian God crystal clear. House of Commons prayers, perfunctory and ill-attended though they may be, reinforce the idea that Parliament acknowledges that its authority derives in the last instance not from the will of the people but from God, to rule justly and wisely according to his will. The design of the British flag and the national anthem reinforce this worldview.

The role of the monarch captures this fundamentally accurate vision of church and state as separate institutions under the authority of Christ. 'The Sovereign, acting according to the laws of the realm, is the highest power under God in the kingdom and has supreme authority over all persons in all causes, ecclesiastical as well as civil.'[6] But just as, in practice, the political rule of the Queen is exercised on the advice of her political ministers, and legislation is only passed with the consent of Lords and Commons, so also the Queen may not be a minister of the Word and sacraments (Article 37 of the Thirty-Nine Articles) and may only exercise her ecclesiastical judicial function through duly appointed judges. By convention the Queen also assents to measures of Synod presented to her. The detail might cause concern here but the broad picture is correct.

The Christian consecration of the monarch could conceivably be performed by any Christian denomination, since non-conformist objections to establishment for the most part concern Anglican attitudes to church government and membership. However, problems might arise with a (conservative) Roman Catholic consecration in that this vision of church and state could imply subordination of the state to the authority of the Pope.

Establishment

But may the state go further, and instead of establishing an *ideology* as foundational, establish an *organization* as best suited to serve the spiritual needs of the nation? That is the question of establishment. Now establishment is a matter of degree. The role of the state, as we have already seen, is to enable all people to come freely into relationship with God in Christ, but it must not use means that God has not sanctioned in a well-meaning but misguided attempt to do this, and it must not prevent the church from being the church. If these conditions can be fulfilled, there is nothing wrong in principle with establishment.

Some would suggest that in practice the conditions just outlined cannot be fulfilled. Any conceivable organizational recognition would tempt the church to adjust its message to the wishes of the state and produce an unfortunate confusion of understanding of the nature of the church as the servant of all with the nature of the state as the master of all. Any connection damns the church by association. But this is to misunderstand the nature of the state, which is in principle a God-ordained institution for the maintenance of peace and the promotion, within its means, of godliness. The church is not damned by association with the state as an institution, although it might be by association with any particular state officeholder. Every establishment must be looked at in detail first.

An arrangement where people are free to seek spiritual guidance where they please, but where there is a bias towards the established church, is institutionalized in prisons, hospitals and the armed services. For example, a prisoner who has declared a *bona fide* religious allegiance is to be granted access to a minister of his religion and allowed to follow his faith to the degree that that is practicable. But each prison has an Anglican chaplain who may be seen at the request of any prisoner, regardless of allegiance, and who has a duty to visit the sick and those under special confinement, given that the prisoner is willing.[7] The way in which the state deliberately makes it easier for the Church of England to reach those likely to respond to the gospel while protecting the freedom of each person to worship as they see fit is structurally superb. The assumption that the established church must have access coupled with a basic commitment to fairness actually protects the interests of other faiths. Of course, if at some stage in the future, a government sought to use the chaplaincy to promote a particular anti-Christian view, the church would have to reject the existing opportunities.

The Church of Scotland represents an alternative model of establishment, which only just extends beyond mere symbolic commitment. It has always maintained that its head is Jesus Christ and no earthly ruler, and that it exercises a jurisdiction complementary to and not derived from the jurisdiction of the state. In fact, the jurisdiction of the Pope was ended by Act of Parliament in 1560, and by the General Assembly Act 1592 spiritual and ecclesiastical jurisdiction was vested solely in the church. The royal claim and interest was preserved by the right to attend the General Assembly and appoint the meeting of the next Assembly, the residue of which right is still maintained by the fact that the Lord High Commissioner informs the monarch of the date of the next meeting. Apart from that, the Church of Scotland Act 1921 appears to concede the total autonomy of the Church of Scotland in spiritual matters.

Complete Unity

Finally there is the model of complete unity found typically in medieval Christendom and defended in sixteenth-century England by Hooker. The state and the church are united. The one consists of the people governing themselves in temporal matters and the other those same people acting in spiritual matters. The last whispers of this approach can be found in the old joke: 'Religion (if none write C of E)'. Such models can still be found today in fundamentalist Islamic states, African tribal societies and Christian Orthodox states.

This model is unacceptable for a number of reasons. First, it assumes that membership of civil society, largely an accident of birth, carries with it membership of religious society. For a religion which consists of outward ceremony, this is plausible – sacrificing to Caesar is then little different from casting a vote – but true faith consists in the free commitment of one's life to Christ and cannot be tested by physical location in a 'Christian' state. In other words, the model does not leave the church free to be the church by excluding non-Christians and confronting the state where necessary.

Second, the model tends towards religious persecution, even in the case of Christianity. The weapon of the state is the sword, but to extend the kingdom of God Christians may not use 'the weapons of the world' (2 Corinthians 10:4). However, the temptation to enforce faith is often too strong for weak human beings, and church discipline is confused with peace and good order.

Issues within the Establishment Debate

The prime benefit of the present establishment lies in the symbolic commitment of the United Kingdom to Christianity.

The alternative to this is not religious neutrality but secular humanism as a foundational ideology. The establishment gives church and people a remarkable degree of access to each other. The division of the whole of the country into parishes and the assumption that the parish church is a first port of call for those seeking help is invaluable. In addition, one could point to certain semi-institutionalized features of establishment such as Remembrance Day services. Of course, this is largely a by-product of the historical significance of the Church of England and is not itself a feature of the establishment as such. It is very hard to assess what effect disestablishment would have on this attitude.

However, any establishment of Christianity must leave the church free to be the church. Concern has been expressed that the structures of the Church of England deviate unacceptably from this ideal in four areas: membership and membership rights, the appointment of officers, financial management, and legislation. In assessing the impact of establishment, one must remember that where the church has the power to change some undesirable feature of its life, the fault lies with the church and not with the establishment.

Membership and Membership Rights

In former times all the inhabitants of a parish were deemed to be members of the Church of England, in the absence of evidence to the contrary. But a current definition is that members are those 'baptised persons giving general allegiance to the ordinances and liturgy of the Church of England as by law established and not owing allegiance to a religious body whose tenets are inconsistent with those of the established church'.[8] Membership is not lost by irregular attendance, although it may be by total failure to attend. A minister may only refuse to baptize an infant from his parish for the purposes of preparing and instructing parents, guardians and godparents, and so in effect may not go behind the professions of faith required from sponsors during the baptismal service. Concerns are raised at this point on two fronts: there is no discretion on the part of the minister to refuse baptism where the sponsors' behaviour gives the lie to their profession, nor is there any way of disciplining the errant member. However, it must be remembered that the issue of who is to be baptized is one internal to the church (appeal lies to the bishop, who decides as he thinks fit) and since the only acceptable way of disciplining an errant member is by exclusion (1 Corinthians 5:13), their non-attendance is barely significant here.

People resident in a parish and not members of the Church of England have certain rights, namely to take part in the election of churchwardens, of marriage in the church and of burial in the churchyard. The first will be dealt with below. It is an offence for a clergyman to refuse to marry a qualified person resident in his parish, unless one party is divorced and the former spouse survives. Since marriage is an institution of God valid regardless of faith (Genesis 2:24) this is in principle not problematic, but at one point in the marriage service the couple are addressed as 'servants' of God, and there is the symbolism of taking vows in the sight of God. Burial is more difficult since the minister must, unless otherwise re-quested, say divine service over the corpse or ashes of the departed unless (in strict law) they were unbaptized, excommunicated or had committed suicide while sane. In fact, the wording of the service is remarkably uncommitted on the question of the salvation of the de-parted. The only clear sign is that he is addressed as 'brother'. The point is that the acceptability of these public functions of the church depends on whether they can be fulfilled with integrity. If one considers a rewording of these services possible such that no impli-cation of faith is made, the question resolves itself into one of state restrictions on church legislation.

The Appointment of Officers

Various links with the state can be found in the procedures for appointing churchwardens, deacons, priests and bishops. Church-wardens must be actual communicant members of the Church of England on the electoral roll of the parish to which they are appointed. This means that as well as being members on the defini-tion above, they must have attended the church for at least six months and have taken communion at least three times in the preceding twelve months according to the use of the Church of England. Two are appointed annually at a meeting of the incumbent

and parishioners, consisting of those on the electoral roll and anyone resident in the parish and registered for the purposes of local
elections by virtue of that residence. If the minister and the parishioners cannot agree, one warden is elected by each. It is thus
possible for non-members to be influential in who becomes church-
warden. Yet it must not be forgotten that they can only appoint a
regular church member, who can always refuse to stand. Any possible conflict between non-members and incumbent must therefore
also be a conflict within the church. Our only concern, then, is the
possibility of non-members supporting a minority of members and
overriding the wishes of the majority. One suspects that this hardly
happens in practice.

The incumbent of a parish is appointed by whoever has the gift
of the benefice, and quite often this can be a non-member of the
church. This was the issue that dogged the Church of Scotland
throughout the eighteenth and nineteenth centuries, leading to the
Disruption of 1843. The Parochial Church Council can now make
suggestions (without naming names) as to the type of person suitable, but these suggestions are not binding. Of course, the choice of
incumbent is limited to ordained clergy who fulfil the church's own
requirements as to suitability. Although the bishop has an absolute
discretion as to whom he shall ordain, that person must (among
other qualifications) 'be found on careful and diligent examination
to possess a sufficient knowledge of holy scripture, of the doctrine,
discipline and worship of the Church of England, and be of virtuous conversation, without crime, of good repute and a wholesome
example and pattern to the flock of Christ'. Thus, the system of
patronage carries with it a danger that a particular skill or need will
not be correctly considered, but no danger that these basic qualifications will not be met. But the issue of patronage is not straightforwardly a feature of the establishment. Even where held by the
Crown, a right of patronage is a type of private property right that
may be held and transferred (but not sold) by private persons. In
the normal course of affairs, the church must bargain for increased
powers of appointment. Legislation disestablishing the church
need not carry with it an expropriation of these rights for the benefit of the church, although the disestablishment of the Church of
Wales in 1920 had precisely this effect. Non-member patronage is
thus more a historical accident than a necessary feature of
establishment.

Bishops are appointed by the Sovereign on the advice of the Prime Minister. The Ecclesiastical Appointments Commission forwards two names to the Prime Minister, who is free to choose either. As with ministers, the general qualifications must be fulfilled. Both must be 'godly and well-learned men, persuaded that they are truly called to this ministration according to the will of our Lord Jesus Christ and the order of this realm; and that the holy scriptures contain sufficiently all doctrine required of necessity for eternal salvation through faith in Jesus Christ ...' But the non-Christian Prime Minister might differ from the body of the church in his view as to the preferable of the two. In this context, the suggestions of the van Straubenzee Committee on senior church appointments (1992) are to be welcomed.[9] If these proposals are implemented, the Prime Minister will be by-passed, and certain senior appointments (suffragan bishops, deans and others) will be made by the Crown on the advice of the Archbishops alone. It is at least arguable that the Human Rights Act 1998 has this effect anyway.

Thus, non-members of the Church of England have a small part to play in the appointment of the church's servants. This deviates from the New Testament ideal, but not to the extent of foisting un-qualified men and women on the church. At most there will be a difference of view as to suitability.

Financial Management

A sizeable proportion – around 25 per cent – of the church's finances are held and managed by the Church Commissioners, and concern has been expressed about who these are and the way they operate.

The Church Commissioners consist of a large body of people, some holding their position *ex officio*, some being appointed. Every lay Commissioner must declare that he is a member of the Church of England, except those lay Commissioners who hold their position *ex officio*. These amount to 12 people holding high state office. The powers of the General Meeting of the Commissioners are similar to those of shareholders in a large PLC, and in practice the funds and property are managed by five committees under the oversight and guidance of the Board of Governors. This latter body consists of the two Archbishops, the three Estates Commissioners, six diocesan bishops, two deans, six clerks in holy orders and eight laymen, six of whom are appointed by the General Synod. In practice, those Church Commissioners who are not members of the Church of England and thus hold their posts *ex officio* play no part in the government of the church's funds.

In 1991, the Bishop of Oxford and others brought legal action further to restrict on ethical grounds the possible investments the Assets Committee (consisting entirely of clergy and lay members of the church) might make.[10] While the court agreed that it was proper for any trustees of property to avoid investments that directly contradicted the purposes of the trust (e.g. a temperance society investing in a brewery), their prime duty was to maximize their returns consistent with commercial prudence. They could not make a less advantageous investment where its ethical quality was at best controversial. But it is important to remember that these restrictions apply to all religious organizations that have property to administer for the purposes of the organization. The only way a financially detrimental but ethically acceptable investment policy may be followed is if provision is specifically made for this in the trust deed or by legislative change. The problem of ethical investment is thus one of the general law, and indeed the Church of England may be best placed to campaign for change.

Legislation

At various points we have seen that an issue is not properly to be counted part of the establishment if it can be controlled by the church alone, nor is it part of the establishment if it is part of the general law applying to all religious groups. The key issue thus becomes the restrictions placed by Parliament on the church's autonomy.

The General Synod can legislate by canon or measure. A canon requires the royal assent (which by convention it always receives, and the Sovereign must be a communicant member of the Church of England anyway) and may not be contrary to the royal preroga- tive or the statutes, laws and customs of the Realm. These restric- tions apply to every organization, religious or otherwise, and so are irrelevant for our purposes. Measures must be considered and reported on by the Ecclesiastical Committee of Parliament, and must pass both Houses before receiving royal assent. Parliament may only accept or reject a proposed measure; there can be no amendment. Measures have the force of an Act of Parliament and are capable of affecting any matter of law except the procedure just outlined. Thus the General Synod can (in theory) initiate legislation on any matter of UK law. This justifies the need for Parliamentary scrutiny and approval. But approval of a largely non-Christian Parliament is also required for any change to those aspects of church life regulated by the general law, which in any other denomination would be matters private to that denomination, and there have been times when Parliament has thwarted the wishes of the General Synod in such matters, most notably in the proposed reform of the Book of Common Prayer in 1927–8 and the Clergy Ordination Measure 1989 (actually passed the following year). The fact that one might welcome the outcome is no reason to defend the procedure. Indeed, one might speculate whether such resistance against the wishes of the church in matters of doctrine and worship would not now breach various international commitments to religious freedom. Since the Church of England (Worship and Doctrine) Measure 1974, the church has achieved a large degree of autonomy in this area, except that a provision to abolish, replace or amend the Book of Common Prayer must be contained in an Act or Measure. The overall effect of these provisions is thus not centrally the control of Parliament over the affairs of the church, but an obstacle to change desired by the church. And the significance one attaches to that depends on one's view of the necessity for change.

Conclusions

There is a tendency to blame the weaknesses of the Church of England on its established position. In reality, the establishment imposes minimal restraints on the life of the church. There is little that a spiritually vigorous Church of England could not achieve. Within the Church of England there is a fear that any changes to the current structures will 'cause the whole thing to unravel'. This fear is well-founded as the process of constitutional reform continues. Disillusionment with the monarchy, executive tyranny, the neglect of fundamental rights and European integration all conspire to make the option of a continental-style written constitution in the liberal-democratic tradition, avowedly neutral on issues of religion, an increasingly attractive option to many. Should such a state of affairs come to pass, it will be hard to maintain any explicit constitutional recognition of the lordship of Jesus Christ.

However, it is at least arguable that total constitutional regeneration is the only way to remove the principles of Scottish and English establishment contained in the Act of Union 1707. On this view, the Protestant succession, Scottish Presbyterianism and the Westminster Confession, English Episcopalianism and the Thirty-Nine Articles are matters of fundamental law which even Parliament cannot change. Nevertheless, some of the concerns outlined in this chapter can be met without undermining the basic commitment to establishment. The franchise for the election of churchwardens could be restricted to those on the electoral roll, private patronage could gradually be recovered and placed in the hands of church and congregation, and a measure could be introduced to enable the Church Commissioners to adopt a more ethical investment policy. Such reform is necessary if the church is to be free. Yet at the same time, the fundamental subservience of the state to the authority of Christ – expressed organizationally where appropriate – should not lightly be abandoned.

1 See Colin Buchanan, *Cut the Connection* (Darton, Longman & Todd, London, 1994), for a vigorous critique of the present establishment.
2 For a thorough and elegant defence of the principle of establishment defended here, readers are directed to Oliver O'Donovan, *The Desire of the Nations* (Cambridge University Press, Cambridge, 1996).
3 *The Functions of a National Church*, Latimer Studies 19 (1984).
4 Lord Hailsham, *The Dilemma of Democracy* (Collins, 1978).
5 A. Bradney, *Family Law*, vol. 19, 408 (1989).
6 *Halsbury's Laws of England*, vol. 14 (Ecclesiastical Law), para. 352.
7 St John A. Robilliard, *Religion and the Law* (Manchester University Press, 1984), Chapter 8.
8 Halsbury *op. cit.*, para. 346.
9 See *Senior Church Appointments* (Church House Publishing, 1992).
10 *Harries v Church Commrs for England* [1993] 2 All ER 300 ChD.

Chapter 7

ROOTS

Biblical Norm or Anachronism?

MICHAEL SCHLUTER

We are witnessing a historic decline in the significance of place to human life.

Alvin Toffler, *Future Shock* (Bodley Head, 1970)

Summary

Western society at the end of the twentieth century values individual mobility as highly as any in history. Christians in the past have not questioned that mobility is desirable. If anything, the New Testament (NT) seems to endorse a culture which holds lightly to place, and to encourage Christians to find their roots in Christ and in the fellowship of believers. However, the Old Testament (OT) appears to teach that 'roots' in place are important for personal identity and social stability.

This chapter will argue that Old and New Testament perspectives on roots are compatible. Christians must hold in tension the practice of roots in their personal lives and the promotion of roots through public policy, while recognizing that Christ may require them at any time to leave home and even family to follow his calling.

Introduction

Writing about the trial of Rosemary West on ten counts of murder, *The Economist* (7 October 1995) commented:

Orwell blamed the decline of the English murder [sic] on the fragmentation of society. It is precisely this that has made serial killing possible.

The women whom Mrs West is accused of murdering were mostly drifters. Bed-and-breakfasting here, taking a short-term job there, they had lost touch with families and roots. That was why their disappearances went unnoticed for so long. In a less mobile society, where children stayed at home, couples stuck together and people kept tabs on each other, so many women could not have disappeared without a grand fuss being made.

High levels of mobility have been a feature of Western European societies since 1945, and of the United States for much longer. Many households change home frequently, so that the movement resembles not a tidal wave but an electron dance. While such mobility may have contributed to broadening individual experience, and to the breakdown of class divisions and regional parochialism, research has shown that it has had a strongly negative impact on neighbourhood solidarity and family cohesion.[1] How should Christians respond to the culture of mobility? Does the Bible encourage strong ties to land in its teaching on the Jubilee, or weak ties to property and other earthly possessions through Christ's example and teaching on the kingdom? Are roots a biblical norm or a cultural anachronism?

Old Testament Teaching on Land and Roots

Throughout Israel's history, land stands as the symbol of the special relationship God has with his people. The land was a divine gift, Israel's inheritance as God's first-born among the nations. It was held in tenancy, not from the king as owner, as in surrounding nations, but from God. If the land as gift gave the people rights, this 'tenant' status also laid on them responsibilities, both to obey God and to love neighbour.

To explore the 'roots' theme in the Old Testament, a brief description of Israel's land-holding system is necessary. When Israel entered Canaan, every clan and family (except those of the Levites) was allocated a piece of land within its tribal land block (Joshua 13–19). This initial allocation was made permanent by the Jubilee year provisions; every fiftieth year each family was to return 'home' to occupy its ancestral land which, if leased out or lost, was returned free of charge. The prospect of a future Jubilee meant there was no freehold land market; land could only be leased until the next

Jubilee year (Leviticus 25). Several consequences followed. Neigh-bours generally were relatives; names of towns and clans were often interchangeable (e.g. Gilead, Etam); family names were associated with specific pieces of land. Potential parochialism was overcome in part by the required triennial visits to Jerusalem for the feasts, and by strong national religious integration.

Thus, at the family level, ownership of a piece of land symbol-ized membership of the covenant community (except for Levites). This is seen in the Naboth incident (1 Kings 21). If land had been merely an economic asset, and if the Jubilee had been primarily about a redistribution of those assets, Naboth would not have objected so strongly to Ahab's offer of cash or an alternative piece of land. Naboth, however, viewed his 'ancestral land' as symbolizing his membership among God's people, his roots and identity as an Israelite. To remove his land would not only strike at his relationship with God, but would threaten the future of the Naboth family line as secure and supported members of the Jezreel community; perhaps this is why the judgement on Ahab for seizing Naboth's land is for his own family to be extinguished (1 Kings 21:21).

These long-term attachments to a specific locality in God's social design for Israel would have profoundly influenced social relation-ships to the extent that they were obeyed. The approximate equality of land distribution, preserved by the Jubilee, would have inhibited growth of rural elites and prevented long-term landlessness, ensur-ing fewer class divisions in the community. Land distribution was the foundation of economic justice in Israelite society. In addition, the overlap of kin and neighbours would have reinforced continuity and obligation in the local community and contributed to long-term, committed and multi-faceted relationships. Every individual and household would have been bound into, and supported by, an extended family and a specific community through their permanent stake in the land. Indeed, if an individual could not support himself on the land, the neighbours were urged to provide help so as to prevent mobility (Leviticus 25:35-7).

At a national level, also, the land played a central role in defining social identity. When Israel repudiated God, judgement involved the nation being uprooted from the land (Deuteronomy 29:28). Equally, return from exile to the land would result from their renewing allegiance to Yahweh (Deuteronomy 30:1-5). In OT thinking, land and those who live on it are so closely intertwined that the word 'land' gradually ceases to mean the physical place and instead becomes a concrete way of talking about society (e.g. Amos 8:8; Zechariah 12:12).

Clearly, the land in Israel did more than provide the basis of family and national identity. The Jubilee was not just about roots, but about wealth and income distribution, and guaranteed all members of society the resources for self-employment. However, the Naboth incident and other OT references to land make it clear that roots and identity are not just a by-product of the Jubilee law but part of its primary purpose.

New Testament Teaching on Land and Roots

Christopher Wright has argued for three levels of fulfilment or application of OT teachings under the new covenant: 'typological, eschatological and paradigmatic'.[2] Using this framework, we explore how OT teaching on land and roots is applied by NT writers within the context of the new covenant.

Foreshadowing of Christ (Typological)

In the New Testament, the land of Palestine ceases to have its former theological significance; it is not an aspect of God's relationship with the new Israel. The role of the land is now taken by Christ, who becomes the source of security, status and cultural identity for the people of God.

Jesus teaches that the Jews can no longer claim to be planted as vines in the land, as taught by the OT prophets (e.g. Isaiah 5:1–7). Instead, they have to be grafted into himself as the true vine, and he in turn is rooted in the Father (John 15).[3] In the same way, Paul constantly uses the term 'in Christ' for the roots and identity of the Christian where the Old Testament might have referred to being 'in the land'.

The land also prefigures the *koinonia* – the fellowship of believers. Those with a stake in the land under the Old Covenant prefigure those who are a part of the fellowship under the New. Those who depart from the fellowship, like those who left their land, show that they have no real part among God's people (1 John 2:19). Both the land and the fellowship entail shared experiences and shared responsibilities such as concern for the poor and needy (e.g. Leviticus 25:39–43; Acts 2:44–5). There is the same 'prophetic indignation' at those who defile the land as there is against those who harm the fellowship (e.g. Jeremiah 16:18; Acts 5:1–11).

Signpost to the Future (Eschatological)

As well as the typological fulfilment of the land in the New Testament, there is also an eschatological fulfilment. The land of Israel, the dwelling place of God's people, is fulfilled in the new Jerusalem (Revelation 21:4ff.). Jesus insists that his followers must be willing to leave their roots, their home and even the closest of their human relationships if they are to be his disciples, but promises them eternal life if they make such sacrifices (Mark 10:29–30), as well as a home in heaven (John 14:2).

In the epistles, also, there is stress on Christians not finding their home and roots on the earth, but in heaven. Peter writes to 'God's elect, strangers in the world, scattered throughout Pontus' and speaks of their inheritance as one that 'can never perish, spoil or fade' and which is 'kept in heaven' (1 Peter 1:1–4). The writer of Hebrews uses the example of Abraham, who 'by faith made his home in the promised land like a stranger in a foreign country … he was looking forward to the city with foundations, whose architect and builder is God' (Hebrews 11:8–10).

Example for Society (Paradigmatic)

All this NT fulfilment of the motif of the land would seem sufficient for the Christian to look no further for contemporary application of OT teaching. Indeed, this is where much Christian discussion of the land issue ends. However, OT law can also be interpreted as a set of interconnected principles which form a coherent pattern for the ordering of society. Israel's sharply distinctive social pattern was part of its role as an example to other nations, to demonstrate what love and justice mean when translated into social, political and economic life (Deuteronomy 4:8). Thus, in Isaiah the task of Servant who is a 'light to the Gentiles' (Isaiah 42:6) refers both to his role of generating the social blessings which should have been found in Israel as well as to his role in salvation (Isaiah 42:1–7; Luke 4:18–21). Jesus teaches that the key to applying OT law under the new covenant is to consider its implications for relationships with God and neighbour (Matthew 22:34–40).

OT law instructs Christians about social order in a way the NT does not. Although set in a covenantal context, it is given to a society most of whom are characterized by Jesus as having 'hardness of heart' (Matthew 19:8), a description applicable to any fallen society. NT teaching is addressed to Christians; extrapolation from the church to society is dangerous as secular society has neither the motivation nor the help of the Holy Spirit to attain standards laid down for Christians.

Without the paradigmatic application of OT teaching of the law, many OT provisions concerning land would lack contemporary relevance. Yet Jesus urges his disciples not to lose sight of even the smallest detail of the law's teaching (Matthew 5:13–19). For example, why should urban and rural land be treated differently in the year of Jubilee? Why was leasehold transfer permitted but not freehold sale? Why does the land legislation so obviously complement the interest ban and year of debt remission in providing a safety net for the poor?

The one ethical principle which we wish to draw here from OT teaching on land is that roots are important for individual, family and social relationships. God arranged that Israel should not be for ever nomadic but should have roots in land, and ordered the ownership and distribution of land to ensure each person and household would have long-term roots in a specific place. From this the principle may be derived that it is important for all societies to foster and promote a long-term association for each family and individual with a specific place or locality. This is to create conditions favourable to the sustaining of 'community': that is, long-term, committed, stable relationships.

NT writers, while stressing that the land of Israel finds spiritual fulfilment in Jesus, are not unaware of the importance of place in people's lives. Just as Jeremiah urges the exiles to 'seek the welfare of the city', even when the city is the home of their arch-enemies the Babylonians, Peter urges the Christians of his day to become socially involved wherever they find themselves (Jeremiah 29:4–7; 1 Peter 2:11–17). Paul sends most of his letters to Christians in specific cities, recognizing the particularities of each situation. Even in Revelation, each church's life is assessed in the light of its specific local and spiritual context (Revelation 2 and 3).

The Roots Issue Today

The Christian Church has not generally had the political and economic influence necessary to implement biblical teaching on land distribution and rootedness in society. After the Reformation in Britain when such an opportunity did exist, the church's continuing position as major landowner stifled any radical critique of landowning structures such as those by the Levellers or Fifth Monarchists. Thus, the later enclosure movement, which resulted in large-scale population mobility and contributed to class antagonisms past and present, went largely unchallenged by the church. Only the Methodists seriously addressed issues of land reform, and then not until the nineteenth century.[4]

The reason why so few people in Western societies today can identify roots in a place is due to the contemporary culture of mobility. This has a long history. Indeed, MacFarlane has traced the origins of English individualism back to a period prior to 1200.[5] Western liberal philosophy, stressing the freedom of the individual, 'searched for universals in every sphere, and recognized no particularism or uniqueness, least of all of a geographic-religious kind'.[6] As Christopher Lasch argued, for certain elites in the Western intellectual tradition, 'progress *is* mobility'.[7]

In neo-classical economic theory, not only is land a commodity to be traded like any other commodity, but mobility is regarded as essential to maximize labour productivity; to encourage rootedness would create skill scarcity in growth areas and thus slow economic progress. Mobility is an essential feature of a capitalist economy.

Both occupational and residential mobility have become accepted as a necessary, inevitable and even desirable aspect of contemporary culture. Mobility contributes to freedom from restricting obligation to family and neighbour, freedom to do as you like with no danger of social censure. This is why urban life for some is so appealing; no-one knows who you are, where you come from or what is your business.

The pattern of university education and career progression has helped inculcate a mobile culture among the better-educated. In Britain, university applications are cleared nationally; graduates rarely return to their former home areas. Thereafter, moving house becomes part of career progression. Thus, in the United States about a fifth of the population change their address annually.[8]

In Britain, even under present difficulties, there were over 1.25 million housing transactions in 1994.[9] For those on low incomes or trapped by negative equity, long-distance commuting is sometimes the only way to obtain work, and while not requiring house relocation equally disrupts family and neighbourhood relationships.[10]

Mobility is linked to stress-related physical and mental ill-health; symptoms include irritation, somatic complaints, tension, anxiety, depression, smoking and heart disease, with women often the worst affected; it is also a recurring feature of marriage breakdown.[11] A study of hospital doctors documented the effects of mobility on their families:

> These wives found that mobility was isolating because it both severed established ties with relatives, friends and neighbours and placed them in new and unfamiliar situations. When moves were frequent, feelings of non-belongingness were ongoing ... building up new relationships was usually a lengthy process.[12]

Mobility also often creates relationship difficulties for children as they move school and neighbourhood. For the elderly, the mobility of their adult children often leaves them isolated and lonely. It becomes impossible for adult children to fulfil obligations to elderly parents, simply because they live too far away.

The overall impact of high mobility is greater superficiality in personal relationships. Durkheim deplored the cult of the individual and coined the term 'anomie' to describe the condition of individuals no longer satisfactorily relating to one another. Immundo, in his phrase 'the mobility syndrome', extends Durkheim's principle to explain a way of behaving that is geared to developing only temporary relationships. Toffler describes the 'modular man' who establishes a fragmented network of limited, functional relationships, in which he plugs into a module of another's personality rather than engaging the person; 'the knowledge that no move is final ... works against the development of relationships that are more than modular'.[13] Thus, mobility directly undermines the sustained and multi-faceted relationships which are required to achieve social integration and personal development.

Implications for Personal Lifestyle Decisions and the Local Church

Against this background of a high-mobility, placeless culture, how can Christians reaffirm the biblical emphasis on roots? At the personal level, clearly the norm of roots is not antithetical to all mobility. Some may choose to broaden their experience and pursue career development before putting down roots. Often, hard choices must be made between making roots the priority for the benefit of family and local church as against career advancement for the breadwinner. There are no rules here; the balance between relationship priorities and the best use of personal talents for God's glory has to be weighed by each individual and household. However, Christians must face the fact that if they choose mobility to pursue career opportunities there will be long-term relational costs, both for themselves and for others in their family, church and neighbourhood.

Principles for personal lifestyle decisions might include the following. First, those asked to move for job reasons should weigh up carefully the long-term relational implications. Second, Christians generally should stay in one town, and if possible in one house, as long as possible so that they can develop relationships in the locality. Third, families need to develop a long-term 'roots' strategy; couples on marrying might be encouraged to plan where their roots should be (perhaps even where they plan to retire) so that they can organize their long-term career decisions accordingly.

However, Christians must be ready for God's call to override the desire for roots here on earth: Christians must be ready to go anywhere, any time. Such mobility is essential, for example, for the evangelization of unreached billions in Asia and nearer home to strengthen Christian witness in inner cities. This ambivalence towards roots is part of the paradox Christians face as they live with one foot in the 'present age' and the other in the 'age to come'.

For those Christians who have been compelled to lose their roots by political upheaval or other tragic circumstances, the biblical perspective can be a source of encouragement. Ultimately, roots which provide meaning, belonging and identity are found in Christ, and as the Israelite exiles discovered in Babylon, God is able to help build new relationships in the local community to provide a sense of plan and purpose (Jeremiah 29:4–14).

It is difficult for Christians to implement the NT vision of the local church when a high proportion of the congregation is transient. Eclectic congregations in suburbs or city centres undermine the claim that Christian faith transcends class and culture. The vision of the sharing and caring community is hard to bring about where relationships last for months rather than years. So local churches need to teach and encourage rootedness among their members. Equally difficult is the church's task of penetrating local communities which are highly mobile. It is tempting not to bother to seek friendship with a family which is likely to move on shortly. Deliberate strategies are needed to befriend short-stay households if they are to be presented with the gospel.

Implications for Corporates and Governments

The corporate sector could play an important role in reducing levels of mobility. Personnel departments would probably be less enthusiastic to relocate staff if they appreciated fully the impact indirectly on the employee's family and directly on employee productivity. Also, corporations could make greater effort to take capital to depressed regions rather than expecting labour to move to growth areas. However, it is only if a new consensus develops in society about the benefits of strong roots to individuals, families and wider society that companies are likely to reduce levels of relocation.

At the level of government, there are a range of options. As a major employer, government departments can act directly to reduce mobility – for example, among NHS and military personnel. In schools, governments could introduce 'family education' into the core curriculum, including discussion of the relational costs of high levels of mobility. Indirectly, the government could discourage mobility through fiscal policy, housing policy and strong regional policy. For example, because much job mobility results from capital being transferred out of depressed areas by national-level financial institutions, economists have begun to call for establishment of regional banks as a means of stemming the outflow of funds from the periphery to the core.[14]

The reason governments fail to tackle mobility is not primarily an absence of policy instruments. It is the failure to appreciate the true economic and social costs of mobility, or the personal and relational benefits of roots. Our task as Christians who wish to be salt and light in society, based on a biblical agenda, must be to actively promote roots in both public and private life, however much this contravenes the prevailing social ethos.

1 For a summary of this research, see Helen Hayward, *The Impact of Mobility on Personal Relationships* (Jubilee Centre, Cambridge, 1992).
2 Christopher J.H. Wright, *Living as the People of God* (IVP, 1983).
3 See Gary M. Burge, 'Territorial Religion, Johannine Christology, and the Vineyard of John 15', in J. Green and M. Turner (eds), *Jesus of Nazareth: Lord and Christ* (Eerdmans, 1994).
4 Helen Hayward, *Christian Attitudes to the Ownership and Distribution of Land in Britain 1500–1930* (Jubilee Centre, Cambridge, 1992).
5 Alan MacFarlane, *The Origins of English Individualism* (Basil Blackwell, Oxford, 1978).
6 W.D. Davies, *The Territorial Dimension of Judaism* (University of California Press, London, 1982), p. 13.
7 Kenneth Anderson, 'Heartless World Revisited: Christopher Lasch's Parting Polemic against the New Cross', *Times Literary Supplement*, 22 September 1995, p. 3.
8 Daniel Bell, 'The Disunited States of America', *Times Literary Supplement*, 9 June 1995, p. 16.
9 Central Statistical Office, London.
10 Philippa J. Semper, *Weekly Long-Distance Commuting: Its Effect on Family and Community Life* (Jubilee Centre, Cambridge, 1989).
11 Helen Hayward, *The Impact of Mobility on Personal Relationships* (Jubilee Centre, Cambridge, 1992), p. 53.
12 Faith Elliot Robertson, 'Mobility and the Family in Hospital Medicine', *Health Trends*, vol. 13 (1981), pp. 15–16.
13 Alvin Toffler, *Future Shock* (Bodley Head, London, 1970).
14 S. Dow, *Financial Markets and Regional Development* (Gower, Aldershot, 1990).

PART III

CRIME AND
JUSTICE

Chapter 8

THE MORALITY OF PUNISHMENT

CHRISTOPHER TOWNSEND

My object all sublime
I shall achieve in time –
To let the punishment fit the crime –
The punishment fit the crime.

The Mikado

Summary

The moral foundation of punishment is a problematic issue which has prompted several competing views. A biblical perspective is anchored in the principle of retribution: punishment is deserved in proportion to the seriousness of an offence. However, the biblical endorsement of retribution is qualified and carefully nuanced. The fundamental aim is not to inflict suffering on offenders but to reassert the existence of the moral order that governs human life. That moral order emphasizes the connections between justice, right relationships and seeking after community well-being. For this reason, punishment should normally aim both at making reparation to victims and at restoring offenders into the community. Taken together these priorities highlight shortcomings in our criminal justice system and suggest directions for reform.

Introduction

Punishment is a universal phenomenon. No human society confronted with infringements of its laws or customs leaves itself powerless to impose sanctions. For all this accumulated experience of dealing with offenders, punishment remains a problematic matter under constant debate.

At the turn of the century, the Gladstone Report of 1895 set the tone for penal policy, affirming that prison had a deterrent function and ushering in the 'rehabilitative ideal'. In 1910 the Home Secretary, Winston Churchill, expressed this ideal by encouraging 'a desire and eagerness to rehabilitate ... tireless efforts towards the discovery of curative and regenerating processes, and an unaltering faith that there is treasure, if only you can find it, in every man'.[1]

This ideal had its heyday in the 1950s and 1960s but, in time, collapsed under the weight of sustained critique and practical observation. As C.S. Lewis trenchantly argued, the apparent benevolence of compulsory rehabilitation masked the potential for injustice.[2] How long must a petty thief be incarcerated before his habit of stealing has been 'cured'? Reviews of the general efficacy of treatment programmes in penal settings reached negative conclusions: the phrase 'nothing works' summed up the collapse of penal confidence.[3] At the beginning of the 1990s, in *Punishment and Modern Society* David Garland wrote:

> For nearly two decades now, those employed in prisons, probation, and penal administration have been engaged in an unsuccessful search to find a 'new philosophy' or a new 'rationale' for punishment. They have been forced to rethink what they do, and to reopen foundational questions about the justifications and purposes of penal sanctions, without so far having found a suitable set of terms upon which to rebuild an institutional identity.[4]

Why Punish?

The philosophical debate has tended to focus on the issue of finding a moral justification for infliction of punishment by the state on individuals. This debate has been dominated by two broad schools of thought, the utilitarian and the retributive.

Utilitarians

The utilitarian tradition treats an act's good and bad consequences as its only morally significant features. For classical utilitarians, consequences are assessed by reference to people's mental state or happiness. Punishment is (normally) unpleasant for the offender and so, to quote Bentham, 'in itself an evil' only justified if outweighed by its positive effects. The right approach is to maximize the net benefits of the penal system for society, typically understood in terms of reducing the future incidence of crime. The method might be incapacitation (e.g. imprisonment, removing a reckless driver's licence); general deterrence (i.e. deterring others from criminal activity); individual deterrence (i.e. deterring the offender from repeat offending) or rehabilitation (e.g. probation orders or psychiatric care). For utilitarians, parsimony is an important principle: to achieve a given reduction in crime the minimum hardship should be imposed on the person punished.

A utilitarian justification involves no essential link between crime and punishment. If our aim is to reduce crime, it is an open question whether a system of punishment should exist at all. Might not some other form of 'social hygiene' be more efficient? Furthermore, a strict utilitarian must contemplate the punishment of the innocent as an open moral option. After the commission of some heinous crime the punishment of an innocent scapegoat might be deemed necessary to maintain the deterrent effect of the law. Rawls's rule-utilitarianism (under which, broadly, rules which nearly always produce the best result should always be followed) claims to overcome this problem but depends on diverging from strict utility-maximizing criteria.

The typical solution to these difficulties is a hybrid approach under which the pursuit of utilitarian aims provides the positive justification of a system of punishment but independent values act as constraints. For example, punishment might only be imposed if deserved for some past wrongdoing. Guilt would be a necessary (but not sufficient) condition for punishment. However, H.L.A. Hart, the most famous proponent of this approach, based his constraints on a concern for fairness and the maximization of freedom, making no recourse to retributivist principles.[5]

Retributivists

A wide range of theories have been labelled retributivist, but all try to establish an essential link between punishment and wrongdoing. Punishment is the morally right response to an offence in the past. In its pure form, this view holds that punishment should be imposed, regardless of whether any beneficial consequences will ensue. For Kant, punishment was linked to the categorical imperative that we respect persons as persons and, accordingly, ought to treat them as ends, not means. Retribution owes its etymology to the Latin *retribuo*, 'I pay back', and conveys the idea that there should be an 'equivalence' between the punishment and the crime. However, given the conceptual problems associated with achieving such an equivalence, retributivists in practice argue that the severity of a penalty should merely be 'proportional' to the seriousness of the offence. By itself, this permits relative, but not absolute, degrees of punishment to be determined.

The justification for punishment is often stated to be simply that offenders deserve to be punished. An assessment of desert will take into account both the harm done and the offender's culpability. The focus on culpability is based, crucially, on the presupposition that people are morally responsible for their actions, and requires the court to take account of mitigating factors or excuses such as diminished responsibility, duress or provocation. Critics argue that, whatever its intuitive appeal, this approach merely asserts an unargued claim that offenders deserve to suffer and provides no justification for the stronger claim that the state should inflict such suffering.

Retributivist theories can be traced to ancient times but have in the modern era tended to be viewed as morally and conceptually deficient by academic commentators on the ethics of punishment. However, since the 1970s there has been a revival of 'modern retributivism'. An American report, *Doing Justice: The Choice of Punishments: Report of the Committee for the Study of Incarceration* (Hill and Wang, 1976), launched 'just deserts' theory, in part as a reaction to excessive discretion over sentencing in the rehabilitative era: proportionality would limit punishment to the amount deserved and ensure that those guilty of similar crimes faced a similar punishment. In *Doing Justice* retribution was not the sole justification for punishment, deterrence being an aim, but retributivist thinking was placed firmly on the agenda.

One approach adopted by modern retributivists is to justify punishment in terms of removing the unfair advantage an offender gains by his offence.[6] The criminal law, by prohibiting anti-social acts, confers benefits on everyone in society but imposes the burden of compliance with the law. The offender gains an unfair advantage over law-abiding citizens by throwing off the burden of self-restraint. Punishment removes that unfair advantage and restores the equilibrium of benefits and burdens. Whether this theory can justify punishment in contemporary societies, given their skewed distribution of benefits and burdens, is controversial: how can there be just deserts in an unjust society? In any case, this theory relies on an unconvincing account of crime and inchoate offences (i.e. crimes which are attempted but not completed). Many crimes are the result of unplanned violence, not a calculated attempt to secure a benefit; we do not envy child abusers for their illegal self-gratification but rather despise or perhaps pity them; attempted murder produces no unfair advantage and yet punishment seems appropriate.

There is, however, a different version of the retributive approach, which sees punishment as the community's way of repudiating or censuring the wrongdoer's actions and upholding the values society wishes to defend. Andrew von Hirsch, in moving away from the benefits-and-burdens approach, writes: 'Punishment connotes censure.'[7] He anticipates that this will reinforce people's desire to be law-abiding. Even if it does not, 'the sanction should still express blame as an embodiment of moral judgements about criminal conduct'.

Communicators, Denouncers, Educators

Punishment does indeed have an expressive function, communicating in a symbolical fashion messages to the offender (condemning their deed), the victim (assuring them that society disapproves of the offender's deed and stands by the victim) and society at large (vindicating the law and reasserting the values it embodies).[8] Communication may be a defining characteristic of punishment, but why communicate these messages, and why communicate in this way?

Lord Denning, commenting on capital punishment, stated that: 'The ultimate justification of punishment is not that it is a deterrent, but that it is the emphatic denunciation by the community of a crime.'[9] Denunciation may be instrumental (e.g. intended to reduce crime by emphasizing its wrongness and by fostering obedience to the law), or expressive (i.e. simply expressing society's condemnation, regardless of any impact on crime). In other words, behind denunciation appears to lurk either an essentially utilitarian or retributivist justification.

For others, punishment is intended to have an educative effect, either on the public or on the offender. In the Court of Appeal in *R v Serjeant* it was declared that the courts need not follow, could not ignore, but perhaps, above all, had a duty to *lead* public opinion.[10] Alternatively, punishment is seen as an endeavour aiming to bring the offender to realize the wrongness of their crime, and to establish in them a proper respect for the law and its values. This differs from utilitarian rehabilitation which aims at obedience to the law by the humane methods most likely to succeed. Here, the offender is viewed as a responsible moral agent who should be persuaded to adopt a new moral outlook to undergird any change in behaviour.

A Ceaseless Debate?

There is, in short, a welter of differing views on the basic justification of punishment. Each has appealing elements; none is immune from telling criticisms. It is perhaps not surprising that traditionally the approach of the English judiciary has been unashamedly eclectic. Our task is to uncover whether an examination of the Bible's teaching on punishment can shed light on this debate, allowing us to discriminate between options and possibly leading us in new directions.

An Eye for an Eye?

It is not uncommon for Christians to cut the Gordian knot of this debate by affirming that the *lex talionis* ('an eye for an eye, a tooth for a tooth') expresses the biblical view of punishment. This principle supports the retributivist view: an offence calls for punishment and its severity should be determined by the offence committed, not by the criminal's characteristics or social policy objectives. Nonetheless, the principle had from the outset a social function, serving to limit the revenge which might otherwise be extracted in a blood feud (cf. Genesis 4:24). An emphasis on desert, implicit in the *lex talionis*, is explicit elsewhere. If corporal punishment was to be administered, the guilty man was to receive 'the number of lashes his crime deserves' (Deuteronomy 25:3).

Some objections can be defused by a sensitive reading of the basic texts. When first stated, the principle is immediately followed by a creative application. A person who injured his servant was to let him or her go free as compensation (Exodus 21:23–7). In other words, no charter for judicial mutilation was given: the aim was proportionate not imitative retribution, often by way of compensation or restitution. There are hints that the principle was flexible, as some passages forbid any reduction of the penalty (e.g. Deuteronomy 13:8; 19:13), suggesting that normally a certain latitude was available. Finally, it is anticipated that often punishment would have a deterrent effect: 'never again will such an evil thing be done among you' (e.g. Deuteronomy 13:11).

From this material it appears that punishment should be imposed on an offender – normally and certainly no more than – in proportion to what their offence deserves. However, subject to this overriding principle, punishment may have other ends to serve, notably restitution and deterrence. Thus, for many Christians, the idea of retribution is the cornerstone of justice in punishment. Not a few, however, consider that retribution springs from a desire for revenge, that it sanctions state cruelty and is morally unacceptable.

Howard Zehr in *Changing Lenses* (Herald Press, 1990) argues that a biblical conception of justice calls for a paradigm shift from 'retributive justice' to 'restorative justice'. Crime should be seen as a violation of people, not rules; social factors should be given greater weight in assessing individual responsibility; the administration of justice should focus not on 'inquiry into guilt' but on 'a search for solutions'; sentencing should aim not at 'infliction of pain' but on 'making right'; justice should be based not on desert but on need; our aim should be not to maintain but to transform the status quo and to build *shalom*.

Timothy Gorringe's thesis in *God's Just Vengeance* (Cambridge University Press, 1996) is that over the centuries the satisfaction theory of the atonement has led to a cultural milieu that endorses the infliction of suffering. A proper grasp of the overall direction of the biblical texts, he argues, points away from such a doctrine. Historically, the church, particularly when part of the establishment, has tacitly – or expressly – supported harsh penal regimes. For Luther, magistrates were 'God's hangmen'. Now, Gorringe urges that 'the church, on the ground of its founding texts' should aim to deconstruct the ideology of retributivism and instead promote 'a conception of human life grounded not on violence, and the logic of an eye for an eye, but on forgiveness' (p. 265).

These writers are wrong to deny an integral role to retribution. However, as we shall see, their misgivings are not entirely misplaced.

The principle of retribution in the Old Testament is derived from the natural phenomenon of blood-vengeance. The rights and duties of vengeance are transferred from the private to the public sphere when the human judge assumes communal responsibility for vindicating the victim's claim, as appears particularly in passages dealing with cities of refuge (e.g. Numbers 35; Deuteronomy 19). On the one hand, 'by giving judgement, and thus discriminating between innocence and guilt, and rewarding the offender proportionately to his offence, the judge transforms the originally blind and impassioned act of vengeance into an occasion for public disclosure of truth'. However, the 'derivation of retribution from the wrath of the injured party helps to explain the persistent ambivalence with which it is viewed. It can neither be dismissed nor absolutized, for it is a feature of human judgement which takes place under the broken social and cosmic conditions of the fall.'[11]

Such an evaluation of retributivism rightly pays no heed to the chestnut that Jesus countermanded the idea of 'an eye for an eye' in the Sermon on the Mount, as there is a clear distinction between personal and public ethics. Yet it helps us to avoid uncritical enthusiasm for the concept of retribution. The Bible's teaching on punishment cannot, however, be reduced to an exposition of judicial vengeance. A broader canvas is filled and, in particular, its distinctive perspective builds on a theology of the state.

Punishment and the State

For the political philosopher the state usually acquires the right, or duty, to impose suffering on offenders by virtue of some form of social contract. Kant's autonomous man acts as a rational co-legislator in the formation of society's laws, and consents in advance to punishment; the individuals in Locke's state of nature hand over to the state their right to exact satisfaction from persons who harm them. The Old Testament, as we have seen, suggests a process whereby victims' 'rights' are adopted and endorsed by the community. By contrast, the New Testament unambiguously accords to the state a penal role which owes its origins to the divine ordering of human affairs.

The governing authorities are established by God and the one in authority 'is God's servant, an agent of wrath to bring punishment on the wrongdoer' (Romans 13:1, 4). The person liable to punishment is 'the wrongdoer': the Greek present participle suggests habitual wrongdoing rather than a solitary offence. C.E.B. Cranfield comments that 'Through the state there takes place a partial, anticipatory, provisional manifestation of God's wrath against sin.'[12] It is partial (no sin escapes God's judgement but the state punishes certain outward actions and apprehends only some offenders); anticipatory (foreshadowing a future day of judgement); and provisional (no human tribunal can evaluate with precision an individual's moral guilt). None of this is to say that all penal action by the state is legitimate – moral constraints must limit, and practical considerations influence, how and when the state exercises its unique authority. For the authorities, as God's servants, are accountable to him and, in Calvin's words, do not 'have unbridled power but power that is restricted to the welfare of their subjects'.

For Christians, punishment has a 'vertical dimension' ignored by secular accounts. Indeed, Christians have a coherent explanation for the persistent intuition that the guilty deserve to be punished, an intuition which secular writers find hard to justify. The fact that pagan Rome could serve as an agent of God's wrath indicates that even a penal system untutored by Christian thought can serve valid purposes. If punishment by the state – when imposed on the wrongdoer – is a manifestation of God's wrath, such punishment should serve as a 'public disclosure of truth', a reminder of the moral order that governs human life and our ultimate moral accountability.

The Old Testament counterpoint to Romans 13 is, perhaps, the role of the king as supreme judge after the monarchy is established. The king is the personification of the state, and the ideal he was meant to fulfil was articulated in the opening words of the coronation psalm, Psalm 72:

> Endow the king with your justice, O God,
> the royal son with your righteousness.
> He will judge your people in righteousness,
> your afflicted ones with justice.

Notwithstanding the messianic overtones of this psalm, it reinforces the impression that human government when punishing should echo in some respects the qualities of divine justice.

Divine Justice

Justice, Wrath and Mercy

The wrath of God is the personal reaction of a holy God to human sin, an indispensable aspect and expression of God's righteousness. The wrath of God is never cruel or capricious but always the action of God as judge, punishment administered to maintain justice. God, while already active in judgement, often refrains from exacting due punishment now in the hope that his patience will lead us to repentance (Romans 2:4). However, on 'the day of God's wrath, when his righteous judgement will be revealed', God 'will give to each person according to what he has done', resulting in eternal life for some and wrath for others (Romans 2:5–11; cf. Revelation 20:11–15). Texts such as this led J.I. Packer to state that 'when the New Testament speaks of the final judgement it always represents it in terms of retribution'.[13] There will be degrees of punishment (e.g. Matthew 11:22, 24), and culpability will be assessed according to how much a person knows of God's will (see, for example, Romans 2:12; Luke 12:47ff.). But, while judgement at God's hands is bitter and painful, the Bible insists that God takes no pleasure in the death of a sinner (Ezekiel 33:11; 2 Peter 3:9). Moreover, not one person condemned on that last day will be able to find fault with God's justice – every mouth will be silenced (Romans 3:19).

We must, however, integrate all this with the great truth that salvation comes 'by grace ... through faith ... not by works' (Ephesians 2:8). We are all 'by nature objects of wrath' but believers escape deserved judgement because God, rich in mercy, saves us by grace (Ephesians 2:3–4). A Christian's deeds do not merit salvation but they are weighed to provide evidence of his inward allegiance to Christ (Matthew 25:34ff.) and to assess their faithfulness in serving Christ (2 Corinthians 5:10). Yet the New Testament insists that salvation arising from God's mercy in no way renders God unjust. How is this?

Paul's triumphant claim in Romans is that 'a righteousness from God' has arrived (Romans 1:17; 3:21). The three main meanings ascribed to this phrase have been: in the medieval tradition, God's justice (as in vv. 25–6); according to the Reformers, a righteous status bestowed by God – in a word, justification; and according to some modern scholars, God's dynamic saving activity (a view based on Old Testament passages, such as Isaiah 45:21 where 'God's righteousness' and 'God's salvation' are synonyms).[14] While the second is almost certainly correct (the righteousness of God is the righteous standing which God gives to those who believe in Jesus), the others may enrich our overall understanding (this gift is only available because of God's dynamic saving activity and the whole operation is consonant with God's justice).

God's mercy is consistent with his justice: first, as there is at least a hint that mercy is an aspect of divine justice. Second, through Christ's atoning sacrifice God 'demonstrate[s] his justice at the present time, so as to be just and the one who justifies those who have faith in Jesus' (Romans 3:26). Christ's death on the cross satisfied the demands of God's justice in full. He bore our sins in his own body and broke the iron logic by which guilty sinners must face retribution at the hands of a holy God. That the cross 'demonstrates' God's justice is revealing: justice must be seen to be done and the broken moral order must be reasserted.

Justice, Relationships and Social Harmony

Judgement in the New Testament is by no means always described using metaphors drawn from the courtroom. The presence or absence of a relationship with Christ is the touchstone of divine judgement; the issue is whether we are 'in Adam' or 'in Christ'. It is not necessary for us (as some do) to infer that the language of retribution in the New Testament is merely intended to emphasize that God's judgement is never arbitrary.[15] A synthesis might build on the organic links existing between whether we know Christ, what we are and what we do. Indeed, as has been suggested, it may be appropriate to understand justification not merely as a forensic action but as 'rectification' of a broken relationship, given the OT background to the word righteousness (*dikaiosyne*).

In the Old Testament, *tsedeq/tsedeqah* are the words usually translated as 'righteousness' or 'justice'. The root meaning is 'straightness' in a physical sense and implies conformity with a norm, but the word develops over time a richer texture. Arising from the idea that God's righteousness is his intervention on behalf of his covenant people (1 Samuel 12:7), and his people's righteousness is their loyal obedience to him, the essential idea emerges that righteousness is the fulfilment of the demands and obligations inherent in a relationship between two persons.[16] The companion to righteousness/justice (*tsedeq*) is justice-in-action (*mishpat*). In C.J.H. Wright's words, '*Mishpat* is what needs to be done in a given situation if people are to be restored to conformity with *tsedeq/tsedeqah*.'[17] In a human context *mishpat* has a wide range of possible meanings and can refer to a legal ordinance, a person's cause of action, the process of litigation, the verdict which emerges, and execution of that verdict. There is, finally, an intimate connection between *tsedeq* and *shalom*, for as the Psalmist tells us 'righteousness and peace kiss each other' (Psalm 85:10). *Shalom*, usually translated 'peace', comes from a root meaning 'to be complete' and conveys a sense of the wholeness, harmony, fulfilment in the community which God desires. This is the fruit of *tsedeq*, things and people as they ought to be, the all-rightness God intends. In short, 'righteousness and justice in Old Testament thought are not abstract ideas. They are highly personal and relational terms.'[18]

Punishment, Justice and Community

An examination of penal provisions of Old Testament Israel ('OT Israel') affords an indication of how some of the values which distinguish the biblical conception of justice from simple retributivism can find their expression in a human society. Indeed, OT Israel is offered by the Bible as a paradigm or model from which ethical and practical insights may with due care and sensitivity be drawn and applied to other societies.[19] The backdrop to OT Israel's penal code was a blueprint for social life which, though little achieved in practice, sought to foster substantial economic equality, family cohesion and moral education. The administration of justice emphasized community participation: alleged offenders were brought to trial by the victim, a relative or an eye-witness, rather than public prosecutors; matters were often settled at the town gate by community elders. In terms of punishment, three prominent themes which emerge are now considered.

Reparation

For many offences, particularly theft and personal injury, Old Testament law required the offender to make restitution (e.g. Exodus 22:1, 4). As between offender and victim, justice had to be restored. Atonement for a wrong done to another person involves, so Richard Swinburne argues in *Responsibility and Atonement* (Clarendon Press, 1989), repentance, apology, reparation and 'penance', which together aim to remove, so far as possible, an action's malevolence and harmful results. In a penal context, reparation might typically be exacted by compulsion and should include compensation for the wrongdoer's malevolence which has not been addressed by apology or penance: hence the Old Testament's requirement that reparation after theft should involve paying back more than the amount stolen. To make the victim 'whole', to restore relations in formal terms, helps to build a just community. Notably, the Hebrew for restitution (*shillum*) is derived from the same root as *shalom*. Restitution was so important that a thief who had nothing was to be sold to pay for his theft: he became the tied servant of the injured party for up to seven years or was, possibly, sold to a third party who would give a sum of money to the victim (Exodus 22:3; Deuteronomy 15:12–15).

Reintegration

The extent of capital punishment in OT Israel is sometimes regarded as problematic. However, OT Israel resorted to capital punishment only after the stringent evidential requirements had been satisfied: two eye-witnesses were needed (Deuteronomy 19:15). In OT Israel, unlike Mesopotamia, no property crime ever warranted this ultimate sanction. Human life was always more precious than mere property. Even so, OT Israel was prepared through capital punishment to carry out the permanent removal of an offender from the community. Nonetheless, a key feature of OT Israel's penal code is that normally punishment, whether by restitution or corporal punishment, involved no severing of family or community links. The principles governing corporal punishment involved respect for the offender: he was a 'brother' whose punishment must be limited to ensure he did not become 'degraded in your eyes' (Deuteronomy 25:1–3). There are hints here of 'reintegrative shaming', a process which John Braithwaite claims is the hallmark of successful crime reduction strategies, and requires expressions of community disapproval to be followed by gestures of reacceptance into the community of law-abiding citizens.[20] This contrasts with disintegrative shaming, or stigmatization, which divides a community by creating a class of outcasts.

The form of punishment conspicuous by its almost complete absence from OT Israel is imprisonment. Manslaughter led to temporary exile in a city of refuge until the high priest's death. Apart from this, compulsory exclusion from community life for a period was not practised, an omission which invites a critical re-examination of the role prison plays today.

The New Testament practice of excommunication sheds interesting light on these themes of removal and reintegration. C.K. Barrett, commenting on 1 Corinthians 5, notes: 'Any community inculcating moral standards ... is bound to recognise a degree beyond which transgression of its code becomes intolerable because destructive of the foundations on which the community itself rests, so that exclusion becomes necessary.'[21] However, in 2 Corinthians 2, possibly a sequel, Paul urges the Corinthians in relation to someone who has been disciplined: 'reaffirm your love for him' (v. 8). If punishment is to be part of a process whereby a person is restored fully to the life of the community, the community will need to demonstrate its reacceptance of the erstwhile offender.

Reformation

OT Israel's penal code contains no express references to seeking to reform an offender. However, in some cases, penalties appear to 'fit' the crime and so serve to communicate something about the nature of the offence. Studies suggest that a factor behind offending behaviour is an inability to grasp the impact of such behaviour on others, a lack of empathy for victims. Double repayment for theft, for example, forces the offender to stand in the victim's shoes, suffering a loss equal to the victim's loss at their hands (Exodus 22:8–9). In God's dealings with Israel, when he punishes his people, his long-term goal is to foster a renewed commitment to himself (e.g. Hosea 5). Similarly, where God intervenes to judge individuals, an accompanying dialogue may seek to sensitize the culprit to the true character of his deed (e.g. God's interaction with Cain in Genesis 4:9–12) and so prompt repentance (e.g. Nathan's visit to David in 2 Samuel 12:1–12). In short, there is wide-ranging, if indirect, support for the principle that punishment, particularly if tailored to the offence, can serve as an element in an offender's moral illumination and, thus, reformed behaviour.

Punishment: A Biblical Synthesis

Our discussion prompts the conclusion that a biblical account of punishment must be anchored in an understanding of retribution which seeks to communicate moral truth by censuring wrongdoing. Punishment must be just and the fundamental aim should be not to impose suffering on offenders but to reassert the broken moral order which lies behind any defensible code of law. Such an endeavour may on occasions allow the setting aside of strict proportionality, so providing a pale reflection of the aspect of mercy within divine justice. Where an offender demonstrates genuine remorse, their acknowledgement of the deed's wrongness helps to communicate moral truth, and special considerations apply in the case of young offenders.[22] Punishment must be seen to be just, and great pains should be taken to ensure, so far as possible, that the entire process of trial, sentencing and punishment is free from grounds for legitimate complaint by those punished: free, that is, from the taint of injustice.

While punishment is determined by retributive principles in that desert should govern, or in any event set an upper limit on, the degree of punishment which may be imposed, punishment must be 'consequence-sensitive'. More than this, punishment administered justly pays heed to the importance of maintaining, or restoring, relationships in society characterized by justice, mutual respect and, wherever possible, full participation in community life. Thus, punishment should acknowledge the place of the victim and in many cases will demand reparation by wrongdoers. For offenders, the aim, in most cases, will be full readmission on equal terms into the community's life.

Punishment Today

The biblical perspective on punishment summarized in this chapter can provide a basic orientation in assessing policy issues in the penal system. Naturally, applying such a perspective to a modern, largely urban society with an increasingly plural culture is a complex matter. A burgeoning criminological literature bears witness to the diversity of people, situations, factors and issues which penal policy must address. Further, punishment cannot be viewed in isolation from the distinct but related matters of judicial process, crime prevention strategies, social justice and welfare concerns. Our aim here is briefly to explore a limited selection of shortcomings in our penal system and possible ideas for constructive change.[23]

Sentencing
While judicial discretion can lead to inconsistency and, hence, injustice, sentencing guidelines are a more appropriate response than mandatory sentences which are sometimes advocated at the highest level (e.g. by former Home Secretary Michael Howard). Meanwhile, unemployed and black people are exposed to some likelihood of more punitive sanctions than others for the same offences, indicative in many cases of a bias which has nothing to do with assessing deserts and which needs to be remedied.

Using Prisons Less
The prison population in England and Wales has risen from 39,708 in 1971 to 61,114 in May 1997 and is projected to rise further.[24] We have been told 'prison works', and an extensive prison-building programme is planned. Yet in many cases it is doubtful whether imprisonment is the most suitable punishment. The majority of prisoners have committed offences involving no violence and are not obviously a threat to public safety. Imprisonment is expensive: the average cost per prison place was £25,096 in 1998/99.[25] Imprisonment can lead to unmerited hardship for dependants, place great stress on family relationships, result in permanent job loss, and multiply contacts in the criminal world. Moral and pragmatic arguments suggest we should use prisons less.

Better Prison Regimes
Imprisonment will remain part of the penal scene, and for some offenders is the only realistic option. For most prisoners, prisons should be run as 'pre-release centres'. Offering prisoners productive, properly paid work should be explored so that they can make payments to their victims – and their own families. Prison is a form of temporary exile. This could be ameliorated by establishing 'community prisons' close to prisoners' homes as Lord Woolf recommended, by building better links between prisons and communities, by permitting more meaningful visits, and by introducing community reintegration programmes.

Non-Custodial Punishments

In 1996, 22 per cent of indictable offenders in England and Wales were imprisoned, 28 per cent given supervisory sentences (e.g. probation orders, community service orders) and 45 per cent non-supervisory penalties (e.g. fines).[26] Increasing further the use of non-custodial penalties is hampered by rhetoric from Westminster, established habits on the Bench, and public perception of non-custodial penalties as a 'soft option'. Changing this would require sustained political effort, increased resources to provide adequate supervision, and ongoing research to develop and assess methods and results. So too would attempts to promote reparation (see below).

Reparation

A comparison of the statistics for 1990 and 1996 shows that the likelihood of an order to pay compensation being imposed for indictable offences has been falling in both magistrates' courts (from 29 per cent to 19 per cent) and in the Crown Court (from 14 per cent to 8 per cent).[27] Frequently, the offender's lack of means stood in the way of making such an order. However, this is a worrying trend and there is scope for increased use of reparation in kind (or community service as a form of 'displaced reparation'). A few schemes (typically associated with diverting young offenders from the courts) already exist; many more could be developed.

The Role of the Victim

If justice is to be done as between victim and offender, the knotty question of victim participation in the process from arrest to sentencing needs careful examination. Direct or indirect communication between victim and offender, as offered by mediation schemes, can help sensitize offenders to the hurt crimes cause to a fellow human being, and help victims work through their often varied reactions to an offence.

The Future of Punishment?

Policy towards offenders has been growing more punitive since the 1970s. Political calculation has been a factor, but so have deeper social trends. Braithwaite has argued that the ideology of individualism – and one might add features of modern economic life – has been eroding the informal sanctions which intermediate social networks can apply to anti-social behaviour. It is tempting to baulk at the uphill task of reinvigorating those social networks, not least by harnessing community resources in responding to crime, and to resort instead to the coercive apparatus of the state. Winston Churchill's oft-quoted words that the 'mood and temper of the public in regard to the treatment of crime and criminals is one of the most unfailing tests of the civilisation of any country'[28] may be true in more ways than he had in mind.

1   *House of Commons Debates*, 5th series, vol. 19, col. 1354, 20 July 1910.
2   C.S. Lewis, 'The Humanitarian Theory of Punishment' reprinted in *Undeceptions: Essays in Theology and Ethics* (Geoffrey Bles, 1971).
3   The phrase was coined after a celebrated article by R. Martinson, 'What Works? – Questions and Answers about Prison Reform', *The Public Interest*, 35 (1974). Martinson in fact never used this phrase and later asserted that 'some treatment programs do have an appreciable effect on recidivism'.
4   David Garland, *Punishment in Modern Society* (Clarendon Press, 1990), p. 6.
5   H.L.A. Hart, *Punishment and Responsibility* (Clarendon Press, 1968). Note, too, some accounts which see reducing crime as the basic justification of punishment are not utilitarian at all but based in human rights theory.
6   See, for example, H. Morris, 'Persons and Punishment' in J.G. Murphy (ed.), *Punishment and Rehabilitation* (Belmont, 1973).
7   A. von Hirsch, *Past or Future Crimes* (1985), quoted in N. Walker, *Why Punish?* (Oxford University Press, 1991), p. 78.
8   See, for example, Joel Feinberg, 'The Expressive Function of Punishment', in *Doing and Deserving* (Princeton University Press, 1970), and Chapter 6 on 'Punishment' in R.C. Lucas, *On Justice* (Oxford University Press, 1980), especially pp. 132–5.
9   Gowers, *Report of the Royal Commission on Capital Punishment*, Cm. 8932 (HMSO, 1953).
10 Serjeant, *60 Criminal Appeal Reports* (1970), p. 74.
11 O. O'Donovan and R.J. Song, 'Punishment' in S.B. Ferguson *et al.* (eds), *New Dictionary of Theology* (IVP, 1988), pp. 458–9.
12 C.E.B. Cranfield, *The Epistle to the Romans*, International Critical Commentary, vol. II (T & T Clark, 1979).
13 J.I. Packer, *Knowing God* (Hodder & Stoughton, 1973), p. 158.
14 J. Stott, *The Cross of Christ* (IVP, 1986), pp. 208–10.
15 See, for example, S. Travis, *Christ and the Judgement of God* (Marshall, Morgan & Scott, 1986).
16 See, for example, W. Eichrodt, *Theology of the Old Testament* (SCM Press, 1967), vol. I, pp. 240–41.

17 C.J.H. Wright, *Living as the People of God: The Relevance of Old Testament Ethics* (IVP, 1983), p. 134.

18 *Ibid.*, p. 135.

19 The idea of OT Israel as a paradigm is explored in *ibid.* and in several papers published by the Jubilee Centre, Cambridge.

20 J. Braithwaite, *Crime, Shame and Reintegration* (Cambridge University Press, 1989).

21 C.K. Barrett, *The First Epistle to the Corinthians* (A & C Black, 1971), p. 123.

22 The biblical theme of 'disciplining' wayward children lies outside the scope of this chapter but may shed important light on the principles relevant to dealing with young offenders. See, for example, Ian Sparks 'Taking Time Out: Juvenile Crime and Justice', *Third Way* (November 1988), pp. 20–22.

23 An overview of the penal system may be found in M. Cavadino and J. Dignan, *The Penal System* (Sage, 1997, 2nd edition). Policy ideas sketched here are considered more fully in J. Burnside and N. Baker (eds), *Relational Justice* (Waterside Press, 1994), and *Relational Justice: A Reform Dynamic for Criminal Justice* (Jubilee Policy Group, 1994).

24 *Prison statistics England and Wales 1997* Cm. 4017 (The Stationery Office, 1998), p. 3.

25 *HM Prison Service Annual Report and Accounts April 1998 to March 1999* (The Stationery Office, 1999), p. 9.

26 *Criminal statistics England and Wales 1997* Cm. 4162 (The Stationery Office, 1998). Derived from Table 7C 'Percentage of offenders sentenced for indictable offences, who received various types of sentence by type of court and period, 1992 to 1997', p. 146.

27 C. Flood-Page and Alan Mackie, *Sentencing Practice: an Examination of Decisions in Magistrates' Courts and the Crown Court in the mid-1990s* (Home Office Research Study 180) (Home Office, 1998), p. 57 and p. 108.

28 *House of Commons Debates*, 5th series, vol. 19, col. 1354, 20 July 1910.

Chapter 9

BLASPHEMY LAW IN THE SECULAR STATE

JULIAN RIVERS

Summary

The English blasphemy law is often criticized for being anachronistic. This chapter argues for a two-tier approach. This would involve the creation of a new offence of incitement to religious hatred, which would encompass all faiths, while retaining a distinct and specifically Christian blasphemy law.

Introduction

In 1979, Mrs Mary Whitehouse proved ultimately successful in her prosecution of *Gay News* for the publication of a blasphemous libel.[1] Many at the time were disappointed that the House of Lords had not taken the opportunity to declare the offence dead. There had not been a conviction in England for over fifty years. Such a discriminatory protection of a religious minority was felt to be an anachronism in the modern secular state, an unwarrantable restriction on the individual's freedom of expression. About a decade later, Salman Rushdie published *The Satanic Verses*, to the indignation of many Muslims both in this country and abroad. But the High Court held that the Chief Metropolitan Magistrate was correct in refusing to issue a summons for blasphemous libel.[2] It was a straightforward application of the law as stated by Lord Scarman at the Whitehouse prosecution:

Every publication is said to be blasphemous which contains any contemptuous, reviling, scurrilous or ludicrous matter relating to God,

Jesus Christ, or the Bible, or the formularies of the Church of England, as by law established. It is not blasphemous to speak of or publish opinions hostile to the Christian religion, or to deny the existence of God, if the publication is couched in decent and temperate language. The test to be applied is as to the manner in which the doctrines are advocated and not as to the substance of the doctrines themselves.

This time the protests were different. The law of blasphemy was not too wide but too narrow. Surely in our multi-faith society the religious feelings of all should be respected? Either too wide or too narrow, our law of blasphemy is generally perceived to be unsatisfactory. While recognizing the need for the greater recognition of religious groups, this chapter will seek to demonstrate that good arguments can still be made for retaining a specifically Christian blasphemy law.

A Christian Position

In the Bible, we find that the word 'blasphemy' covers a spectrum of wrongdoing. 'Misusing the name of the Lord' includes both cursing God and living in a manner inconsistent with one's status as the people of God (e.g. Ezekiel 36:22–3). Blasphemy also covers the taking of false oaths and other instances of profanity. But we are particularly concerned with the central case of blasphemy as cursing God. A number of important aspects of this should be noticed.

First, it is never a trivial matter. The third commandment carries the added warning that 'the Lord will not hold anyone guiltless who misuses his name', and the offence, which was one of very few restrictions on speech, was punishable by death in the Israelite community.

Second, although one might have expected such a punishment in a society which rested so clearly on a covenant relationship with God, it was not restricted to members of that society. Thus, after some doubt on the part of the assembly, it is established that even the alien who blasphemes the Name must be put to death (Leviticus 24:1–16). God is seen carrying out the punishment himself against the Assyrian army after Sennacherib's violent abuse (2 Kings 18 and 19).

Third, blasphemy is to be distinguished from heresy in that it must contain an element of violence or mockery. In mourning the desecration of the temple, the Psalmist is particularly distressed by the way in which God is reviled and mocked (Psalm 74:10; 18, 22). The apostle Peter captures this violent aspect in his condemnation of the false prophets who 'blaspheme in matters they do not understand. They are like brute beasts' (2 Peter 2:12). While the advocacy of falsehood may be a matter of discipline within the church, the sincere heretic is not automatically a blasphemer.

Finally, blasphemy is not just a matter of individual responsibility. The curses uttered on Mount Ebal are uttered against Israel as a nation if they cease to live up to their new status as the people of God (Deuteronomy 27). But the concept of national responsibility does not stop there. In the Revelation of John, the evil kingdoms of the world are represented as 'a woman sitting on a scarlet beast that was covered with blasphemous names' (Revelation 17:3). Judgement occurs not only at the end of time but within time. As mankind refuses to glorify God, he gives them over to an increasing spiral of depravity and corruption (Romans 1:18–32). The consequence of despising the good authority of God is an unhappy oscillation between anarchy and tyranny. For blasphemy is the supreme expression of sinful humanity's rebellion against their Creator and rejection of their Saviour. The nation that tolerates it will not survive.

Convincing the World

This position is problematic for the Christian legislator. The act of blasphemy operates in a vertical plane: that is, it is directed against God, and yet it results in catastrophic harm both to the individual and to society. Because it requires the agency of God, the causation of this harm is visible only to the eye of faith. Thus the claims set out in the last section would be simply incomprehensible to most people in Britain today. And it is a fundamental requirement of respect for individuals created as rational beings in the image of God, however marred, that the grounds of our criminal law are at least comprehensible to those subject to them, even when controversial and violated.

The dilemma arising when the Christian conscience declares behaviour wrongful which society in general accepts has led some to abandon the battle for social reform in favour of exclusive concentration on evangelism. Only when society has turned to God can just law be enacted. While we must affirm the primacy of the proclamation of the gospel, this approach is unsatisfactory. For then, if social reform is ever to be achieved, one must assume that society will indeed grow more and more Christian. In God's grace, this can, and does occasionally, happen, but this cannot be presumed upon. As a rule, Scripture suggests the contrary (e.g. 2 Timothy 3:14). At best there will always be a residue of unbelievers to whom an argument based on the agency of God will be incomprehensible. Second, one might doubt whether just laws will simply appear, given a largely Christian society. The abolition of slavery was undoubtedly made easier by the eighteenth-century revival, but it still had to be fought for – and, sadly, among many who saw themselves as following the same authoritative Scripture. The obligation to be salt in our communities is expressed in the search for arguments which, while they may not be the compelling motives for our concerns, are nonetheless sound ones which the majority of people can assent to.

A Brief Survey of Justifications

Not surprisingly, this tension between the Christian case for blasphemy law and the need to justify it to unbelievers can be seen in the variety of justifications of the present offence. A justification that was often used, particularly around the end of the eighteenth century, was that an attack on Christianity was an attack on general morality; the one could not survive without the other. This was often linked with the idea that a blasphemous statement somehow endangered the faith of the intellectually weak.

Around the start of this century there were judicial hints of a need to find a threat to public order in the statement. On this view, the law of blasphemy prevented civil unrest among the (largely) Christian population.

But the growing, and now predominant, rationale is that the material is 'calculated ... to outrage and insult the Christian's religious feelings' (per Viscount Dilhorne in *R v Lemon*). This is a type of harm which the law will not permit.

Finally, one must note the original justification for criminalizing blasphemy which was, in Sir Matthew Hale's memorable words, that 'Christianity is part of the law of England ... to reproach the Christian religion is to speak in subversion of the law' *(R v Taylor* 1676).

We can therefore summarize the potential justifications for a blasphemy law as follows: support of society's moral code, protection of the intellectually weak, prevention of public disorder, protection from outrage and insult, and maintenance of the law. These must be considered in greater detail.

The Support of Society's Moral Code

It is plain that this argument will be extremely controversial. Most would want to maintain that morality is possible without, or is in some way prior to, God. It no longer appears obvious that without God there can be no moral imperative. For instance, philosophers such as J.L. Mackie argue strongly for a system of ethics which depends solely on reason interpreting the human condition. But since I am, presumably, free to be irrational, in what sense am I bound to be morally upright, even when I am capable of establishing what that requires? Reason, intuition, social practice and the criminal process are no substitute for the all-seeing eye of a just and powerful God. Perhaps without God everything is indeed permissible. So there is still currency in the argument from morality, but few at present will be convinced by it.

The Protection of the Intellectually Weak

This argument had only a short currency, and for good reasons. It is true that the law does try to protect members of society from the persuasive presentation of some ideas, for example in regulating advertising. This cannot apply to matters of faith. For one must then assume that the faith of less intelligent people is weaker than that of the more intelligent. But the connection between faith and intelligence simply does not exist (1 Corinthians 1:26–8).

The Prevention of Public Disorder

The problem with the public disorder justifications is that they are speech-content neutral. In other words, they look solely to the effect the speech is likely to have on others, regardless of its intrinsic merit. They have nothing particularly to do with blasphemy, and if found convincing would lead to protection for all religions. Using public order reasons to justify restrictions on expression is always dangerous, because the person primarily responsible is the rioter. No-one ever has to riot because he is told to. In addition, there should always be a concern about the heckler's veto, lest a person's right to speak is controlled by the intolerance of his audience. Nonetheless, the law is quite restrictive of speech on the grounds of public order. At its most extreme, anyone who uses threatening, abusive or insulting words or behaviour within the hearing or sight of any person likely to be caused harassment, alarm or distress is guilty of an offence (Public Order Act 1986 *s.5*). This is already wide enough to cover speech with religious overtones.

Arguments from Outrage and Insult: Incitement to Religious Hatred

The argument from offensiveness is generally perceived to be the most convincing argument for restrictions on blasphemous speech. But Muslims were as much offended by *The Satanic Verses* as Christians by Professor Kirkup's poem in *Gay News* – what they heard about it. As Lord Scarman recognized, if offensiveness is the only rationale, there would be good grounds in a multi-faith society for a multi-faith blasphemy law. But such a position is only possible if the relevance of the content of the speech, rather than its manner, is so suppressed as to be almost non-existent. The question then becomes whether the offensive speech is orientated against 'religions', a broad and hazy category, not 'Christianity', which is relatively easy to define. And again, it cannot be blasphemous both to assert and to deny that Jesus of Nazareth is the Son of God. The law would then have started to use 'blasphemy' in a sense too far removed from current practice. For 'blasphemy' is inextricably linked to exclusive truth-claims. And if the content is indeed irrelevant, are we not talking about another offence altogether, such as obscenity? For as we have seen, blasphemy in the Bible is concerned with a vertical man–God relationship, not a horizontal one between people. The offensiveness argument is concerned precisely with this latter relationship.

Some legal theorists would indeed like to see potential cases of blasphemy dealt with under the obscenity laws. In a liberal democracy, people must be thick-skinned enough to withstand whatever criticisms are made of them and their beliefs. Thus under the United States constitution, a restriction on speech by virtue of its content is not permissible. The law will only intervene when the manner of speech becomes unacceptable – that means, primarily, obscene.

But this line of reasoning underestimates the strength and nature of religious commitment. Christians stand together with those of other faiths at this point. For the sceptic, religion is essentially a matter of uncontrolled, and thus arbitrary, choice. But from within a religion, the commitment stems from a recognition of the truth. Unbelievers are blind, not mistaken. One's own faith cannot simply be changed at will. In addition, at least in the religions of Islam, Judaism and Christianity, an attack on God is peculiarly personal to the believer in a way that an attack on a philosophy or ideology is not. These two characteristics of irresistibility and personality demonstrate that religion is far more akin to race than, for example, career. This provides a strong case for the introduction of an incitement to religious hatred law similar to the present racial hatred laws. It is foolish to deny that British Muslims form any less a homogeneous grouping than Jews simply because they do not come from one ethnic stock.[3] An unsuccessful attempt was made by Lord Lester to introduce such a change in the course of passage of the Criminal Justice and Public Order Act 1994.

It is unlikely that Salman Rushdie would ever have been successfully prosecuted under such a law. While the boundaries are awkward to draw, his work would appear to constitute Islamic heresy rather than the vicious abuse of Islam as such. Although the people of minority faiths need to be assured that their identity as a religious grouping is recognized and respected, statements of heresy alone cannot be criminalized.

Cases of Christian religious hatred may be cases of blasphemy too. Part of the confusion noted at the start of this chapter stems from the fact that in the past these two categories could be assimilated. Christianity was the only religion permitted in Britain. The Salman Rushdie affair highlighted the need to separate them.

A Blasphemy Law – In Theory

We have already noted how a blasphemy law is primarily concerned with the content of a particular expression, and only secondarily with its manner. Many today would find any restriction on expression by reference to its content alone unacceptable. No truth claim should be stifled in the marketplace of ideas. But this model of freedom of speech requires at least one restriction on speech. Since the concern is with truth, it requires the speech enshrining truth-claims to be answerable; that it does not, by its manner, render the recipient 'dumb with outrage'. Thus obscenity can be seen as the unanswerable promotion of gross violence or sexual immorality. The question is whether this is the only necessary type of restriction on freedom of speech. If it is, one must seek to explain every justifiable limitation on speech in terms of the language or visual impact of expression, and not the root idea which is being communicated.

There are two reasons for doubting whether this is possible. First, in our law we find restrictions which seem right but which cannot be justified in terms of manner alone. Instigating soldiers to desert in time of war is always a crime, however rationally and politely done. Second, the model of freedom of speech just outlined itself rests on certain (controversial) truth-claims. It presupposes that unrestricted discussion is a better means to the perception of truth than state-controlled, or majority-controlled, discussion. It presupposes that it is best for the individual to decide what is good for himself. It presupposes that an individual commitment to truth is, in general, more important than social harmony. But it must be stressed that these value judgements are not shared by everyone. It is thus possible that speech which challenges these presuppositions must be discriminated against in order to preserve maximal freedom of speech.

In a secular state – one that attempts to hold the balance between competing religious claims – it is clear that no one religion can be forced on people. But a religion could be prioritized, by being awarded special protection, if it promoted the basic values on which the state itself rested. In order to maximize general freedom of speech, the state can legitimately restrict particular instances of speech that attack religions themselves committed to that freedom.

Maintaining the Law: Modern-Style Christendom

This conclusion points us back to the oldest rationale for criminalizing blasphemy: that Christianity is part of the law of England. We can now recast that argument in the form outlined above. The state is justified in prioritizing Christianity to the extent that there is a coincidence between the values underpinning the modern secular state and those promoted by Christianity.

To mount an argument that Christianity and the law still have this special relationship is going to be controversial. A vigorous exponent of this view was Lord Denning.[4] Nor would we want to claim that the present law approaches a perfect embodiment. While the history of Britain would lead us to expect such a relationship, this understanding is generally weakened by the belief that the modern state is value-neutral, that freedom of expression and religious toleration, to name but two ideals, somehow grow out of scepticism, or a bare commitment to treating individuals equally, whatever that means. Such a claim must be open to serious doubt.

To demonstrate the presence of Christian values in the law would be a lengthy process, so a few comments must suffice. One could point to the fact of religious toleration itself, which can only find a secure home in Christianity. The tension we find in Scripture between individual responsibility and individual helplessness can be seen mirrored in the blend of free enterprise and welfare state, however much we might disagree exactly where the boundaries should lie. Concern for the economically weak has led to careful regulation of potential exploiters. Equality before God is seen in the ideal of equality before the law, however hard that is to achieve. Elements of procedural justice, which are still neglected the world over, appear already in the trial of Adam and Eve (*audi alteram partem:* the accused should always be heard) and throughout the Old Testament: for example, in the need for two concurring witnesses. The list is endless. The abusive denigration of Christianity will ultimately undermine the freedom of people to disagree about matters of faith at all.

For an example of this we need only look to the states of the former Communist bloc. A commitment to economic equality coupled with atheism led to a loss of freedom not just for Christians and those of other faiths, but also for intellectuals, scientists and artists alike. What the Western countries have to offer these states is not capitalism, but an uninterrupted, albeit declining, heritage of Christian values. Market economies coupled with atheism are no better substitute for the old order and will only lead to similar bondage. One's quality of life can be as impoverished in a corporation as in a collective.

Given that Christianity could plausibly be prioritized in the secular state in this way, what about other faiths? This would have to be done by legislation. There could be little problem with Judaism, although the need is not so pressing, since Jews qualify for protection under the racial discrimination laws.

The vexed question is undoubtedly that of Islam, the problem being compounded by the wide diversity of views within it. While most British people could identify with the high moral standards enshrined in Islam, other features, such as the role of women, would be unacceptable. And since conversion to Islam is largely a matter of correct form, rather than correct relationship, it cannot share Christianity's commitment to religious toleration. The subversion of our democratic process by the formation of the so-called Muslim Parliament is also profoundly disturbing. One must conclude that an offence of incitement to religious hatred outlined above provides as much protection as we can afford to give.

However, even if protection for a faith other than Christianity is justified on value-supporting grounds, we are still left with the problem that what will be prosecuted will not be blasphemy. Blasphemy is inextricably linked to a creed. Where two creeds conflict, to vilify both might be unjustifiable, but it cannot be blasphemy in both cases.

Various Objections

The common popular objection to retaining a distinctively Christian blasphemy law is that the state ends up fighting the church's battles. Put more bluntly, is not God capable of looking after himself? The objection contains more than a grain of truth. It is precisely because God will vindicate himself that we all have an interest in preventing the violent abuse of his name. It is out of self-preservation that the state criminalizes blasphemous speech, not misplaced evangelistic zeal. Whoever thought that preventing people blaspheming turned them into Christians?

Then it is objected that the state must be neutral on matters of religious commitment. This presupposes that religious neutrality is possible. It is of course true that any particular law, for example the law against murder, might be equally acceptable to those of different faiths or none (although even here there will be disagreements about the correct limits of such a law). In that sense law can be neutral. But the idea that justice stands outside of competing religious worldviews and can arbitrate between them is flawed. Consensus is desirable, but not always achievable.

Perhaps, then, the law of blasphemy shows insufficient tolerance on the part of the Christian legislator?[5] It is certainly the case that Christians are limited in the use of state force, and if the biblical warrant for criminalizing blasphemy were found only in the covenant with Israel, then one might have cause to question its continuing validity. But as we have seen, blasphemy appears as a theme and supreme expression of humanity's rebellion against God throughout Scripture. Its significance is quite independent of any special national relationship with God.

Finally, there is the pragmatic objection. However much one might legitimize the criminalization of blasphemy in theory, in practice it has been used to persecute heretics and the insane. Historically one has to accept the force of this objection. But it is not true nowadays. The prime function of the law of blasphemy today is to prevent the publication of films and books that abuse God and Christ in disgusting fashion. Quite simply, we are better off as a result of such censorship.

The Way Forward

The ideal way forward would therefore seem to be this. A law should be introduced protecting all recognizable religious groups from threatening, abusive or insulting words or behaviour used with the intent to outrage, or likelihood of outraging, the feelings of a significant number of the group. Exactly what a religion is has to be left to the courts to decide on a case-by-case basis. Such an exercise has been done before in the case of charity law, and the vast majority of instances are obvious. The simplest way of achieving this reform is to insert the word 'religious' into the relevant sections of the Public Order Act 1986 containing the existing offence of incitement to racial hatred.

The old offence of blasphemy should not be simultaneously abolished, but left as a largely symbolic reminder of the Christian basis to our law. For the British secular state ignores both the power of religious commitment and its heritage of Christian values at its peril. The Christian community too must fulfil its God-given obligation to be the salt of social justice. If we do not, we cannot complain if we lose the privileges we once had (cf. Matthew 5:13).

1 *R v Lemon* (1979) AC 617.
2 *R v Chief Metropolitan Magistrate ex p. Choudhury* (1991) QB 429.
3 See S. Poulter, 'Towards Legislative Reform of the Blasphemy and
   Racial Hatred Laws', *Public Law* 371 (1991).
4 Lord Denning, 'The Influence of Religion on the Law', Earl Grey
   Memorial Lecture No. 33, Kings College, Newcastle upon Tyne, 1953.
5 See Ian Leigh, 'Towards a Christian Approach to Religious Liberty'
   in Paul R. Beaumont (ed.), *Christian Perspectives on Human Rights
   and Legal Philosophy* (Paternoster, 1998).

Chapter 10

BEYOND THE MORALITY OF RIGHTS

JULIAN RIVERS

The Christian is a totally free lord of all, subject to none;
The Christian is a servant of all, fully subject to everyone.

Martin Luther, *Treatise on Christian Freedom* (1520)

Summary

This chapter considers the current tendency to talk about justice in terms of rights. It analyses biblical material and suggests that in spite of the immoral tendency of rights-language, rights can perform a useful role in identifying aspects of human dignity. After briefly considering the UK Human Rights Act, it concludes with three strategies for dealing with rights.

Introduction

The language of rights has become endemic within Western societies. It is no longer good enough to say, 'Thou shalt not kill'; instead we have rights to life. If animals are to be treated compassionately, they too must have rights. From the Universal Declaration of Human Rights to the Patients' Charter, rights have become the *lingua franca* of modern moral discourse. Christians tend to be unhappy with this trend. Is it not inherently selfish, always to be insisting on my rights? Does not Christ command us to give up our rights? How do rights fit within a Christian worldview? [1]

A Brief History of Rights

The concept of a right first emerged within European culture about eight hundred years ago when medieval jurists combined two Roman law concepts, *dominium* and *ius*.[2] *Dominium* (owner-ship) in Roman law was not a set of rights to an object, but prim-arily a relationship of real power over an object. *Ius*, by contrast, was either justice in the abstract or the legal consequences attaching to a contract or property: 'the what's right',[3] rather than a right. When *dominium* and *ius* were eventually combined, one could be said to have power over a particular legal consequence or aspect of justice. Bits of justice could start belonging to people as their rights. A right, then, was a piece of 'moral property' (H.L.A. Hart).

Rights entered moral and political discourse generally through the works of seventeenth-century writers. The Authorised Version of the Bible (1611) was translated just before this period, which partly explains its relative lack of rights-language. A vigorous flow-ering during the eighteenth-century Enlightenment in the form of natural rights theory issued most notably in the English Bill of Rights (1689), the Bill of Rights of Virginia (1776) and the French Declaration of the Rights of Man and the Citizen (1789). Rights theories then collapsed in the nineteenth century under the on-slaught of utilitarianism, recovering only after the Second World War in the guise of the international human rights movement, and after 1972[4] in political theory generally.

Rights, Duties and Virtues

Rights as Interests or Benefits

A small but increasing minority of theorists have argued that rights are fundamental interests.[5] This makes the scope of rights extremely broad. Children, animals and even plants could conceivably have rights on this account. 'Third generation' rights in international law become possible, such as the right to peace and to a clean environ-ment. More prosaically, the criminal law can also become a matter of rights, instead of duties owed to society, because we undoubtedly benefit from our mutual restraint in not killing, wounding and defrauding each other.

In one sense, adopting the interest-theory is the easy route out. Since morality is always in somebody's interest – it always benefits somebody – it ought to be possible to restate any moral position into interest-theory rights. However, the 'interest-theory' is flawed because having an interest, or benefiting, is neither necessary nor sufficient for having a right. It is not necessary, because we all have many rights in which we have no interest at all (e.g. for me, the right to worship at a mosque), although of course rights are usually in somebody's interest. Having an interest is not sufficient, because we are all beneficially affected by other people's behaviour in myriad ways, without having rights to that behaviour. I benefit from the birthday presents I am given, without having rights to them.

Since the interest theory is analytically flawed, rights-language inevitably carries with it a moral flavour properly associated with a more limited conception. It is the morality of this more limited conception that we need to address.

Rights as Justified Powers over Others

We have already seen that historically a right is a piece of normative property. That sounds like a relationship between a person and a thing, but this is shorthand for what is really a relationship between people. My property right to sit quietly in my back garden is a right that no-one disturb me. My contractual right to a salary is a right that my employer transfer the appropriate sum of money. So rights are better seen not as basic interests but as forms of legitimate control over other people's behaviour, and the two examples given illustrate two basic types of right: defensive or liberty rights (stopping others from doing things to me) and entitlements or claim rights (making others do things for me). From the point of view of the other person, my right implies their duty – a duty not to interfere in my enjoyment of property, or a duty to keep their side of the employment contract. The correlation is not always one-to-one, but any coherent statement of a right can always be worked out in terms of the set of duties that correspond to it, the behaviour required of the people over whom the right-holder has legitimate power.

Legal and moral rights are distinct. A legal right formally recognizes an element of justice as it applies to an individual and empowers that individual to achieve justice through a legal system. The granting of legal rights may not necessarily be the best way of achieving justice; in the case of criminal law, for example, it is the state that seeks to ensure that wrongdoers are punished, not the individual. A moral right, by contrast, is a justified power that one person has over another because of who they are. In short, legal rights are granted and moral rights are 'inherent', and it is possible to accept the practical need for legal rights while denying the existence of moral rights.[6]

Virtues

Virtues are good dispositions or character traits. The New Testament has many lists of virtues (e.g. Galatians 5:22–3), which can be seen as aspects of the godly moral character modelled on Jesus Christ. It has recently been suggested that the distinction between rights and virtues matches that between 'perfect' and 'imperfect' obligations or duties.[7] A perfect obligation is one owed to another specified individual, over which that other has control, and hence a right. An imperfect obligation is one not owed to a specific individual, such as the duty to be charitable or patient. Justice and virtue, the right and the good, are distinguished by their concern with two different types of obligation.

In one sense, all obligations are perfect, in that we have a duty to God to be completely virtuous. Nonetheless, my duty (to God and to you) to give back the car you lent me is different from my duty (to God alone) to forgive you when you wrong me. For in the case of the first duty, you do have legitimate control over me. And while you also owe duties to God as to how you go about dealing with my forgetfulness, unwillingness or inability to hand back your car, I cannot complain if you ask it from me. You have a right to the car, but you do not have a right to be forgiven. The mistake is to assume that any situation can be evaluated solely in terms of one relationship between two people; in fact we are caught up in networks of relationships with God and each other, and the same action can be a matter of right as regards one relationship, but duty or virtue as regards another. There can be vicious and virtuous uses of one's rights.

Rights in the Bible

The Old Testament

In common with all ancient legal systems, Hebrew contains no word that corresponds to our concept of a right. *Dîn* comes from a root meaning to act as a judge, advocate or ruler, and can refer to the place of judgement, the cause of action and the judgement itself. Where *dîn* means cause of action, it gets quite close to our concept of a right. In Proverbs 31:8, King Lemuel is urged to advocate the *dîn* of the destitute, and Jeremiah criticizes his people for failing to plead the *dîn* of the fatherless in such a way as to succeed (5:28). So a *dîn* can be a justified plea, which is almost a legal right. *Tsedek*, by contrast, refers to justice and righteousness as abstract qualities, and only in Isaiah 5:23 could it plausibly be translated by 'rights'.

Where English translations use rights-language, the commonest Hebrew word is *mišpat* or *mishpat*. *Mišpat* has a large range of meanings, covering everything to do with justice from *dîn* to *tsedek*. It can refer to the practical aspects of litigation, to abstract justice, to a law, to a series of legal decisions, and to that which is customary and conventional. Hebrew dictionaries also state that it can refer to a person's legal right, but this is anachronistic. *Mišpat*, indeed, is often linked to certain categories of people (e.g. the *mišpat* of daughters), but here it always appears in the singular (this is the other reason why the Authorised Version prefers 'my right' to 'my rights'). And it is rare to find *mišpat* with an object, as we would say rights to life, property, etc. There would appear to be only three examples, namely the *mišpat* of 'firstbirth' (Deuteronomy 21:17), redemption (Jeremiah 32:7) and possession (Jeremiah 32:8). The content of *mišpat* is thus usually worked out not in terms of specific rights over others, but as divine commands or rules which benefit certain categories of people.

If one accepts the interest-theory, that to have a right is simply to benefit from a duty owed by one to another, then *mišpat* can be translated quite often with rights-language. Follow God's law and people will get their *mišpat*. If, however, key to rights is the idea of legitimate power over the behaviour of others, then clear instances of *mišpat* as a right are rare. In the case of the Jeremiah passage just cited, one needs to know the extent to which the redeemer was free to choose to redeem the property, and the New International

Version (for example) is ambiguous on this point, referring to the right and duty to buy (cf. Leviticus 25:25 with Ruth 4:4). Indeed, in the clearest instances of rights in the Old Testament, there is no normative word at all. For example, the various rights of redemption contained in Leviticus 25:29, 32 and 48 are properly so called, because they are powers held by original proprietors over existing ones. Yet in the Hebrew, the original owner simply has 'his redemption'. In short, *mišpat*, like the Latin *ius*, is better seen as 'the what's right' for a person, and although we, with our twentieth-century concepts, can identify cases where individuals had what we call rights, the Old Testament does not think like that.

The New Testament

In most cases where 'right' is used in modern translations of the New Testament, it is a translation of *exousia* (power, authority).[8] Power in this context means not physical force but the power to command legitimately. In the New Testament this refers to the complete authority of God over all creation (Luke 12:5), Christ's authority, granted to him by the Father (Matthew 28:18), and also other forms of 'devolved' authority such as that of apostles and political rulers (1 Corinthians 9:4ff.; Romans 13:1). Where this authority relates to a specific action or object, it looks very like a right.

Paul's first Corinthian letter is key to the understanding of *exousia* as rights. Already in chapters 6 and 7 he has given advice on how the Corinthians are (not) to use what we would see as their legal rights, rights to bring lawsuits, to sleep with prostitutes and to marry. Then in chapter 8 he considers how believers are to use their *exousia* to eat food sacrificed to idols: although they have this right because idols are nothing, they are to have regard for those whose consciences are weak. Paul continues in chapter 9 with the way in which he also has not used his *exousia* as an apostle to food and financial support. While he had rights to these things from the Corinthian church, his Spirit-filled love for them enabled him to surpass justice and forego his rights. Authority – justified power over others – is not denied; but it is to be used in certain ways.

The Christian, then, can accept the existence of rights, but must move beyond rights to consider how they should be exercised. Living the Christ-like, virtuous life involves reflection on how I can make best use of my 'normative property' in the knowledge that I am accountable to God for that use. This applies straightforwardly to the exercise of legal rights. Christ teaches that his followers must be prepared to give up their rights to life, physical integrity, liberty and property (Matthew 16:24; 5:39; 5:41; 5:40). While Paul suffered at times as an outcast, at other times he could insist on his rights as a Roman citizen, undoubtedly for the benefit of the fledgling church (Acts 16:37). Moreover, other non-legal relationships can also be considered in terms of rights and virtues. As Son of God, Christ has the right to be worshipped. But first he came in love, not insisting on this right, and he will come again and every knee will bow, whether willingly or not (Philippians 2:6ff.). True moral authority comes not from having no rights, but from having them and using them in love.

The Morality of Rights

Regardless of how closely particular concepts in the biblical languages correspond to modern notions of rights, much modern rights-talk has connotations that are egoistic, licentious and antagonistic: in short, that are profoundly anti-Christian. For rights carry an inherent bias favouring individualism over collectivism, autonomy over heteronomy, and conflict over consensus.

Individualism

Rights belong to particular people, so the use of rights-language favours individual interests over group interests. In constitutional thought, the purpose of rights is to protect the individual from governments that are (at best) over-zealous in pursuing common interests. For example, there is undoubtedly a common interest in national security, but the pursuit of national security can lead to infringements of the democratic right to question government policy. Dangers start arising when the right is seen as more important than the common interest, or when the existence of common interests is denied altogether. This was well exemplified by the difficulties arising from the Sunday Trading debate, in which a concrete individual interest (the freedom to trade when one pleased) had to be set against an abstract common benefit (a day of quiet, free from commerce). The only way to start arguing against a relaxation of the law was by identifying those individual interests that were adversely affected (rights of shop-workers); once a majority had accepted that these were going to be adequately protected, the battle was effectively lost.

Christians would want to straddle the individualist–collectivist divide, the usual image being of one body with many parts. We are one in Christ, yet we have diverse gifts and roles (1 Corinthians 12:12–31). Rights are apt to protect one side of this tension – the element of individuality and diversity – but not the other – the element of community.

Autonomy

To be autonomous is to set laws for oneself, to be in control of one's own life; to be heteronomous is to be subject to another. Modern interpretations of autonomy tend to create a conflict with morality, since they see autonomy as the desirable capacity to set standards of morality for oneself (consistent with everyone else setting *their* own standards of morality). Thus, it has been claimed, there is a 'right to moral independence',[9] and particular rights identify those areas of life in which the individual is free to decide 'what is good for them'. So, for example, while there could not be a right to assault another – since that would interfere with their autonomy – there might be a right to pornography, since why should you be subject to the wishes of others (heteronomy) in the privacy of your own sitting-room? Thus freedom drifts towards licence.

The autonomy–heteronomy divide is difficult to evaluate, since a key idea in Christian morality is the continually voluntary submission of self to God and each other (Ephesians 5:21). Such a person is simultaneously autonomous and heteronomous. In the political and legal context, there must be rights to certain freedoms, such as the freedom to worship God as one sees best, if not because it is good to choose how to worship God, at least because it is bad for the state to choose for you. However, since moral perfection is commanded (Matthew 5:48), there can be at root no right to moral independence. Yet even though virtues such as love, patience and generosity are commanded by God, there is an element of human creativity and freedom in how we live out those virtues; in the classic example, the devotion of a mother is incompatible (in one life) with the devotion of a nun. Moral rights can be understood as preserving individual creativity in living diverse virtuous lives, free from the pressures of an authoritarian community.

Conflict

The adversarial flavour of rights derives from the fact that rights developed first in a legal context, and only later became transferred to the realm of morality. A major function of law is dispute-resolution, and this resolution is traditionally achieved in the Western world not by negotiation and compromise, but by declaring one party in the right, by upholding their pre-existing rights. When rights get transferred to the moral realm, relationships with others suffer. For relationships flourish when people not only give others their due, but spontaneously give them more than their due in countless acts of unrequested goodwill. By contrast, an insistence on rights leads to inflexibility in relationships; each must give the other their due, no more and no less. Given human sinfulness, this leads to perpetual personal conflict.

Once again, the Christian is caught in the middle. There is a time to differ and a time to defer. Of course, there are appropriate ways of agreeing and disagreeing, and when it comes to the enforcement of rights, we should be quick to uphold the rights of others and slow to uphold our own. Yet rights are apt to express that which is non-negotiable as a matter of justice, that for which it is worth fighting.

In short, human beings, created in God's image, have an inherent dignity, which has consequences for the structure of our moral relationships and is expressed in an individuality and creativity that needs upholding and protecting.[10] Rights-language used properly protects specific aspects of that human individuality and creativity by recognizing the moral power potential victims have over potential oppressors. The tragedy is that in much modern thought, rights have become a vehicle for the perversion of these values: individuality becomes egoism, creativity becomes licentiousness, and courage in upholding these values becomes antagonism to threats, whether perceived or real.

The Human Rights Act 1998[11]

The Human Rights Act 1998 incorporates the European Convention for the Protection of Human Rights and Fundamental Freedoms into domestic law. It extends the right of individuals to challenge governmental actions before the courts. Although it does not empower judges to invalidate Acts of Parliament, it does permit them to declare Acts incompatible with the Convention, which will lead to their rapid repeal. It also empowers judges to strike down government decisions that breach the Convention, and interpret laws to give effect to the Convention where possible. The Convention contains a standard set of civil and political rights, such as the right to life; freedom from slavery; the right to a fair trial; respect for family life; freedom of religion, conscience, expression, assembly and association; and the prohibition of discrimination. Many rights are limited by the need to preserve common interests such as national security, public health and morality.

The Human Rights Act will be useful where it prevents the government from 'cutting corners', causing unjust harm to the individual. The problem is that it is being enacted into a culture in which individual rights are already overemphasized, strengthening that trend still further. Rights of freedom and privacy can also be interpreted as expressions of the modern concept of autonomy that insulates the individual from the demands of personal morality. And rights that are primarily protections from unjustified governmental interference can be interpreted as structuring all relationships. Current fairly conservative interpretations of the ECHR by the Strasbourg Court will not necessarily be followed by an increasingly liberal British judiciary.

The UK is already obliged under international law to respect the standards set out in the ECHR, and the individual already has recourse to the Court of Human Rights. A good argument can be made that this is adequate. Furthermore, as Christians we must be quick to emphasize that society will only function well when individuals are prepared to forego their rights. Of course, there must be an individual right to demonstrate, and the government must also have the power to intervene when necessary to preserve public order, but best of all – as the marching season in Northern Ireland regularly shows – we must be prepared to forego these rights for the sake of our neighbour.

Conclusion: Three Strategies for Dealing with Rights

We have considered three different accounts of rights. First, we noticed a trend to redefine rights as fundamental interests or benefits, resulting in a massive expansion of potential rights. Then we sought to find an acceptable place for rights-language as expressive of elements of authority over others in a broader context of obligations and virtues. Finally, we rejected the morality implicit in much modern rights-talk, while recognizing that the faults identified were perversions of something valuable.

Each of these accounts gives rise to a strategy. We could attempt to subvert the language of rights by adopting such an expansive definition via the interest-theory that we get nowhere. Just how do we balance the 'rights' of apple trees, maggots and human beings? The proliferation of rights-language is becoming increasingly bizarre and hence useless in the resolution of moral disagreement. The second strategy is to abandon rights-language out of protest at its current immoral tendency. If not conclusive, the relative absence of rights-language in the Bible should give us pause for thought, and at least in our own lives we can insist on thinking in terms of duties (What ought I to do?) and virtues (How will what I do impact on my character?). The third strategy is to reform rights-language. This involves challenging those who use rights to identify the persons against whom those rights are claimed, to specify the corresponding duties, and to consider whether there may not be vicious and virtuous uses of those rights.

Christians need not commit themselves to adopting the same strategy in every situation. The concept of a right is a powerful tool for doing certain limited moral and legal jobs. Like any powerful tool it needs to be used carefully, but it should be neither overworked nor abandoned.

1 K. Cronin, *Rights and Christian Ethics* (Cambridge University Press, 1992); M. Cromartie (ed.), *A Preserving Grace: Protestants, Catholics and Natural Law* (Eerdmans, 1997), Chapter 4.
2 R. Tuck, *Natural Rights Theories* (Cambridge University Press, 1979).
3 J. Finnis, *Natural Law and Natural Rights* (Oxford University Press, 1980), Chapter 8.
4 J. Rawls, *A Theory of Justice* (Oxford University Press, 1972).
5 E.g. N. MacCormick, 'Children's Rights: A Test-Case for Theories of Rights' in C. Nino (ed.), *Rights* (Dartmouth, 1992).

6   E.g. P. Marshall, 'Does the creation have rights?' in *Studies in Christian Ethics*, vol. 6, no. 2 (1993).

7   O. O'Neill, *Towards Justice and Virtue* (Cambridge University Press, 1996), Chapter 5.

8   D. Foerster, *Theological Dictionary of the New Testament*, ed. G. Kittel, translated and edited by G. Bromiley (Eerdmans, 1965), pp. 557–72.

9   R. Dworkin, 'Do we have a right to pornography?' in *A Matter of Principle* (Harvard UP, 1985).

10 J. Montgomery, *Human Rights and Human Dignity* (Canadian Institute for Law, Theology and Public Policy, 1986).

11 A.J. Rivers, 'A Bill of Rights for the UK?' in A. Beaumont (ed.), *Christian Approaches to Law Reform* (Paternoster, 1997).

Chapter 11

HELL: A DISPUTED DOCTRINE

CHRISTOPHER TOWNSEND

Why then have so many theologians abandoned the traditional doctrine of hell? The answer to this is straightforward: the doctrine is widely regarded to be morally indefensible.

Jerry Walls

It is one of the weaknesses of a great deal of contemporary Christianity that we do not speak of the last judgement and of the possibility of being finally lost.

Lesslie Newbigin

Summary

This chapter focuses on the doctrine of hell, examining the main features of the Bible's teaching and considering a number of debated issues, notably the argument over annihilationism and eternal punishment. The chapter goes on to explore the apologetic challenges and opportunities which arise from the doctrine of hell, and reflects on the 'strange silence' of the modern church on this topic.

Introduction

For most of Christian history, it has been axiomatic to mainstream Christianity that those who died without Christ would suffer eternal, conscious torment in hell. There have always been competing views, but today 'an overwhelming reluctance to address any eschatological topics, and especially the topic of hell, characterizes most pulpits and books. Among those few who are willing to reflect on this ominous doctrine, the disagreements have become increasingly sharp in recent times.[1]

If we look back to the patristic era, three different accounts of the fate of the unrighteous find early exponents. Universalism, the view that ultimately all will be saved, can be traced to Origen (c.185–c.254) and Gregory of Nyssa (c.335–c.394). For those who have not embraced Christ already, the sufferings of hell have principally a remedial quality (purging us of our sin) leading ultimately to restoration to God. Conditional immortality, the view that immortality is not intrinsic to human nature but a gift conferred on the righteous through Christ and, some argue, its corollary that the unrighteous suffer destruction and cease to exist, may be traced to Irenaeus (c.130–c.200) and Justin Martyr (c.100–c.165). Unending retribution, taking the form of physical suffering in hell, characterizes the Apocalypse of Peter (written before AD 150) and found advocates in Tertullian (c.160–c.225) and, above all, Augustine (354–430).

Augustine's view prevailed, and led to what may be termed the 'traditional doctrine of hell': the unrighteous suffer unending physical torment as retribution for their deeds. This 'traditional' view dominated Western Christendom from the Middle Ages until the mid-nineteenth century. This doctrine came to be challenged in an environment informed by the penal reform movement and optimistic expectations of human progress. The former, based on Bentham's utilitarian philosophy in which all suffering is seen as evil, implied that retribution serves no purpose and compromises God's goodness. The latter encouraged ideas of the unending possibility of an individual's moral and spiritual improvement. The challenge, when it came, addressed the duration, quality, finality and purpose of hell within the traditional view. Thus, the case for conditional immortality was promoted (duration), an emphasis on mental anguish rather than physical pain took root (quality), the existence of a 'second chance' beyond the grave was accepted in many circles (finality), and many felt unable to attribute retributive motives to God (purpose).

These debates were, in part, a pale reflection of deep-rooted changes in Western culture. If Christians still debate hell, critics dismiss the notion altogether. For Bertrand Russell, the fact that Jesus believed in hell was a moral blemish on an otherwise noble character,[2] and human destiny after death is simply to rot. Generally, today, the possibility of hell is evaded rather than examined, or mocked as a relic of bygone beliefs or, in the world of literature, reinterpreted as a metaphor for the bitterness of the human condition. The irony is that the underlying intellectual trends which have undermined the credibility of divine judgement have also eroded confidence in the possibility of finding a shared morality or an authentic source of meaning for human life.

Today, within the church, universalism has become the 'unquestioned dogma' of liberal theology and the 'secretly cherished hope' of many more conservative theologians. Among evangelicals, a modified-traditional view (with hell as eternal non-physical torment) is under challenge in a vigorous, sometimes intemperate, debate with those who believe that conditional immortality or annihilationism better reflects the New Testament's teaching. Against this backdrop, we turn to consider biblical teaching on the fate of the unrighteous, those who do not receive salvation, but without attempting to address how the 'righteous' will be distinguished from the 'unrighteous' or the relative size of the two groups.[3]

Biblical Teaching

The Great Separation

Throughout the Bible people are presented as accountable to God for their actions and, unless God's mercy intervenes, deserving judgement at God's hands. That some turn to God and find mercy, but others turn away and endure judgement, is reflected in the Bible's repeated division of humanity into two groups: wise and foolish, children of light and children of darkness, and so on. What the New Testament brings into focus is that the day of judgement at the end of history will render this division both public and final. When Christ returns, and the dead are raised, all people and all actions – and omissions – will be brought into judgement, the culmination of a process which begins even now.[4] The people of all nations will be separated, as a shepherd separates sheep from goats: the former will go away to eternal life but the latter to eternal punishment.[5] The basis of judgement will be retributive (a requital of deeds done in life) and relational (whether a person is in Christ or not).[6]

Universalists seeking biblical support turn to texts which, it is argued, affirm God's desire to save all people, the unlimited atonement of Christ, the universal life-giving implications of Christ's work, and the ultimate restoration (or *apokatastasis*) of all things to God, when 'in Christ all shall be made alive' and 'God may be all in all'.[7] The claim is that the New Testament's overriding theme of universal redemption must govern the interpretation of references to eternal damnation. For some, the two-group passages speak of a painful interim period before all is well. For others, the graphic imagery of these texts springs from the existential urgency of the apostolic message and the imperative to call people to decision.[8]

However, a biblical case for universalism is not sustainable. 'Universalist' texts, read in context, teach universally accessible salvation (available to Jews and Gentiles, powerful and poor alike), the final supremacy of God's kingdom and (some hold) the objective reconciliation of all people in Christ (but which is appropriated by faith). New Testament texts indicate a final division of humankind. Some will never know salvation: '… anyone who speaks against the Holy Spirit will not be forgiven, either in this age or in the age to come' (Matthew 12:32). Far from eternity serving as a 'vale of soul-making', our ultimate destiny is fixed at death.[9] Attempts to conclude otherwise from notoriously difficult texts such as 1 Peter 3:18–22 (Christ's preaching to the spirits in prison) and 1 Corinthians 15:29 (baptism for the dead) are unconvincing, and at best speculative.

The Existence of Hell

In the Old Testament, life after death was generally understood as a shadowy, limited existence in Sheol, a place of darkness, silence and forgetfulness.[10] In the New Testament, where the prospects of heaven and hell are delineated, the standard term for 'hell' is *gehenna*.[11] It referred, in the first instance, to the Valley of Hinnom, south of Jerusalem which was notorious for child sacrifices offered to Molech (2 Chronicles 28:3), and later where Jerusalem's refuse was burned. In the light of prophetic warnings (Jeremiah 7:30–3) it became a symbol for the eschatological fire of judgement.

N.T. Wright's extensive investigation into the identity and aims of Jesus includes the thesis that Jesus's own eschatological horizons were limited to the near future. For Jesus's hearers, the argument goes, apocalyptic language served as 'an elaborate metaphor-system for investing historical events with theological significance',[12] and passages such as Mark 13 have their significance exhausted by the fall of Jerusalem in AD 70. Thus, when Jesus 'spoke about "Gehenna" … His warning was that those who persisted in going the way of nationalist rebellion rather than the way of peace would turn Jerusalem into a foul extension of its own rubbish-dump.'[13] Nonetheless, N.T. Wright does not infer that judgement outside time is an unbiblical concept. While it lies outside the scope of this chapter to interact properly with N.T. Wright's work, aspects of the Old Testament concept of the 'Day of the Lord' and early New Testament letters which anticipate Christ's second coming jar with N.T. Wright's reading, as does evidence of contemporary belief in an eternal afterlife.

The New Testament speaks of hell as a place, the 'lake of fire' into which, after the dead are raised, the unrighteous and even Hades are thrown.[14] However, it is a 'place' originally made for spirit beings[15] and as the New Testament imagery of 'fire' and 'darkness' is mutually contradictory, if understood literally, much of the descriptive material should be understood metaphorically. In the age to come, the focal point of the universe is Christ on his throne, and around him the elect gathered from all the nations, in the new heaven and earth. Hell, though not 'nowhere', is utterly 'elsewhere'. Indeed, some have speculated that hell will be barely discernible: 'a speck upon the infinite azure of eternity'.[16]

The Duration of Hell

Annihilationists hold that after the resurrection, and (typically) after a time of punishment experienced as conscious suffering, those outside Christ will have their existence brought to an end by God. Conditionalists argue that God alone possesses immortality in himself but reveals and gives immortality to us in the gospel but not otherwise.[17] Four lines of argument are common to both approaches.[18] First, the final state of the lost is often described in terms which suggest complete obliteration, such as annihilation (*apoleia*), destruction (*olethros*), death (*thanatos*), end (*telos*), disintegration (*phthora*). Second, the imagery of fire speaks of pain but, more importantly, of destruction; hence Edward Fudge's annihilationist treatise bears the title *The Fire that Consumes*.[19] Third, for God to permit people to suffer unending torment in hell is incompatible with the justice of God, let alone the love of God. The biblical concept of justice stresses that any penalty imposed must be commensurate with the evil done and there would be a serious disproportion between sins committed in time and torment experienced throughout eternity. Fourth, the unending existence of a region of rebellion and torment would be incompatible with the ultimate victory of Christ when God will be 'all in all'.

However, none of these arguments is compelling. None of the terms which appear to speak of 'destruction' uniformly bears a meaning consistent with total extinction. For example, the *apoleia* word-group has a range of meanings, dependent on context, and is applied to the 'lost' son, a 'ruined' wineskin and a 'waste' of expensive perfume.[20] When fire burns up a log, the result is not the total disappearance of the log into non-existence but its transformation into ashes, some sort of residue. There are difficulties inherent in any human attempt to assess what action by God would or would not be just, and the logic that annihilationism must be more just is open to doubt.[21] Finally, the New Testament writers do not regard the co-existence of heaven and hell as problematic, so neither should we.

New Testament references to 'eternal fire' and 'eternal punishment' require us to explore the meaning of the adjective 'eternal' (*aionios*).[22] Annihilation, it is argued, represents eternal punish*ment* as the consequences endure for ever and Jesus's words do not demand eternal punish*ing*. There is a debate over whether Jesus's words in Matthew 25:46 have an inherent parallelism so that as 'life' is experienced for eternity, so therefore must the 'punishment'. Such discussion tends implicitly to understand eternity as the endless prolongation of time *as we now know it* but that is not a safe assumption. The Hebrew concept of time emphasizes content rather than duration. The adjective *aionios* means, simply, 'pertaining to an age', that is, the age to come. While it normally carries temporal/eternal overtones, where Jesus offers a 'definition' of eternal life, he speaks of 'knowing' God 'and Jesus Christ whom you have sent' (John 17:3). Relationship with him is central to the idea; the unending continuation of 'time' may well not be. We do not know how 'eternity' will be experienced.

One underlying issue is whether the formulation of orthodox Christian belief in the patristic era was distorted by the Platonic concept of an immortal soul. The legacy, some contend, of reading the New Testament through 'glasses ground in Athens' is a reorientation of all the relevant New Testament terms and an *a priori* rejection of the possibility of extinction of being. However, against this, Jewish concepts of the afterlife developed during the inter-testamental period and, incidentally, underwent a process of hellenization. Thus, by the beginning of the first century AD, the Pharisees had absorbed the doctrine of immortality and held that the wicked suffer eternal torment. The New Testament nowhere endorses the Platonic or Pharisaic belief in a never-dying soul. Nonetheless, Jesus's hearers would have taken references to *gehenna* and 'eternal punishment' to signify unending torment. Jesus must have known that his words would be understood in this way, and if he had wanted to distance himself from that view, he failed to take up many opportunities to do so.

In the end, the annihilationist case, while appealing in many ways, is not quite convincing. Problematic texts, such as Revelation 14:10–11, invite serious doubts: ' … the smoke of their torment rises for ever and ever. There is no rest day and night for those who worship the beast and his image ...' The typical structure of annihilationism suffers from a telling weakness. For annihilationists: '… God's final sentence begins with banishment, continues with a period of conscious suffering, and ends with destruction. In fact, not a single New Testament passage teaches exactly this sequence …'[23]

So, this chapter concludes – with some emotional reluctance – that on balance the biblical material endorses the view that hell endures for eternity. However, the traditional emphasis on punishment does need formulation in a way which gives appropriate weight to each of the different images which hint at the same eschatological reality.

The debate between annihilationists and (to coin a term) 'eternalists' is bound to continue. John Stott has recently urged that these matters are among the *adiaphora* ('matters indifferent') on which evangelicals can tolerate differences of opinion.[24] This is so, provided that both annihilationists and eternalists endeavour honestly and energetically to submit to Scripture: showing respect but not uncritical attachment to tradition, and resisting undue influence from emotion or the 'spirit of the age'. Annihilationism could lead – though one must add that it need not do so – to the supposition that to miss salvation in Christ matters little because the only penalty is non-existence. The New Testament insists that the consequences of facing God's judgement on the last day are dreadful.

The Experience of Hell

As we have noted, the New Testament imagery of hell falls largely under three heads: punishment, destruction and exclusion: '[those who] do not obey the gospel of our Lord Jesus … will be punished with everlasting destruction and shut out from the presence of the Lord …' (2 Thessalonians 1:8–9).

The language of punishment underscores, first, that hell involves pain[25] and deprivation and, second, that these experiences are not merely the outworking of our own choices but also the decisive act of God. It is important to note that there will be degrees of punishment in hell, proportional to the degree of culpability.[26]

For the eternalist destruction speaks perhaps of utter ruin, dissolution, even of becoming less than human. Blocher speaks of eternal fixity, a total loss of animation but the never-changing 'feeling' of remorse; C.S. Lewis speaks of the 'remains' of someone who was truly human; N.T. Wright speaks, tentatively, of the loss of the image of God.[27]

On that day Jesus will say to some, 'I never knew you. Away from me, you evildoers!' (Matthew 7:22–3). While the imagery of exclusion is, comparatively, less prominent in the New Testament, it reflects a deep vein of biblical truth. The result of sin was exclusion from the Garden of Eden, and exile from the Promised Land and the Temple. Hell is being cut off from Jesus Christ and kept out of the kingdom of God. In John Donne's words:

> What hell of hells, the torment of torments, is the everlasting absence of God, and the everlasting impossibility of returning to his presence … to fall out of the hands of the living God, is a horror beyond our expression, beyond our imagination …[28]

Sinners who desire to live apart from God are given over to the full implications of this decision. Made for relationship with God and others, sin leads to a state of absolute self-absorption in which attempts to find satisfaction are futile. If we are not known by God, even our identity loses any solid basis: we are lost indeed.

The Didactic Function of Hell-Imagery

A proper handling of the doctrine of hell requires us not only to discern what the Bible teaches about hell but also the purposes to which the doctrine, at least in its more graphic forms, is put in the New Testament.

There are times when Jesus warns the crowds, the towns and villages in glaring terms.[29] More often, though, Jesus is speaking to his disciples. The language of *gehenna* reinforces Jesus's words when he warns of the danger of an angry spirit, urges the importance of reconciliation before religious ceremony, stresses the radical steps necessary to avoid sin, and exhorts his followers to fear God, not persecution.[30] Some of Jesus's starkest use of hell-imagery is reserved for confronting the spiritual hypocrisy of the Pharisees and the religious complacency of the Jews.[31]

In the sermons recorded in Acts there is considerable emphasis on the role of Christ as Lord – and judge – demonstrated through his resurrection from the dead, and on the need for repentance.[32] In the epistles, the outworking of God's wrath, the fact of judgement and spiritual death are all represented. However, the graphic imagery of hell found on Jesus's lips has largely disappeared. Where it appears, it is reserved particularly for those who harm the church, whether through persecution or false teaching, and for those at risk of falling away from the faith.[33]

So, while startling New Testament hell-imagery is sometimes used in the hearing of the crowds, often its purpose is to spur the believer to faithfulness (by pursuing holiness, persevering in the face of adversity, resisting the drift to apostasy or the allure of false teaching) or to shock the 'religious' out of misplaced self-confidence.

The Apologetic Challenge

The existence of hell presents a major challenge to the Christian apologist: 'How can a God of love send people to hell?' A satisfactory response is difficult, and calls for a consideration of the moral fabric of the universe, the character of God, and the interplay of human freedom and divine sovereignty.

A Moral Universe

Human attitudes to the prospect of hell are ambivalent: anguish in many cases, but not always. Faced with a world with genocide, brutal torture, sexual exploitation of children, callous oppression in the name of profit, money-laundered millions of drug pushers, we long not only for a heaven but for a hell so that our sense of justice can be vindicated. Peter Berger suggests such experiences are 'signals of transcendence', pointing beyond our own reality, representing sensitivity to moral evil and its just recompense.[34]

Hell is part of a matrix of truths, which in the West once set the parameters for human life, under which God stands at the heart of the universe, the source of meaning and morality. Since the Enlightenment, philosophers have sought to build a system of ethics on auto-nomous human reason. But, instead of moral consensus, the result has been the rise of relativism and postmodernity's flight into heterogenous 'worlds' of self-manufactured meaning. A cogent system of ethics needs a legitimate source of moral authority. The Bible insists that God, creator and sustainer of the universe, is just that. The significance of hell is that God is also a moral referee, able to enforce sanctions and ultimately uphold the moral values essential for human flourishing.

The Holiness of God

God's holiness is reiterated in the Bible, if anything, more repeatedly than his love. God's implacable opposition to all evil, and his burning purity, are set in sharp contrast to the moral ambiguities and unseemly compromises that mar even the best human endeavours. Indeed, God himself is experienced as a 'consuming fire'[35] by recalcitrant sinners. So, for the biblical writers confronted with the corruption embedded in human nature, the profound problem, which divine wisdom alone could solve, is how anyone can enter and enjoy the presence of God. Typically, all this is overlooked by critics who claim that hell reveals the 'cruelty' of God. Nonetheless, the question gnaws away: if God redeems some, why not all?

In exploring this question, God's utter majesty, and 'otherness', should prompt us to expect *some* difference in the outcome of moral reflection which regards God's glory and human experience, respectively, as paramount. To define the highest good by reference to the sum total of human happiness is not a biblical idea. Biblical ethics are theocentric, not anthropocentric. Like Job, we may be commended for the integrity of our questions but silenced when God himself appears, and able only to say, 'Surely I spoke of things I did not understand ...' (Job 42:3).

Human Freedom

Modern apologists for hell tend to emphasize, above all, human freedom. So for C.S. Lewis, arguably the best-known advocate of this approach, 'the doors of hell are locked on the inside'.[36] That is, the lost 'enjoy forever the horrible freedom they have demanded ...' In the end, humankind is divided into 'those who humbly say to God, "Thy will be done" and those to whom, God says, in the end, "Thy will be done".'[37] Hell emerges as the greatest monument to human freedom.

This argument has considerable appeal. It allows the apologist to argue that hell, far from revealing how badly God can treat people, shows the radical degree to which God respects human decision. Moreover, this argument has substantial biblical warrant. God deals with us as people who can – and must – choose, and whose choices matter: '... I have set before you life and death, blessings and curses. Now choose life ...' (Deuteronomy 30:19). Jesus, in deep sorrow over Jerusalem, exclaimed: '... how I have longed to gather your children together, as a hen gathers her chicks under her wings, *but you were not willing*!' (Luke 13:34). The Bible sets before us people who are able to refuse – and do refuse – God's tender and persistent appeal.

However, the argument from human freedom can become lop-sided. Stressing human freedom can aim at discharging God from the responsibility of punishment. Hell becomes nothing less – and nothing more – than the natural outcome of choices made during our lifetime. In such an account, the figure of Christ the judge may disappear from view. J.I. Packer, commenting on John 3:18–20, strives to maintain the right balance: '... we choose to retreat from God rather than repent before God, and God's judicial sentence is a ratifying for eternity of the sentence of separation from God we by our own choice have already passed on ourselves'.[38] Moreover, the argument from human freedom can prove too much: biblically, perfect freedom is obedience to God, not power to disobey God, and disobedience leads to slavery to sin.[39] Further, a mishandled emphasis on human freedom might diminish the grace of God: does salvation turn upon the wise exercise of our autonomous freedom rather than God's effective call?

Divine Sovereignty

This leads us into a fundamental issue at stake when the human freedom argument is deployed. C.S. Lewis is quite candid about the implications as he sees them:

> It is objected that the loss of a single soul means the defeat of omnipotence. And so it does. In creating beings with free will, omnipotence from the outset submits to the possibility of such defeat ...[40]

C.S. Lewis is not speaking here of inherent lack of omnipotence (assumed, for example, by process theology) but rather the voluntary self-limitation of divine omnipotence. This idea has been developed in recent years into the idea of the 'openness of God' or 'free will theism': God lacks foreknowledge of or sovereignty over future free acts.[41] However, quite apart from involving a substantial reorientation of our understanding of God,[42] this view is difficult to square with the biblical phenomenon of predictive prophecy. The Bible never relinquishes the claim that God exercises ultimate control over all things. He is the one 'who works out everything in conformity with the purpose of his will' (Ephesians 1:11).[43]

However, if divine sovereignty is extrapolated with mechanical logic, and salvation is traced (as it is) to divine election, the inference (some argue) is a doctrine of reprobation (i.e. that some individuals are ordained by God from before time to end in hell). This doctrine, the *decretum horribile*, has been defended on the basis of various passages.[44] However, its scriptural basis is not as secure as may first appear. The language of a 'realized eschatology' of condemnation is arguably being employed in some cases: present unbelief leaves one under the wrath of God (cf. John 3:36), a foretaste of the destiny that awaits persistent unbelief. C.E.B. Cranfield's close analysis of Romans 9 argues that the dominant concept is the free and *merciful* will of God (not any unilateral right or inclination to make capricious decisions with human destinies) (v. 15), that hardening at God's hands (vv. 17–18) refers to a process which assists the manifestation of God's mercy in time/history rather than one that seals the ultimate fate of an individual, and that 'objects of wrath' (v. 22) may be prepared (in the sense of 'ripe') for destruction but may yet become objects of mercy (ch. 10).[45]

The biblical worldview insists on holding in tension both divine sovereignty and human responsibility. This 'compatibilist' approach is easier to state in the negative: man's responsibility is never developed into a doctrine of free will in the sense of absolute power to foil God's will, but neither is it suggested that God's sovereignty renders us no more than puppets. The existence of hell forms part of the problem of evil and no easy solutions exist. If a risk-free view of divine providence is followed in the light of biblical texts, hell as a dimension of the problem of evil leads to various paths of reflection. The quality of human freedom implicit in a compatibilist universe may be impossible to combine with salvation for all (a form of free will defence). The fall, and even hell, may find a rationale in the context they provide for the manifestation of the depths of divine love and justice (the idea of *felix culpa*). But in the end, one must acknowledge that there is an element of impenetrable enigma in the counsels of God.

The Love of God

Surely, if God is love he must find the suffering of even one human soul in hell, even a Judas Iscariot, intolerable? The classic view of God's 'impassibility' implies that his eternal bliss cannot be disturbed by his creatures' pain. The suffering of God at the cross and even the emotional terms in which the Bible describes God's reaction to human plight undermine this view. Indeed, our struggle with the existence of hell reflects God's compassion which finds an echo in our hearts. However, if God were to suffer for ever if some are lost, he would become the emotional hostage of recalcitrant sinners. God wants us to be saved for our sake, but does not need us to be saved for his sake.

The eternal relations of the Trinity lie behind the truth that 'God is love' (1 John 4:8), unlike his wrath which arises as his holy response to the actions of sinful humanity. As God is love in all that he is and does, punishment imposed by justice is – indeed, can only be – compatible with, and not a contradiction of, God's love. C.S. Lewis argues that judgement plants the flag of truth in the citadel of rebellion: 'In a sense, it is better for the creature itself, even if it never becomes good, that it should know itself a failure, a mistake … if evil is present, pain at recognition of the evil, being a kind of knowledge, is relatively good.'[46] We easily imagine that love will always seek to shield a person from pain – but is that so?

However, the link between hell and God's love is easier to see at the cross. Christ died in our place, was punished for our sins and shut out from intimacy with his Father: 'My God, my God, why have you forsaken me?' (Matthew 27:46). Hell is, unexpectedly, the measure of God's love for us, for in Christ he, quite literally, went through hell for us.

The Ministry of the Word

The cleric preaching fire and brimstone is an unmistakable figure in church history. The flavour of such preaching can be gathered from Jonathan Edwards' sermon 'Sinners in the Hands of an Angry God' from the Great Awakening in eighteenth-century Massachusetts:

> The wrath of God burns against them, their damnation does not slumber; the pit is prepared, the fire is made ready, the furnace is now hot ready to receive them; the flames do now rage and glow.[47]

His aim, of course, was to move people to flee the wrath to come and seek shelter in Christ from the coming storm. Today, by contrast, it is rare to hear a sermon that deals head-on with the topic of hell.

The Strange Silence

The apparent reluctance to address the topic of hell invites inquiry and may reflect a host of trends and pressures. Indeed, the Bible itself encourages some reserve when speaking of the ultimate destiny of those without Christ and, in any age, an unpopular topic requires both skill and some courage from the preacher. Nonetheless, other factors may be at work:

Our Preoccupation with the Present
It is ironic that, while academic theology has seen a revival in eschatological thought this century, at a popular level the church has become more preoccupied with the 'here and now'. A deep

awareness that we live this life on the threshold of eternity is rare. Sermons on heaven, and the pivotal role of hope, are almost as uncommon as sermons on hell.

The 'Irrelevance of Holiness'

This startling phrase introduces David Wells' analysis – written in a US context – of the church's loss of a sense of God's holiness.[48] Modernity has rendered God 'weightless' for our culture, society has embraced 'therapeutic' responses to human behaviour which diminish our sense of personal responsibility for our actions, and both trends have infected the church. Modern evangelicals, he argues, have carelessly imagined that 'God is love' is an adequate theology by itself. He adds:

> Modernity's God is not nearly so morally angular as the God of the Bible. His sharp edges have all been ground down to make him less threatening, more comfortable, more tame … The gospel of Our Time frequently is unthinking and superficial, frequently is believed and preached without urgency, and the reason is that it has yet to dawn on many in the church that God in his holiness is deeply and irrevocably set in opposition to the world because of its sin.[49]

Barriers to Communication

The idea of hell is somewhat implausible to the modern mind. The very term 'hell' is laden with the baggage of centuries and may suggest the irrelevance of the church (still wedded to medieval ideas) and the unacceptability of its views (not merely old-fashioned but barbaric).

Preaching Hell …

The discipline of expository preaching will help us speak of hell neither less nor more than the New Testament and apply the doctrine as the New Testament writers do. Beyond this, if we are to speak of hell, given that the Bible does, how are we to do so?[50]

Theological Coherence

The existence of hell coheres with God's self-revelation of his nature (his sovereign majesty, holy opposition to evil, eternal self-consistency, and justice). Thus the ongoing proclamation of the person and character of God should provide the bedrock for a comprehensible account of divine judgement and its consequences.

Gospel Proclamation

The fact that people are under judgement, and face an unwelcome destiny, is both the *context* and part of the *content* of the gospel.[51] So preaching hell is never an end in itself but the backdrop to making known the way to life. Moreover, while the New Testament proclamation of the gospel to the *outsider* underlines the fact of judgement, it eschews lurid accounts of the experience of judgement. The *focus* of gospel proclamation lies elsewhere: on the identity of Christ as Lord, his saving work on the cross, and the arrival and future consummation of the kingdom of God.

Tearful Compassion

To preach hell, appearing to want to see others punished by God, is an ugly distortion of Christianity. There is rather a prophetic tradition of sorrow over people's rejection of God's Word and the resulting inevitability of judgement. Indeed, Jesus himself wept over the impenitent city of Jerusalem, crying out: 'If you, even you, had only known on this day what would bring you peace …!' (Luke 19:41–2). Are we, like our Master, prepared to weep?

Pastoral Sensitivity

When we speak of hell, we must be sensitive to the pain – and the challenges to faith – which may be caused. For any congregation will include Christian believers with loved ones who have so far refused to embrace Christ. The future, however, is in the hands of a God to whom we can and should pray. He may yet win over those who stubbornly or nonchalantly reject him; none of us knows the state of a person's heart in their dying moments; we trust a God who is just and merciful. And in the end, God promises to 'wipe away every tear from [our] eyes …' (Revelation 21:4).

Cultural Transposition

The Bible, in relation to hell, uses evocative imagery rather than literal description. A portrayal of hell can seek, with gravity and without sensationalism, to expound the biblical imagery. This will take us a long way indeed from the depictions of hell generated by medieval imagination. There will remain a tension between faithfulness to the 'God-given symbols' used to convey the reality of hell and finding language which resonates with our contemporaries.

The Significance of Hell

Uncomfortable though the process will be, we need to reverse the perceptible loss of interest in hell in both popular and more academic Christian circles. Hell is simply too important to neglect. It is a doctrine which interacts with more central theological issues. Neglect, or inappropriate changes, may result in a subtle reshaping of the whole body of theological belief. Indeed, the meaning of salvation turns on beliefs about the fate of the lost: if we overlook the eschatological consequences of refusing Christ, salvation can increasingly focus on personal fulfilment in this life. Finally, this doctrine is integral to the vitality of the church, promoting holiness and faithfulness, and reinforcing the motives for mission to a needy world.

1   K.S. Harmon, 'The Case against Conditionalism' in N.M.de S. Cameron (ed.), *Universalism and the Doctrine of Hell* (Paternoster Press, 1992), p. 193.
2   B. Russell, *Why I Am Not a Christian* (Unwin Paperbacks, 1979 edn).
3   For a survey of views on the scope of salvation, see J. Sanders, *No Other Name: Can Only Christians Be Saved?* (SPCK, 1994).
4   Matthew 16:27; John 5:28f.; Romans 1:18–32.
5   Matthew 25:31–46.
6   Romans 2:5–11; Romans 8:1.
7   1 Timothy 2:4; 2 Peter 3:9; Hebrews 2:9; 1 John 2:2; Romans 5:12–19; Acts 3:19–21; 1 Corinthians 15:22–8.
8   E.g. John Robinson, *In the End God* (Collins, 1968).
9   Hebrews 9:27; Luke 16:23.
10 Job 10:21; Psalm 94:17; Psalm 88:12. A few OT texts indicate blessing or condemnation after death (e.g. Psalm 16:10; Isaiah 66:24; Daniel 12:2).
11 Occasionally *hades* (especially Luke 16:23) and *tartaroo* (2 Peter 2:4) are translated as hell, but these terms appear to denote the intermediate state between death and final destiny.
12 N.T. Wright, *Jesus and the Victory of God* (SPCK, 1996), p. 96. Cf. *The New Testament and the People of God* (SPCK, 1992), ch. 10.
13 N.T. Wright, *Following Jesus* (SPCK, 1994), pp. 78–9.
14 Revelation 20:14–15.
15 Matthew 25:41.

16 W.G.T. Shedd, *Dogmatic Theology* (Edinburgh: T. & T. Clark, 1889), Vol. II, p. 745.
17 1 Timothy 6:16; 2 Timothy 1:10. Some annihilationists prefer to be described as conditionalists (e.g. Edward Fudge, Philip E. Hughes).
18 See e.g. D.L. Edwards and J. Stott, *Essentials* (Hodder & Stoughton, 1988), pp. 312–20. For a recent in-depth annihilationist argument, see D. Powys, *'Hell': a Hard Look at a Hard Question* (Paternoster Press, 1998).
19 E. Fudge, *The Fire that Consumes* (Providential Press, 1982).
20 Luke 15; Matthew 9:17; 26:8.
21 If a time of punishment is needed to satisfy, and does satisfy, God's justice, why should the individual not then be accepted by God? If it does not satisfy God's justice, why does the time of punishment not continue?
22 Matthew 18:18; 25:46; Jude 7.
23 K.S. Harmon, *op. cit.*, p. 213.
24 J.R.W. Stott, *Evangelical Truth: a Personal Plea for Unity* (IVP, 1999), pp. 141–3.
25 Given resurrection bodies, the possibility of physical pain cannot be excluded.
26 Luke 12:47–8; Matthew 11:20–24.
27 H. Blocher, 'Everlasting Punishment and the Problem of Evil' in N.M.de S. Cameron, *op. cit.*, pp. 304–12; C.S. Lewis, *The Problem of Pain* (Fount Paperbacks, 1940), pp. 113–14; N.T. Wright, *Following Jesus*, pp. 80–81.
28 J. Donne, *Sermons IV*, p. 86. Cf. NT references to 'weeping and gnashing of teeth'.
29 E.g. Luke 13:22–30.
30 Matthew 5:21; 5:23–4; 5:29–30; 10:28.
31 Matthew 8:5–13; 23:33.
32 Acts 2:14–39, 17:31.
33 1 Thessalonians 1:6–10; 2 Peter 2; Jude 13; Hebrews 10:26–31.
34 P. Berger, *A Rumour of Angels* (Anchor Books, 1969), p. 53.
35 Deuteronomy 4:24; Hebrews 10:27; 12:29.
36 *The Problem of Pain*, p. 115.
37 *The Great Divorce* (Fount Paperbacks, 1977 edn), p. 58.
38 'The Problem of Eternal Punishment', *Crux* XXVI, No. 3 (September 1990).
39 Romans 6:18; John 8:34; Galatians 3:22.
40 *The Problem of Pain*, p. 115.
41 See e.g. C. Pinnock et al., *The Openness of God* (InterVarsity Press, 1994).
42 See e.g. Norman L. Geisler, *Creating God in the Image of Man?* (Bethany House, 1997) for a critique of the 'open' view of God.

43 Cf. Psalm 135:6; Isaiah 46:8–10.
44 Romans 9:17–22; 1 Peter 2:8; Jude 4. *Horribile* indicates fearful, awe-inspiring.
45 C.E.B. Cranfield, *Romans: A Shorter Commentary* (T. & T. Clark, 1985).
46 *The Problem of Pain*, p. 110.
47 Quoted in A.E. McGrath (ed.), *The Christian Theology Reader*, (Blackwell, 1995), pp. 361–2.
48 D.F. Wells, *God in the Wasteland* (IVP, 1994), pp. 133–45.
49 *Ibid.*, pp. 136–7.
50 Cf. B. Milne, 'Preaching Hell' in *Preaching the Living Word* (Christian Focus, 1999).
51 Romans 1:1–3:31, especially 2:16.

Part IV

ECONOMICS
AND FINANCE

Chapter 12

SHOULD CHRISTIANS SUPPORT THE EURO?

MICHAEL SCHLUTER

He is the king of the country whose coin is current in the country.

Talmud

Europe will be created via a currency or not at all.

Jacques Rueff

Summary

On 1 January 1999, the ten currencies of the eleven countries entering Economic and Monetary Union (EMU) became denominations of the euro at irrevocably fixed exchange rates. While monetary unions have been attempted in the past, this is by far the most ambitious project of its kind in history. Its success or failure will determine the prosperity, and perhaps the peace, of Europe for decades to come. This chapter examines what the Bible has to say about monetary systems and then derives biblical principles to evaluate political and economic developments of this kind. EMU is assessed against these principles. The conclusion is that because the euro is unlikely to succeed without political integration, Christians should be wary of giving their support.

Background to the EMU Debate

The European Economic Community (EEC) began in 1957 at the initiative of Christian Democrat politicians in France and Germany, with the aim of ensuring Europe would never again destroy itself by war. It started as a free trade area with six member states. The UK joined in 1973 with confirmation in a 1975 referendum.

From 1992 the EEC, now the European Community (EC), became a 'single market' area with capital and labour able to cross internal boundaries, theoretically without restriction. The free flow of capital within the EC created a presumption in favour of monetary union since currency fluctuations would otherwise hamper internal trade and permit competitive devaluations.

In the 1992 Maastricht Treaty, member states agreed to foster not just economic integration but an 'ever closer union among the peoples of Europe'.[1] In the process, the EC became the European Union (EU). Maastricht provided for the abolition of border controls among member states, a common EU foreign and defence policy and co-operation on matters of justice and home affairs, as well as the process and timetable for EMU. A unitary fiscal authority is not yet envisaged. Each nation still contributes to a central budget, but the European Commission and Parliament lack independent tax-raising powers.

The Choice of Monetary System

Since 1996 the process of establishing EMU has been put into effect. Eleven countries have joined in the first round, including Germany, France and Italy but excluding Britain, Sweden, Denmark and Greece. The entrants' independent currencies will be abolished from the beginning of 1999, although they will still exist as denominations of the euro, and electronic transactions may be denominated in euro. Notes and coins will begin to circulate in 2002.

Short-term interest rates will be set for the whole euro area by the Governing Body of the European Central Bank (ECB) on which each of the governors of the member central banks will have one vote alongside the six members of the ECB's Executive Board. Voting on interest rates will be secret for sixteen years. The ECB is charged with maintaining price stability; its independence from political interference is strongly enshrined in the Maastricht Treaty. The euro will fluctuate against other currencies (such as the US dollar and the pound) but it is not clear whether or how member states' finance ministers will be able to influence the euro exchange rate. Members must pool some of their currency reserves to be managed by the ECB and governments will be limited in how much they are permitted to borrow each year, or risk fines. Euro notes will not depict any national symbols. Prices and wages will still vary across countries in EMU according to local conditions and tax rates, but it will be easier to compare prices between countries because they will be in the same currency.

The alternative to EMU that the UK has recently adopted is to have domestic interest rates set by the Monetary Policy Committee (MPC) of the Bank of England, with an inflation target set by the Chancellor. This is a variant of the system that has been relatively successful in achieving low inflation in the US, Canada, Australia, New Zealand and Sweden. The exchange rate of the pound varies without being explicitly targeted and there is no requirement for a limit on the government's freedom to borrow. Minutes of MPC meetings, including the results of votes, are published two weeks later.

These alternatives do not seem very different. Does the question just boil down to which committee of central bankers is given the job of setting interest rates? While the two formats appear much the same, the effective differences are profound, as the rest of this chapter will seek to demonstrate in the light of biblical teaching.

The Monetary System in the Bible

While direct biblical teaching on monetary systems is limited, it offers some useful pointers.

Precious Metals Were Used as the Monetary Base

Money originally acted as an aid to trade through avoiding the need for direct barter by substituting a portable, inherently valuable commodity for one side of an exchange. Initially, precious metals were used for the purpose. The first record of metals being used in this way in the Bible is Abraham paying 400 shekels of silver for Sarah's burial site (Genesis 23). Gold and silver were chosen for their scarcity, malleability and decorative qualities. But desire for their ownership runs deep in human nature and gives them an intrinsic value that is widely recognized.

The Old Testament gives no direct teaching on the form of money to be employed in Israel. The value and use of precious metals in fixed weights seems to have been assumed and legislated for (e.g. Deuteronomy 22:19, 29). A metallic monetary base generally provides a long-term anchor for the price level. The price of people and land stayed roughly constant over several centuries in Israel. For instance, Jesus was betrayed by Judas for thirty silver coins (Matthew 26:15). This was approximately the value of a slave in the Mosaic period (Exodus 21:32; cf. Genesis 37:28). The same sum was used by the chief priests to procure a field in Jerusalem (Matthew 27:7–10); Jeremiah had bought a field in Jerusalem for seventeen silver shekels centuries earlier in a depressed land market (Jeremiah 32:9).[2]

A long-term anchor for the price level is important for both moral and economic reasons. Modern economies seem endemically prone to rising inflation due to their reliance on debt contracts to finance consumption and investment (see Chapter 13). This is an immoral aspect of modern economic life, in that the inflationary process redistributes wealth between creditors and debtors, savers and borrowers, and those on fixed and inflation-linked incomes. Inflation is in effect collective theft by one group against another. It also erodes the incentives for long-term saving, investment and risk-taking, and confuses price signals within an economy, leading to inefficient decision-making.

Political Sovereignty Is Closely Tied to Issuing Currency

The next major monetary development was to mint coins of precious metals of set weights so that a coin was known to have a certain intrinsic value. Unfortunately, minted coins were vulnerable to debasement, leading to inflation. State-controlled mints were established to attest to the inherent value of the coin while their designs and inscriptions attested to the reliability of the issuer. But cash-strapped states soon realized that they could procure easy revenue by debasing their coinage themselves and passing it off for its face value. The implicit tax that a state receives through increasing money in circulation in excess of its production costs is known as seignorage. The process continued when governments began printing paper money unbacked by gold or silver. This is a lucrative source of revenue even today.

While an absolutely fixed link is maintained between a currency and its metallic base, the monetary system remains 'automatic' and apolitical. However, the possibility of debasement and seignorage makes money creation an inherently political process. On the one hand, states saw it as a mark of their trustworthiness and reliability that their currency circulated widely and was exchanged for its face value. On the other, if debasement was occurring, it was important for a state to be able to force the use of its currency on the populace to maximize seignorage.

This connection between political control and the issuing of currency informs Jesus' answer to the vexed question, 'Is it right to pay taxes to Caesar?' Requesting a Roman coin, Jesus asked whose inscription and portrait were on it. He then gave his famous reply, 'Give to Caesar what is Caesar's, and to God what is God's' (Matthew 22:15–22). This teaching makes clear that the state has legitimate but limited claims upon the resources and loyalty of Jesus' disciples. But the inference drawn by Jesus is groundless unless the use of a government's coinage by its citizens legitimates its tax-raising claims; if the Jews are to enjoy the economic benefits of the Pax Romana, as exemplified by their use of Roman currency, they should accept the taxation required to maintain it.

This connection between political authority and issuing currency has been remarkably close throughout history once debasement and seignorage became involved. Almost invariably, currencies are issued by the government of the state in which they circulate, although control over the amount of money in circulation is now exercised through setting short-term interest rates. Modern banking systems effectively can lend into existence as much credit as is demanded at the prevailing interest rate, so most governments now opt to control the amount of credit in their economy by setting the price for short-term credit to the banking system via the central bank. The fundamental questions are whether this control is better exercised on a country-by-country or EU-wide basis, and what the political consequences of pooling decision-making are likely to be.

A Christian Analysis of EMU

For a Christian evaluation of EMU, our approach will be to seek guiding themes from biblical teaching as a whole. As biblical teaching is always set in a specific historical and cultural context, it is not possible generally to lift precepts out of their context and apply them immediately today (see Chapter 6). Jesus himself seems to have used 'principles' in teaching how difficult ethical problems should be addressed. For example, when confronted on the Sabbath with a disabled person, he asks his critics what principle should govern their response (Mark 3:1–6).

While Christians can and should agree about principles, they may legitimately disagree about the appropriate action to take as a result. For example, almost all Christians agree on the principle that discrimination on the basis of skin colour is morally offensive. However, Christians disagreed as to whether sanctions against South Africa in the 1980s were an effective response. Such disagreement about appropriate action is legitimate. Principles are moral absolutes; policies are the practical means to apply those principles today. Principles are derived from biblical reflection; policies are a matter of pragmatic judgement.

The value of applying biblical principles to a contemporary problem depends on how thoroughly we understand biblical teaching, as well as the quality of our judgement with regard to political and economic realities. So with some trepidation we shall propose seven relevant biblical principles and then use each to make an assessment of the ethical implications of Britain joining EMU.

Seven Biblical Principles

The Identity of Peoples and Nation-States

Many today are sceptical about the significance of the nation-state, defined as a people identified by language and cultural affinity existing in an independent political entity. Throughout history there have been many realignments following invasions and colonization. The United States and Britain each share a language and cultural traditions but are a polyglot of peoples. China and India have a multitude of languages and cultures. Germany and Italy each have a common language but only relatively recently became single political entities. Add to this the undoubted danger of nationalism as a form of idolatry and current trends towards globalization, and it is no wonder many are reluctant to defend the continuing role of the nation-state.

Despite these complexities, biblical teaching portrays national identities and diversity as ordained by God and something to be celebrated. Israel is nurtured by God to become a nation, and her self-determination is seen as a blessing from God (Deuteronomy 28). In the New Testament, Paul reminds the Athenians that 'From one man [God] made every nation of men ... and he determined the times set for them and the exact places where they should live' (Acts 17:26). At Pentecost, God celebrated rather than obliterated this diversity by enabling people to understand the gospel in their own language, rather than substituting one universal language. In the New Jerusalem, too, people will be differentiated by culture, language and national identity (Revelation 5:9–10; 21:24–5). Shared ethnic awareness is nowhere condemned in Scripture, only communal arrogance.

Loss of national sovereignty through absorption into empire is regarded as a judgement, both for Israel (e.g. Deuteronomy 15:6) and her neighbours (e.g. Amos 1). God may use empires as instruments to achieve his purposes (e.g. Isaiah 40) but they are nowhere extolled as part of God's social design. Rather, diversity of language is a means of restraining evil (Genesis 11).

So we need to ask, what impact will EMU have on the strength and diversity of national identities, cultures and languages across Europe, since these are part of God's design both in creation and in the providential restraint of evil?

Many of the proponents of EMU on continental Europe unashamedly seek to foster economic and political integration within the EU, for laudable reasons. The economic case for EMU is unproven (see below) but they see it as a calculated risk worth taking to intertwine the trading relations and economic structures of Europe so completely that exit from the EU, let alone war in Europe, becomes too costly to contemplate.

The demarcation of current borders in Europe is no more sacrosanct than elsewhere in the world: the break-up of the USSR and Yugoslavia, for example, has rightly reconstituted several nations. But, as these processes have demonstrated, large and homogenous people groups cannot be denied a significant degree of national sovereignty indefinitely. The centralizing forces that accompany EMU will significantly diminish decision-making powers of existing nation-states. This increases the likelihood of internal conflict within Europe (see below) and weakens the ability of nation-states to resist pan-European dictatorship. Too often the states of Europe have been the focus of nationalistic idolatry, but at the same time their existence has repeatedly prevented the rise of lasting pan-Continental Empires as, for example, under Louis XIV, the Hapsburgs, Napoleon, Kaiser Wilhelm III, Hitler or Stalin. If the EU bypasses nation-states by replacing them with a single executive and devolving administration to regional governments, the risk of continent-wide dictatorship increases.

Solidarity of Family and Local Community

As William Temple noted:

> Each individual is born into a family and a nation. In his maturity he is very largely what these have made him. The family is so deeply grounded in nature and the nation in history that anyone who believes in God as Creator and as Providence is bound to regard both as part of the divine plan for human life.[3]

Much of Old Testament law is designed to protect and give function to the family and local community. For example, the Jubilee laws worked to protect a family's roots in the local community and specific locality as well as providing it with a long-term asset. Laws on debt and interest protected families from penury, while welfare was organized primarily through families and local communities.[4] Although Jesus makes clear that the demands of his kingdom must take precedence over family loyalties, he nevertheless underlines family obligations for welfare in his teaching (e.g. Mark 7:9–13) and by example (e.g. John 19:26–7). Paul does the same (e.g. 1 Timothy 5:3–8).

So, will EMU protect and strengthen the institutions of the family and local community which lie at the heart of stable and healthy relationships in society?

One of the economic motivations behind EMU is to remove currency differences and volatility so as to foster a single EU-wide labour market. Workers will be able to see where wages are highest and companies where costs are lowest. Indeed, in the absence of fiscal transfers within EMU, greater mobility is probably the only way that regional divergences of economic performance within EMU can be evened out. This runs counter to the need to reduce social isolation and welfare dependency, both of the elderly and of young families, which arises as a result of the disintegration of the extended family through spatial job mobility. A major flaw of the US economic system is that it undervalues the role of 'rootedness' in bolstering the extended family and local community as supports for the nuclear family. Societies should attempt, wherever practicable, to move jobs to people. EMU will operate to do the opposite.

Avoidance of Concentration of Political and Economic Power

The third principle is closely tied to the first two. If Israel's political and social design was intended to teach general normative principles for social organization, one of its most obvious lessons is the importance of diffusion of political and economic power. Politically, the Law tightly controls the military and economic power of the king (Deuteronomy 17:14–20). It makes no provision for tax-raising powers or a standing army. When the people want a king 'like the nations round about' (totalitarian Canaanite city-states), Samuel uses the strongest possible language to warn them of the consequences of centralized state power (1 Samuel 8). The theme continues through the period of the prophets (e.g. 1 Kings 21). The Law also seeks to ensure diffusion of economic power through laws such as the Jubilee (Leviticus 25:1–34), the seventh year remission of debt (Deuteronomy 15:1–6) and the ban on interest (Deuteronomy 23:19–20) – laws preventing property accumulating in the hands of an elite, and slowing down individual accumulation of capital.

Decentralization of power facilitates the widespread participation in political and economic decisions, which is a necessary expression of every person being made in God's image. It is also important to ensure accountability in the exercise of power, given the reality of human fallenness, and prevents the state abrogating to itself the glory that rightly belongs to God (cf. Revelation 13).

So, will EMU help protect European societies from concentration of political and economic power and make public decision-making more accountable?

The delegation of decision-making over interest rates to non-elected appointees shifts power away from elected politicians. This is in the well-founded belief that politicians would otherwise make inflationary decisions for electoral gain. The special feature of EMU, however, is that this decision will be made at the EMU-wide level rather than by individual economies. In some countries, this represents an increase in influence, since their monetary policies have had to shadow closely that of Germany. However, for Germany, the UK,

Italy and Spain, EMU entry entails a diminution of independence over interest rates. This is problematic in that, no matter how wise the decisions of the ECB, divergences among EMU economies will mean that monetary policy will be simultaneously too tight for some and too loose for others. For those countries that have sacrificed a degree of independence over interest rates, EMU automatically entails a loss of decision-making autonomy.

Of far greater importance, however, is the centralizing of economic decision-making that will result if EMU succeeds in creating transparent product and labour markets and a more mobile capital market. Countries in EMU will be fined if their government deficit exceeds 3 per cent of national income, while the prospect of EMU is already prompting calls for harmonized rates of tax on profits and savings for fear of competition from low-tax areas. The same logic points to harmonized income tax rates, excise duties and welfare systems. Once agreed by the majority, it will be impossible for one country in isolation to negotiate a change to the system. By its nature and its intended effects, EMU is designed to centralize economic decision-making away from national governments.

EMU is a further step towards the centralizing of economic and political decision-making on matters that affect the whole EU. As noted, the Maastricht Treaty already envisages the establishment of a common EU defence and foreign policy. It will be much more difficult for concerned organizations or individuals to influence EU decisions than national decisions. Although the views of those calling for a change in UK monetary policy can be given some weight by the Bank of England's MPC, their influence would be minimal on the ECB. Regarding the European Parliament, most MEPs have constituencies of over half a million voters, so the time available for each constituent is around a sixth of that of a Westminster MP. As yet, there are no pan-European parties to counterbalance the executive. In such an environment, only the largest and most highly resourced lobbying groups will influence policy.

Effective Stewardship of Resources

Christians generally understand the command to 'subdue the earth' (Genesis 1:28) as a mandate for the effective stewardship of the earth's economic and human resources. The same theme underpins the Parable of the Talents (Matthew 25:14–30). Stewardship is partly a matter of making the best possible use of the resources God has given us, so maximizing economic growth and wealth creation. However, it is also concerned with the long-term sustainability of the growth process and the care we take of the environment. Since the natural world belongs to God rather than ourselves, we are under an obligation to use it both productively and responsibly.

So, will adopting the euro result in a more efficient and sustainable use of the economic and human resources God has given us?

The strongest arguments in favour of EMU are that it will foster more efficient use of resources. By eliminating internal currency movements within Europe, longer-term investment horizons should become feasible due to the greater degree of certainty over relative prices.[5] Local monopolies that are protected by pricing in local currencies should be eroded. Transparent prices should foster even greater trade and specialization within the EU, leading to larger production volumes and greater economies of scale. A more efficient and integrated financial capital market is now developing in continental Europe. Although often exaggerated, there will be some saving of resources through eliminating the need for cross-currency transactions and risk-hedging.

However, the efficiency case for EMU is far from proven:

EMU is not necessary to foster trade and cross-border investment and could easily raise costs and prices. Economists have not, in practice, found a strong link between currency stability and growth of international trade. Even if such a link were significant, currency risk can now be hedged more cheaply than previously; also the Internet and electronic payment systems are dwarfing any impact of EMU in furthering international trade and transparent pricing.

The EU probably trades too much with itself anyway to be truly efficient in trade terms due to its tariff wall and agricultural protectionism.

The transition costs of changing the currency and IT systems are likely to amount to 3–7 per cent of GDP.[6] Even on the most optimistic scenarios this will take 15–20 years to recoup in higher growth. The move to unfamiliar prices for goods and services will not only lead to temporary confusion of consumers and opportunities for fraud, but probably also higher prices as producers round their prices up and have to change production runs.

The pragmatic case against EMU does not stop there, particularly for the UK. The borrowing restrictions in EMU will limit the degree of freedom for fiscal policy (government spending and taxes) just when giving up interest rates autonomy makes an active fiscal policy more necessary. There is no clearly defined 'lender-of-last-resort' for the banking system and so EMU increases the risks of contagious financial crises. The UK's different trade and economic structure, relative to the rest of the EU, means that the UK would suffer more currency volatility relative to the US dollar, when stability against the dollar rather than the euro is more important for the majority of UK exporters and importers. The UK's greater exposure to short-term interest rate movements (owing to greater corporate and personal debt at variable interest rates) means that a disproportionate share of the effect of interest rate changes will be felt in the UK. As a result, the UK's economic cycle could easily become more, not less, volatile following EMU entry. We could go on. Suffice it to say, from an economic viewpoint, the 'stewardship' case for EMU is far from proven and runs the risk of major costs, especially for the UK.

Equity in Distribution of Wealth and Income

Every person is made in the image of God. From this foundation stems the obligation to ensure the welfare of every person. This in turn raises concerns about both absolute and relative levels of wealth and poverty, in particular how the structures of political and economic organization impact on the distribution of wealth and power. The concern for some measure of equity in society is clearly evident in Israel's economic and social order. Every family received a piece of land at the time of entry into Canaan; the land was given out in roughly equal amounts, and the Jubilee laws were given to ensure the land was held by those families in perpetuity (Numbers 33:54; Leviticus 25:8–13). The prophets spoke out strongly when actions by the wealthy resulted in families being robbed of home and farm (e.g. Micah 2:2).

So, will EMU bring greater equity in the distribution of resources across regions, ethnic groups and social classes?

Proponents of EMU hope it will lead to the swifter 'catching-up' of some of the poorer peripheral regions of the EU. Certainly, there is evidence that the constraints of EMU preparation have led to better governance in Spain, Portugal and Greece. The greater visibility of lower wages in the periphery could lead to greater outside investment than otherwise.

However, this is not a foregone conclusion. Persistent regional imbalances remain even now within EU countries despite a single internal currency and large fiscal transfers (e.g. Italy). These hopes would certainly be dashed if, as some trade unions hope, EMU results in a levelling up of wage and benefit rates to German levels. If this does occur, the lesson from highly protected labour markets in Europe, combined with a non-inflationary monetary policy, is that it leads to high structural unemployment. Harmonization of currency, wage and benefit rates at unwarranted levels during German unification has resulted in Eastern German mass unemployment, dependency and the re-emergence of fascism.

There is a role for richer EU nations to help their poorer neighbours but this does not require EMU. Indeed, at a wider European level, EMU will increase income disparities between countries inside and outside the EU as it raises the entry requirements for Eastern European countries wishing to join the EU. Meanwhile, they will remain discriminated against in their agricultural exports to the EU. Making EU markets more accessible to former Communist countries would raise incomes and bolster democracy. EMU will delay that process.

Peaceful Relationships between Nations

It is almost a platitude to say that God is concerned that there should be peace between nations. Perfect harmony of understanding and purpose is the hallmark of relationships within the Godhead (e.g. John 5:19–23). Jesus' concern for peace is central in the Beatitudes (Matthew 5:9) and one of the signs of God's coming kingdom will be the end of war (Micah 4:1–4). The desire for peace, however, must be compatible with the demands of justice – God does not want 'peace at any price'.

So, will EMU help to promote peaceful coexistence among the EU member states, and between the EU and other countries around the world?

The original goal of the Christian founders of the EEC was to foster peace in Europe so as to make another war in Western Europe inconceivable. Although NATO must take most of the credit for the past fifty years of peace, the EU has played its part by fostering closer political and economic ties. EMU is a logical progression from that start. By unifying the EU nations' currencies, EMU will not only make them more economically interdependent but also make exit from the EU virtually impossible.[7]

Unfortunately, EMU may well foster conflicts and increase nationalism among EU countries. If the system works well and an active fiscal policy compensates for the lack of an independent monetary policy, some countries will need to raise taxes in order to cool their economy even though the government is in strong surplus. Quite correctly, electorates will blame the system. However, if EMU fails, endemic unemployment will result in some countries due to an overvalued exchange rate for their needs and excessively high interest rates. Wage cuts in, or labour movements from, the countries thus affected seem unlikely, and the current treaty does not provide for fiscal transfers from a prospering country to a depressed one as a result of EMU. Hence, some countries will feel neglected in the interest rate setting process, and will demand restitution from the centre. To make matters worse, they could be having to cut spending and raise taxes in a recession to avoid being fined for an 'excessive' deficit, while having to bail out a collapsing banking system due to inappropriate interest rate levels.

If a country faces an unsustainable fiscal situation, it may be forced to threaten default on its debt or request help from other members. If a transfer or debt guarantee is granted, those populations in solvent countries may resent their taxes being used to bail out irresponsible governments elsewhere. If these payments have no democratic mandate, resentment of neighbouring countries within EMU may result. Such a scenario has prompted some US economists to place a high probability of civil strife within Europe as a result of EMU.[8] Lessons from history are being ignored. The American Civil War was at root a conflict about whether the states would remain a single economic entity rather than divide to follow their divergent economic interests. Single currencies did not hold the artificial political creations of Yugoslavia and the USSR together. The first action of the newly independent states was, of course, to create their own currencies.

Acknowledgement of God's Sovereignty over Political Life

All Christian thinking about society must begin not with man but with God. Contrary to the ideas of Rousseau that political sovereignty lies with the 'general will' expressed through an autonomous state, a biblical understanding of government is that ultimate sovereignty lies with God (Romans 13:1). A fundamental Christian concern, therefore, is that the Word of God should be acknowledged, or at least taken into account, when laws are made and society structured, and that there should be a sense of submission to God in the making of law and policy. Although this becomes increasingly difficult in pluralistic European societies, as Christians we still have to ask whether closer European integration will help or hinder keeping God and his values as an influence on the political and economic system.

Is the economic and political integration that EMU will encourage likely to strengthen or weaken the acknowledgement of God in the political and economic decisions which govern our lives?

From a Christian viewpoint, political integration of the UK into the EU could be advantageous. In many cases, the constitution and legislation of other EU countries embody a stronger Christian Democratic or Christian Socialist outlook than those of the UK. Some prominent examples include laws governing abortion and embryo experimentation as well as Sunday working. However, counter-examples can be cited, such as pornography legislation and control over TV channels. Of greater significance, in most of continental Europe the trend towards secularization is even stronger than in Britain (notwithstanding the choice of an overtly Catholic symbol for the EU flag). While British Christians may have a strategic role in the re-evangelization of the continent, closer integration of Britain into the EU through EMU is unlikely to bring about greater acknowledgement of God's sovereignty in temporal affairs, particularly if it results in weaker ties with the US.

Conclusion

Based on the biblical principles we have derived for judging economic and political structures, our conclusion is that any pragmatic benefits to EMU are outweighed by both the economic costs and risks, and the centralization of power that will result.

Of course, although we feel that the weight of argument from our biblically derived principles is contrary, Christians may favour greater EU integration on purely pragmatic grounds or they could derive this position from some of the principles already outlined. However, if political integration is the goal, the irony is that monetary union should be introduced *after* political union has received democratic validation. Then, a far more workable currency union could be designed without the inefficiencies and internal contradictions of EMU. It is perfectly possible to be pro-EU but EMU-sceptic.

Due to the divergent nature and structure of the UK economy compared with the Deutschmark bloc, entry would almost certainly be economically damaging for the UK, while remaining out of EMU is a tenable position. Recent financial market turbulence has shown that the UK now has a credible monetary regime that can be exercised independently of EMU. Thirty-year rates of interest in the UK – a good test of credibility – are even now much lower than in the EMU-area. Switzerland, Canada and Norway continue to prosper without participating in larger currency blocs nearby.

Our greatest concern is that EMU cannot work without substantial political and economic centralization. The near-universal observation from economic history and current practice is that currency areas follow the boundaries of sovereign political entities. This realization even seems to have informed Jesus' teaching on the legitimacy of tax-raising authority. The clear inference is that either EMU will break up in a costly and acrimonious way, or that sovereignty over national fiscal policy will have to be sacrificed – first by mutually guaranteeing other governments' debts and then by agreeing to large-scale fiscal transfers to regions in recession. This in turn will require a much higher degree of political integration.

That the political implications of EMU are not being fully spelled out to the electorates of Europe is deeply concerning to Christians who believe in democracy. It is no coincidence that the German people, who have most to lose economically from an unsuccessful EMU, have not been given the opportunity to express direct support for the project. We conclude that the foundations of EMU are suspect, and Christians in Britain should be wary of joining.

Acknowledgements

The author would like to acknowledge the assistance of Dr Paul Mills in providing technical economic advice for this chapter.

1   Article A of the Maastricht Treaty.
2   A similar degree of price stability was enjoyed in Britain from the end of the seventeenth century to the end of the gold standard in 1931. Subsequently, the price level has risen approximately sixty times.
3   William Temple, *Christianity and Social Order* (1942, republished SPCK, 1976), p. 64.
4   Michael Schluter and Roy Clements, *Reactivating the Extended Family* (Jubilee Centre, Cambridge, 1986).
5   An undoubted weakness of the current system of floating exchange rates is that foreign exchange markets tend to overshoot in their adjustments to shocks due to self-sustaining speculation. This disrupts trade and capital flows by introducing relative price uncertainty.
6   European Research Group, *The Euro: Bad for Business* (London, 1998), p. 49.
7   Essentially, once in EMU, a country could only contemplate withdrawal if it was prepared to exit from the EU altogether and reinvent its currency – an immensely costly process.
8   E.g. Martin Feldstein, 'EMU and International Conflict', *Foreign Affairs*, November 1997.

Chapter 13

THE BIBLICAL BAN ON INTEREST[1]

Dead Letter or Radical Solution?

PAUL MILLS

Summary

Financial disasters are currently everyday occurrences. Many are attributable to the workings of a debt- and interest-based economy. Rather than argue the case for and against the biblical prohibition of interest from the texts themselves, this chapter attempts to demonstrate the injustices and problems that have arisen because we have ignored traditional Christian teaching on finance. In so doing, a pragmatic case is made for taking seriously what the Bible teaches on this aspect of economics, rather than dismissing it as an ancient irrelevancy.

Introduction

Bankruptcies are at record levels. Thousands of houses are repossessed each month. Banks and building societies increase their interest rate margins to cover their bad debts. Only the debt counselling and pawnbroking industries prosper. Financial disasters seem to dominate the economic headlines. Indeed, it is not difficult to argue that the explosion of indebtedness in the mid-to-late 1980s has been largely responsible for the recent boom and bust of Western economies, particularly in the English-speaking countries, Scandinavia and Japan.

What have Christians had to say about the issue? Apart from a vague sense of uneasiness about the materialism embodied by credit-financed spending, the Christian response has been woefully inadequate. This reflects the absence of a well-developed Christian analysis of economics in general, and finance in particular. Such was not always the case. For three-quarters of her history, the church upheld the prohibition of interest found explicitly in the Old Testament (e.g. Deuteronomy 23:19; Ezekiel 18:8, 13) and implicitly in the New (Luke 6:34, 35; 19:22, 23).[2]

The church sought to universalize the ban on interest that applied originally only within the Jewish community. It sought to replace interest-bearing loans with either profit-share financial partnerships, rental charges for the use of physical property or charitable, interest-free loans. In addition to the early and medieval church, the ban was subscribed to by Luther and Melancthon in their early writings, as well as by many English Puritans before 1640. Now, only orthodox Jews and some Muslims regard the prohibition of interest with any seriousness.

Rather than discuss the relevant biblical texts in detail, this chapter will seek to question the legitimacy of interest with reference to the current state of financial conditions. Are the workings of interest responsible for our current mess? Would a non-interest system be more just and efficient? If so, a favourable reappraisal of the biblical prohibition of interest seems in order.

An Illustration: Low Income Country (LIC) Debt

Perhaps the most obvious example in which the interest-based financial system has manifested most of its undesirable traits is that of LIC debt. Christian opinion in rich and poor countries alike has condemned the injustice of billions of dollars being paid by the poorest countries to the richest without recognizing that this is how an interest-based financial system typically operates.

The immediate causes of the crisis are well-known. Banks lent and LICs borrowed heavily in the late 1970s when interest rates were low and commodity prices were increasing rapidly. In the early 1980s, rising world interest rates coincided with a collapse in the prices of commodities produced by the most heavily indebted LICs. In order to maintain their interest payments and receive International Monetary Fund (IMF) emergency loans, most LICs have been forced to increase exports dramatically and submit to austere IMF 'adjustment' programmes. The results have included the degradation of the world's environment (to produce more cash crops for export); the net transfer of resources from poor to rich countries (despite aid and further loans); and cuts in the living standards of the world's poorest societies, to pay for loans from which they have derived little benefit. The lives of millions have been lost as a direct result.

Responsibility for this tragedy must be shared. Banks lent huge sums without adequately considering the potential for circumstances to change, the uses to which the loans were put and the lending of other banks. LIC governments oversaw the misuse of borrowed resources in the funding of public deficits, capital flight, imports of arms and luxury goods, corruption and 'white elephant' development projects.

That such errors could be perpetrated, however, can be fundamentally attributed to the cost of debt finance being unrelated to the profitability of its use. If lenders had been rewarded with a profit-share return rather than interest, the loan demand would have been tempered prudentially, while lenders would have taken far greater care over what projects they were investing in. If these proved to be failures, the suppliers of capital would have shared in these losses rather than being able to impose greater and greater interest burdens on the world's poorest peoples. To the critic of interest, it is no surprise that banks have been able to survive only by governments providing generous tax reliefs, deposit insurance and a powerful debt-collection agency in the form of the IMF.

The LIC debacle illustrates many of the side-effects of the workings of interest. This example is not a one-off occurrence. It is a typical consequence of the unrestrained workings of an interest-based financial system, as the following discussion will attempt to demonstrate.

Preliminary Definitions

Before the question at issue can be addressed, some preparatory definitions are required.

A 'loan' is the temporary transfer of property from a lender to a borrower. It is repaid when the same property, or its equivalent in value and quality, is returned to the lender. For the loan's duration ownership, and hence the risk associated with the use of the property, is transferred to the borrower.

'Interest' is the amount that the borrower repays the lender in excess of the original sum lent ('principal'). Interest is usually charged as a percentage rate per unit of time, irrespective of how the money is used. The loan may be 'secured' on 'collateral' – that is, property of the borrower that must be forfeited to the lender if the loan and interest payments cannot be met.

A rental or hire arrangement is also the temporary transfer of property from the owner ('lessor') to the user ('lessee'), but one in which the legal ownership and risk of accidental damage and depreciation remain with the lessor. A hire or rental charge covers payment for the use of the property and the risk of its loss, damage or depreciation. Such a distinction between loan and hire arrangements seems to have been drawn in Exodus 22:14, 15.

A profit-share partnership is an arrangement whereby a commercial enterprise is financed by two or more partners who receive a proportionate share of the enterprise's profit or loss in return. Ownership of the financial capital, and hence risk of its loss, is retained by the partners. Public or private limited companies are variants of such partnerships, in which the share of the profit paid out to shareholders ('dividend') is at the discretion of the board of directors, and in which the shares are transferable.

The Fundamental Issue

At the heart of the interest debate is a moral question. Is it just for lenders to receive back more than the amount lent simply because they have been deprived of their property for the duration of the loan? Conventional wisdom and economic theory of course believe it is. After all, interest is the reward for 'abstaining' from immediate consumption; a sum of money now is automatically 'worth' more than the same sum in the future because people are impatient creatures, and because the sum can be invested profitably in the meantime; without interest, no-one would save and everyone would want to borrow; if rent can be charged for the use of property, why can't interest be charged for the use of money? Notwithstanding the morality of the use, how can finance be efficiently allocated without interest to act as a price signal?

Many of these objections are valid. However, they do *not* apply to the traditional Christian position on interest, but to that of socialism. Put simply, this regards the exercise of labour as the only true source of all economic value. Consequently, all income that is not derived from the exercise of labour – that is rent, interest, dividends and most profit – are the fruits of exploitation of the workforce. The logical conclusion of this result is that charges for the use of property should not exist. Many of the criticisms of the previous paragraph then apply. If no charge can be made for loans or the use of property, then a market for financial capital cannot exist. Some other mechanism is needed to determine the level of savings and the use of capital. This has usually taken the form of a state planning bureaucracy.

While some Christian socialists have interpreted the ban on interest in this way, it has not been the traditional approach. Rather, the legitimacy of a return being made on financial capital (e.g. dividends) or property (e.g. rent) has been accepted, on condition that these contracts involve direct risk of loss – reflecting the retention of legal ownership rights and responsibilities by the original owner. For instance, when cash is invested in a business on an equity or profit-and-loss share basis, the owner of the money is risking its loss for the prospect of eventual gain. The return, if forthcoming, can be seen as a reward for bearing risk. Similarly, in a rental arrangement, ownership, and hence the attendant risk, remains with the lessor who is compensated by the rental payment.

This sanctioning of returns on risked capital answers most of the aforementioned objections. A price for capital can be established in the market for shares[3] and rented property, and in fluctuations in the profit-share ratios charged for the supply of risk capital in partnerships. Such returns provide an incentive to save and economize on the use of finance, and a mechanism whereby capital can be allocated to those ends in which it will be used most efficiently.

In a loan arrangement, ownership risks and responsibilities are temporarily transferred to the borrower, who is then under a legal responsibility to repay at the specified time, irrespective of how wisely the property has been used in the meantime. (Of course, the lender suffers risk of non-repayment but this is not inherent to the loan arrangement, and can be catered for by specifying collateral and/or penalties for default.) This fact prompts the question as to what service interest pays for. Why should my voluntary and temporary relinquishment of my ownership rights be *always* deserving of reward, especially considering that the borrower bears the risks of use and ownership in the meantime? Given that the alternatives of profit-share or rental contracts exist, the traditional Christian response has been that the lender of funds had no just grounds for claiming such a reward.

Another way to view the issue is to examine what the loan is needed for. If it is to finance hopefully productive investment, then a profit-related arrangement can be used instead. Such a contract does not assume that future profitability is a foregone conclusion, as an interest-based loan implicitly does (cf. James 4:13–16). If the loan is to finance the acquisition of property that the borrower needs now, but cannot afford (e.g. a house), then either a rental, hire purchase or income-share arrangement can be devised. These would share risk more fairly between the consumer and the financier than with a consumer loan or mortgage. Finally, if the borrower is too poor to pay the rental equivalent to acquiring the good, the loan should be charitable (i.e. interest-free), or not granted at all. Scripture is replete with references to the potential for interest-bearing loans to oppress the poor (e.g. Exodus 22:25; Leviticus 25:36, 37; Nehemiah 5:1–11).

The Consequences of Permitting Interest

All this comes as something of a shock to the modern mind grown accustomed to the omnipresence of interest. After all, if interest was so iniquitous or inefficient, would it not have been dispensed with centuries ago? However, a number of our economic ills can be ascribed to our economic system being reliant upon interest-based debts rather than non-interest financial arrangements. Like most diseases, however, only the symptoms of the interest malaise are recognized. The acceptance of interest is now so deeply ingrained in conventional thought we cannot conceive that interest is the underlying cause of the symptoms. We have ruled out that diagnosis before the patient enters the examination room. Here, however, are some of the results that can be attributed to the workings of interest:

The Unjust and Destabilizing Allocation of Returns between the Users and Suppliers of Finance

Economic theory claims that the long-term rates of profit and interest are inexorably linked. No-one claims that such a connection exists over the short or medium term. This leads to obvious injustices. When a borrower's profits are rising, the lender receives no extra reward for having the foresight to lend to a successful business in excess of the basic rate of interest. Yet when a borrower's profits are falling, small or non-existent, the responsibility to pay interest at the going rate remains. The lender does not suffer for financing an unsuccessful business, and may foreclose on a business that could continue to survive if it need not pay interest. Hence, we observe that banks deepen the recessions by bankrupting firms unnecessarily. As bank depositors, we tend to forget that the banks are acting in this way on our behalf.

This same aspect of interest actually tends to amplify the economic cycle. On the upswing, businesses that borrow heavily retain a greater proportion of their profits, and will be encouraged to borrow and invest even more. On the downswing, these businesses will find themselves burdened by high interest costs when profits are low or negative. Most will reduce their investment and production – many will be bankrupted unnecessarily. If businesses were more heavily dependent on forms of finance that shared profits (or losses), and spread these widely to savers, the financial system would destabilize the economy far less.

The Misallocation of Finance to the Safest Borrowers Rather Than to the Most Productive

A frequent claim of orthodox economics is that the market for loans will allocate finance to those borrowers most likely to use it most profitably or well because they are prepared to pay for most of it. Unfortunately, lenders have no direct incentive to ensure that this happens because they only receive the going rate of interest, no matter how profitably or well their loan is used. However, they will suffer losses if borrowers default or are forced into bankruptcy. Consequently, lenders have a direct incentive to slant their lending towards those borrowers who pose least risk of default. Of course, the level of anticipated profit has a bearing on this risk, but it is not the overriding consideration. Rather, it is the size of the borrower's assets that the loan can be secured upon that is paramount.

This is why the loan market is biased towards those who have already acquired valuable assets (i.e. large firms and wealthy individuals). Meanwhile, small firms and less wealthy borrowers are lent less, at higher rates of interest, despite offering the prospect of using the funds more productively. This is how lenders are *forced* to operate in an interest-dominated system. If they were to lend on a profit-share basis, however, they would have a direct incentive to lend to those borrowers offering the best prospects of a high return, rather than those that posed the least risk. Indeed, given that a non-interest/profit-share system would place more emphasis on the expected profitability of the investments funded, it might even allocate finance *more* efficiently than an interest-based alternative (if one accepts that profitability is a satisfactory signal of efficiency). This much was recognized by *The Economist* when discussing (non-interest) Islamic banking:

> Islamic banking is not merely consistent with capitalism (i.e. with a market-driven allocation of capital, labour and other resources), but in certain respects may be better suited to it than western banking.

> 'Banking behind the veil', *The Economist*, 4 April 1992, p. 76

A Propensity to Finance Speculation in Assets and Property

A further misallocation of funds that can occur in an interest-based economy is the financing, and exaggeration, of speculative booms and busts, as seen in UK housing and Japanese shares in the late 1980s, to give but two examples. When the price of an asset in relatively fixed supply begins to rise, buyers borrow to purchase more of it, so as to maximize their capital gain. Lenders comply because the value of their collateral is rising and they face little risk of loss even if the borrower defaults. The process spirals, with more lending causing higher prices, which encourages even more lending. However, when the 'bubble' bursts (due to sharply increased interest rates or the publicizing of a financial scandal or crisis), and asset values begin to fall, speculators are forced to sell their assets on a falling market in order to pay their debts, and lenders are reluctant to finance the purchase of depreciating assets. These factors depress prices even further, leaving many borrowers with debts greater than their assets are worth, as with 'negative equity' in the UK housing market in the early 1990s.

Throughout their history, interest-based credit markets have displayed a remarkable penchant for financing speculative booms, and exaggerating the ensuing slumps, when governments have been foolish enough to give them the opportunity. Financial arrangements whereby risk and speculative return, if any, were shared between borrowers and lenders would make both more cautious when asset values were rising, and force fewer 'fire sales' when they were falling.

An Inherently Unstable Banking System that Can Only Survive with Government Guarantees

It is all very well to say that it would be better if lenders bore more risk, but wouldn't this make banks and building societies vulnerable to collapse? The fact is, however, that banks and building societies are already unstable by their very natures. This vulnerability partly stems from the interest-based arrangements that they undertake with their depositors. Currently, banks offer deposit terms whereby the nominal value of the deposit is guaranteed, interest is paid on the deposit and withdrawal can be instantaneous, or at short notice. These conditions may be convenient to both bank and depositor, but they render the bank open to collapse on two counts. Either it could sustain losses on its loans in excess of its reserves and capital, and go bankrupt because it has guaranteed the nominal value of its deposits, or it could suffer a 'run' where depositors demand immediate repayment, and be unable to satisfy them, because most of the money has been lent out

Only the first of these threats is definitely the result of operating on an interest basis. By guaranteeing the value of its depositors' funds, the bank gives the impression of keeping them safe and secure. And yet, if a return is to be made for depositors, this money must be risked by being lent out. A conventional bank tries to give the impression of doing these two irreconcilable things simultaneously. That banks have largely succeeded with this legerdemain is due partly to their ability to diversify their lending, and partly to the guarantees that central banks and governments have been forced to give banks to protect them from losses of confidence by the public. Central banks often act as 'lender-of-last-resort' for private banks unable to acquire emergency funds from elsewhere.

Governments often provide deposit insurance protection, thus pledging taxpayers' money to bail out the depositors of a collapsed bank in part (e.g. BCCI). No other private sector operation enjoys such generous guarantees from government, and it is generally agreed that these 'safety-nets' encourage banks to take excessive risks in some circumstances (witness the US Savings and Loan crisis).

The problem of potential bank insolvency would be addressed in a non-interest economy by insisting upon depositors sharing in some of the risks of the investment process through receiving a profit-or-loss related return on their invested deposits. Consequently, when the bank makes a profit or loss on its assets, this is shared *pro rata* with depositors. Hence, if a bank deposit is liable to receive a return, there must be some possibility of it incurring a loss. In this way, the bank cannot become insolvent because losses are shared with depositors, who would then also take far greater care over which bank they entrusted their money to. (For current accounts, banks could guarantee the nominal value of deposits, but be unable to invest these funds, or pay a return on them.)

A 'Short-Termist' Investment Strategy

Interest promises that a compound return can always and everywhere be made on the loan of money. 'Real' investment projects are forced to match up to this rate of return in each period, or risk being neglected in favour of the money being deposited with a bank. Consequently, the pervasive influence of interest tends to bias business investment towards quick-return, short-term projects even though longer-term, more risky ones may offer greater benefits in the long run. This is one of the reasons for the perceived 'short-termism' of the UK stock market and business managers. The more successful financial postwar systems (e.g. Germany, Japan pre-1985) have been those that have ensured that banks have stakes in the long term of their business customers.

A related point is that the existence of an interest rate, against which the return on every other asset is compared, can lead to the over-exploitation of natural resources. For instance, a high rate of interest encourages owners of nonrenewable resources (e.g. oil-fields) to exploit their resource more quickly, and to bank the proceeds. Such an outcome could severely damage the interests of future generations. In the case of renewable resources, however (e.g. forestry, fish stocks), the resource may be physically incapable of growing or reproducing at a rate equivalent to the rate of interest. In such circumstances, the owners will maximize their return by exploiting the resource to such a degree that its price continually rises so as to reflect its growing scarcity. In extreme cases, a high rate of interest could even indicate that profits would be maximized by the extinction of the resource.

The Concentration of Wealth into Fewer and Fewer Hands

Interest automatically acts to transfer wealth from net borrowers to net lenders. Not surprisingly, the former tend to be the less well-off and the latter tend to be the richer members of society. This tendency arises in any society that permits unearned income to exist, including a non-interest one. However, interest works to exaggerate the process in two ways. First, it permits the augmentation of wealth in a relatively risk-free manner, so enabling interest to compound upon itself and funds put out at interest to grow exponentially. This means that, so long as they do not spend extravagantly beyond their income, rich individuals will always remain rich. Second, those who borrow at interest and fail to make their businesses pay, or keep up with their interest payments, are penalized heavily. They may be forced into bankruptcy, or into financial stringency for an indefinite period, and still be unable to extricate themselves from the debt trap due to their outstanding debt growing at a compound rate. (In circumstances where the supply of credit is uncompetitive, the concentration of wealth can be further increased by lenders deliberately seeking the default of poor borrowers so as to permit the seizure of undervalued collateral, usually land or property.) By allocating risk so unevenly, interest ensures that the rich can largely protect themselves from uncertainties, while the poor can be legally subjected to financial servitude.

Both of these features would be moderated under a non-interest system that would share the risks of investment more equitably. (However, the inclusion of periodic debt cancellation in the Old Testament Law – Deuteronomy 15:1–11 – suggests that the prohibition of interest may not be sufficient to prevent the polarization of wealth through lending and borrowing.)

A Rapid Flow of Financial Capital Across Regions and Countries

It is of the nature of interest that it economizes on the information necessary for funds to be transferred from saver to borrower. Only the rate of interest and the quality of the collateral need be known for a transaction to occur. With profit-related or rental contracts, however, because investors are incurring more risk, they need more information before committing their capital (e.g. on the trustworthiness of the borrower or the exact amount of profit being made with their funds). Such information is most readily available at the local or regional level. Consequently, interest permits financial flows to occur on a far greater scale than would otherwise occur. Economic theory may believe that this will improve the efficiency of investment, but it contributes to the erosion of community and regional cohesion as jobs tend to follow flows of financial capital.

The Fallacy of Compound Interest

Although economists have rarely recognized the point, scientific observers of economics have often been puzzled by a logical contradiction posed by the existence of interest. This is that the ability to charge a positive compound rate of interest means that money wealth can increase at an exponential rate if left unspent.[4] However, natural resources are physically unable to sustain exponential rates of growth for anything other than a short period of time. If productivity cannot be increased at a perpetually compounding rate, something, somewhere, has to give. A financial system cannot sustain the exponential growth of debt claims indefinitely:

> An economic system that includes the positive feedback of compound interest can only endure if it also includes a counteracting force such as inflation,[4] bank failures, confiscatory taxes, robbery, bankruptcy, revolutions or repudiations of debts. Conventional wisdom considers these events are pathological. Understandable they may be; but at least one such force must be included … if the system is to endure.
>
> G. Hardin and C. Bajema, *Biology: Its Principles and Implications*, W. H. Freeman, San Francisco, 1978, 3rd edition, p. 275.

But …

The preceding discussion illustrates what goes wrong when a society permits a rate of interest to exist on money loans. State intervention has usually been required to prevent interest-based financial systems from periodically destroying themselves. Such an outcome is unsurprising given that exponentially growing debt claims are unsustainable over long periods.

This is not to suggest, however, that a non-interest system would be easily achievable. Its practicability is qualified in a number of ways. First, a complete change of attitude would be needed on the part of lenders. The notion of interest is so ingrained in our thinking that savers will always expect the 'something for nothing' deal that interest offers. Consequently, it would come as an enormous shock to find that one couldn't receive a return on one's savings without incurring some risk. Savers might respond by trying to move their money to countries where a risk-free return was still offered, or hoarding cash rather than investing it with a financial intermediary.[5]

Second, the relationships between lenders and borrowers would have to be closer than they are now. For instance, if a bank finances small businesses on a profit-share basis, it would have to take more care over who it lends to and whether the accounts of its borrowers are trustworthy. Similarly, depositors would have to take more care over which bank they chose, since their return would directly depend on the success with which their bank invested their money. With risks shared more evenly between lenders and borrowers in a non-interest system, more information must flow between the two parties. Although these are grounds for believing that a more efficient allocation of funds would be the result, and that the costs of producing this information would diminish over time, there would unquestionably be an initial period in which these costs would outweigh the benefits of moving to a non-interest system.

Third, interest enables some highly convenient financial arrangements to be devised. For instance, companies and individuals often find it useful to have access to overdraft and short-time credit facilities which ease the transacting of awkwardly timed payments. Non-interest revolving credit arrangements can be devised, often on a co-operative basis, but their availability would be much more restricted than those offered by current banking operations.

Perhaps the most important implication of non-interest operations, however, is for the running of government finances. For it is impossible to devise non-interest substitutes for government debt for anything other than revenue-raising public projects (e.g. toll roads). Since there is no profit to share in most of its spending arrangements, a government could not borrow to finance education, health, defence, welfare or whatever. Many see in this restriction implicit support for the belief that governments ought not to be allowed to spend beyond their tax-raising means. Such borrowing often imposes unwarranted burdens upon unrepresented future generations of taxpayers and/or gives government an incentive to permit inflation so as to alleviate its debt burden. However, sustaining the required government surplus necessary to repay the accumulated national debt would require a radical change in the way government finances are currently administered.

Assessment

Undoubtedly, a non-interest financial system – built along the lines suggested by the traditional Christian critique of interest – would have many costs. It would involve the repudiation of the illusion that financial capital can be both return-bearing and 'safe' simultaneously. As a result, wholesale changes to current financial institutions would be required.

A non-interest financial system is perhaps too radical a solution to be realizable in the near future. However, some of its lessons could still be applied within our current ways of operating. For instance, the economy would become more stable if less reliance was placed on interest-bearing debt in favour of profit-sharing and rental arrangements. This process ought to be fostered by the removal of the remaining tax incentives to incur debt – notably mortgage tax relief and the deductability of interest payments against corporation tax. Banks could be permitted to offer chequeable unit trust accounts, so as to provide them with a long-term stake in the profitability of their business clients. Less reliance could be placed on the expansion of credit to finance consumer spending.

Nevertheless, while interest continues to operate, injustice and inefficiency will remain, even if governments re-regulate financial markets to protect them from their own self-destructive urges. The current plight of many Western and LIC economies is eloquent testimony to the damage wrought by reliance on debt finance. The foundation for an alternative that offers greater fairness, efficiency and stability is the biblical prohibition of interest, and the Christian analysis developed from it. The detractors of Old Testament economics need to take care. Experience has shown that there is far more wisdom in this biblical teaching than Christians have realized for the last five centuries. Without it, we have no cogent response to the financial chaos that rages about us.

1   This paper was originally published in March 1993.

2   The Parables of the Talents (Matthew 25:14–30) and the Ten Minas
    (Luke 19:11–27) are often cited as examples of Jesus implicitly
    sanctioning the receipt of interest by Christians. A different reading of
    the texts is possible, however. The lazy servant is 'judged by his own
    words': if he had truly believed that his master was a 'hard man', then
    he should have put the money on deposit at interest, for this is what a
    'hard man' would expect. The receipt of interest is effectively 'reaping
    where one has not sown' (Luke 19:22, 23). Detailed discussion of the
    biblical texts can be found in S.C. Mooney, *Usury: Destroyer of
    Nations* (Theopolis, Warsaw, Ohio, 1988), and P.S. Mills, *Interest in
    Interest: The Relevance of the Old Testament Ban on Interest for Today*
    (Jubilee Centre Publications, Cambridge, 1990).

3   Although shares have the advantage of sharing risk, this is not to
    say that the current workings of the stock market are above moral
    censure. The dilemma for the Christian responding to the prohibition
    of interest and yet cognizant of the ethical shortcomings of the stock
    market is explored in P.S. Mills, *Christian Principles for Saving and
    Investment* (Jubilee Centre Publications, Cambridge, 1992).

4   The extraordinary power of compound growth rates has often been
    commented upon. A recent illustration was given when the newly
    independent republic of Ukraine sought to reclaim a barrel of gold
    deposited at the Bank of England in 1723 by a Ukrainian nationalist.
    Using compounded market rates of interest, the claim came to
    £16,000,000,000,000, or 130 times Britain's national income
    ('Ukraine Claims Gold', *Financial Times*, 23 July 1990).

5   It is sometimes claimed that the existence of inflation means that
    interest must exist in order to compensate savers for the erosion of
    the real value of their wealth. This is an inadequate justification for
    interest, however, because interest would exist even if the price level
    were stable, and profit-related or rental returns on finance could offer
    as good as, if not better, inflation-proofing as nominal interest rates.
    It must also be considered whether the existence of interest, and the
    type of banking system thereby permitted, is responsible for persistent
    inflation in the first place.

Chapter 14

CHRISTIANS AND FINANCIAL SECURITY

Faith Versus Prudence?

PAUL MILLS

Summary

This chapter is the first of two concerned with financial management from a Christian perspective. It confronts the tension in biblical teaching enjoining the exercise of personal faith and prudence with respect to wealth. It then addresses some of the practical issues involved in determining the appropriate level of savings and insurance. The following chapter discusses the relative ethical merits of the variety of savings instruments available, including bank accounts, shares, pension funds and housing.

Introduction

Do not store up for yourselves treasures on earth … Look at the birds of the air; they do not sow or reap or store away in barns, and yet your heavenly Father feeds them.

Matthew 6:19, 26

Go to the ant, you sluggard; consider its ways and be wise! … it stores its provisions in summer and gathers its food at harvest.

Proverbs 6:6–8

Which is the more 'spiritual' province of the animal kingdom – the 'birds of the air' who trust in Providence, or the ants who make provision for the future? The question sounds frivolous, but it highlights one of the most difficult issues that each Christian must address when applying biblical teaching to everyday life – just how much wealth is it right for me to own? The dilemma arises because the Bible contains two strands of teaching on the subject that seem to run counter to one another. For instance, Jesus explicitly enjoins his followers not to accumulate treasure on earth (Matthew 6:19); yet elsewhere the Scriptures commend prudent foresight and the responsible stewardship of possessions.

Given the prominence of this seeming paradox, one might have anticipated Christians to be well versed in its practical resolution. However, while the issue of the personal ownership of wealth has provoked heated debate throughout the church's history, it is now largely ignored by Western Christians.[1] We have been infected with the mores of our age that regard personal finance as too sensitive a matter to be broached outside the confines of the cash dispensing confessional. It is only on the question of giving that the Christian can be guaranteed frequent financial instruction!

This chapter addresses the seeming impasse in the Bible's teaching on wealth in the context of decisions concerning savings and the insurance of life and possessions. Pointers to the resolution of this dilemma will then be suggested.

Reasons for the Biblical Warnings against Accumulating Wealth

Wealth Is a Rival Deity Vying for Our Worship

The foundation of the Scripture's misgivings about the ownership of wealth *per se* is that material possessions are an idol competing with the true God for our worship. Jesus expressed the idea most powerfully when he made a sharp distinction between the love of God and love of money ('Mammon'):

> No-one can serve two masters. Either he will hate the one and love the other, or he will be devoted to the one and despise the other. You cannot serve both God and Money.
>
> Matthew 6:24

By personifying wealth as a slave-owner in competition with God for our allegiance, Jesus places it in the ranks of the spiritual powers of evil used to seduce us away from adherence to God. Possessions can, quite literally, 'possess'. Its ability to act as a demonic force therefore means that wealth cannot be treated as morally neutral when interacting with our fallen human natures. It is apt to tempt us to evil (1 Timothy 6:10) and facilitates the satisfaction of other sinful desires. We, naturally, crave to compromise between the service of God and Mammon, but Jesus so framed the choice to make this impossible – if his disciples do not 'hate' Mammon, they will 'love' it.

Wealth Is a Positive Barrier to Faith in Providence

One of the traits of the worship of Mammon is to regard it as the ultimate source of security in one's life. Precautionary saving, insurance and holding on to wealth are motivated by the instinctive human desire for material security and certainty in the future. Yet true security is only to be found in God's provision.[2] The accumulation of riches can not only lead to the withering of faith in this providential care but also results in the self-reliance and pride of unregeneracy.[3] It is all too easy to pay lip-service to the idea of God's daily provision for our needs, but if this makes no impression on the level of security we arrange for ourselves, our declarations of faith will ring hollow:

> Ultimately, there is no way to share: either our confidence is in God or it is in our savings account. To claim that we can thus insure ourselves and still put our trust in God is to add hypocrisy to mistrust.
>
> J. Ellul, *Money and Power*, Marshall Pickering, 1986, p. 105.

Wealth Is Deceitful

As with other idols, wealth ultimately fails to deliver. For instance, despite being christened with such reassuring epithets as 'secured', 'bond', 'index-linked' and 'guaranteed', every financial or real asset involves some degree of risk – inflation erodes, debtors default, markets crash, governments renege, thieves steal, companies collapse, currencies devalue, assets depreciate, taxes rise, wars ravage, disasters strike, crooks defraud and banks fold.[4] It is therefore pointless to search for the totally safe asset and foolish to rely on wealth as the ultimate source of one's security. Risk is ubiquitous. Also:

The Appetite for Wealth and Security Is Never Satisfied

Since the completely safe asset does not exist, a person can never accumulate enough to feel totally safe. The search for such security is a chasing after the wind – we are never satiated, no matter how much we possess. It is wiser not to begin the pursuit (e.g. Ecclesiastes 5:10; 6:7).

Wealth Cannot Buy Happiness

Outside meaningful relationships, wealth has severely limited currency in the procurement of fulfilment (e.g. Ecclesiastes 4:8).

Death Robs Everyone

Eventually 'Life assurance' is something of a misnomer, for wealth makes no difference beyond the grave:

> Our life is but an empty show,
> naked we come and naked go;
> Both for the humble and the proud,
> there are no pockets in a shroud.[5]

Wealth Is a Bad Investment

But perhaps the most surprising element of the Bible's denigration of wealth is couched in purely self-interested terms. In the spiritual scheme of things, the long-run return on worldly savings is worse than non-existent. For instance, Jesus is sure that a new age is dawning in which this world's wealth will be worthless[6] – sterling futures of that maturity trade at zero. Consequently, the smarter investor patronizes the *Banque Celestiale* by choosing savings media that will survive the looming financial crisis. However, the only asset with the requisite durability is the good done to others. Hence, Jesus' cryptic advice:

> Use worldly wealth to gain friends for yourselves, so that when it is gone, you will be welcomed into eternal dwellings.
>
> Luke 16:9; cf. 12:33; 1 Timothy 6:18, 19

Such advice may disqualify Jesus from certification as an independent financial adviser, but if we really believe in the coming kingdom of God, it is the only realistic advice on the market:

It is want of faith that makes us opt for earthly rather than heavenly treasure. If we really believed in celestial treasures, who among us would be so stupid as to buy gold? We just do not believe. Heaven is a dream, a religious fantasy which we affirm because we are ortho-dox. If people believed in heaven, they would spend their time preparing for permanent residence there. But nobody does. We just like the assurance that something nice awaits us when the real life is over.

J. White, The Golden Cow, Marshall, Morgan & Scott, 1979, p. 39.

Unsurprisingly, these teachings have continually prompted Christians not only to regard wealth with suspicion but, in many cases, to renounce its individual ownership altogether. For instance, the Rule of Saint Benedict was typical of monastic orders:

The vice of private property is above all to be cut off from the Monastery by the roots. Let none presume to give or receive anything without the leave of the Abbot, nor to keep anything as their own, either book or writing tablet or pen, or anything whatsoever.

Chapter 33

This school of thought views the accumulation of savings, and the insurance of property, as a clear betrayal of trust in God's daily providential care.

Biblical Support for Savings and Insurance

Before a radical Christian critique of private property can be in-ferred, however, these teachings need to be balanced by further considerations. For instance, all of Jesus' teaching on wealth is con-demnatory, yet he was supported in his itinerant ministry by a group of women of independent means; neither Nicodemus nor Joseph of Arimathea were required to relinquish their possessions as a condition of discipleship; and, while the early church in Jerusalem held its wealth in common, the incident of Ananias and Sapphira shows that this was neither a universal nor a compulsory requirement. These observations force many commentators into a more or less common position:

> There are two sides to Jesus' attitude to private property ... Emphatic black-and-white statements and commands suggest that no true disciple should own property, while incidental comments and inferences from both his teaching and his practice indicate that private ownership is normal, and indeed essential, not only for society at large, but for the majority of Jesus' disciples.
>
> R.T. France, 'God and Mammon', *Evangelical Quarterly*, 1979, p.13.

In addition, if the ownership of wealth was inherently immoral, Scripture would endorse poverty. However, while it may be a 'blessed' estate (Luke 6:20), poverty is never positively advocated. The Christian is urged to relieve penury, not embrace it. Rather, trustworthy stewardship of,[7] and contentment with,[8] the provision that God has afforded are the recurring themes.

These observations provide grounds for the Christian ownership of wealth by default. However, a more positive justification for savings and insurance also exists. While this strand of teaching is not as rich as that condemning wealth (for good reason, given the natural inclination of the human heart towards the idolatry of Mammon), it is nevertheless present.

Godly Wisdom Is Marked by Prudence and Foresight

A theme running throughout the book of Proverbs is that prudence and foresight characterize the wise.[9] A mark of such wisdom is abstinence and saving:

> In the house of the wise are stores of choice food and oil, but a foolish man devours all he has.
>
> Proverbs 21:20; cf. 6:6–8

The ability to subjugate current desires in favour of future needs is one that the ungodly often lack – 'let us eat and drink ... for tomorrow we die' (Isaiah 22:13). Consequently, the adjunct to the Christian suspicion of debt is the prudent saving up for necessary purchases. The most dramatic example of God's advocacy of prudential provision was in the prompting of Joseph to store the surplus from seven Egyptian harvests (Genesis 41), for these not only enabled Egypt to survive the ensuing famine, but preserved the descendants of Abraham. Truly, saving saved the people of God.

Savings Are Necessary to Fulfil One's Family Obligations

Scripture is adamant that the fulfilment of extended family responsibilities is the Christian's paramount practical religious duty.[10] This is primarily effected through the earning of daily income. However, there are some circumstances, such as one's death, where it is hard to envisage how one's dependants could be provided for without the prior accumulation of wealth or insurance against such risks. Although trust in God's provision on a hand-to-mouth basis is possible, even admirable, as a single person, the task becomes much more difficult when one has dependants. Indeed, not saving when required by such circumstances could be construed as presuming upon God. Freedom from such concerns is one of the reasons for Paul's commendation of Christian celibacy (1 Corinthians 7:32–3).

The Duty to Avoid Dependence on Others

While mutual dependence in times of trial among Christians is to be welcomed, it is irresponsible for the spendthrift deliberately to place him- or herself in a position of vulnerability. It runs contrary to the teaching in Paul's letters that the Christian should work diligently in order to avoid dependence on others and be in a position to assist the needy.[11] This liberating aspect of saving was a favourite theme of Victorian Christian moralists:

> A store of savings is to the working man as a barricade against want; it secures him a footing, and enables him to wait ... until better days come round ... But the man who is always hovering on the verge of want is in a state not far removed from that of slavery. He is in no sense his own master, but is in constant peril of falling under the bondage of others, and accepting the terms they dictate to him.
>
> S. Smiles, *Self-Help*, John Murray, 1859, reprinted 1958, p. 285

Today, this would not just apply to the need to avoid dependence on personal charity but also on the state.

A Reconciliation?

The Truncated Spectrum

Given this diversity of teaching, it is tempting to believe that any number of attitudes to savings and investment can be justified. The spectrum could range from giving everything away and living a purely hand-to-mouth existence, with no thought of the future, to accumulating as much as possible to guard against any possible contingency.

However, the spectrum can be narrowed a little by eliminating variants of these two extreme positions from the range of alternatives. The first is a form of fatalism disguised as Christian spirituality. It accepts that 'what will be will be' – any exercise of foresight, in the form of planning or saving, is regarded as a lack of faith in Providence. Yet, taken to its logical extreme, this way of thinking yields the absurd conclusion that any action we take on our part for our own preservation and sustenance, such as looking before crossing a road, betrays a lack of faith in God's ability to provide for us. But this, in the main, is not how God has chosen to act in this world. In numerous areas of Christian experience (e.g. evangelism, healing) God has chosen to act mainly through, and in response to, the prayerful actions and efforts of his people. Hence, exercising foresight and acting in response does not necessarily betray a lack of trust in Providential oversight.

Conversely, however, protecting oneself from every contingency through high levels of savings and insurance, under the guise of 'prudence' and 'self-reliance', is indistinguishable in practice from resorting to wealth as the ultimate source of one's security. We must examine our hearts before God. For the Christian is required not only to hold to doctrines in theory, but to embody them in the way he or she lives (e.g. James 2:17).

Consequently, rejection of the worship of money must result in a lower level of financial accumulation than would otherwise be the case.

The Need for Diversity

Despite eliminating both *de facto* fatalism and Mammonism, a huge range of possible approaches nevertheless remains. This is somewhat disconcerting. It runs counter to the natural human desire for simple, unified rules by which to judge what is right and what is wrong. Hence the numerous attempts to squeeze the diversity of teaching on wealth into a single, universally applicable norm.

Those who make such attempts ignore the likelihood that a diversity of view and practice on this issue is not only inevitable but divinely intended. Such a conclusion is prompted by various indications in the New Testament that the appropriate attitude to wealth depends on the Christian's situation and calling. Notably, when witness is to be given of the imminence and power of the kingdom of God, a 'reckless' attitude towards wealth and possessions is entirely appropriate in order to display more powerfully Christian love and faith. However, greater prudence is required when physical conditions are more hostile and endurance is the order of the day. It is a question of finding where to strike the balance between the practicalities of living in the 'world' while living in the light of the age to come.

Some of Jesus' teachings highlight the different attitudes to wealth that may be appropriate depending upon circumstance. For instance, when anointed at Bethany, Jesus commended Mary's extravagance as fitting, even though Judas was technically correct in his advocacy of alms-giving (John 12:1–8; cf. the correct times to fast, Matthew 9:15). However, the contrast in fortunes between the wise and foolish virgins (Matthew 25:1–13) illustrates the advisability of prudence and preparation when awaiting the age to come. Most clearly, when sending out his disciples on their first missionary campaign, Jesus ordered his disciples to 'Take nothing for the journey – no staff, no bag, no bread, no extra tunic' (Luke 9:3); and yet, with the crucifixion looming, he gave precisely the opposite instruction (Luke 22:36). With the onset of persecution and hostility, a different attitude towards possessions was needed.

This diversity of approach is also found in the practice of the early church. The extravagant sharing of property in the Jerusalem congregation was entirely appropriate as a sign of the power of the Spirit to change lives and as a means of support for the pilgrims converted at Pentecost (Acts 2:45; 4:32–7). Yet the communal sharing of property is not mentioned in the epistles, save in the context of interchurch alms-giving (2 Corinthians 8 and 9). Indeed, Paul chastises members of the Thessalonian church for forsaking work, probably in anticipation of the imminent arrival of the kingdom of

God (2 Thessalonians 3:6–12). They were suffering from an 'over-realized eschatology' and not planning for the long haul.

Hence, there is no warrant nor need for the assimilation of biblical teaching on wealth into a 'grand unified theory'. A diversity of approach, that depends on circumstance, the Spirit's prompting and the message to be given to the outside world, is entirely tenable.

Practical Pointers in the Savings and Insurance Decision

Discern One's Calling with Regard to Wealth

The diversity of approaches that Christians can take towards wealth and lifestyle immediately leads on to the need personally to discern God's will in the matter. For instance, if a Christian is without weighty obligations to dependants and is unlikely to incur them in the future, a relatively 'reckless' attitude towards wealth might be appropriate. Similarly, Christian communities and missionaries wishing to demonstrate their mutual love and trust can do so through a common purse. However, Christian individuals and organizations with obvious commitments and obligations will need, if possible, to maintain a level of wealth necessary for their fulfilment.

Deliberately Set Limits to One's Material Security

The accumulation of wealth can only be justified if it is motivated by the need to fulfil specific obligations or anticipated future needs (e.g. saving up for necessary purchases rather than borrowing). Merely saving to achieve ever-greater levels of financial security equates to the worship of money. The motivation for possessing wealth is crucial. It is no coincidence that the harshest scriptural condemnations of wealth are aimed at hoarding for selfish purposes:

> Do not store up *for yourselves* treasures on earth.
>
> Matthew 6:19

> Now listen, you rich people, weep and wail … Your wealth has rotted, and moths have eaten your clothes. Your gold and silver are corroded. Their corrosion will testify against you … You have hoarded wealth in the last days.
>
> James 5:1-3; cf. Luke 12:21

Now, we may save more through building up financial assets than hoarding durables and cash, but the same considerations apply. The need to avoid pure hoarding and bondage to possessions implies that Christians need to be crystal clear about the purpose for which they are saving, or continuing to own valuable assets (e.g. a large family house). Once that purpose has been achieved, saving should cease and the surplus be given away. For instance, the level of savings and life assurance needed to provide for one's dependants in case of one's death should be limited to that necessary to provide for their maintenance at a predetermined level, given a reasonable estimate of the risks of the relevant savings schemes. Savings should not be piled up merely for the sake of providing protection against every imaginable contingency.

Develop the Church and Extended Family as Substitutes for Impersonal Savings and Insurance Schemes

In capitalist countries, insurance through state provision and financial intermediaries has virtually dispensed with the need for the local church or extended family to play a role in this area. Indeed, the appropriation of the financial support role from the extended family is one of the main reasons for its demise within Western society.

The absence of an obvious financial role, combined with the cultural reticence to discuss matters sacred (i.e. pecuniary), has resulted in many congregations too embarrassed to broach the subject of monetary need in their midst, let alone act upon it. This contrasts strongly with the New Testament picture of a mutually supporting body that feels and acts upon the material needs of its members.[12] The place of individualized saving can be taken, in part, by mutual risk-sharing within the congregation through the establishment of grant and interest-free loan funds, consumer durable goods pools (e.g. gardening equipment, children's clothes) or an *ad hoc* self-contributory insurance pool to cover periods of illness or unemployment. By such acts, a congregation can give practical expression to the mutual care it pays lip-service to.

However, as with individualized wealth, the accumulation of collective congregational and denominational wealth, through endowment, also poses great spiritual dangers. The hoarding of wealth by churches, to provide security for the future, leads to the temptation of thinking that the collective body can survive indefinitely, when this, too, is dependent on God's grace (e.g. Revelation 3:16, 17). The endowment of churches dilutes the incentive and necessity of the present congregation to give sacrificially to the church, or in support of one another. The allocation of large sums of capital always brings the potential for internal strife, while their investment in order to receive an income is fraught with ethical dilemmas (seemingly unbeknownst to many church treasurers). Most difficult of all, if the flow of income is to be preserved into the future, the capital sum must go untouched. And yet, there are always more calls on a congregation's resources than can be met at any one time. Hence, an endowed church is continually placing the prerequisites of its own survival above pressing, current needs.

Maintain the Distinction between Savings and Insurance

To advocate honesty with regard to insurance claims may seem trite and obvious, but there is a popular fallacy abroad in this regard that is gaining ever-greater currency. This is the supposed right of claimants to inflate their claim in order to regain the value of the premia they have paid. This attitude turns catastrophe insurance into a form of savings scheme, whereby withdrawals are to be made through claims against damage or theft. Yet, clearly, this is not how such insurance schemes are structured. They pool the risks and premia of numerous policyholders in order to pay out much larger compensation to the minority who suffer mishap. Only life assurance policies are designed to act as both an insurance and a savings medium.

The fallacy is most apparent in the widespread belief that people have a right to National Insurance benefits (state pensions and unemployment benefit) *because* they have made their contributions. Unfortunately, National Insurance contributions have long since ceased to cover the benefits paid, and the system was never established on an actuarially sound basis in any case. They are simply taxes by another name. There is no pool of assets from which contributors have a right to repayment.

Conclusion

Both the 'birds of the air' *and* the ant teach valuable spiritual lessons. The Christian is both to trust God wholly for material security and to be ready to save prudently when the circumstances require it. While there may be tension within the biblical teaching on wealth, there turns out to be no contradiction. As far as faith versus prudence goes, the Christian is faced not by either/or, but both/and.

1   The last major evangelical discussion of the issue was initiated by the Lausanne Congress on World Evangelization in 1974. The resulting Covenant commended a simple lifestyle for the furtherance of poverty relief and evangelism. The ensuing debate ranged widely over the causes of world poverty and the supposed culpability of capitalist nations in its continuation (e.g. R. Sider, *Rich Christians in an Age of Hunger*, Hodder & Stoughton, 1977; cf. D. Chilton, *Productive Christians in an Age of Guilt Manipulators*, Institute for Christian Economics, 1985). However, the practicalities of deciding the level and instruments of saving were barely touched upon.

2   E.g. Psalms 62:8–10; Matthew 6:25–34; Luke 12:22–31; cf. Proverbs 3:5–6.

3   E.g. Deuteronomy 8:13, 14; Mark 4:19; Luke 12:16–21; 18:18–25.

4   Cf. Proverbs 23:5; Matthew 6:20; 1 Timothy 6:17.

5   Attributed to James Hill. See also Ecclesiastes 5:15; Zephaniah 1:18 and 1 Timothy 6:7, 19.

6   Matthew 6:19–21; Luke 12:33–4; cf. Zephaniah 1:18; James 5:1–3.

7   E.g. Genesis 1:28; 2:15; Matthew 25:14–30; Luke 16:1–9; 19:11–27.

8   E.g. Proverbs 30:3–6; Ecclesiastes 5:18, 19; Philippians 4:11, 12; 1 Timothy 6:6–8.

9   E.g. Proverbs 14:15; 22:3; 27:12; cf. Luke 14:28–33.

10   Mark 7:9–13; 1 Timothy 5:8; cf. 2 Corinthians 12:14.

11   E.g. Ephesians 4:28; 1 Thessalonians 4:11–12; 5:14; 2 Thessalonians 3:6–12.

12   E.g. Acts 4:34, 35; 1 Corinthians 12:26; 1 Timothy 5:3.

Chapter 15

INVESTING AS A CHRISTIAN

Reaping Where You Have Not Sown?

PAUL MILLS

Summary

Who should you trust with your savings? Is the highest return all that counts, or should this be sacrificed to moral principle? This chapter discusses the appropriate ways for Christians to save and invest by outlining general and specific biblical instruction on the subject. Although there are few forms of saving that can be wholly endorsed, biblical principles offer far more discriminating guidance on financial investment than is commonly supposed.

Introduction

Consult any financial advisor about where to put your savings and four things will guide their counsel – risk, return, personal circumstance and tax. It is unlikely that the ethical status of your investments will enter into their calculations. This outlook is shared by the financial markets. Modern capitalism is founded on the belief that the maximization of financial return is its own justification. Ethical considerations have no place in determining how and where resources are invested, since the free play of market forces is meant to ensure the greatest overall benefit to society. The profitable end justifies any (legal) financial means.

Surely Christians should strongly challenge such a view. Is not *how* a return is made on savings more important than *how much*? However, while some Christians, such as the present Bishop of Oxford, have been at the forefront of the 'ethical investment' movement, teaching on these issues at grass-roots level remains surprisingly scarce. In the main, Christians (and church treasurers) are given precious little guidance on where and how to invest their resources.

This chapter attempts to redress the balance by outlining the biblical teaching concerning savings and investment, and then assessing how the most widely available forms of saving compare.[1] It will not seek to give detailed financial advice but rather an ethical framework against which the advice of others can be evaluated.

General Biblical Principles for Personal Saving and Investment

Stewardship

The most widely quoted principle of biblical teaching to the practical issues of saving and investment is that of stewardship. The Creation narrative teaches that, while God is the source of all material resources, he has condescended to entrust their preservation and development to humanity.[2] In a number of parables, Jesus develops this theme by picturing his disciples as servants given charge of property. Their performance in its use will be assessed at the consummation of the kingdom.[3]

These parables apply to our use of all resources, both spiritual and material, entrusted by God to his servants until the coming of the kingdom. The servants' performance is assessed purely on the basis of financial return. Praise is reserved for those servants who have achieved a healthy profit through business ventures. The lazy servant is condemned for not even attempting to make a return. Superficially, this implies that the sole priority for a Christian is the maximization of financial return.

This would be a misguided interpretation of the parables. First, the 'return' spoken of is wider than just the pecuniary and includes the total good done to others. Second, the means by which profit is obtained matters to God. The Old Testament law accepts the legitimacy of trade for profit *per se*, since trade is presupposed but profit is unregulated. However, any wealth that results from dishonesty, theft, monopoly or exploitation of the poor is legislated against[4] and denounced by the prophets.[5] Consequently, the righteousness of any monetary return is conditional on the absence of the exploitation of customers, workers, creditors and suppliers. The ethic of stewardship applies not just to how productively we deploy God's resources, but also influences to what righteous purposes we deploy them.

The immediate problem this poses for most Western Christians is that we have relinquished the stewardship of our savings to intermediaries, such as fund managers and banks. In most cases, we have no idea of the activities and methods used to derive a return on our money. It seems contradictory, therefore, to bemoan economic exploitation and injustice and yet fail to realize that our own interest payments and pensions are being secured by the same exploitation perpetrated in the name of shareholders and creditors.

Financial returns must come from somewhere – they do not spring automatically from the action of impersonal 'market forces'. Rather, investment affects the distribution of assets, the products and services supplied and their relative prices. It has an inherent moral dimension. In practice, there are few morally flawless forms of investment. We have to choose the least of numerous evils. However, the absence of a first best option does not mean that we are absolved from the responsibility of making such a choice.

The Cultivation of Relationships

Scripture is unequivocal in preaching the subjugation of wealth to the cultivation of loving relationships. Not only does it teach the ever-present duty of supporting one's dependants[6] but Jesus specifically urges the use of this world's wealth to develop friendships, since the good done to others will be the only return on investment that will ultimately last (Luke 16:9).

Knowing exactly who is using your savings and for what purpose is a prerequisite for this. Not only do the close ties between saver and investor ensure a ready flow of information about how the money is used and how the business is going, but investing in this manner may help to cement the original relationship. By contrast, the trend of financial investment has been away from saving with people that you know to channelling savings through anonymous middlemen in order to reduce risk.

Presumption on the Future

Investment decisions are almost entirely guided by expectations of the future. Although there is no contradiction between believing in God's providential care and simultaneously making plans to meet financial needs, the wise are humble in their attitude towards the future[7] whereas the foolish presume upon future profits.[8] To believe that one can know the future, and to incur financial obligations on that basis is, in a way, to claim an attribute of God for oneself.

The need for humility in one's attitude towards future events leads to circumspection when borrowing, especially in order to speculate. It also produces a suspicion of speculative schemes that require specific future events to occur in order to generate a return (such as funds that invest in futures and options).

Specific Biblical Principles for Personal Saving and Investment

The Prohibition of Interest[9]

Contrary to popular assumption, the Bible *does* prohibit all interest on loans within the domestic economy, and not just 'usury' or 'excessive interest' (see Deuteronomy 23:19).[10] Subsequent Old Testament references indicate no exceptions to the prohibition while underlining its moral gravity by associating it with bribery and theft.[11] In addition, Jesus commends a radically liberal attitude towards lending (Luke 6:34, 35).

Crucially in this context, the Parables of the Talents and the Ten Minas do *not* reverse the Old Testament opposition towards interest. While the master chastises the lazy servant for burying his talent, and unfavourably compares this with putting the money out at interest, he judges the servant 'by his own words'. If the servant had truly believed that his master was a 'hard man', then he should have put the money out at interest, since this is what would be expected. Receiving interest is 'reaping where one has not sown' – it is what hard men do (Luke 19:22, 23). Implicit in this parable, therefore, is a distinction between risking money actively in a business venture and putting it on deposit at interest – reaping where one has not sown.

This hints at why such antipathy is reserved for interest-bearing loans. In such a loan, the lender takes no explicit share in the risks of the business, yet requires a return. Not only does this presume that future profit is certain but, if the venture fails, it is the entrepreneur rather than the lender who is liable. Similar problems arise when interest-bearing loans are incurred to finance consumption or house purchase – little consideration is given to changes in borrowers' circumstances by the inexorable logic of compound interest.

The Sanctioning of Risk-Taking and Profit-Share

The corollary of this criticism of interest is that financial contracts that explicitly share risk, through partnerships or equity shares, can be positively sanctioned. No specific biblical warrant exists for such contracts and so their legitimacy must be inferred from the support given to reasonable commercial profit fairly obtained, the acceptance of rental contracts (see below) and the support given to trade and risk-taking.[12] However, two of the previous principles point to the validity of such profit-sharing contracts. First, they explicitly acknowledge that profit is uncertain and is not presumed upon. Second, a profit-share contract is more risky for the provider of finance. This necessitates greater information flows between the user and supplier of capital, so reinforcing their relationship.

Rent and Hire Contracts

Interest on money and rent on property derive from different forms of contract. In a loan, the ownership of the money and its associated risks are transferred to the borrower, whereas in a rental contract, ownership and ultimate risk remain with the original owner. This distinction is set out in Exodus 22:14–15 where hire charges act as compensation for the owner retaining the risk of the objects used by another (see also Leviticus 25:14–16; 29–31). These precedents give tacit sanction to the renting or leasing of property for a return.

Hoarding and Speculation

Hoarding can range from stuffing banknotes in a mattress to amassing valuables in a bank vault. Although the practicalities of life require some degree of storage, hoarding to protect one's wealth receives short shrift from the biblical writers.[13] Hoarding is an anti-social act in that it deprives the economy of the employment-generating consequences of the resources being spent, donated, lent or invested.

A related activity is that of speculation, whereby assets are acquired solely in the expectation of their appreciating in value. This can range from investing in shares that are thought to be takeover targets to borrowing heavily in order to 'invest' in property, futures contracts, art or antiques. To the extent that such speculation achieves a return, it is the result of favourable circumstances and superior knowledge rather than productive activity. Risks are taken not in providing benefits to others but in gambling upon future events. Indeed, in volatile markets, speculation is essentially motivated by the desire to gain at the expense of the next sucker who buys high and sells cheap. As such, it is merely redistributive and presumes upon the future.

Savings Alternatives in the Real World

These general and specific principles give various pointers to how a Christian should invest. How do the most widely available forms of savings and investment match up?

Bank Deposits

The ethical status of money-lending is no longer questioned. Commercial banks lend to a wide variety of ventures, from the smallest of businesses to multi-national corporations, in whatever activity is expected to yield the bank the highest return. Depositors have no control over whether their money is being used to finance employment creation in the inner cities or international arms deals, other than through occasional boycotts (e.g. over Barclays' involvement in South Africa in the 1980s).[14] Neither do depositors have any influence over how their bank conducts its relations with its borrowers vis-à-vis the level of collateral, interest rate margins or the severity of foreclosure. Banks have been widely criticized for their non-forgiveness of low income country debt, for lending too freely in booms and foreclosing too harshly in recessions. Yet it is in the interest of the great bank-depositing public that such deeds are done.

Building Society Deposits

Fewer of these concerns apply to building society deposits. Regulations ensure that societies can only lend to property-related activities and for consumer purchases. Also, societies are mutual organizations, so depositors are members with a stake in the reserves and assets of the society and voting rights at the AGM. Hence, a greater degree of stewardship can be exercised through a building society deposit, while there is less chance of involvement in 'unethical' business operations.

Nevertheless, through their involvement in interest-based lending, societies share some of the failings of banks. For instance, in order to keep their savings returns competitive, societies resort to standard repossession procedures despite the membership status of their borrowers and do not lend readily in deprived housing areas. Also, the influence that any one member can have on society policy is marginal.

Government Debt

UK government debt is held directly by the public through National Savings deposits and holdings of bonds ('gilts'). The debt is the accumulated borrowing of governments since the seventeenth century, largely to finance wars but more recently to cover recurring budget deficits.

The whole gamut of government spending from overseas aid to defence spending is financed by government borrowing, since it makes up the shortfall in taxation that would otherwise be needed. Essentially, public borrowing takes current savings and uses them to finance the present and past unwillingness of governments to impose upon their taxpayers the full costs of their spending decisions. As such, buying government debt serves little productive purpose. The interest payments are merely transfers made by taxpayers to current debt-holders for the 'time value' of their money. (Government debt interest is the fourth largest expenditure programme, exceeding defence.) There is not even the risk of default to justify this return, and future generations of taxpayers are burdened to finance current expenditure.

Property and Other Durables

Wealth is often accumulated through durable assets that have either a practical use (housing, antique furniture) or aesthetic appeal (jewellery, art). They are often a hedge against inflation and may offer the prospect of capital gains. Owner-occupied housing clearly serves a useful purpose, contributes towards rootedness, and can be used for the benefit of others. However, other objects acquired purely as inflation hedges or as a speculative gamble provide few practical benefits. As such, they cannot represent a 'stewardly' use of one's savings, and face the criticisms of hoarding and speculation. One of the evils of high inflation is the encouragement it gives to speculate in durables rather than to invest in productive activity.

Company Shares

The principles outlined earlier seem to sanction individual investment in shares. Their return is related to the profitability of the business through dividends and is a reward for supplying risk capital. Shareholders can influence company policy – they receive the company's accounts and statements, they can put forward motions and can vote at AGMs on the composition of the board and on the outcome of takeovers. If the company is involved in an unethical practice or product, the matter can be raised formally with the company and the share sold if no change is forthcoming. It would seem, therefore, that shares are a more principled outlet for a Christian's savings than a bank deposit, especially if they are owned in a small local or family business where sufficient time can be devoted to be concerned with the management of the firm ('Business Angel' investment).

These ethical benefits are also enjoyed by workers who own shares in their company. Not only is return related to risk-taking, but employees are in a better position to know how their company is behaving and to object if this is immoral. (The one caution about employees owning a substantial part of their savings in the form of their company's shares is that they are very vulnerable if company bankruptcy means they lose their jobs, shares and maximum pension rights.)

However, a blanket commendation cannot be given to investment in shares. Buying shares is risky. Their prices are more volatile than those of other assets because the tax system encourages firms to borrow heavily and pay out their return in capital gain rather than dividends. This prompts shareholders to diversify across a number of companies, so diluting their 'stewardship' interest in any one firm.

There are other concerns. Principally, shares can only be widely traded because the liability of shareholders for the firm's debts is limited to the value of their holdings. In the case of the bankruptcy of such a company, shareholders are not obliged to make good the debts incurred in their company's name. Although limited liability facilitates trading in shares and the growth of large corporations, it breaches one important ethical principle – the small matter of paying one's debts.

This is the root of the other ethical qualms with shares. Limited liability permits the separation of a firm's ownership from the exercise of managerial control. This allows shareholders to treat their shares as purely financial investments and take little interest in how their company is being run. Indeed, they will own so little of a large company that it is not worth their while making the effort to monitor the management. It is easier to sell their shares if they dislike management performance than to make an effort to improve it.

In addition, the impression that the stock market is another arm of the gambling industry is strengthened by the prevalence of takeovers as the principal form of corporate discipline in Anglo-Saxon economies. Not only are takeovers one of the least successful forms of improving company performance in practice, they also permit absentee shareholders to determine the destinies of thousands of employees on the basis of the largest speculative return.

Consequently, although individual shareholdings seem to fulfil more of the initial biblical criteria for personal investment, in practice limited liability and the development of a liquid market in shares make it increasingly difficult for shareholders to discharge their stewardship responsibilities.

Pensions, Endowments and Unit Trusts

Some of these difficulties of shareholding can be overcome by investing through shareholding intermediaries – notably private pension funds, endowment policies and unit trusts. These hold a diversified portfolio of shares, so reducing risks and dealing costs. Between them, UK fund managers control around 70 per cent of the shares in UK quoted companies and so should, collectively, be able to exercise sufficient discipline over company managers to ensure the long-term efficiency of most businesses.

Unfortunately, this is generally not the case. Diversification of risk means that individual fund managers often hold too small a proportion of shares in any one company to make close monitoring worthwhile in the long run. It is usually easier to sell shares (especially in takeovers) than to try to influence company policy. 'Index-tracking' funds do not even pretend to monitor companies but just mechanistically buy and sell shares based only on their size relative to the benchmark index.

The situation is made even worse for the Christian investor through the vast majority of funds being managed with the sole intention of maximizing the funds' return, irrespective of the activities that the companies concerned are involved in. Hence, as with bank depositors, most pension fund holders and endowment policyholders are given little information on the means by which their profits are made.

This problem has recently been addressed by the establishment of 'ethical' and 'green' funds for both pension funds and unit trusts. These limit the range of shares that can be invested in through use of a variety of criteria. 'Negative' funds will not invest in companies in certain areas of business (e.g. tobacco, alcohol, arms, pornography, etc.). 'Positive' funds are those that seek out companies that are a definite benefit to the community or environment, or which operate their trading and working practices according to various ethical criteria. These funds constitute a small (around £1 billion, 0.1 per cent) but growing share of UK funds under management and have tended to perform at least as well, if not a little better, than their competitors since establishment.[15]

Ethical funds offer a definite improvement on ordinary funds, but they are not a panacea. Some funds apply mechanistic criteria to particular business activities but do not discriminate concerning business methods (e.g. predatory pricing, late payment of suppliers). Neither do all funds employ a long-term strategy of trying to influence managers rather than simply selling out at an acceptable return. Consequently, care must be taken in the choice of ethical fund, just as in the choice of individual company shares. Nevertheless, the steps taken thus far are in the right direction and offer a more principled alternative for those without the time or expertise to engage in the stewardship of specific shares.

Conclusion

Christian principles for investment rest uneasily with most of the widely available savings media in the UK. That the range of options is not, in general, congruent with the principles of biblical teaching is no coincidence. At virtually every turn, UK laws and regulations are biased against investing one's money on these principles. Banks are effectively underwritten by the taxpayer through deposit insurance and the Bank of England as 'lender of last resort'; the prospect of short-term windfall payouts is sounding the death-knell of a viable building society sector; companies are encouraged to borrow by the corporate tax system; and tax relief for ISAs and pension funds encourages saving through institutions rather than direct shareholdings. CREST, the new electronic share-dealing system, has made the responsible ownership of shares even costlier by charging more for individual registration.

Clearly, the ethical drawbacks of the various forms of saving need to be traded off. For instance, scrupulousness on the interest question might lead to foregoing opportunities for charitable lending to credit unions or Christian development agencies (e.g. Shared Interest). Alternatively, sensitivity over the 'gambling' aspects of shares could entail relinquishing the chance to invest in a local company and create employment or aid the cause of ethical investment. To facilitate such choices, the table below gives a subjective ranking of the alternatives against some of the criteria discussed here.

Table of investment instruments measured against various ethical criteria

	Personal stewardship	Knowledge of use	Equity/rent v interest	Non-hoarding	Non-speculation
Employee share ownership/ 'Business Angel' investment*	✓✓	✓✓	✓✓	✓✓	✓
Owner-occupied housing	✓✓	✓✓	✓✓	✓	–
Personal shareholding	✓	✓	✓✓	✓	?
Ethical unit trust/fund	✓	✓	✓	✓	–
Building society deposit	✓	✓	✗	✓	–**
Pension fund/ unit trust	✗	✗	✓	✓	–
Govt debt/ National Savings	✗	–	✗	✓	–
Bank deposit	✗	✗	✗	✓	–
Cash	–	–	–	✗✗	–

*   'Business Angel' is the term used to describe an outside shareholder in a small business who also supplies managerial advice and expertise.
** Some building societies have attracted depositors speculating on whether the society is to change its mutual status.

As ever, the Christian has the challenging task of living in the world without being part of it. While there are still no easy answers, the Bible gives more down-to-earth financial advice than is usually presumed. It may not offer the secret of financial success, but at least reaping and sowing will be more closely related.

1   This chapter works from the assumption that someone has spare resources to save and invest – an irrelevant presumption for many. The preceding chapter discussed the grounds for a Christian to own wealth legitimately.

2   Genesis 1:26–30; 2:15.

3   Matthew 25:14–30; Luke 19:11–27; cf. Matthew 24:45–51; Luke 12:42–7 and 16:1–12.

4   Leviticus 19:13, 35–6; Deuteronomy 19:14; 24:15; 25:13–15; 27:17.

5   Isaiah 10:2; Jeremiah 17:11, 22:13; Ezekiel 18:12–13, 22:12–13; Amos 2:6–8.

6   Leviticus 25:25; Mark 7:9–13; 1 Timothy 5:3–8.

7   It is those 'without knowledge' who claim that 'tomorrow will be like today, or even far better' (Isaiah 56:11, 12) whereas Solomon urges 'Do not boast about tomorrow, for you do not know what a day may bring forth' (Proverbs 27:1).

8   Luke 12:16–21; James 4:13–17.

9   Chapter 13 outlined the undesirable economic consequences that arise from an interest-based economic system.

10   Exodus 22:25 and Leviticus 25:35–8 state the prohibition in the context of charitable loans, whereas Deuteronomy 23:19 puts it in terms of loans to all fellow citizens (cf. v. 20).

11   Psalm 15:5; Ezekiel 18:13, 22:11, 12; cf. Proverbs 28:8; Nehemiah 5:7–11.

12   Proverbs 31:10–31; Ecclesiastes 11:1–6.

13   Luke 12:16–21; James 5:3; see also Psalm 39:6; Ecclesiastes 5:13; Zechariah 9:3.

14   Since 1992, the Co-operative Bank has followed various ethical criteria in determining which activities it will not finance. These include oppressive regimes and the sale of arms to them, animal experimentation for cosmetic purposes, factory and fur farming, and tobacco.

15   A full description of ethical funds and their track record is given in R. Sparkes, *The Ethical Investor* (HarperCollins, 1995).

Part V

SCIENCE AND MEDICINE

Chapter 16

SCIENCE: FRIEND OR FOE?

DENIS R. ALEXANDER

Summary

This chapter examines the contemporary relationship between science and Christianity. The exaggerated claims of secular scientists and Christians concerning the nature and scope of scientific and religious knowledge occasionally lead to conflicts. Overall, however, it is concluded that science and Christianity are mutually supportive. Historically, the scientific enterprise has strong Christian roots and Christians have a firm commitment to truth-telling about God's world. Most importantly, both science and Christianity are sceptical about relativistic theories of knowledge, a shared scepticism which has been brought into sharp focus by the rise of postmodernism. The inroads of such relativism into Western thought stimulate the provocative question: 'Can science survive without Christianity?'

Introduction

Contemporary Western societies are profoundly ambivalent about science. On the one hand science is invested with exaggerated expectations and inflated hopes. The vision is for a high-tech universe in which we manipulate its powers to serve our own ends. At the other extreme a vigorous anti-science lobby perceives science to be the source of all our current woes. Scientists are viewed as dangerous meddlers, wresting secrets from nature that are best left well alone, playing God as they pry into the secrets of the human genetic code and uncover the fundamental forces that hold the universe together. How should Christians respond to these opposing currents?

Science Not Technology

One potential confusion in any discussion about science is the modern tendency to fuse the twin concepts of 'science' and 'technology' as if they referred to the same phenomenon. Although it must be admitted that the distinction is not always clear-cut, there are some important differences. 'Science' is an intellectual endeavour to explain the workings of the physical world, informed by empirical investigation and carried out by a community trained in specialized techniques. Its task is to produce testable ideas. In its modern version, complete with experimentation, scientific journals and societies, science has been with us only since the seventeenth century. In contrast, 'technology' refers to the practical arts with their goal of the production of usable objects, and is therefore as old as the earliest human artifacts. Only in the last two centuries has science had a dramatic impact on technology. Today there is even a case for suggesting that if a scientific discovery is made, then, sooner or later, for better or for worse, it will find some application. Yet the underlying fatalism inherent in such a view should be treated with some suspicion. In the final analysis, it is human societies that choose the technological applications of scientific discoveries.

Christians have a great responsibility to contribute clear biblical thinking to the ethical debate about the myriad applications of modern technology. However, it is science, not technology, which is the focus of this chapter, because if science is intrinsically an enemy of Christianity, then clearly its applications in technology will be tarred with the same brush. Conversely, if science is at heart an ally, or neutral in its stance towards Christianity, then its technological applications can be assessed dispassionately on their own individual merits without prejudice stemming from hostility to the scientific enterprise *per se*.

Science As Foe

There have occasionally been times in the history of science, as also today, of conflict between Christian faith and the scientific enterprise. In most cases such conflicts arise from exaggerated claims about the nature and scope of either scientific or religious knowledge.

Conflicts Arising from the Secular Misuse of Science

Ideological and Political Uses

The use of science for political or professional reasons has been a key factor in generating the 'conflict thesis', the idea that science and faith are innately hostile.[1] The *Philosophes* of the French Enlightenment used science as an ideological weapon to attack the power of the church. Similarly T.H. Huxley and his friends in the X-Club in late Victorian Britain campaigned vigorously for scientists to obtain the degree of financial support and intellectual kudos which society invested in the church. While the old 'warfare' metaphor to describe the relationship between science and religion has long been discarded for lack of historical support, the use of science in these campaigns of the past has left a lingering feeling in popular culture that science and faith are in conflict, an idea still promoted by a small but vocal group of anti-religious scientists.

Science and Scientism

Hostility towards science frequently arises from a confusion between 'science' and 'scientism'. The essence of scientism is the belief that scientific descriptions of reality are the *only* descriptions which matter or which are acceptable as *real* knowledge. Scientism is illustrated well by the zoologist Richard Dawkins when he claims that:

> We are machines for propagating DNA, and the propagation of DNA is a self sustaining process. It is every living objects' sole reason for living.[2]

The aim of such scientistic statements is to exclude other levels of explanation. There is, however, no reason why *methodological reductionism*, a research strategy essential for the scientific enterprise in which the component parts of phenomena are dissected and investigated systematically, should lead to *ontological reductionism*, a fallacious claim that such phenomena are 'nothing but' the descriptions generated by such investigations. As it happens, scientific journals deliberately exclude vast domains of human knowledge and experience. Steve Jones, Professor of Genetics at University College, London, summarized the reasons for this well in his recent Reith lectures:

Science cannot answer the question that philosophers – or children – ask; why are we here, what is the point of being alive, how ought we to behave? Genetics has almost nothing to say about what makes us more than just machines driven by biology, about what makes us human. These questions may be interesting, but scientists are no more qualified to comment on them than is anyone else.[3]

Conflating Categories

A further cause of conflict between science and religion comes from the tendency by some scientists to conflate scientific and theological descriptions as if they were offering rival explanations. For example, Stephen Hawking comments in the closing words of *A Brief History of Time* that if we discover a complete theory linking all the fundamental physical forces, then 'it would be the ultimate triumph of human reason – for then we would know the mind of God'.[4] But this mixing of scientific and theological categories is not a triumph of human reason and leads to confusion. Cosmological theories, however elegant and successful, provide complementary explanations to those concerning ultimate meaning and value which are provided by theology. Equations *per se* are not theological. Dawkins falls into the same trap when he states that 'The claim of the existence of God is a purely scientific one.'[5] Yet if there is one question that science is woefully inadequate to address, it is precisely such a metaphysical question. It is this type of category-confusion which brings science into disrepute and generates unnecessary antagonism.

This is not to imply that God's world can be divided into autonomous 'secular' and 'sacred' spheres, but rather that the appropriateness of different types of explanation is dictated by the context. The stone that was rolled away from the tomb of Jesus was a very significant stone, a significance which is best expounded by the theologian. Yet the properties of stones in general are the province of science and have no particular theological significance. No amount of scientific analysis of stones in general provides insight into the meaning of that one particular stone, any more than generalizations about human physiology can provide a basis for assessing individual human worth.

Conflicts Arising from the Christian Misuse of Science

Christians, too, are sometimes guilty of generating conflict with science where none need or should exist. The tendency of some Christians to criticize science without being well informed can be embarrassing. Two areas in particular provide unnecessary sources of conflict.

Conflicts Due to a Mishandling of Scripture

The Christian natural philosophers who laid the foundations of modern science in the seventeenth century campaigned to deliver Scripture as well as science from their Aristotelian interpreters, exhorting their contemporaries against the scholastic habit of extracting science from Scripture. John Wilkins, an early member of the Royal Society in England, who repeatedly referred to Calvin's commentaries in his writings, maintained that:

> It were happy for us, if we could exempt Scripture from Philosophical controversies: If we could be content to let it be perfect for that end unto which it was intended, for a Rule of our Faith and Obedience, and not to stretch it also to be a Judge of such Natural Truths as are to be found out by our own Industry and Experience.[6]

The early Christian scientists saw their science as a process of truth-telling about how the world *actually* worked, in contrast to the 'ancients' and their rationalistic followers who expounded how the world *ought* to work. Uncovering such natural truths was a matter for 'our own Industry and Experience'.

Unfortunately, the twentieth century has witnessed a revival of biblical scholasticism in some circles, often alienating the scientific community from the gospel quite unnecessarily in the process. To take a specific example, following centuries of 'Industry and Experience' the scientific evidence that the earth we inhabit is many millions of years old has become overwhelming. It requires a deliberate refusal to face the evidence, worthy of an ostrich, to continue to believe that the earth is, for example, only ten thousand years old. An obscurantist clinging to such a belief runs counter to the commitment, common to both science and Christianity, to tell the truth about God's world. Furthermore, the idea that the Bible expounds science is difficult to reconcile with the contemporary understanding of the nature of scientific knowledge, for reasons that will become clearer below.

Conflicts Due to an Over-Dependence on Natural Theology

The attempt to invest science with secular ideologies which are not intrinsic to the scientific enterprise has already been criticized. On occasions, however, the boot is on the other foot, as Christians try to extract far more theology from their scientific knowledge of the world than it can possibly provide, in the end bringing their faith into disrepute. The biblical perspective on such natural theology is that it has very limited scope in its ability to bring people from unbelief to faith. The maximum information that unbelievers can obtain by looking at the physical world is of 'God's invisible qualities – his eternal power and divine nature' (Romans 1:20). Attempts by Christians to pin their theology to the latest cosmological or quantum mechanical theories have a habit of back-firing; as the scientific model changes (as it inevitably will) so the rationalistic prop for theology is removed. Good theology does not need scientific props.

Science as Friend

A very wide range of reasons could be cited for the mutually supportive relationship between science and Christianity. For example, Christianity has played a key role in the historical development of modern science.[7]

Furthermore, the Christian doctrine of creation, which inspired earlier generations of scientists, continues to provide a strong motivation for empirically based 'truth-telling' in science. This is not just any old world, but *God's* world.

Critical Realism Versus Postmodernism

Perhaps the most striking congruence which occurs between Christian and scientific ways of thinking concerns their common commitment to 'critical realist' views of the world, a congruence stemming from their close historical links and today brought into sharp focus by the rise of postmodernism, a currently popular form of relativism. To appreciate this shared commitment it is first necessary to outline some of the important changes in our concept of scientific knowledge which have been taking place during the course of this century.

The Nature of Scientific Enquiry

The 'standard view' of science comprises a commonsense inductivist picture of scientific progress that started with Bacon, was continued by the empirical approach of the mechanical philosophers, and was expressed in its most extreme form by the logical positivists. According to this view, the natural world is regarded as real and objective, and the preferences or intentions of its observers make no difference to its characteristics. The task of the scientist is to make a large number of accurate experimental observations, and then induce from such facts a general theory which, providing it is supported by a large body of consistent data, is viewed as an 'immutable law of nature'. Discovering a law, in this view, is like discovering a new continent.

This 'naive realist' view places the authority of science firmly in the techniques involved in the method of enquiry itself. Subjective value-judgements are consigned to a realm outside of science, making science itself the realm of *facts*. The positivists took this approach a step further by defining meaning and rationality using criteria of empirical verifiability. However, this century has witnessed a gradual loss of confidence in the naive realist view. First, Karl Popper launched a frontal attack on one of its key tenets in his *Logic of Scientific Discovery* (Routledge, 1934) by claiming that, far from gaining more credibility as they are buttressed by increasing quantities of empirical evidence, scientific theories are really only useful to science insofar as they can be *dis*proved. The difference between scientific knowledge and other kinds of human intellectual and artistic endeavour, according to this view, is that the former is potentially falsifiable. It should be noted that Popper's influential perspective on the nature of scientific knowledge shifts the focus of attention away from the 'facts in the external world' which force the theory upon us, on to the scientific community, whose logic and expertise generate better theories and methods for testing them. Data thus become 'theory-laden' since they are collected in the context of this attempt to falsify particular theories.

A second major assault on naive realism has come from critics of Popper, in particular Thomas Kuhn in his seminal work *The Structure of Scientific Revolutions* (University of Chicago Press, 1962). Kuhn pointed out that the history of science does not support Popper's view that science advances by the systematic refutation of theories. Instead, Kuhn introduced the idea of 'paradigm-shifts' to describe the way in which science develops. A paradigm comprises the framework of beliefs which are accepted in common by a community of research scientists. When anomalies accumulate within this framework, science gradually enters into a process of crisis which continues until the revolutionary creation of a new paradigm. In making such a paradigm choice, Kuhn claims, 'there is no higher standard than the assent of the relevant community'. It is this phrase in particular that sets Kuhn's philosophy of science aside from its predecessors. No longer is there a particular set of methods which gives to scientific knowledge its special status. Instead, the final scientific authority now lies in the hands of the scientific community itself, which decides between competing paradigms on grounds that go well beyond the mere application of rules. Pressed to an extreme, such a view leads to an anti-realist sociological reductionism which regards scientific knowledge as determined more by the prejudices and foibles of a scientific community than by the properties of the physical world under investigation.

Critical Realism in Science and Faith

'Critical realism' is a view of scientific knowledge which rejects both the naive realism of the older 'standard view' of science as well as the relativism of some of Kuhn's followers, yet also accepts many of the insights that both Popper and Kuhn have provided. Probably most scientists are critical realists in practice. Critical realists believe that their data reflect the properties of the real world 'out there', but also acknowledge the important role of the scientific community in selecting and interpreting data. The 'theory-laden' nature of data and the processing effects of techniques and instruments are frankly acknowledged. In the critical realist view, far from being immutable laws, good scientific theories provide a series of reliable maps which make the workings of the physical world intelligible and which have predictive powers enabling scientists to explore new territory. Although far from perfect, the maps are nevertheless congruent with the data derived from the physical world as presently understood; they are not mere social constructs, and a strong commitment to the current map is therefore entirely appropriate.

It is this congruence which provides the strongest argument in support of the critical realist position. In the final analysis, science *works*. A major weakness of the more extreme sociological interpretations of the advance of science is that they are unable to explain why science has been so successful. For example, if it is the case that all forms of human knowledge are equally valid social constructs, why is modern medicine more successful than the theories of witch-doctors in curing the sick? And why do those sociologists who believe most fervently in cultural relativism still entrust themselves to the laws of aerodynamics and fly to international conferences at 30,000 feet?

The 'critical realism' espoused by most scientists sits very comfortably with a closely analogous form of critical realism adopted by most Christians. According to biblical theism there is a real world, which is not an illusion, having physical properties which are consistent and reproducible because contingent on God's continued activity. This world can therefore be investigated by the methods of science. At the same time, however, there are 'data' derived from human experience and observations which require a canvas much broader than scientific knowledge alone can provide. These 'data', which are beyond the self-limited horizons of the scientific map, are just as much part of the real world as the data about the physical world generated by the scientist in the laboratory. They include the saving acts of God in history and a whole host of features of human existence and awareness which are rendered more coherent by a theistic than by an atheistic worldview (moral sense, personal relationships, the arts, etc.). The Christian theist, however, is a *critical* realist who is acutely aware of the fallenness of human reason and who realizes that our understanding of the world is invariably filtered through all kinds of cultural and philosophical assumptions. Nevertheless, despite such caveats, our observations and experiences of the world, according to this view, are not merely social constructs, but provide data that enable us to evaluate rationally the truth-claims of conflicting worldviews.

The beliefs of scientists about the physical world, however incomplete, are in the final analysis shaped by the structure of that world. Similarly the beliefs of Christians, also incomplete, are shaped by what God has said and done in history as described in the biblical record. In the final analysis, both scientists and Christians respond to reality; they do not construct it.

The Challenge of Postmodernism

The position of the critical realist, whether in science or in religion, is quite incompatible with that of postmodernism. One strand of postmodernism that has proved highly influential argues that language is purely conventional and specific to a particular community. More radically, there is no way of knowing whether a language mirrors reality, since the criteria for its correct use are internal to a particular linguistic community. The suspicion is that all language, and thus all articulations of 'knowledge', are masks for power relationships. The result is a profound scepticism about all claims to objectivity.

If modernism was epitomized by rationality and science, then postmodernism, as Professor Roger Trigg comments, 'dethrones science by attacking the very human rationality which has produced science'.[8] An expounder of one particular stream of postmodernist thought, Jean-François Lyotard, echoes Kuhn when he writes that:

> It is recognised that the conditions of truth, in other words the rules of the game of science, are immanent in that game, that they can only be established within the bounds of a debate that is already scientific in nature, and that there is no other proof that the rules are good than the consensus extended to them by the experts.[9]

According to this view, there is no 'grand narrative' which could validate one set of rules or the beliefs of one linguistic community above another. Postmodernism is therefore defined by Lyotard as 'incredulity toward meta-narratives', disbelief in the idea that knowledge can be anything but rooted in a particular historical context and culture. The possibility of universally shared human experiences is excluded. Even were such shared experiences possible, we could not discover them since we have no universal means of communication.

At first sight it might appear that the ideas of postmodernism could provide a fruitful way of reinterpreting the relationship between science and religion. After all, if all forms of constructed knowledge are 'language-games', why should it not be possible for science and religion to busy themselves in isolation with their own 'set of rules'? The drawback to such a view is that if the postmodernist worldview is valid, then both science and theism must abandon their claims to map objective reality. This probably explains why postmodernism has had some influence in the arts, and is popular among enthusiasts for pantheistic mysticism, but has made little impression on scientists, for the very good reason that their profession would cease to exist were the beliefs of postmodernism accurate! For example, science operates on the assumption that the created world is consistent in its properties and therefore that experiments will work in the same way irrespective of the cultural, linguistic or social context in which they are carried out.

The reality of gravity means that people fall out of trees with the same acceleration irrespective of their language, although they may interpret their experiences differently. The properties of DNA are not time-bound, geography-bound, cultural artifacts. And so the 'game of science' is worth playing for the very good reason that its models and maps claim to say something which is true about the physical structure of the universe, something which anyone in the world would be right to believe and wrong to disbelieve. Science *does* have a 'grand narrative' which validates its knowledge, an elegant 'mathematical narrative' written into the structure of the universe which expresses those physical realities which ultimately dictate what will be believed by scientists following a process of investigation and rational argument. Language for the scientist, therefore, is not what the 'game' is all about, but rather an essential tool through which the character of the world is encountered. Language may be a human construction, but what we talk about is certainly not.

Conclusion

The echoes of the late Victorian 'conflict thesis' relationship between science and Christianity are finally disappearing. They are being replaced by a renewed awareness of the common commitments shared by science and biblical theism. Indeed, the question may now even be: 'Can science survive without Christianity?' Strong inroads have been made into Western cultures by relativistic modes of thought. At present the scientific enterprise appears to have sufficient momentum to carry on regardless. The 'space-capsule of science' speeds on, apparently no longer needing the 'launching rockets' provided by a Christian worldview. But the day may yet come when the trivialization of knowledge promoted by postmodernism undermines the motivation to investigate the physical world to such an extent that science will wither away in the absence of a solid metaphysical foundation.

There are strong grounds for believing that science and Christianity are mutual allies, particularly in their shared commitment to a critical realist view of knowledge and their mutual hostility to relativistic modes of thought. If tensions do still occasionally occur, requiring dialogue for their resolution, there will at least be a common conviction that there is something real to argue about.

Acknowledgements

I am grateful to Dr Oliver Barclay, Professor Brian Heap, Professor Colin Russell and Brenda Stone for their helpful comments.

1 See C.A. Russell, 'The Conflict Metaphor and Its Social Origins', *Science and Christian Belief*, vol. 1 (1989), pp. 3–26.
2 See R. Dawkins, Christmas Lecture Study Guide, *Growing Up in the Universe* (BBC Education, 1991), p. 21.
3 See S. Jones, *The Language of the Genes* (Flamingo, 1993), p. xi.
4 Bantam Press, 1988, p. 175.
5 *The Independent*, 16 April 1992.
6 See John Wilkins, *Discourse Concerning a New Planet*, 1640.
7 See J.H. Brooke, *Science and Religion – Some Historical Perspectives* (Cambridge University Press, 1991); C.A. Russell, *Cross-Currents – Interactions Between Science & Faith* (IVP, 1985).
8 *Rationality and Science* (Blackwell, 1993).
9 See J.-F. Lyotard, *The Postmodern Condition: A Report on Knowledge* trs. G. Bennington and B. Massumi (Manchester University Press, 1985), p. 29.

Chapter 17

GENETIC ENGINEERING

Exploring Its Role in God's World

DENIS R. ALEXANDER

Summary

This chapter provides a brief summary of genetic engineering (GE) and considers some ethical issues raised by applications of GE to humans. GE is distinguished from novel reproductive technologies, such as cloning, which are not discussed. The doctrines of Creation, Fall and Redemption provide a Christian framework within which to evaluate the appropriate goals and limitations of GE. As God's 'earth-keepers' Christians have a responsibility to use all the tools he has provided to tackle disease and feed a hungry world. But knowledge of the world's fallen state also makes Christians wary of exaggerating the benefits of new technologies, and acutely aware of their potential for evil.

Introduction

DNA, with its double-helical structure, has become one of the cultural icons of the late twentieth century. In books, films and everyday speech, genetic metaphors are used to express diverse and even contradictory concerns.[1] Genetics is used to justify both social harmony (based on common ancestry) and social division (based on race). The DNA of popular culture is surrounded by mystique. The genetic engineers have become media constructs, either with two horns, bent on subverting the natural order, or as genetic wizards delivering the future to humankind on a plate as they sweep away hunger and disease.

DNA and Genetic Engineering

The DNA of biology is very different from the DNA of popular culture, yet even stripped of its mystique it remains a remarkable molecule.[2,3] Each of the 10,000,000,000,000 somatic (non germ-line) cells in our body contains six feet of DNA, packaged with proteins to form 23 pairs of chromosomes. If all the DNA in all the cells in a single human being were stretched out, it would reach to the moon and back 8,000 times. As millions of our cells divide every second, each individual produces thousands of miles of newly-copied DNA every minute.

Human DNA contains 3,000,000,000 nucleotides, the 'letters' which comprise the genetic alphabet, encoding about 50–100,000 genes. There are only four 'letters' in this alphabet. Each gene consists of a sequence of nucleotides which encodes a different protein. Only about 3 per cent of human DNA encodes genes – the function of the rest is not yet well understood. The Human Genome Project (HGP) aims to determine the complete DNA nucleotide sequence, a task which should be accomplished soon after the year 2000. If this information were printed in books of 200 pages each, 5,000 books would be required. Only when the HGP is complete will we be sure how many genes our DNA encodes. But we already know that DNA sequences in different individuals (except identical twins) vary to such an extent that everyone alive today is different, not only from everyone else, but from everyone who has ever lived or ever will live. On average, two people differ in about one DNA letter per thousand, or about 3,000,000 nucleotides in total, due to naturally occurring mutations. DNA is not a static molecule but is in a state of flux. Fortunately this flux is not very fast, otherwise we would not be here to discuss it.

The genetic code is essentially identical for all living organisms from bacteria, yeasts and viruses to dandelions, kangaroos and humans. This is the most powerful argument for the unity of all living things and is what makes genetic engineering (GE) possible. GE refers to the techniques whereby recombinant DNA, that is hybrid DNA made by artificially joining pieces of DNA from different sources, is produced and utilized. Strictly speaking, therefore, novel reproductive technologies, such as those used in the cloning of sheep like Dolly,[4] do not involve GE. Instead, such techniques involve the manipulation of whole cells or nuclei, rather than the generation of novel DNA as in GE. Reproductive technologies raise important issues beyond the scope of this chapter.

All the 'tools' of the genetic engineer are natural products, such as the various enzymes which act like scissors to cut the DNA at precise points and then paste the pieces together again. Recombinant DNA by itself can do nothing unless it is incorporated into a cell to make a protein. To do this the DNA is packaged into a carrier, normally a plasmid or virus, disabled so that it cannot damage the host cell. Thus, GE mimics processes already occurring in the natural world, in which DNA is transferred into new cellular locations.

GE is routinely used in research in thousands of laboratories world-wide. Most manipulations are carried out on cell-lines or bacteria, applications which have raised little ethical controversy. In the human context the handling of GE by the media has often been alarmist and sensationalist, deflecting attention from that small proportion of situations in which the new technology does raise serious and immediate ethical issues. It is these which form the focus of this chapter. Safety issues, important as they are, will not be discussed, since questions of risk are common to all novel technologies.

A Christian Framework for Thinking about Genetic Engineering

Three doctrines are crucial:

The doctrine of Creation reminds us that God, the almighty Creator, is not only distinct from his creation (transcendence), but also actively involved in sustaining it moment by moment (immanence). God made the universe through his Son, and it is the Son who now in the present 'sustains all things by his powerful word' (Hebrews 1:2–3). 'All things were created' by Jesus and 'in him all things hold together' in the present (Colossians 1:16–17). Peter wanted his listeners to know that they had 'killed the author of life' (Acts 3:15; cf. also John 1:3).

So the DNA which underlies all biological diversity is as much the product of God's authorship as any other of creation's myriad aspects (Genesis 1). The Bible invites us to see God's handiwork in every detail of its biological diversity, whether mundane or exotic (Psalm 104). DNA in God's world is no icon but just one more example of his creative handiwork, demythologized of any mystique that popular culture might wish to bestow. Furthermore, human beings are made in God's image (Genesis 1:26–7), and therefore have a special value independent of the genetic variation which exists between them. The value and special status of humans is reflected in the weighty responsibility that God has given us to care for his creation (Genesis 1:26–8; 2:15), using our God-given gifts to explore his world (Psalm 24:1).

The doctrine of the Fall reminds us of how far the world is from what God intended. The entry of sin into the world has ensured that human earth-keeping will never be fully as God intended, at least not in this present evil age (Genesis 3:16–19). The exploration of God's created order for the good of humankind is one of the joys and privileges of being a scientist, but Christians are acutely aware that human knowledge tarnished with sin can be used for evil purposes. Christians will therefore be suspicious of arrogant or naively optimistic attitudes towards the exploitation of the natural world.

The doctrine of Redemption reminds us that God's plan is not only for the salvation of individuals, but encompasses the whole created order. Why is the creation which has 'been groaning as in the pains of childbirth' waiting 'in eager expectation for the sons of God to be revealed' (Romans 8:19, 22)? Surely one answer to this question is that 'the sons of God', his new family, are being redeemed to become the kind of earth-keepers that God intended. As God's people join in his work of liberating creation from its bondage to decay, so they act as an eschatological signpost pointing forward to the new earth which God is one day going to bring into being (Revelation 21:1). Earth-keeping in the present is only a pilot-project compared to the full redemption which God promises in his new earth, but it is that future-full redemption which gives the present pilot-project both its rationale and its hope.

Objections to Genetic Engineering

The implications of these theological reflections can be illustrated by considering some common objections to GE.

'Genetic Engineering Is Dangerous'

There is no doubt that GE, as with any other technology, has great potential for misuse. Humanistic science has not been immune from arrogance in its utopian ambitions. The history of the eugenics movement provides many unfortunate examples of such human folly. In the first half of the twentieth century, for example, 30 states in the United States enacted eugenic laws that included directives for compulsory sterilization. It is therefore vital that the debate about GE remains firmly in the public domain, and that Christians in particular remain active and well informed in their contributions.

'Genetic Engineering Is Unnatural'

Ironically, in marked contrast to other recent technologies, the 'toolkit' of the genetic engineer is entirely derived from products found naturally within the created order. What people mean by 'natural' often turns out to mean 'what I am personally used to'. Flying, watching TV and car-driving all appeared unnatural at first. Furthermore, 'naturalness' does not necessitate desirability. Pathogenic viruses, bacteria and mosquitoes are all natural but people generally approve of destroying them whenever possible. 'Naturalness' is therefore irrelevant to the ethical debate about GE.

A more substantial argument suggests that we should not change the inviolable *ousia* (essence) or *telos* (goal) of any living organism. Both concepts come directly from Aristotelian philosophy. The GE of female turkeys to make them less broody (so that they lay more eggs), has been attacked by Jeremy Rifkin as 'a serious violation of the intrinsic value of the creature'.[5] The precise definition of this 'essence' or 'goal' is, however, problematic. The domestication of animals and the breeding of new crop strains for food has been going on for many millennia. Is the 'essence' of a species supposed to refer to its original state or its present state? Is the 'essence' of doghood better represented by a Pekinese or by a Great Dane? Both belong to the same species. If 'essence' is taken to refer to the genome of a plant or animal as if a static entity, then this is simply false. DNA is always changing, albeit slowly. In practice the applications of GE are not to change the identity of species but to introduce minor genetic modifications into plants and animals to make them more productive in farming or, as discussed below, to prevent and cure human disease.

'Genetic Engineering Involves Playing God'

The term 'hubris' was used in Greek philosophy to refer to the supposed impiety involved in delving into the realms of the gods.[6]

Similar ideas are apparent in some contemporary ecological think-ing which views nature as sacred and therefore inviolable. However, the biblical doctrine of creation has demythologized nature of these semi-divine overtones and given humankind a very specific man-date to care for the earth and its biological diversity (Genesis 1:28, 30; 2:15–20), a mandate that, if anything, was made even more ex-plicit after the Fall (Genesis 9:1–3).

We are called not to 'play God' but to be responsible stewards of all that God has given us. As Donald MacKay has written: 'In place of the craven fear instilled by a pagan theology of nature … the Christian who finds scientific talents in his toolbag has quite a different fear – the fear that his Father should judge him guilty of neglecting his stewardly responsibilities by failing to pursue the opportunities for good that may be opened up by the new develop-ments.'[7] We should approach such responsibilities not with the arro-gance implicit in the phrase 'playing God', but with prayerful concern that we should be responsible earth-keepers under God.

The applications of GE to farming provide good examples of what such stewardship can involve. About one-third to one-half of all agricultural production world-wide is lost to pests and diseases, and there is enormous scope for GE to render crops resistant to pests, drought and frost, to improve yields and to enable food to be produced in harsh environments.[8] The central Christian concern will be to utilize the new technology to feed a hungry world and to distribute its benefits more equitably.

'Genetic Engineering Will Remove the Challenge of Suffering'

Some fear that GE will ultimately remove the opportunity for moral growth which the demands of caring for the sick and disabled pro-vide. Such fears, however, are based on an exaggerated view of the scope and potential of GE. The most that GE can achieve is to gen-erate some useful new drugs and remove some lethal genes from human populations. Even if all this were achieved, it would only represent the removal of a drop in the ocean of human suffering. Besides, Jesus did not leave human diseases untouched to preserve the moral benefits that caring for the sick might generate. Rather, he drove diseases out as a demonstration of the kingdom of God (e.g. Matthew 9:35; Luke 9:2; 10:9). We do not know whether any diseases Jesus healed had a genetic basis, but the gospel record certainly provides no basis for genetic fatalism. As members of God's new family we are called to identify with Christ in his work of liberating creation 'from its bondage to decay' (Romans 8:21).

Specific Ethical Issues in the Applications of Genetic Engineering to Humans

This section flags some of the weightier issues arising from the main application of GE to humans – the detection and cure of disease. There are about 5,000 different inborn diseases which are due to genetic mutations. Probably we all carry at least one lethal gene, but fortunately most of our genes come in pairs and usually both members of the pair have to be defective for a disease to develop.

Screening

The earliest immediate practical application of the Human Genome Project is likely to be an increase in the number of tests available for screening defective genes. Mass screening has usually been counterproductive, unless a particular population has a very high prevalence of a defective gene. More usually screening is carried out for families where a risk of genetic disease is already established. Different ethical issues are raised depending on whether screening is prenatal or postnatal.

Prenatal screening of foetuses can involve abortion, a thorny question about which Christians have disagreements. Prenatal screening *per se* does not depend on GE and has been carried out since the 1970s. Typically it is offered to a pregnant mother in cases where both parents are known to be heterozygous ('carriers') for a specific lethal genetic disease. This means that any child born in that family has a 1 in 4 chance of being affected by that disease. Tests are carried out using a tiny sample of cells obtained from the foetus. If the foetus is found to carry the disease then the pregnancy may be terminated. Such terminations comprise less than 3 per cent of the 200,000 abortions performed annually in the UK.

Some Christians are strongly against a liberal policy on abortion and yet believe that termination of pregnancy is preferable to giving birth to a child who, in many cases, will appear normal at birth, but who is then certain to die a slow and painful death within the first decade of life. Such is the outcome, for example, of most lysosomal storage diseases.

In contrast to such 100 per cent certainties, one effect of using DNA tests for prenatal diagnosis will be to increase the number of cases in which percentage risk factors of developing a disease in later life can be estimated. It is this latter class of information which is most fraught with ethical dilemmas. Similar dilemmas are already raised by the availability of prenatal diagnosis for the chromosomal abnormality which leads to Down's Syndrome, a condition with unpredictable effects ranging from mild to severe abnormality.

Ethical issues are also raised by preimplantation diagnosis (PD). As with other forms of prenatal diagnosis, this procedure is usually carried out when both parents are known carriers of a lethal disease. PD involves *in vitro* fertilization (IVF)[9] followed by growth of the embryo to the stage at which it contains 4–8 cells. One or two cells can then be removed without damaging the embryo, and defective genes identified. Clearly defective embryos are discarded and only the healthy embryo is implanted in the mother. Only a few hundred PDs have been carried out so far, but this number is likely to increase markedly as more DNA tests become available. The procedure has the great advantage that it avoids the need for aborting an affected foetus post-implantation, as required by current prenatal diagnostic procedures. In assessing the ethical implications involved, it should also be kept in mind that more than 80 per cent of all embryos fail to implant following IVF or natural fertilization. Some of these embryos demonstrate severe chromosomal abnormalities, apparently 'nature's way' of preventing the birth of children carrying genetic defects. It could therefore be argued that in PD, human intervention is merely refining this natural process of viable embryo selection.

Postnatal screening raises rather different issues. Where prevention or treatment of diseases is possible, there seems every reason to proceed. Every baby born in the UK, as in many other countries, is screened for the genetic disease phenylketonuria. If untreated this disease results in severe mental retardation, but once detected is easily prevented by minor dietary adjustments. This is a good example of a genetic outcome being radically altered by a small change of environment. Knowing that defective genes are present can enable affected individuals to change diet and lifestyle in an attempt to counteract their effects.

Where no treatment is available, different issues arise.[10] Receiving general information about the genetic basis for human disease is very different from the momentous implications of hearing that *you* personally carry a defective gene. For example, Huntington's Disease develops in people aged 40 to 50. After some years of increasing loss of motor control, death occurs 10–15 years after the first onset of symptoms. A DNA test can now tell a person at risk that they carry the defective gene. Some might conclude that such information is too heavy a load for anyone to bear. However, Christians in particular might view the situation differently from the secular world. Knowledge that one is carrying a lethal gene could enable a choice not to have children and the pursuit of a different career. With professional counselling and support from the Christian community, the prospect of future suffering might accentuate the need to use the years of health even more fruitfully for God's glory. It is surely far better to have a fruitful short life than a fruitless long one, Jesus himself providing us with the perfect example.

As postnatal screening becomes more widespread, two urgent ethical issues require attention. First, screening may lead to people having information about their lives about which they can do nothing. Such information may increase stress and may also be misused by others if confidentiality is breached. The right *not* to know one's genetic heritage is as important, perhaps more important, than the right to know. Second, screening may create an underclass of carriers of deleterious genes who will become increasingly marginalized from the benefits of society, for example by being unable to obtain mortgages or life insurance. Christians, however, will view all people as having equal value, irrespective of their genetic inheritance, and will press for insurance practices which allow the equitable pooling of risk.[11]

Therapy

There are two types of potential genetic therapy: those in which defective genes are replaced, and those in which the goal is to add additional qualities to the individual which lie beyond the normal range of genetic variation currently found within human populations.

Replacement therapies could, in principle, be carried out in either germ-line or somatic cells. Somatic cell replacement therapies have already been used with limited success since 1990, as an experimental approach for treating several genetic diseases. Ethically such procedures are no different from other novel medical technologies.

Germ cell replacement therapies are proscribed and are technically hazardous at present. In principle the therapy could involve, for example, IVF for parents who are known carriers of lethal genes, followed by genetic surgery of a defective 4–8 cell embryo. In practice, however, there would be little point in carrying out such a procedure, since PD would be available. In theory it might seem more acceptable ethically to heal the defective embryo. In practice, however, Christians who take an 'absolutist' view of the value of such very early embryos should realize that their stance may encourage development of the DNA technology for manipulation of human germ-line cells, which could increase social pressure for the use of additive therapies. A futuristic alternative is the screening of sperm and eggs for defective genes prior to fertilization, followed by IVF using only healthy gametes. Such an advance could eventually make ethical discussions about embryos and abortions redundant.

Additive therapies, whether at the somatic cell or germ-line cell level, are currently technically impossible and are proscribed in the UK, as in other countries. The aim of such procedures would be to add to the individual specific qualities not already encoded by their genome. Additive therapies therefore represent a very different set of goals from those which aim to prevent or cure human disease. Fortunately the human genome is immensely complex, and numerous genes interact to generate human capacities in ways that we understand only dimly. There is, as far as we know, no single gene 'for' intelligence, or musical ability, or homosexuality. In fact, any genetic contribution at all to these and many other facets of human behaviour remains hotly disputed. The complexity of the human genome remains its best protection against doomsday scenarios.

More importantly, the fact that we are now, with our current genetic endowment, made 'in the image of God' (Genesis 1:26–7) defines clear boundaries. Accepting the term 'image of God' to refer to all those qualities which distinguish humans from animals, in particular our spiritual capacity for fellowship with God, the dangers of trying to add to what God has given us become apparent. The builders of the tower of Babel (Genesis 11:1–9) thought that their improved technology would allow them to reach up to heaven using their own human wisdom, but the result was confusion (v. 9).

The biblical record, not to speak of human history since, makes it clear that human pretensions to self-grandeur invariably end in disaster. It is vital that we do not misuse God's good gift of GE to repeat such mistakes.

Conclusions

The creation of humankind in God's image means that every individual has an absolute value in God's sight which is independent of variations in their genetic heritage. Christians persistently need to draw attention to this fact. GE can make a significant contribution to the prevention and cure of human disease, and to the feeding of a hungry world. If used wisely it can function as yet another signpost pointing forward to the day when God will bring about creation's complete redemption. But, like other human attempts to improve health care and nutrition, the applications of GE, important as they may be, will never represent more than a patching-up operation, and are certainly no panacea for all ills.

Acknowledgements

I am grateful to Dr Caroline Berry, Professor Derek Burke and Professor Lord Winston for their helpful comments on an earlier draft of this chapter.

1 D. Nelkin and M.S. Lindee, *The DNA Mystique – the Gene as a Cultural Icon* (W.H. Freeman, Oxford, 1995).
2 S. Jones, *The Language of the Genes* (Flamingo, 1994).
3 E. Russo and D. Cove, *Genetic Engineering – Dreams and Nightmares* (W.H. Freeman, Oxford, 1995).
4 I. Wilmut *et al.*, 'Viable Offspring Derived from Fetal and Adult Mammalian Cells', *Nature*, 385, 810–13 (1997).
5 Cited in M.J. Reiss and R. Straughan, *Improving Nature? – The Science and Ethics of Genetic Engineering* (Cambridge University Press, 1996).
6 R. Hooykaas, *Religion and the Rise of Modern Science* (Scottish Academic Press, 1972).
7 D.M. MacKay, *The Open Mind and Other Essays* (Inter-Varsity Press, 1988).
8 The important applications of GE to farming are beyond the scope of this chapter. For a helpful survey see M.J. Reiss and R. Straughan, *Improving Nature? – The Science and Ethics of Genetic Engineering* (Cambridge University Press, 1996).

9 The overall livebirth rate per cycle of IVF treatment is currently 14 per cent. See A. Templeton *et al.*, *Lancet*, 348, 23 November, 1402–6 (1996).

10 See *Genetic Screening: Ethical Issues* (Nuffield Council on Bioethics, London, 1993). Also P.R. Reilly *et al.*, *Nature Genetics*, 15, 16–20 (1997).

11 This complex issue is helpfully discussed in 'Human Genetics – Uncertainties and the Financial Implications Ahead', a booklet obtainable from The Royal Society, 6 Carlton Terrace, London, SW1Y 5AG.

Chapter 18

CAN SCIENCE EXPLAIN EVERYTHING?

Scientific Naturalism and the Death of Science

DENIS R. ALEXANDER

Experiments are the only means of knowledge at our disposal. The rest is poetry, imagination.

Max Planck

Summary

Scientific naturalism is the view that only scientific knowledge is reliable and that science can, in principle, explain everything. This chapter surveys the inherent weaknesses in this philosophy, illustrated by the naturalistic attempt to extract ethics from biology. Different Christian responses to naturalism are considered. It is argued that the Christian worldview provides a more coherent explanation than naturalism for the properties of the universe and for the richness of human experience. Ironically, naturalism itself puts at risk the future health of science.

Introduction

Peter sits on a government committee which advises Parliament on issues such as genetic engineering and cloning. Peter believes that science provides the only source of real knowledge for his committee and that any other inputs are mere opinion. Human cloning, for example, should be allowed provided the technology is safe.

Susan is a doctor who has imbibed the writings of the philosopher James Rachels. Rachels sees no reason to prefer the value of a human baby with severe brain damage over the life of a healthy monkey.[1] Susan is now working on a ward for severely handicapped infants and objects to the effort and expense involved in keeping alive such badly damaged human beings.

Jonathan is a first-year university student doing religious studies. He accepts the convictions of his lecturer, who thinks that religions are worthy objects for cultural study but not actually true. Jonathan believes that science has shown that miracles are impossible, and the idea of 'supernatural interference' by a god is ridiculous.

Peter, Susan and Jonathan are united in a metaphysical commitment which remains surprisingly common in our so-called postmodern society. This commitment is called 'scientific naturalism', or sometimes 'metaphysical naturalism'. *Scientific naturalism refers to the view that only scientific knowledge is reliable and that science can, in principle, explain everything.* Science can be defined as an intellectual endeavour to explain the workings of the physical world, informed by empirical investigation and carried out by a community trained in specialized techniques.[2] Scientific naturalism, however, is a philosophy which goes well beyond science. Naturalism is appealing because it promotes human rationalism and moral autonomy, specifically excluding the possibility of God or other supernatural agencies acting in the world. As Professor Peter Atkins comments: 'Humanity should accept that science has eliminated the justification for believing in cosmic purpose, and that any survival of purpose is inspired solely by sentiment.'[3] Nevertheless, scientific naturalists are not atheistic in a merely negative sense, but actively seek to answer all types of human questions by recourse to science. In striking contrast to much recent philosophizing, naturalists discuss classical problems in philosophy, such as mind and body, justification for moral beliefs, and so forth.

Scientific naturalism runs through contemporary society like a mineral seam through rock, appearing in different guises to influence critical decisions in education, the media, and the economic and political arenas. Implicitly, if not explicitly, the presupposition that real knowledge is scientific knowledge, and none other, remains firmly embedded in the Western psyche.

A Critique of Scientific Naturalism

Scientific naturalism can be criticized for reasons which do not require prior religious commitments.[4] For example:

Naturalism Is Self-Refuting

Scientific naturalism claims that science is the only true source of knowledge. It is therefore fair to ask whether science itself can be used to justify naturalism. It cannot. The data which science generates can provide no support for or against such a philosophy. Since the truth of scientific naturalism cannot be scientifically demonstrated, it cannot be a valid form of knowledge, and so is hoist by its own petard.

Naturalism Is Self-Defeating

Science has shown that the properties of the universe depend on the remarkable fine-tuning of the cosmological constants which define the properties of matter. Turn the dial even slightly to change one of these critical parameters and the universe would be completely different from the one we inhabit and, in most cases, incompatible with life. As the physicist Steven Weinberg has commented: 'There is reason to believe that in elementary particle physics ... there is simplicity, a beauty, that we are finding in the rules that govern matter that mirrors something that is built into the logical structure of the Universe at a very deep level.'[5] It is a remarkable fact that conscious beings have appeared who can understand and describe the properties of this mathematically elegant universe. Yet there is no explanation for the existence of such a universe within the framework of scientific naturalism.[6] To say that it 'just happened' displays a startling lack of curiosity. The more science uncovers of the remarkable universe we inhabit, the more pressing becomes the need to explain the reason for its existence, and the more obvious becomes the failure of naturalism to provide any satisfactory explanation.[7]

Naturalism Excludes Too Much

The task of science is to develop generalized statements of increasing sophistication which explain physical phenomena. But the construction of scientific knowledge has a cost: the tendency to exclude the particular in favour of the general, and of the subjective in favour of the objective. The scientist as observer of other human beings, for example in psychology, aims to construct increasingly accurate theories of human behaviour by recourse to data based on large sample numbers. In the process of quantification and generalization the human individual as a conscious agent is reduced to an

'it', the object of scientific investigation. Merely as a research strata-
gem for investigating human behaviour, this is perfectly acceptable.
But if science is the only form of real knowledge, then knowledge
derived from the individual's personal biography tends to be down-
graded. Scientific descriptions exclude the joy of the first kiss, the
exhilaration of reaching the top of the mountain, and the depths
of despair at some personal tragedy. They also exclude aesthetic
appreciation, love, beauty, poetry, art, friendship and moral judgements. Brainwaves and hormonal levels can be measured in individuals experiencing all these normal aspects of everyday life. But they
are not the same as the experiences themselves. Such reflections
have generated the influential perception in contemporary Western
society that science dehumanizes. However, it is not science which
dehumanizes, but the naturalistic philosophy which is parasitic
upon it.

So concerned was one scientific naturalist, Professor Richard
Dawkins, about the reactions of his readers to the 'cold, bleak message' of his earlier writings, that he wrote a book extolling the 'deep
aesthetic passion' of science which ranks 'with the finest that music
and poetry can deliver'.[8] The aesthetic experiences of scientists are
not in question, but Dawkins should admit that the existence
of 'aesthetic passions' cannot be adequately accounted for by the
creed of scientific naturalism. Francis Crick was more faithful to
the creed when he wrote that science has shown that '"you", your
joys and your sorrows, your memories and your ambitions, your
sense of identity and free will, are in fact no more than the behaviour of a vast assembly of nerve cells and their associated molecules'.[9] Scientific naturalism is a bleak creed which excludes
precisely those experiences in life which, for most people, make it
worth living. In practice no-one lives as if science were enough.

Evolutionary Naturalism – A Case Study

No society, and no scientist, can live without ethics. Yet naturalism
seems to deprive us of ethics. Naturalists have fought hard to plug
this breach in their philosophical dyke. But the plug is rationally
flimsy and insufficient to cope with the ethical challenges arising
from the current rapid pace of biomedical research. If naturalistic
assumptions are dominant, then care and protection for the handicapped, the newborn and the elderly are all likely to come under

threat. The case study that follows is no mere academic exercise, but an insight into the forces that may reshape our law and morality during the course of the twenty-first century.

Evolutionary naturalism is a particular brand of scientific naturalism which attempts to explain all aspects of current human behaviour by recourse to evolutionary explanations, utilizing the resources of sociobiology and, more recently, evolutionary psychology. Its approach is exemplified by the philosopher Michael Ruse who, in *Taking Darwin Seriously*,[10] attempts to argue his way from evolution to ethics in five steps.

In Step 1, Ruse maintains that complex human behaviours, such as moral decision-making processes, can be inherited. In Step 2, it is claimed that these innate dispositions have, or once had, adaptive value: they increased the chance of parents passing on their genes to their descendants. In Step 3 Ruse proposes that the force of the 'ought' which is implicit in all genuine ethical discourse is based on such innate biological drives derived from our genetic inheritance: 'Morality is a collective illusion foisted upon us by our genes ... the illusion lies not in the morality itself, but in its sense of objectivity' (p. 253). In Step 4 we are informed that such biological drives result in ethical impulses which, as a matter of fact, are broadly in line with traditional morality, promoting the 'values cherished by decent people of all nations' (p. 272). Finally, Step 5 of the argument tells us that we have a moral duty to aid the process of evolution since it has generated moral beliefs rooted in 'the very essence of living beings' which are truly international in scope.

Two types of critique may be levelled at Ruse's position: empirical and philosophical. The empirical critique relates to Steps 1, 2 and 4 and the philosophical to Steps 3 and 5. Steps 1 and 2 are not impossible in principle, but suffer from poor experimental support. There are currently no firm data supporting the genetic inheritance in humans of any complex forms of behaviour, though this is a controversial research field which awaits clear resolution. If there is no genetic basis for human moral convictions then neither, of course, can they have any inheritable adaptive value.[11] An alternative position to that of Ruse agrees that moral convictions could have adaptive value, but via the fast process of cultural transmission, rather than by the 'slow-track' of genetic change. A commonly held view among biologists is that genetically encoded behavioural programmes are dominant among animals, but that in humans the acquisition of language and of conscious intellectual processes has enabled such a rapid transmission of behavioural norms as to make arguments based on slow genetic changes redundant.

In Step 3 Ruse starts to run into philosophical problems. The 'is–ought' distinction (which Ruse refers to as the 'naturalistic fallacy'), pointed out forcefully by Hume and later expounded by the Cambridge philosopher G.E. Moore,[12] is not so readily circumvented within a naturalistic framework. Moore pointed out that all attempts to justify moral claims by reference to descriptions of the physical world are doomed to failure. In short, you cannot derive an 'ought' from an 'is'. Ruse tries to side-step the fallacy by redefining 'ought' so that the word no longer has its traditional sense of an implicit appeal to an objective yardstick of morality, but instead refers merely to innate dispositions. But in the process of redefining 'ought' as a biological disposition, the force of the concept vaporizes. Moral obligations founded on a disposition to do something are not really obligations at all. Furthermore, if our sense of objectivity about morality is, as Ruse claims, a genetically programmed illusion, now that this deception has been revealed by science, we can choose to ignore it.

The weakness of the naturalistic argument at this point is highlighted by Step 4 of Ruse's argument, since it is not clear how 'traditional morality' can be maintained by appeals to innate dispositions. In fact Step 4 is empirically false. In practice people are not robots – they make genuine moral choices which vary from ethnic cleansing to caring for lepers. The biological perspective is simply that people have different urges to do different things, but biology provides no criteria for deciding why one set of urges should be labelled more 'moral' than another. Armed only with Ruse's presuppositions, we could be left describing the atrocities of the Nazi regime as yet another 'interesting' manifestation of humankind's innate dispositions. The value of the human individual is at severe risk within a naturalistic framework. Rachels draws the correct conclusion from his naturalism when he comments that 'The abandonment of grandiose ideas about the place of humans in the scheme of things, inevitably diminishes our moral status. God and nature are powerful allies; losing them does mean losing something.'[13]

With regard to Step 5, it is odd that we should need urging to support the process of evolution when Ruse then spends the rest of his thesis arguing that moral values are as innately natural to us as having two legs. If values were really that innate, then people would promote the processes of evolution naturally by their genetically influenced moral behaviour and would require no exhortations to do so. Promoting belief in evolution as a 'moral duty', with the aim of demonstrating that evolution itself generates innate moral beliefs, sounds incoherent.

Science, Christianity and Nature

How does the Christian understanding of nature differ from that of scientific naturalists? Christians who are scientists believe that God is the creator and sustainer of everything that exists. Through the Word, Jesus Christ, 'all things were made; without him nothing was made that has been made' (John 1:3). God is the prime first cause of all things. Scientists can study only the secondary causes which God has used to bring the universe, with all its diversity, into being. The scientific enterprise is possible only because of God's faithfulness in creation and there is nothing that scientists can investigate which has not been made by God. Therefore, there cannot be anything intrinsically 'naturalistic' about their enterprise. The Bible has no developed concept of 'nature', with all its Enlightenment-derived overtones of autonomy, for the simple reason that the word is redundant in biblical thought – the word 'creation' renders it unnecessary. Augustine expressed the biblical view succinctly: 'Nature is what God does.'[14] By uncovering more of the wisdom and majesty of God in his creation (which naturalists call 'nature'), scientists who are Christians bring their new-found knowledge to him as part of their worship, just as artists bring their art or historians bring the fruit of their research. Naturalism is excluded by definition.

Does this mean that there is, or should be, something called 'Christian science' or 'Christian algebra' or 'Christian gardening'? Not necessarily. Christians can share with non-Christians a perfectly acceptable common discourse as they experience God's common grace to humankind. The Christian gardener may analyse the state of his vegetable patch with his non-Christian gardening neighbour without recourse to explicitly theological concepts. The scientist who is a Christian does the same with her secular colleagues, since all scientists, whether they admit it or not, are studying God's creation with a shared set of methods and approaches. Therefore, finding a common discourse in the scientific language of secondary causes has no naturalistic implications. It is their prior metaphysical commitment which makes someone a naturalist. Furthermore, Christians who are scientists will wish to avoid the danger of invoking God to explain something in science as if he were simply another secondary cause. In biblical thought, God is the author of creation – the prime cause of all that exists.

Christian Responses to Naturalism

Christian responses to naturalism have been quite varied:

'Science Is Intrinsically Naturalistic'

The least helpful response of Christians to naturalism has been the attempt to equate it with the scientific enterprise itself. This includes the misuse of the adjective 'naturalistic' as a synonym for 'scientific', and a critique of the scientific community as being inherently naturalistic. But this view is inaccurate. Scientific naturalism is a philosophy held only by some scientists, and is not intrinsic to science itself. Naturalism refers to a prior metaphysical commitment which may or may not be held by scientists, just as it may or may not be held by lawyers, historians, butchers and car mechanics. Many scientists, probably the majority, do not believe that science can explain everything. For example, a group of 13 leading American scientists, including the President of the National Academy of Sciences, explicitly denies the naturalistic view in saying that 'Religions and science answer different questions about the world. Whether there is a purpose to the universe or a purpose for human existence are not questions for science ... No one way of knowing can provide all of the answers to the questions that humans ask.'[15] The expression of such views by scientists is not uncommon.

Some scientists are vocal in the media in using science ideologically to promote their naturalism, but the proportion of Christian believers is in fact high in many segments of the scientific community. There are strong resonances, both historical and contemporary, between Christianity and science.[16] In 1916, 42 per cent of American scientists believed in a personal God who answered prayer. In 1996 a repeat survey using identical questions found a figure of 39.3 per cent, hardly suggestive of a massive swing to naturalism in the scientific community during the course of the twentieth century.[17]

'There Are Different Kinds of Naturalism'

A response of some Christians to naturalism is to maintain that there are two kinds of naturalism, the acceptable and the unacceptable. The unacceptable form is labelled 'ontological naturalism' ('ontology': the study of existence, of being), another name for the naturalism as defined in this chapter. The supposedly acceptable form is labelled 'methodological naturalism'. If the term merely refers to the shared methods and procedures used by scientists, whether Christian or non-Christian, in their research, then the concept is benign, but the terminology inaccurate. For Christians who believe that all their science without exception is but 'thinking God's thoughts after him', as the astronomer Johannes Kepler expressed it, the study of God's creation can in no way be naturalistic. The 'heavens declare the glory of God' (Psalm 19:1) and 'the earth is the Lord's, and everything in it' (Psalm 24:1). There is nothing naturalistic about investigating God's heavens and God's earth using the methods of science, so the term 'methodological naturalism' is inappropriate. The Christian scientist should no more exclude the Lordship of Christ from their research than the Christian politician, economist or factory worker.

'Naturalism Is Incompatible with Christian Theism'

A more appropriate response is that scientific naturalism is simply incompatible with Christian faith. Naturalism is a rival metaphysical worldview to Christianity but, in distinction to postmodernism, both the rivals believe that there is a real world which requires explanation. Naturalism attempts an explanation which assigns priority to scientific knowledge, to the exclusion of other valid forms of human knowledge. In contrast, Christian explanation is based on biblical revelation. This undergirds science as one valid source of knowledge, but also goes well beyond science. The existence of a finely tuned universe, and within it conscious observers, is explained by a personal creator God who has plans and intentions for his creation, encompassing both human life and human death. The possibility of science is explained by the faithfulness of God in maintaining consistency in the properties of matter, although on occasion God can and does choose to act unusually in his creation in miraculous events. The worth of each person is guaranteed because based on the personhood of God who loves each individual. In God's creation order, greater value is assigned to a handicapped baby than to a healthy monkey, and the human individual and human relationships have priority in the ethical decision-making process.

So Peter, Susan and Jonathan will generate a very different society if their metaphysical allegiance changes from naturalistic to Christian faith. Their worldview will also become rationally more defensible, for Christianity provides a framework in which the scientific elegance and fruitfulness of the world, as well as human hopes and fears, good and evil, life and death, can all be integrated within a coherent model. It generates a holistic view – science with a human face.

Naturalism – the Death of Science?

Scientists, as well as the general public, often assume that the scientific enterprise will continue indefinitely. But intellectual movements have endings as well as beginnings. On purely pragmatic grounds, the present integration of science and technology into the world economy makes it unlikely that science will be neglected in the near future. In the longer term, however, scientific naturalism provides a very insecure foundation for the future health of science.

There are compelling grounds for thinking that the development of modern science in medieval Europe was facilitated by a justification of human knowledge based on Christian theism. God the creator and law-giver acted as guarantor of the consistency of the properties of his creation. Since scientific knowledge was rooted in God's faithfulness in creation, and human observers were gifted by God with reason and curiosity, it was viewed as reliable knowledge. But scientific naturalism contains no such foundation for the validity of science. Ironically, it is the philosophy which enthrones science which simultaneously subverts it, for science provides no resources for justifying itself.[18] Lacking solid foundation, it is a small step from naturalism to the postmodern trivialization of scientific knowledge.

At an ethical level the scientific community, like the rest of society, can only function as it practises values which resonate with its Christian roots, such as truth-telling and co-operation. Currently these are maintained within the community largely on utilitarian grounds, but those grounds may eventually prove insufficiently robust. Naturalism has no resources to generate or justify such values. As a philosophy it provides a poor option for the healthy functioning of the scientific enterprise.

At the level of public perception, if scientific naturalism becomes equated in people's minds with the scientific enterprise *per se*, then it is likely to create its own backlash: naturalistic philosophy is ultimately dehumanizing and cannot generate an adequate foundation for moral values. Evidence suggests that such a backlash is already in progress in Western societies. Scientists who try to prop up their naturalistic ideology by appeals to scientific advances do science a disservice.

Conclusion

Scientific naturalism has inherent philosophical weaknesses which many secular writers find crippling to its cause. Most importantly, its bleak creed excludes great swathes of human knowledge and experience which play a large role in the daily lives of all people, not least in the lives of scientific naturalists. The weakness of the naturalistic position is well illustrated by the failed attempt to extract ethics out of biology. Despite the incoherence of the naturalistic position, it is still propagated vigorously in public and educational discourse. Christian responses have sometimes failed to hit the target, by mistakenly identifying naturalism with science *per se*, or by implying that scientific methodologies are intrinsically naturalistic. A biblically based response will emphasize a robust theism in which God is seen as the creator and sustainer of all the secondary causes which scientists investigate. The Christian worldview succeeds where naturalism fails: it provides a coherent explanation for the origin and consistent properties of the universe, which make science possible, and for the richness and ultimate purpose of human existence, which make life worth living.

Acknowledgement

I am grateful to Michael Poole of King's College, London, for his comments on an earlier draft of this chapter.

1   J. Rachels, *Created from Animals – The Moral Implications of Darwinism* (Oxford University Press, 1990).

2   See Chapter 16.

3   P. Atkins, 'Will Science Ever Fail?', *New Scientist*, 8 August 1992, pp. 32–5.

4   S.J. Wagner and R. Wagner (eds), *Naturalism – a Critical Appraisal* (University of Notre Dame, Indiana, 1993).

5   S. Weinberg, *Nature*, 1987, vol. 330, pp. 433–7.

6   The standard riposte to this point – the 'many worlds hypothesis' – has severe problems e.g. A.E. McGrath, *The Foundations of Dialogue in Science & Religion* (Blackwell, 1998), pp. 111–18; P. Dowe, *Science and Christian Belief*, 1999, vol. 11, pp. 67–8.

7   See Keith Ward, 'Why God Must Exist', *Science and Christian Belief*, 1999, vol. 11, pp. 5–13.

8   R. Dawkins, *Unweaving the Rainbow* (Penguin, 1998), pp. ix–x.

9   F. Crick, *The Astonishing Hypothesis: The Scientific Search for the Soul* (Simon and Schuster, 1994), p. 3. For a Christian alternative to the views of Crick, see W.S. Brown, N. Murphy and H.N. Maloney (eds), *Whatever Happened to the Soul? Scientific and Theological Portraits of Human Nature* (Fortress Press, 1998).

10 M. Ruse, *Taking Darwin Seriously: A Naturalistic Approach to Philosophy* (Blackwell, 1986).

11 Space does not allow the full discussion these points deserve. For a potent secular critique of sociobiology, see P. Kitcher, *Vaulting Ambition – Sociobiology and the Quest for Human Nature* (MIT Press, 1985).

12 G.E. Moore, *Principia Ethica*, 1903.

13 J. Rachels, *op. cit.*, pp. 204–5.

14 Augustine, *Literal Commentary on Genesis*, c. 391.

15 *Teaching About Evolution and the Nature of Science* (National Academy Press, 1998), p. 58.

16 See chapter 16.

17 E.J. Larson and L. Witham, 'Scientists Are Still Keeping the Faith', *Nature*, 1997, vol. 386, pp. 435–6.

18 R. Trigg, *Rationality and Science: Can Science Explain Everything?* (Blackwell, 1993).

Part VI

HISTORY AND PROVIDENCE

Chapter 19

A BRIEF THEOLOGY OF TIME

PAUL MILLS

What then is time? If no-one asks me, I know;
but if I wish to explain it to one who asks, I know not.

Augustine, *Confessions*, XI, 14

Summary

This chapter reviews the biblical witness that God is both transcendent over time and acting within it. Theological challenges to this view, including the development of 'free-will theism', have recently been allied to the findings of chaos theory and quantum mechanics. However, the traditional view of God's relation to time can accommodate these developments and remains the most satisfying solution to the puzzle of time. The results are a renewed appreciation of God's sovereignty over the universe, greater confidence in prayer and assurance about the future.

Introduction

We are temporal creatures with a finite lifespan. Western lifestyle is dominated by considerations of time to such a degree that the clock is rivalled only by the printing press as the most influential invention of this millennium. In societies less obsessed with temporal flow, we are known as 'people with gods on their wrists'. Time travel is a pervasive theme of our science fiction.

Yet, with Augustine, although we instinctively know what time is and can sense its passing, we have extreme difficulty in defining it. We perceive time as approaching us from the 'future', passing across the vanishingly brief boundary of the 'present', into the 'past', but we cannot sense whether the past and the future exist as realities other than for their moment in the present. Yet physicists now talk of time as if it were akin to a fourth spatial dimension, such that all points on the space-time continuum are equally 'real'.

This chapter cannot attempt a comprehensive discussion of time. Rather, it will focus on the biblical revelation of God's relation to time, how humanity attempts to deny or subvert that relation, and the practical implications for how we are to live 'in time'.

God's Relation to Time

The biblical witness maintains a fine balance between stressing God's transcendence over time and emphasizing that God is actively involved in sustaining the universe within time.

God Exists Eternally outside the Confines of Time

Due to our temporal limitations, we struggle to conceive of a state outside time. It is well-nigh impossible for us to envisage anything without a 'beginning'. Yet within the restrictions of language, the biblical writers convey that God exists eternally. In particular, God's name – 'I AM WHO I AM' – seems to indicate his continuous present existence (Exodus 3:14). Christ is the 'Alpha and Omega ... who is, and who was, and who is to come' (Revelation 1:8). The Lord is 'from everlasting to everlasting' (Psalm 90:2). By definition, the familiar speculation about 'what came before God' is futile.

God Initiated the Passage of Time in the Act of Creation

When God began to create the universe, time was initiated and the succession of moments and events commenced (e.g. Genesis 1:1; John 1:1–3; Colossians 1:16–17). Hence, time as we experience it does not automatically exist but, as with all creation, was dependent on God's creative fiat for its commencement. This is consistent with the current cosmological description of the interconnectedness of matter, space and time such that one cannot exist without the others, a description anticipated by Augustine's meditation that time is a meaningless concept without the existence of a universe in which processes occur: if matter existed but nothing changed, 'time' would have no meaning (*Confessions*, XI, 14).

God Instituted the Sabbath to Remind Us of His Sovereignty Over Our Time

The Sabbath was established to emulate God's ceasing from creative activity in time and to limit our working time (Exodus 20:8–11; Deuteronomy 5:12–15). In conjunction with the seasons, the Sabbath established a rhythmical pattern within time and was a weekly reminder of God's sovereignty over time. Just as payment of a tithe is an acknowledgement of God's material provision and ultimate ownership of our possessions, so observance of a day of rest affirms God's 'ownership' of our time.

God Is Immutable over Time

Whereas the created universe is subject to change within the temporal process, God remains 'the same' despite the passage of time. The second law of thermodynamics marks the direction of 'time's arrow' by describing the tendency of the universe to dissipate energy and progressively to decay, but God is untouched by the process. In contrast even to the heavens and the earth which will 'pass away', God is 'the same' (Psalm 102:25–7). He 'does not change like shifting shadows' (James 1:17). Unchangeableness is an attribute shared by Christ, who 'is the same yesterday and today and for ever' (Hebrews 13:8). This, however, does not exclude the possibility of 'events' occurring within the timeless being of the Godhead.

God Is Not Constrained by the Passage of Time and Sees All Moments Simultaneously and with Equal Clarity

'With the Lord a day is like a thousand years, and a thousand years are like a day' (2 Peter 3:8; cf. Psalm 39:4; 90:4). For us, every day is 24 hours. We can neither speed up the passage of time nor slow it down. Even travelling close to the speed of light would not change how we experienced the passage of time – only how we perceived it in relation to others. God, however, is free from the limitations that we face in experiencing time in indivisible and inexorable units. He not only possesses both 'fast forward' and 'freeze-frame' but stands 'outside' time and is not limited to the succession of moments. To God, all of creation's existence is somehow 'present'. As C.S. Lewis put it:

> If you picture Time as a straight line along which we have to travel, then you must picture God as the whole page on which the line is drawn. We come to the parts of the line one by one: we have to leave A behind before we get to B, and cannot reach C until we leave B behind. God, from above or outside or all around, contains the whole line, and sees it all.[1]

Time Is a Linear Process with a Preordained End

While some biblical writers depict history having cyclical features,[2] the overriding picture is of time within this universe being linear, having both a beginning (at creation), and a definite end (e.g. Acts 17:30–1). We do not know the exact time of the end, but it is already known by the Father (Mark 13:32). History has a fixed end-point, and therefore a destination. This contrasts particularly with the Hindu notion that time is endlessly repetitive and cyclical, which can result in apathy about the consequences of our actions within time. Rather, the belief that time is linear encourages purposive action (Psalm 90:10, 12).

God Alone Knows and Foretells Future Events with Certainty

A consequence of God's freedom from existence solely in 'the present' is that the future is literally an open book. This knowledge has been conveyed to his prophets and apostles: 'I am God, and there is none like me. I make known the end from the beginning, from ancient times, what is still to come.'[3] God's foreknowledge stretches to knowing in advance every detail of our personal existence: 'Before a word is on my tongue you know it completely, O Lord ... All the days ordained for me were written in your book before one of them came to be' (Psalm 139:4, 16).

God Acts within Time to Bring About His Purposes

It would be inaccurate to think of God as disengaged from the temporal flow, as if he had lit the blue touch-paper at creation and then retired into timelessness. Rather, God actively upholds the creation every moment of its existence (e.g. Colossians 1:16), and operates within time to bring about his desired ends, including those foretold through his prophets (e.g. Acts 3:18). The Judaeo-Christian tradition continually looks back to moments in history when God acted in time to further the salvation of his people (such as at the exodus).[4] This is demonstrated most clearly in the Incarnation: 'when the time had fully come, God sent his Son, born of a woman' (Galatians 4:4–5) and in the Crucifixion: a 'testimony given in its proper time' (1 Timothy 2:6). Belief in God's actions within time is the very basis for petitionary prayer – if God is powerless to intervene in time then such prayer is pointless. It is this belief in the 'immanence' of God within time that distinguishes the Yahweh of the Bible from the Allah of the Qu'ran. Since the will of Allah is fixed and inscrutable, Muslims do not pray for him to act in a particular way, but merely seek to conform themselves to Allah's will, whatever that may be.

Hence, the biblical picture of God's relation to time is both of his creative mastery, his total foreknowledge and of his acting within time to fulfil his purposes.

Challenges to God's Sovereignty over Time

This description of God's relationship to time has not gone unchallenged, either inside or outside the church.

Deism

In the seventeenth and eighteenth centuries, deism grew out of a strong belief in the implacability of physical laws – God created the universe in accordance with a set of deterministic laws governing the motion and behaviour of every particle. He does not need to intervene with these particles since their paths within time have been mapped out from the beginning:

> God created substances and gives them the force they need, and after that he leaves them to themselves and does nothing but conserve them in their actions.[5]

God established the initial conditions and laws to be such that they would achieve his intended goal without the need for further intervention. To suggest that God intervened in time implied a limit to his initial omniscience, as well as the abrogation of preordained natural 'laws'.

Two inferences were drawn. First, that there is no such thing as 'chance', in the sense of something occurring without an identifiable cause; and, second, that the future course of the physical universe could, in theory at least, be exactly predicted – if we discovered all the laws governing the particles within the universe, knew their position, direction and velocity and had a sufficiently powerful computer. It was this last assertion (e.g. by Laplace) that underpinned the study of physical laws for over two centuries.

Deism has many attractions. It emphasizes God's pre-eminence over, and distinction from, his creation. It stresses the omniscience and foreknowledge of God over time. It renders the universe intelligible by describing it in a set of observable regularities. And it reduces the perceived complexity of divine activity required at any instant – God has simply created the universe, set it in motion and retired a safe distance. It is logically appealing since it avoids many of the problems associated with believing that God is both 'eternal' and yet acts within time.

However, by assuming that the 'laws' of the physical universe are unbreakable even by the lawgiver, deism is forced to come to conclusions that are incompatible with the biblical witness to God's actions within time. For example, 'miracles' either cannot happen or are a worrying aberration. Similarly, petitionary prayer becomes pointless since God cannot act in time to change the course of events that have been preordained. Rather, prayer becomes a process of moulding one's will to the preset divine plan. Most fundamentally, the action of God in sustaining the universe at every moment is denied.

Divine Ignorance and Human Free Will

Compared to deism, however, the more longstanding and popular objection to the traditional interpretation of the biblical revelation is that God cannot preordain or know the future. This is not necessarily derived from any inherent problem with conceiving of God being outside time. Rather, philosophers from Cicero onwards have rejected belief in God's foreknowledge of events since it is deemed incompatible with human freedom:

> An omniscient being ... knows everything that it is possible to know. There can, however, be no antecedent truth with respect to particular

future free actions of men other than that they might and might not occur. God, accordingly, cannot know whether they will be performed until the time for the performance arrives.[6]

This is a natural conclusion to reach. First, it 'feels' to us as if the future is 'open' rather than on a tightly constrained path moving towards its fated end. The future is 'not there waiting for us but something we make as we go along'.[7] Indeed, it is this feeling that encourages humanity to be creative:

> Time has a sort of successive reality because it allows you to be creative, to do new things. Now the price of that freedom and creativity is that you can't predict the future exactly – not even God can.[8]

Second, if we are not free to make unconstrained choices then we cannot be held accountable for our actions. On this definition of responsibility, freedom of choice is the basis for personal morality – we can only be 'good' if we could choose evil. Finally, we have personal worth only if our choices and actions count for something – if we cannot change the course of events then, in the eternal scheme of things, our existence is meaningless. Indeed, what would be the point of the whole creative process if we cannot 'surprise' God?[9] The obvious conclusion from this is that God 'takes risks' with his plan for the universe:

> If God created man in his own image, he must have created him capable of new initiatives and new insights which cannot be precisely or infallibly foreknown, but which give to the future a perpetual freshness as the inexhaustible variety of possible thoughts and actions, on the part of his children as well as himself, crystallizes into actuality.[10]

Similar sentiments are expressed by 'process theology'. Arising as something of a reaction to classical theism, this position asserts that process and change are indispensable aspects of genuine existence. Indeed, reality is defined to be the experience of change and so any notion that the ultimate reality behind the universe is immutable is rejected:

> to be actual is to be a process ... Since the world as we experience it is a place of process, of change, of becoming ... the contrary notion

that what is actual or fully real is beyond change leads to a devaluation of life in the world.[11]

The corollary drawn from this starting position is that God *must* change over time along with everything in creation. Indeed, some would argue that God is adding to his identity all the experiences that happen anywhere in the universe. God cannot be immutable over time because otherwise our existence would not matter to him.

The more recent school of 'free-will theism'[12] adopts a similar line of reasoning. This position again asserts that God cannot fully know the future, since this would encroach on the free exercise of human freedom.[13] God is not the aloof, immutable monarch who exists in a timeless eternity; rather, he is a loving parent who shares the control of the future with us. God perfectly knows all there is to know (the past, the present and his intended actions in the future), but he comprehends what actually occurs as it happens rather than knowing it in advance, and responds to human actions in order to bring his purposes about eventually:

> The future is determined by God not alone but in partnership with human agents. God gives us a role in shaping what the future will be. He is flexible and does not insist in doing things his way. God will adjust his own plans because he is sensitive to what humans think and do.[14]

Support for free-will theism is derived from various biblical passages. In addition to overriding emphasis being placed on love as the principal facet of God's nature (1 John 4:16),[15] and the evidence that God is deeply and 'emotionally' engaged with the actions of his creatures (see Hosea), support is sought from those passages which depict divinely inspired prophecy as conditional (Jeremiah 18:6–10; Jonah 3), and God as 'repenting' or changing his mind (e.g. Genesis 6:6; 1 Samuel 15:35). The advantages claimed are that the unbiblical baggage of Greek philosophical belief in the impassibility of the divine is discarded; the logical problems of God being 'timeless' and yet acting within time are circumvented; petitionary prayer truly becomes involvement in divine action rather than simply conforming oneself to God's predetermined will; and that evangelism truly 'matters' rather than merely revealing the elect.

The Discovery of Scientific 'Chance'?

While God's foreknowledge has long been deemed incompatible with true freedom, two recent scientific developments are now used to reinforce the case for indeterminism.

First, the discovery of quantum uncertainty early this century has led to the belief that truly 'chance' events occur. Observations of quantum phenomena suggest that, at a subatomic level, events occur without an apparent 'cause'. For instance, there is no way for us to know when a particular uranium atom will decay into a lead atom, even though we can detect this event once it has happened. It seems to occur unprompted. Such reactions are still governed by statistical regularities (allowing us to construct nuclear power stations), but the individual events themselves seem to occur without explanation and appear purely random.

Second, the discovery of 'chaotic' systems with non-linear dynamics has led to greater understanding of why certain events are almost impossible to predict. Such systems display the property that a small disturbance can set off a chain reaction so that its effect on the whole system is disproportionately large. The best-known example of a chaotic system is that of the atmosphere. This can display the 'butterfly effect': the beat of a butterfly's wing could start a series of events that might lead to a hurricane on the other side of the globe.

That such small events can have large effects means that forecasting the state of such a system for any substantial period becomes virtually impossible. Hence, we can forecast tomorrow's weather with a fair degree of accuracy, but that of a month ahead with almost no confidence whatsoever. This is not to say that chaotic systems do not obey the general regularities of cause and effect, just that the interactions within the system are so complex that they do not necessarily follow the usual pattern of reverting to an average expected outcome. Also, if we are to make accurate predictions, we must know the initial conditions of the system very precisely.

These discoveries have led some to doubt the determinacy of the future. For instance:

> The intrinsically statistical character of atomic events and the instability of many physical systems to minute fluctuations, ensures that the future remains open and undetermined by the present.[16]

Certainly, both quantum uncertainty and the existence of chaotic systems pose difficulties for the belief in absolute scientific determinism. For they mean that we will never know enough about the initial conditions or the behaviour of its components ever to 'solve' the universe and predict its behaviour exactly from the outset.[17] Laplace's dream is now seen to be unrealizable.

But these discoveries have also been used to deny that God can either know or preordain every event that occurs within time, including those in our lives, and to reassert the place of human freedom. For instance, as a consequence of quantum uncertainty, Peacocke believes that this 'inherent unpredictability … represents a limitation of the knowledge even an omniscient God could have' of events at a quantum level; indeed, that the future cannot currently 'exist' and that therefore there is no content of future events for God to know.[18] Polkinghorne believes that quantum uncertainty means that the future is 'open' and that God allows the universe a degree of 'independence' in order to enhance its creativity. God is still sovereign but does not know the path the system, including mankind, will take.[19] A favourite analogy is that of the cosmic chess player:

> God is the supreme Grandmaster who has everything under his control … whatever the finite players do, God's plan will be executed; though various lines of God's play will answer to various moves of the finite players … No line of play that finite players may think of can force God to improvise: his knowledge of the game already embraces all the possible variant lines of play, theirs do not.[20]

God may not have entirely relinquished control over the course of events but he does not know which 'line of play' events will take.

The Reassertion of Divine Sovereignty

Philosophers and theologians deny the omniscience of God[21] on the basis that this precludes a place for human freedom, creativity, self-worth and moral accountability. These claims are partly based on the psychological insecurity that comes from the belief that self-worth is derived from the choices we exercise and the 'difference' we make. But they also come from the more deep-seated objection that experiencing personal 'freedom' by definition rules out any form of divine predetermination or prescience over time.

The Christian rejoinder to the former insecurity is that 'self-worth' in the temporal process is derived from a deepening relationship with God, rather than from any lasting impression we make on the space-time continuum. The response to the second is to recognize in it the rebellion of human pride in believing we must be allowed unfettered freedom, and then to reassert the Bible's insistence on both divine sovereignty and human responsibility (e.g. Acts 4:24–8). This can be done either by positing divine foreknowledge of what will cause us to exercise our 'free' choices in a particular way; or by defining human 'freedom' in such a way that we can be held responsible for our choices despite their preordination.[22]

Remarkably, the concept of time implied by relativity theory is consistent with the traditional notion of God standing outside the timeline. Time is conceived as the fourth dimension in space with the whole of history laid out as a changeless continuum – otherwise observers moving relative to one another would disagree about what time 'now' is. Ironically, this concept of the whole history of the universe being 'created' at the inception of both space and time means that it is now easier for astrophysicists to believe in divine foreknowledge than for theologians.[23]

As regards chaos theory and quantum uncertainty, neither development necessarily precludes the foreknowledge of God or his preordination of events. This is clearer with chaotic dynamics since what we observe are not phenomena without apparent causes. Rather, relationships between events exist but are far more complex and less tractable to simple extrapolation than linear ones. Thus, while the computational complexity of divine foreknowledge and co-ordination of events must be that much greater, there is no inherent reason why God could not sustain a universe containing chaotic processes if he could sustain one containing linear ones.[24] After all, Scripture is replete with claims to God's power over the weather (e.g. 1 Kings 8:35; Psalm 78:47–8). He even dictates the fall of the dice (Proverbs 16:33), an outcome that is extremely sensitive to initial conditions.

Quantum uncertainty is of a different order. Here events seem to occur without any apparent cause. One response has been to say that these phenomena do not occur in this fashion – there are 'hidden variables' at work that we cannot yet observe which cause the quantum events we do observe. (Although taken up by Einstein, this position is now held only by a small minority of physicists.) Alternatively, theistic comfort can be taken from the observation that quantum events still accord with statistical regularities and are not observed at a level greater than the atomic. Hence, God could permit truly chance events to occur at the subatomic level, but these will not have a material impact at the macro level at which he ordains events.[25] Again, it has been posited that God himself acts as the 'hidden variable' that is the ultimate cause of quantum phenomena,[26] or that there is a middle ground in which God knows the propensities towards quantum events and may intervene to change them if required for his wider purpose.[27] While quantum uncertainty does raise new questions about the degree to which God ordains the smallest of subatomic events, it does not provide the advocates of 'openness' with a clinching argument. It merely defines the limits of our ignorance of how God operates in the universe.

The position of free-will theism and those who seek to carve out a space for human freedom seems even more difficult to reconcile with a belief in God's ultimate triumph over evil in the light of chaos theory. The discovery of such systems (of which human history appears to be a prime example), means that it is even more difficult to conceive of a God who improvises in response to the 'lines of play' of his creatures, in order to preserve their freedom. In chaotic systems, even small disturbances can result in far-reaching consequences. So, if God does 'play the game' in this way, but has a particular 'endgame' in mind, then he must become progressively more interventionist over time as his degrees of freedom for action diminish.

Free-will theism tries to provide comfort for Christians that their actions and prayers 'matter'. But it fails to engage with the large preponderance of the biblical material that describes God's sovereignty over time, and ignores the longstanding interpretation of the 'repentance' passages that God is accommodating the explanation of his actions to human capacities of understanding.[28] The result is to depict a God who cannot always accurately prophesy the future, cannot know the full consequences of his actions, and cannot know that his purposes ultimately will prevail. Free-will theism deprives Christians of assurance in their own salvation and the triumph of God's will in the future. Ironically, it diminishes one's confidence in prayer: who would be foolhardy enough to pray for God to act if one believed that God did not know the consequences of answering such a prayer? The strange implication of free-will theism is that we can affect God but he cannot affect us.

Living in Time

We have seen that the biblical witness is to a God who is both outside time yet active within it. He preordains and foreknows our actions within time, yet also actively upholds the universe at every instant within the temporal flow. How does this belief affect the way we should live in time?

How *Not* to Live 'In Time' – Usurping God's Sovereignty

A deep-rooted inclination of humanity is to try to emulate some of God's suzerainty over time, particularly with regard to acquiring information about, or control over, the future. The most ancient of these methods is some form of divination to pierce the veil of the future. These have ranged from interpreting patterns in the entrails of sacrificed animals to palmistry, tarot cards and astrology. The widespread use of divination betrays a universal desire to throw off the temporal limitations with which we have been created. Man is not content with his confined temporal position and lays claim to this divine knowledge. Unsurprisingly, the presence of diviners was proscribed (Deuteronomy 18:10) and condemned (Zechariah 10:2) within Old Testament Israel.

Both secular society and the church are too careless with how they treat predictions and forecasts of the future. Too often we seem willing to listen to those prophets, both within and outside the church, who lay claim to knowledge of the future. While God does announce events 'before they spring into being' (Isaiah 42:9), to claim to make such a statement is an awesome responsibility. One of the tests laid down for the discernment of 'true' from 'false' prophecy was, of course, whether the events predicted occurred (Deuteronomy 18:20–22). Prophecy which proved to be false was a capital offence because of the 'presumption' of the false prophet who claimed to speak for God when not inspired to do so. Perhaps we would hear of fewer predictions made within the church if we understood how seriously God takes such presumption.

But the more widespread claims to 'prophecy' come from economists, scientists and sociologists. For instance, economists still

derive equations from past data describing how the economy operates and use these to inform their forecasts of next year's GDP,
despite the signal failure of any one model consistently to predict
much better than forecasts derived randomly. Ultimately, such prediction fails because it must assume that the future will be like the
past. But time and again, we are too prone to believe those who
forecast by extrapolating current experience – be they the doom-
mongers of imminent exhaustion of the world's food supplies or the
optimistic believers in mankind's evolution towards a destiny of
greater technological, genetic and moral progress. It was those
'without knowledge' who proclaimed that 'tomorrow will be like
today, or even far better' (Isaiah 56:12), and 'scoffers' who say that
'everything goes on as it has since the beginning of creation'
(2 Peter 3:4). By taking our experience within time and extrapolating it back or forwards, we are displaying our collective egocentric-
ity – as if only our experience now was valid and we can interpret
the rest of the timeline solely in the light of it. Surely, those cog-
nizant of God's sovereignty over time should adopt a more humble
attitude that leaves room for unanticipated contingencies.

How to Live 'In Time' – Humility, Urgency and Hope

Of course, this is not to say that all planning and provision for the
future is inherently presumptuous. Those who take Christ's injunc-
tion not to 'worry about tomorrow' (Matthew 6:34) as an excuse
for indolence are ignoring the balance of the biblical material (see
Chapter 14). Wise stewardship of the gifts we have been given
requires a degree of planning, anticipation and risk-taking. Rather,
the attitude in which we plan and contract should be one which
humbly recognizes our ignorance over the future:

> Do not boast about tomorrow, for you do not know what a day may
> bring forth.
>
> Proverbs 27:1

James condemned the rich businessman, not necessarily for planning his sales itinerary, but rather for the presumption with which it
was done: 'all such boasting is evil' (James 4:13–16).

The practical application of such an attitude is that we need to
change the way we arrange our affairs to embody a 'contingent'

attitude towards the future. For instance, borrowing (particularly to finance consumption or speculation), involves presuming upon future events to transpire as expected if the debt is to be repaid. Another consequence of our ignorance about the future is that, since we do not know and should not presume that we will be alive tomorrow, we need to make the most of every moment granted to us (e.g. Ephesians 5:16). However, this is always in the context of service to God and others. By contrast, the postmodern obsession with the 'present' also results in trying to make the most of every moment, but more in the spirit of a hedonistic cult of 'eat, drink and be merry, for tomorrow we die'.

Another radical difference that the biblical perspective on time can make to those who live in its light is that Christians, above all people, can be confident about the future – be it our own or that of the whole universe. For instance, in Psalm 139, David takes great comfort from the discovery that God knows every word he will speak before he utters it. Rather than railing against a God who has abrogated his free will, David is comforted by God's intimate fore-knowledge of his life. This belief gives an assurance that the pattern of our lives has been planned instead of being a random outcome of chance events:

> Sov'reign Ruler of the skies,
> ever gracious ever wise;
> All my times are in thy hand, all events at thy command.
>
> He that form'd me in the womb,
> He shall guide me to the tomb;
> All my times shall ever be, Order'd by his wise decree.
>
> Plagues and deaths around me fly;
> Till he bids I cannot die;
> Not a single shaft can hit, Till the God of love sees fit.
>
> John Ryland

But perhaps most clearly in our contemporary society, the biblical theology of time gives comfort that there is a purpose to creation after all and that history is proceeding towards its divinely ordained end (Titus 1:2). For if the future is 'open', and human freedom could ultimately thwart the will of God, then there can be no confidence that evil will not triumph and the plans of God for salvation will not be frustrated.

Hope for the future was not a uniquely Christian trait in the 'modern' age when belief in the inexorable progress of humanity through technological progress, economic growth and moral improvement held sway. But pollution, wars, famine and unemployment have shaken our faith in the future. Even astrophysicists can only offer two alternative futures: either a universe that expands for ever, ultimately cools to absolute zero and suffers 'heat death', or one that eventually collapses in a 'Big Crunch'. In a postmodern era obsessed with the present and disillusioned with the future, hope remains the most attractive feature of the Christian theology of time.

1   *Mere Christianity* (Collins, Glasgow, 1952), p. 144.
2   Both Judges and Revelation contain repetitive themes suggesting that some patterns may be discernible within history. Ecclesiastes 1 describes the cycles within physical processes to emphasize the pointlessness of a godless existence.
3   Isaiah 46:9–10; cf. 41:21–2; 42:9; 44:6–8; 45:21.
4   David Bebbington contrasts the Old Testament's depiction of Yahweh as a God who acts in history to bring about his purposes for individuals (e.g. Genesis 45:8) and for Israel (e.g. Psalm 136), with the Canaanite deities who were associated with spatial location rather than time (*Patterns in History*, IVP, Leicester, 1979).
5   G.W. Leibniz, *Theodicy*, edited by Austin Farrer (Routledge, London, 1952), para. 27.
6   R. Taylor, 'Determinism', in P. Edwards (ed.), *Encyclopaedia of Philosophy* (Macmillan, London, 1967), vol. 2, p. 363.
7   R. Flood and M. Lockwood, *The Nature of Time* (Basil Blackwell, Oxford, 1986), p. 2.
8   Keith Ward, quoted in R. Stannard, *Science and Wonders* (Faber & Faber, London, 1996), p. 139.
9   For instance, see David Pailin, quoted in Stannard, *ibid.*, pp. 140–41.
10 J.R. Lucas, *The Future* (Basil Blackwell, Oxford, 1989), p. 233. See also similar quotations from Hasker, Adams and Swinburne in P. Helm, *The Providence of God* (IVP, Leicester, 1993), pp. 40–42. Helm notes that the common reason why these theologians believe God 'takes risks' is that only then is there a place for human freedom.
11 J.B. Cobb and D.R. Griffin, *Process Theology: An Introductory Exposition* (Westminster Press, Philadelphia, 1976), p. 14.
12 C. Pinnock *et al.*, *The Openness of God: A Biblical Challenge to the Traditional Understanding of God* (IVP, Downers Grove, Illinois, 1994).

13 Pinnock, *op. cit.*, pp. 121–3.

14 *Ibid.*, p. 113.

15 *Ibid.*, p. 15, 23.

16 P. Davies, *The Mind of God* (Simon & Schuster, 1992), p. 201.

17 E.g. see K. Ward, *God, Chance and Necessity* (OneWorld Publications, Oxford, 1996), p. 81.

18 A. Peacocke, 'God's Interaction with the World' in R.J. Russell, N. Murphy and A. Peacocke (eds), *Chaos and Complexity* (Vatican Observatory Publications, Vatican City, 1995), pp. 279–80.

19 J. Polkinghorne, *Science and Providence* (SPCK, London, 1989), pp. 77–84.

20 P. Geach, *Providence and Evil* (Cambridge University Press, 1977), p. 58.

21 One possible way out of some of the questions concerning whether 'time' has an objective existence or is purely subjective is to define time 'relationally'– that is, 'time' is what happens as the persons of the Trinity interact (see L. Osborn, 'Spacetime and Revelation', *Science and Christian Belief*, October 1996, 121–2). This relational perspective may resolve the puzzle of how existence in the 'new heaven and the new earth' can be both 'everlasting' and yet involve perception of the passage of time and change (e.g. Revelation 21:25; 22:2, 5).

22 See Helm, *op. cit.*, Chapter 2.

23 E.g. Stannard, *op. cit.*, p. 144.

24 D. Wilkinson, *God, the Big Bang and Stephen Hawking* (Monarch, Crowborough, 1996), p. 60.

25 'The basic framework of creation is fixed, but the details are not. In the smaller-scale behaviour of things, indeterminacy seems to allow physical systems a degree of freedom which seems to parallel our own sense of ourselves as freely acting beings' (P.J. Bussey, 'Indeterminacy, Time and the Future', *Science and Christian Belief*, April 1997, p. 82).

26 D.M. MacKay, 'The Mythology of Chance' in *The Open Mind and Other Essays* (IVP, Leicester, 1988), p. 204; P. Dowe, 'Chance and Providence', *Science and Christian Belief*, April 1997, pp. 3–20.

27 J.J. Davis, 'Quantum Indeterminacy and the Omniscience of God', *Science and Christian Belief*, October 1997, pp. 129–44.

28 E.g. Calvin, *Institutes*, I, 17, 13. For critiques of free-will theism see 'Has God Been Held Hostage by Philosophy?' *Christianity Today*, 9 January 1995, pp. 30–34, and M.J. Erickson, *The Evangelical Left* (Baker Books, Grand Rapids, Michigan, 1997), pp. 104–7.

Chapter 20

REFLECTIONS ON PROVIDENCE

Can We 'Read' Events?

MARK E. DEVER

Meanings or patterns discernible in 'history' ... are clearest for each of us in the periods he has studied least.[1]

C.S. Lewis, 'Historicism' in *Fern-seed and Elephants*

Summary

There is an assumption in society, and increasingly in the church, that the events of our lives cannot be placed in a larger context of meaning. This chapter considers the obvious moral problems raised by Christian claims to meaning, and suggests some biblical guidelines which may help us to 'read' events.

The Question Set

'AIDS is the judgement of God.' This is one of those statements which is best known by its denial. No sooner is it uttered today than the speaker is surrounded by people denying it, albeit for various reasons. One of these is a reason which would deny that people are able to discern the hand of God in the events of history at all. This objection is found not only in the expected places – the statements of the philosophical sceptic or the religious cynic – but in the pulpits of even the most conservative Christian churches. What is the root of this hesitancy? What does the Bible have to say about it? Can we 'read' the purposes of God in the events around us?

These days such a question may sound strange. For the last three centuries, academic institutions have increasingly answered the question 'why?' only as if it were the question 'how?' As experiment and observation in the seventeenth and eighteenth centuries discovered the regularity of nature, a decreasing number of occurrences seemed to be inexplicable. Therefore, recourse to explaining events by the absolute power of God came to be seen, as the late seventeenth-century Anglican divine John Wilkins put it, as 'the Receptable of Lazy Ignorance: which any industrious Spirit would be asham'd of' *(Mathematical and Philosophical Works,* London, 1708, pp. 98–9). The God of the universe seemed to shrink to the 'God of the Gaps', and then, by the early nineteenth century, to no more than a largely privatized, subjective deity relevant only to the happenings of the inner soul, and not to the world around. As the natural sciences were reconstructed on an empirical basis, so too history began to move from rhetoric to science. 'Meaning' in history began to go the way of fabulous beasts and legendary heroes.

The History of 'Reading' History

Yet, though the hand of God in history does seem to have become faint to the point of having faded away altogether, there is no doubt that this idea of 'reading' history has been prevalent in the past. Traditionally, people assumed that the events of their own life, and of the world around them, were to be read as one would read the words of a novel. Just as the letters on a page are not simply arbitrarily formed spots of ink, so, too, it has been assumed, the events of history are purposeful. To the discerning eye, there was significance beyond that which first appears.

In the past, to assert the existence of a god was meaningless without an assertion of this god's action in the world. The pagan shipmates of Jonah clearly assumed that the storm that threatened their lives demonstrated the anger of an offended god against one of the people on their ship (Jonah 1:7). The pagans of ancient Rome ascribed her destruction in AD 410 to the anger of their gods at the rise of Christianity. Augustine's response was confidently and meticulously to trace the hand of the one true God in the rise and fall of Rome. Whatever differences earlier generations of Christians had with their pagan contemporaries, the willingness to discern a divine hand in the events around them was not one of them.

Much closer in time to the present day, John Foxe chronicled the hand of God in English religious history in a way which was formative on perhaps every generation between his and our own. Foxe's heirs watched with bated breath as the fate of Protestant Europe seemed for a time to hang upon the actions of Gustavus Adolphus of Sweden. Each victory of Adolphus' forces over the Emperor's was seen as the judgement of God on the Church of Rome. The Puritan minister Thomas Beard and his one-time student Oliver Cromwell, powerfully presented this reading of history as essential to the Reformed understanding of England. At the same time, Roman Catholic observers in Europe were no slower to see God's hand in every reversal in the fortunes of the Protestant forces. Thus, storms and invasions, plagues and wars were all regularly interpreted in the past as 'acts of God' conveying particular divine lessons for humans.

Nor should we think this simply the preserve of a few religious enthusiasts from the long-gone days of religious wars. In the most recent edition of *Hymns Ancient and Modern*, the words of nineteenth-century hymn-writer W.E. Hickson are still present, asking God in the national anthem to 'scatter our enemies, and make them fall; confound their politics'. Do we think, when the 'politics' of our national adversaries are 'confounded', that this is the action of God?

This kind of interpretation of events seems to be encouraged by the Bible. Two Old Testament books are particularly important in this regard – Deuteronomy and Proverbs. Deuteronomy presents numerous blessings and curses which are to follow from the actions of God's covenant people. The prophets, expounding the Deuteronomic view of history, present an account of God's dealings with his people collectively in history, as they neglect his laws, suffer the consequences and experience his grace. Similarly, the book of Proverbs presents many of these same directions from God in aphoristic form, with particular consequences flowing from particular actions.

The Problem with 'Reading' History

The problem, of course, raised by a simple correlation of events with divine meaning – whether it be that someone's contracting AIDS is the judgement of God on them, or that the prosperity of the United States is a sign of divine approbation – is the problem which Job's friends faced. Informed by proverbial wisdom, they reasoned backwards from Job's trials to the sin which these trials evidenced. Yet, in the end, Job's friends were confounded, as God declared their readings wrong. Job was not suffering because of his sins but, ironically, because of his righteousness. The story of Job, then, raises the problem of 'innocent suffering' as it is often called, and thereby sets a question mark against an automatic association of wealth and virtue, of poverty and sin.

This clear lack of a perfect correlation between events and desert disturbs us. In Fyodor Dostoyevsky's novel *The Brothers Karamazov*, Ivan questions his brother Alyosha, a novice monk, about the cruelty which Alyosha's God allows in his world. Ivan recounts a story which he has heard of the atrocities the Turks are committing in Bulgaria:

> They burn, kill, violate women and children, nail their prisoners' ears to fences and leave them like that till next morning when they hang them, and so on ... These Turks ... seemed to derive a voluptuous pleasure from torturing children, cutting a child out of its mother's womb with a dagger and tossing babies up in the air and catching them on a bayonet before the eyes of their mothers.

Dostoyevsky continues with even greater horrors, scarcely imaginable though that may be.

Don't such actions make a mockery of attempts to discern the will of God in events? How can anyone maintain that there is a God of justice ordering a world where such things occur? In the modern age, this has led people to question whether there can be any meaning – any God – at all. In the ancient world, similar observations led people not to atheism, but rather to question the just character of God. This is the question which is put to God repeatedly in the Bible (see Ezekiel 9:9; Malachi 2:17; 2 Peter 3:4).

Can we say then with certainty, as so many Christians have seemed to in the past, that a particular event has happened as judgement for particular sins? Yet, if we can't say that 'X' is the judgement of God, can we say that 'Y' is the blessing of God? In the end, the believer is apparently left on the horns of a dilemma. On the one hand, there must be a meaning to history, to the events of our own lives and the world around us, if life is to have a point at all. In that sense history must be able to be 'read'. On the other hand, to attempt to ascribe meaning to events in our own lives and in the world around us in any coherent way would seem to prove difficult, to the point of being impossible. What can deliver us from this dilemma?

Clues to the Mystery: Five Biblical Statements

Faith is essential to deliver us from this dilemma, because faith is essential to any biblical perception of meaning in events. As the writer to the Hebrews said, 'faith is being sure of what we hope for and certain of what we do not see. This is what the ancients were commended for' (Hebrews 11:1). He then goes on to give numerous examples of those who believed God's promises for the future, and so rightly assessed and acted in their present situations. We believe, then, in order to understand. Thus, we know that should we, for example, miss a train by frustratingly few moments, God 'In all things ... works for the good of those who love him, who have been called according to his purpose' (Romans 8:28). We might not know how God is using this to further his purposes, but have faith according to his self-revelation in Scripture that he is. The alternative is to have a faith-less and therefore fundamentally meaningless and necessarily self-centred existence. To affirm meaning in events, then, is certainly a statement of faith. But it is an affirmation to which our faith, by its nature, calls us. The five statements of biblical truth outlined below may put us in a position to think about this problem more carefully.

God Is Sovereign, Acting Purposively in History

No amount of incomprehension of how God can use events should shake us from the clear statements of Scripture on this. God created all things, and by his power all things are continuously sustained, (Nehemiah 9:6; Hebrews 1:3). More specifically, while Scripture is clear that humans are responsible for their actions, it is also unambiguous in asserting that God is sovereign even over human actions (e.g. Romans 9). 'In his heart a man plans his course, but the LORD determines his steps' (Proverbs 16:9). 'The king's heart is in the hand of the LORD, he directs it like a watercourse wherever he pleases' (Proverbs 21:1). However obscure God's intention in allowing certain things to occur may be, our present perceptions are not the final verdict. There are no chance encounters, nor simple coincidences. Scripture speaks of God's having 'determined the times set for them [every nation of men] and the exact places where they should live' (Acts 17:26). Even the crucifixion of Jesus is described in prayer to God as 'what your power and will had decided beforehand should happen' (Acts 4:28).

Ultimately, God Will Vindicate Himself; Evil Will Be Punished

The problem Job's counsellors had in trying to 'read' Job's history was that they assumed that because the truth of proverbial wisdom was usually obvious, it was always obvious immediately. The truth of proverbial wisdom's proscriptions and prescriptions are evident: tragedy does follow sin, blessing does follow wisdom. But it may take some time for the blessings or misfortunes to be worked out. Indeed, the absolute truth of proverbial wisdom is not ultimately undermined by the story of Job, but is shown to be true only by God, and only at the end. Therefore, the simple fact that God's reasons for acting are inscrutable at present does not mean that God is unjust. He will make the meaning plain, though perhaps not as soon as we might desire. It is interesting to note that in the cases mentioned above (recorded in Ezekiel, Malachi and 2 Peter) when God was charged with moral indifference, his answer was never to explain why each apparently unjust thing happened, but rather to say simply, 'Wait, you'll see.' Good will triumph visibly ultimately.

In the Meantime, Any Adversity Must Be Viewed in the Light of the End

Biblically, there are no good people. Everyone's nature and actions put them ultimately under God's judgement. 'The day of the LORD is near for all nations. As you have done, it will be done to you; your deeds will return upon your own head' (Obadiah 15; cf. Amos 4:11–13). Therefore, difficulties which befall the believer in this life are to be seen as coming from a loving Father, who has his process for bringing us to our goal (Romans 8:28: Hebrews 12:1–11). On the other hand, the adversities experienced in this life by those who do not repent are rightly seen as the beginnings of the outpouring of God's wrath on them which they will one day experience in its fullness.

In the Meantime, Any Good Must Be Understood as God's Gracious Blessing

If we deserve God's wrath, then any good which we experience, however apparently ordinary, must be seen as a gift – undeserved – from God, not as an inherent right. Even the food which we have, Scripture teaches, comes by God's particular providential goodness towards us (Psalm 145:15). As Augustine said, the genuine

Christian 'ascribes whatever there is that may be pleasing in himself entirely to the mercy of the God whom he fears to displease, offering thanks for faults amended, and pouring out prayers for the amendment of faults that still remain' (*The City of God*, V, 20).

Full Judgement and Blessing Will Come Only Finally

The events of our lives are passing. They are significant, yet they are only faint indicators of what is to come. As Jesus clearly taught, those who do not respond to the Word may live now, but they live under his wrath, and they will die (John 3:16–19, 36; Matthew 13:40–43, 47–50). The tares will be burned, and the good wheat will be gathered into the barn (Matthew 13:30). The present state of sheep and goats may look similar, but there will come a separation (Matthew 25:31–46). The unredeemed are passing out of the realm of whatever relative prosperity they have known, and into a woe which is unimaginable. Those who have been redeemed by Christ are experiencing only purging trials in this life, and are increasingly gripped by the reality of the God in whose company they will dwell for ever.

> nothing is less befitting than that we should estimate the wrath of God, according as any one is afflicted in the world, as nothing is more absurd than to take hold of the transient blessings which we enjoy, that we may from them form an estimate of God's favour.
>
> John Calvin, in his comments upon 1 Thessalonians 1:10

The best and worst of times lie in the future.

Reading in the Meantime

Apart from this finally revealed 'reading', can we in the meantime further 'read' the meanings of events which are complex, apparently ambiguous, even horrifying? Certainly there are many examples of providences having been 'read' in the history of the church – from Augustine's conversion by hearing snatches of a child's conversation while playing a game, to the defeat of the Spanish Armada in 1588, perhaps even to some interpretations which readers of this chapter have given to events in their own lives. Yet we obviously have limited ability to 'read' such events as hearing phrases of others' conversations, the outcomes of military struggles, and even the occurrences of our own days or dreams of our own nights. Certainly there are disanalogies between this image of reading and the believer's perception of the hand of God in events.

First, the simple fact that events 'have meaning' need not be evident to all in order for these events to be authentically meaningful. The clearest example of this is found, of course, in the cross. In the death of Jesus God's judgement on sin and his gracious love meet in the most mysterious providential happening of human history. And yet, even that event – central to God's plan for the world – has no 'meaning' self-evident to those who witnessed it, or to those who have heard of it since, beyond the simple fact of the crucifixion itself. The meaning of this event is only understood as God himself explains it to us through the testimony of his Spirit via witnesses and the Word.

There is a second disanalogy between reading and the believer's perception of the hand of God in events. Unlike a written message, such events, even if being taken as providing a message from God, need not be taken as speaking univocally to all. For example, one can imagine a well-timed lightning bolt, which is judged to be an 'act of God' in an even more precise fashion than an insurance policy might suggest. Through this lightning bolt, God could authentically speak messages which were appropriately different, yet not ultimately contradictory, to a bishop being consecrated, a Christian minister wrestling with some sin, a sceptical journalist, a devout executive of a local construction firm, and a young Christian convert. These could be respectively tested, rebuked, shaken, encouraged and confirmed – all by the same lightning bolt.

Perhaps another example would be helpful. American television preacher Oral Roberts recently underwent surgery to remove blockages from his arteries. In a statement released soon afterwards, Roberts was quick to ascribe his survival to God, and interpreted it as evidence that God wanted him to continue preaching his message of healing and prosperity. According to the biblical statements mentioned above, Roberts was right to ascribe his survival to God. His 'reading' of the event beyond that, however, is more open to question. Could it not also be that God had given him life to *repent* of his message of healing and prosperity, or to put in order some personal problems in his life, or even simply to continue to be a husband to his wife? Ultimately, the perfect reading of history implies perfection both in knowledge and in moral judgement. In one way or another, we need God to read history.

And yet, the realization that we can't perfectly read all events should not be taken as conclusive proof that we can't read any. Just as Christians in the past have been eager to see the providence of God in their daily lives, so should we. Whether or not we can 'read' events well according to our questions, we can use them as mnemonics, reminding us of God's actions in and agenda for our lives. We can take occasion to remind ourselves to give thanks, and to repent.

One powerful tool which God has given the believer in this task is the conscience (see Romans 2:15). The conscience often acts as our spiritual ear, or as our eye of faith. In it, we find a part of ourselves which is made to be sensitive to God's pleasure more than our own. In regeneration, God awakens the believer to this spiritual sensitivity. God begins to teach us the vocabulary of his concerns, reorienting us from focusing on ourselves to focusing on him and on others. This has a profound effect on how we understand the happenings of life, whether they are racial tensions (e.g. Ephesians 2:14–18), religious persecutions (e.g. 1 Peter 1:3–2:25), or even death itself (e.g. 1 Thessalonians 4:13).

But most clearly of all, it is in Scripture that God, as it were, both reads history to us and teaches us how to read. He reads history to us through the tremendous sweep of his actions in the nations, and in individuals, as the stories are recounted in the Bible and interpreted according to God's intentions. Though we are not to seek to know God's secret will, that is, what he has declared will happen, God has revealed himself and his moral will to us in Scripture. In Scripture, we learn generally of God's standards, and of the meaning of normal events (e.g. Romans 6:23) and more specifically of the meaning of occasions in the lives of individuals (e.g. Acts 12:19–23; John 9:1–3).

Insofar as he has revealed himself, we should seek to know him. As the Scriptures say, 'The secret things belong to the LORD our God, but the things revealed belong to us and to our children for ever, that we may follow all the words of this law' (Deuteronomy 29:29). Through Scripture, therefore, God also teaches us how to read, though not, of course, as well as he can. Our lack of both the complete sweep of knowledge and perfect moral balance predispose us to perverted, self-centred readings of history. Nevertheless, as we read of his character and will, this revelation of himself is used by his Spirit to re-educate us, to transform our minds (Psalm 19; Romans 12:1–2). Jesus rebuked the religious leaders of his day for understanding meteorology better than they could 'interpret the signs of the times' (Matthew 16:3). The crowds he rebuked for not knowing 'how to interpret this present time' (Luke 12:56). From what God had revealed of his plans, they should have recognized Christ's coming as the coming of the Messiah. So, too, discrete events in our own lives and communities should take on meaning to us as we learn through Scripture to follow God's finger in faith, God's understanding of our lives, as he reveals his plan for our histories, as he teaches us how to live (Deuteronomy 30:15; Micah 6:8).

In all of this the significance of some events – like the vexed question of AIDS with which we began – are clearly left to the individual conscience to discern, according to their honest self-knowledge in the light of God's self-revelation in Scripture. That such individual reading can be difficult is obvious but nonetheless necessary as God continues daily to weave together the events in human history – those more and less obviously meaningful to us – into the rich tapestry of his providential dealings with the world.

Nevertheless, our responsibility to 'read' history in more than in-dividual lives – in the rise and fall of nations and peoples – would seem to be demanded by God's concern with 'the nations' evi-denced from Genesis through the prophets to Revelation. With minds transformed by God's Spirit, re-educated by his Word, living among his people, it would seem that Christians today should accept responsibility for declaring God's concerns to the world in which they find themselves, in the light of the actions which peoples and nations take. Objections to this whole undertaking are rampant in the culture at large and even within the church itself. Can we today go beyond the reading of events as they affect individuals to a Christian reading of history? How would one apply the principles of this chapter to the larger and more complex events of history around us? That is to be the topic of the next chapter.

1 C.S. Lewis, 'Historicism' in *Fern-seed and Elephants* (HarperCollins, 1998), p. 31.

Chapter 21

THE RISE AND FALL OF NATIONS

How far can Christians interpret history?

MICHAEL SCHLUTER

History is not a chaotic, disorderly, fortuitous flux of events, in which there is no pattern or rhythm.

Arnold Toynbee

Summary

In Chapter 20, Mark Dever raised the question of whether it is possible to move beyond seeking God's hand in our personal circumstances to 'reading history' in the rise and fall of nations. This chapter addresses that question.

Christian empiricists, we shall argue, seek to understand historical events through processes of cause and effect, but find the key explanatory factors in biblical moral law. The rise and fall of nations, in political or economic terms, can be traced at least in part to the impact of relational factors in a society's culture, and specifically to the way organizations operate. This puts the onus on to Christians to contribute towards the reform of the society to which they belong.

Interpretations of History

Three main approaches among historians may be distinguished to make sense of the past: the historicist, the individualist and the empiricist. These three provide a helpful framework for considering what may be learnt from biblical teaching about the rise and fall of nations.

The historicist is one who believes history has some hidden purpose, and that some special insight holds the key to its interpretation.

This may be derived from divine revelation, philosophical speculation or scientific observation. For Hegel and the German nationalists there was a mystical Spirit which drove events, while for Marx it was the inexorable laws of dialectical materialism which governed progress from one 'epoch' to the next. The danger is that once a person believes they understand the secret of history, they may believe they can manipulate it. Historicism has too often been the instrument of tyrants.

A second school of historical interpretation might be termed the individualist. Carlyle, for example, in his book *On Heroes*, focused on the role of the individual genius, arguing that his or her significance cannot be understood entirely in terms of the historical circumstances surrounding their emergence. 'Heroes' make a decisive difference to the direction taken by history. Obvious candidates are Alexander the Great, Julius Caesar and Josef Stalin. The world would have been different without them. The danger is that people become politically passive, believing that change must await some messianic saviour. They cease to take responsibility for their own destiny.

A third approach to historical interpretation is the empiricist. No eternal or supernatural plan is at work in the world, it is argued, or if there is, it is inscrutable. And while individuals have influence over historical events, so do technological advance, the distribution of natural resources, and the weather! However, the rational coherence which the scientist discerns in data derived from the natural world, depending as it does on complex chains of cause and effect, can also be observed in social affairs. This falls far short of the kind of all-embracing pattern believed in by the historicist. Gibbon in his *Decline and Fall of the Roman Empire* focused on the structure of social institutions as the key to understanding the rise and fall of Rome. Toynbee also was reluctant to speculate beyond the boundaries of factual data although he clearly believed history 'made sense'.

Biblical teaching gives some endorsement to each of these approaches. The prophets claim a hidden knowledge of where history is going. Amos speaks of God's overruling providence in the affairs of nations other than Israel (e.g. Amos 9:7ff.). Isaiah similarly insists that there is a divine, hidden purpose controlling history. Such inside knowledge of history's meaning, of course, was given only to the prophets, so that it is available to us only at second hand. With hindsight we can see that the Christian historicist Bossuet, writing with the confidence of an Isaiah about events in European history, overestimated his ability to discern the hidden purposes of God.

There is biblical endorsement, also, for the emphasis on the role of the individual. Isaiah sees in Cyrus an individual that God would raise up to accomplish extraordinary historical feats. Cyrus is totally unexpected. So, too, Christians understand the person and work of Jesus. The Incarnation is not the result of socio-economic forces, and yet Jesus changed the course of world history.

While acknowledging the role of these first two approaches to a Christian understanding of history, it is the third which is discussed here. This chapter argues that God deals with societies in an orderly way which can be discerned without prophetic inspiration. The rise and fall of nations can generally be understood as a reflection of their conformity to God's moral law.

Israel's Law as a Social Vision

God is seen in the Old Testament as the creator not just of the human person in the singular but of human society as a collective entity. Human beings are made in God's image. In the moral and civil dimensions of the laws God gave to Israel, after taking into account both the specific historical and covenantal context, the will of God is expressed for the ordering of a society of fallen human beings. God's purposes for social, economic and political life have been revealed, albeit in one specific historical context.

Such a view does not require, or even suggest, literal transposition of individual laws. Christopher Wright has described Israel's law as a 'paradigm', which he defines as a model or example for other cases where a basic principle remains unchanged, although details differ.[1] To move from a thousand years BC to two thousand years AD there is clearly need for careful historical and contemporary social analysis, as well as creativity in identifying underlying principles or norms. However, Christians are encouraged to do so because Jesus regarded the Law as having permanent validity (Matthew 5:17–20). It is technical knowledge and its application, rather than divine or human nature, which have changed over the centuries.

This view of biblical law opens up some intriguing possibilities. If the underlying pattern of Israel's social institutions has general validity, then a normative framework exists within which to develop a social vision. Such a vision is urgently needed in Western democracies, many of which appear to be in an advanced state of social disintegration. For the so-called 'developing countries', the principles of biblical law offer guidelines to help evaluate social policy and prioritize development objectives, urgently required at a time of rapid social and technological transformation.

However, many theologians would not accept the initial premise that Israel's law has contemporary validity. Israel had a unique covenant relationship with God which forms the context of Old Testament law, for which there is no contemporary analogy. So the correct use of the Old Testament law in the New Testament period, they would argue, is to interpret the experience and to order the life of the church which is the true people of God. New Testament support for this understanding cannot be denied. The church is described as 'a holy nation' (1 Peter 2:9), thus drawing a parallel between Old Testament Israel and New Testament church; Paul, too, describes the Galatian church as 'the Israel of God' (Galatians 6:16).

All this seems straightforward, so why the query? The New Testament never suggests a literal parallel between Israel and church; indeed, in some New Testament teaching Israel and church are contrasted. To take one example, Old Testament Israel was a *political* unit, a state, or civil polity. The church was not to be a political entity. So the rules governing the political structure of Israel cannot be expected to apply to the church.

In other significant respects the nation of Israel is unlike the incipient church. God's legal provisions cover cases of murder, theft, adultery, rape, incest and bestiality. As Paul says, such laws are intended not for the just, but for the unjust (1 Timothy 1:9), emphasizing that these laws are not primarily for the church (although one case of incest is recorded in the early church in 1 Corinthians 5). Divorce, too, while permitted by Moses was not part of God's original design, as Jesus points out. It was included only 'because your hearts were hard' (Matthew 19:1–11). The divorce provision was appropriate as a standard of conduct for Israel as a sinful nation, but not for the church as God's elect.

So perhaps the primary analogy lies between the true Israel in the Old Testament, defined as *the faithful remnant* within Israel, and the true church of the New Testament. Jesus emphasizes that it is spiritual rather than physical descent from Abraham which counts before God (John 8:34ff.). Paul often makes the same point. The true Israel are not those with the outward sign of circumcision, but those spiritually circumcised (Romans 2:29); it is the 'faithful remnant' rather than the nation as a whole which prefigures the elect (Romans 11:3–6).

So there is no simple and literal parallel between the nation of Israel and the church. To apply the Law only to the life of the church is to ignore an important dimension of its relevance, just as a reduction of *Romeo and Juliet* to a tale of romantic love would miss out much relating to other themes. The rest of this chapter will now consider how the church might apply those many passages, or aspects of passages, which do not find their primary fulfilment in the life of the church.

Defining the 'Rise and Fall' of Nations

A secular understanding of a nation's rise or fall would generally be measured in terms of material prosperity, specifically economic growth and political influence. The categories provided by biblical law are similar, but wider in scope. They are listed towards the end of the book of Deuteronomy, especially in chapter 28. The rise and fall of nations correspond broadly to what the writer describes as blessings and curses.

Extracting the principle from the detail of the text, obedience to God's law in a society may be said to result in economic prosperity and political status. The blessings listed in Deuteronomy cover livestock and crops, town and country, weather patterns and health. They extend to international relations so that the obedient nation will be in a position to lend, and not require to borrow – what is called in modern parlance a 'balance of payments surplus'. In political terms, the obedient nation will have significance and status, described in terms of being the head and not the tail, the top and not the bottom, and being 'set high among the nations'.

Conversely, disobedience to God's law results in curses in national life, many being the mirror image of the blessings. A society which turns its back on God's law will experience confusion and rebuke. It will be scorned and ridiculed by other nations and will suffer military defeat. Citizens will find themselves overtaken by immigrant communities. There will be widespread frustration and an inability for citizens to enjoy what they have worked for. In particular, there will be acute suffering at the hands of invading armies.

These experiences are to act as a 'sign' to succeeding generations, sending a clear signal that the rise or fall of a society can be traced to its response to the God of Israel and to his law (Deuteronomy 28:46). Possibly, the severity of the consequences may be linked to the privileged covenantal relationship which Israel enjoyed with God. However, the thesis of this chapter is that the results of obedience and disobedience outlined in Deuteronomy are not due entirely to intervention by God from outside the socio-economic order, but arise in part intrinsically, from within the system, as it ceases to function as God intended it should.

The Law's Requirements for Social Organization and Personal Morality

To give a central role to biblical law in the ordering of society is not to follow the route of the theonomists. The ceremonial dimension of each of the laws was for Israel in its covenant relationship; these requirements have been fulfilled in Christ. Sacrifices, Sabbaths and food laws, for example, were part of a system to show Israelites how to approach God and make their lives distinctive from the nations round about. However, the principles underlying the civil and moral dimensions of biblical law have application to all societies (Deuteronomy 4:8), with the caveat that the sanctions imposed for specific breaches of the Law may have been appropriate for the strong family ethos prevailing at the time, rather than representing what is just under all circumstances.

The theme which gives coherence to biblical law, Jesus says, is not economic or financial, but relational. All the law and the prophets 'hang' on the two commandments of loving God and loving neighbour (Matthew 22:34–40). Love is a quality of relationships. Jesus is emphasizing that quality of relationships between God and the individual, and between people, is the key interpretative principle in understanding the Old Testament. It is the basis on which to evaluate public policy as well as personal lifestyle. This emphasis on relationships should hardly be surprising to the Christian: 'The fact that God is Trinity shows that personal relationship is basic reality, that is, that there is nothing more ultimate than personal relationship. Being, carefully considered in itself, is an abstraction. Ultimate, true and real being is and always has been, being-in-personal-relationship.' [2]

Here we can pursue just four areas of application of the insight that quality of relationships is the key to social organization because it is the foundation of obedience to God's law:

Land Is Not Primarily an Asset but a Source of Roots

The contemporary Western view is that land, like any other resource, is worth what you can do with it. In contrast, biblical law recognizes that families need roots in place for cohesion and survival. A close link between land and community is institutionalized through the Jubilee legislation (Leviticus 25). Land was not to be owned by individuals but jointly owned by the family, subject to certain inalienable community rights (e.g. Deuteronomy 23:24–5). Patterns of property ownership play a crucial role in shaping relationships within families and communities: a Cambridge historian has argued it is individual property rights which lie at the heart of English individualism.[3] High rates of population mobility associated with the free market approach to economic development tend gradually to a breakdown in community relationships which runs counter to biblical norms.

Financial Resources Should Be Deployed in a Relational Context

There are problems associated with an interest-based financial system, where the flow of financial resources occurs in impersonal money markets and not primarily on the basis of personal relationship. The Old Testament ban on interest, which would have limited debt finance as we know it today, was not just a concern for the poor; all interest-bearing loans were prohibited except those to foreigners (Deuteronomy 23:19–20). The ban is reinforced by the seventh-year debt remission, further discouraging lending outside the family and community context. The relational overview given by Jesus suggests that the primary purpose of the ban was to maintain financial interdependence as a form of bonding within families and neighbourhoods. For if you had surplus funds in Israelite society, and could not lend them at interest, the alternatives were either to invest them yourself or to lend them to a friend to invest on a profit-sharing basis. A further consequence of the ban would be to ensure economic power did not accumulate in a few hands, for one side-effect of an interest-based financial system is to funnel funds to those who already have the greatest wealth, and who thus appear to offer the greatest security.

Political Power, Like Economic Power, Should Be Widely Spread

The distribution of political power in a society impacts on the economic system through the size and culture of the government's bureaucracy, government allocation of income and expenditure, the degree of urban bias in economic policy, and the level of commitment to family and community self-reliance. While centralizing political power often has advantages in international relations and trade, biblical law is strongly committed to decentralization both in the Deuteronomic code (e.g. Deuteronomy 17:14–20) and in the prophetic tradition (e.g. 1 Samuel 8; 1 Kings 21). Diffused political power gives much greater opportunities for direct and indirect participation in decision-making, strengthening local solidarity and inculcating a sense of responsibility and civic duty among the citizenry. At the same time, it acts as a key constraint on the arbitrary use of power by a head of state, which surely has been one of the greatest curses of society down the ages.

Public Behaviour Is Determined By Private Morality

The Ten Commandments may be regarded as the summary of these norms; they are specified in greater detail elsewhere in Old Testament law. They include a demand for personal honesty and integrity and detailed rules to govern sexual relations, patterns of respect and even personal attitudes within the family. These laws, both of social organization and of personal morality, are closely bound up with the relationship which the individual, and wider society, has with God himself. Love for God and neighbour is tied explicitly and constantly to rejection of idolatry; the vertical cannot be separated from the horizontal.

Contemporary Experience of Social Change

There is a growing body of evidence today for the central importance of right relationships – in both a personal and an institutional context – to economic and political success and environmental stability. Douglass North has been awarded a Nobel prize for his work in this area.[4] He argues that the economic cost structure in any society is determined partly by resource endowments of land, labour and capital, which determine 'transformation costs', and partly by information and contract enforcement costs which he labels 'transaction costs'. The latter, he estimates, now amount to almost half of total costs in the United States economy.

The main factor influencing the level of transaction costs is the way institutions operate. He defines 'institutions' as the rules – formal and informal – which govern the behaviour of organizations and individuals. As so many of these rules are determined by the culture and are not written down, they are difficult to change quickly and not easily susceptible to political manipulation. Thus, a long-term movement towards or away from biblical values in a society is likely to have a major impact on economic performance and the political structure of that society through its influence on the institutional framework. This suggests it was changes in public morality arising from the Reformation, not simply the work ethic of the Weber–Tawney thesis, which gave rise to the industrial revolution.

Examples of these patterns of performance abound, despite the five caveats listed below. Space permits only one or two examples, with all the dangers of abbreviated generalizations. The relative decline in economic performance and political influence of the United States and Britain can be traced to growing secularization of the culture and its impact on public and private morality. In North's terms, lack of trust, integrity and initiative is raising transaction costs and undermining international competitive advantage. The poor economic performance of Africa, despite full churches, may be linked to the failure to transfer biblical teaching into public life. Power is highly centralized and corruption is rife. There is generally not the trust between ethnic groups, nor between individuals beyond the limits of family loyalty, to provide the platform necessary for the capital made available by the West to be employed efficiently. If this analysis is right, it is more urgent for the church to apply biblical teaching so as to transform public and private morality than for the development agencies to pump in further capital. (Capital, however, is still needed, especially for infrastructure development.)

Five Caveats

While a nation's response to biblical law results in either social benefit or decay, the causal relationship is often obscured by a number of factors:

In Old Testament Israel the prophets constantly threaten God's *future* judgement as a result of the people's *present* apostasy. Indeed, if there were no time lag between apostasy and judgement, so that the two were obviously and directly correlated, a significant element of human free will would be lost. The same time lags occur today. Often it takes several generations for a capitalist economy to break down traditional family loyalties, as is evident in Japan today. However, the time-frame required for such changes may be gradually declining as technological change accelerates.

Where a society has had little Christian influence, obedience or disobedience just to the second table of the Law, summed up in 'love your neighbour as yourself', may well be the key factor determining the degree of national prosperity.

The apparently inexorable trend towards social disintegration is not inevitable. There was always the opportunity for national renewal in Old Testament Israel (e.g. 2 Chronicles 7:13ff.; Isaiah 58), and there is today for contemporary societies. In Britain we have seen it happen in the eighteenth and nineteenth centuries; it could happen again today.

The operation of biblical law does not guarantee a clear interpretation of national or international events. There will always be a measure of inscrutability in human affairs, as the writer of Ecclesiastes reminds us. Nations acting in conformity with biblical law will be more robust than otherwise, but will not necessarily be immune from threats posed by international disasters or dictators.

Old Testament laws do not prescribe all aspects of culture. Nor does commitment to a biblical social vision determine the priorities and timescale for social reform. Agreement on *principles* for national prosperity does not imply or necessitate agreement on the *policies* needed for their implementation; principles translate into goals, while policy is a matter of means, not ends.

Conclusion

The social pattern given in biblical law provides the basis to interpret the broad sweep of historical development for particular societies. God judges nations within time, just as he judges individuals outside time. The process of discernment is complicated by the five factors listed above, but in many cases history is not impossible to interpret. On this understanding, there is more of contemporary relevance for the preacher to draw out of Old Testament teaching on society than is generally appreciated. Biblical law enables us to understand and critique our society far more effectively than the historical dialectic of Marx or the evolutionary models of social change now in vogue, such as those of neo-classical economics and capitalist ideology.

The ability to evaluate a nation's social system by the norms of Scripture is what makes it possible to describe Christians today as being in the tradition of the Old Testament prophets (Matthew 5:11–12). Christians are not to be under the influence of dictators with a determinist view of history, nor to be passive passengers waiting for a national hero – or even a religious revival – before attempting social reform. Their task is to get on with tackling social and moral decay (Matthew 5:13–16). The factors to which Christians attribute the rise and fall of nations do not just influence how they understand the past, but become an important factor governing how they respond to the social problems of the present. That is why it matters how Christians interpret history.

1 Christopher J.H. Wright, *Living as the People of God* (IVP, 1983), p. 43.
2 D. Broughton Knox, *The Everlasting God* (Lancer Books, Australia, 1988), p. 130.
3 Alan Macfarlane, *The Origins of English Individualism* (Blackwell, Oxford, 1978).
4 For example, Douglass C. North, *Institutions, Institutional Change and Economic Performance* (Cambridge University Press, 1990).

Chapter 22

JERUSALEM

At the Centre of God's Plans?

PETER WALKER

If you, even you, had only known on this day what would bring you
peace...

Jesus speaking of Jerusalem in Luke 19:42,
the week before his death

This is the most holy land.

Yigal Amir, in the *Washington Post*,
five months before his assassination of
Yitzhak Rabin in November 1995

Summary

In the light of Old Testament history and prophecy, many would
argue that Jerusalem continues to have a central role within God's
purposes today. Yet the New Testament offers a radically new perspective on the city, pointing to Christ as the true temple and the
one in whom the promises of restoration were fulfilled. Jesus himself predicts the imminent end of the temple. The consequences
of this biblical teaching prove to be far-reaching – both for the
church's mission in the world and for religious and political issues
in Jerusalem today.

Introduction

During 1996 there were celebrations in Jerusalem to mark the
3,000th anniversary of David's founding of his capital city. That
was also the year when discussions were supposed to start between

the Israelis and the Palestinians concerning the political status of Jerusalem as part of the Oslo Peace Accord. For various reasons, however (not least the three-year premiership of Benjamin Netanyahu until May 1999), those discussions are still on hold. The issue of Jerusalem is a major modern issue, but its roots lie far back in the past.

For Christians the issue of Jerusalem raises many questions. How does our faith in Christ affect our attitude to this unique city? What precisely is the significance of Jerusalem in God's purposes? Should the events of 1948 (the birth of the state of Israel) and 1967 (the unification of Jerusalem under Jewish rule) be seen as instances of fulfilled prophecy? How much should we support Israel or Zionism? Does it matter to us as Christians who controls Jerusalem? How should we 'pray for Jerusalem' (Psalm 122:6)?

Christian opinion has become polarized, and sympathy with either the Jewish or Arab situation can colour our responses to the Scriptures. Yet, although biblical passages may be distorted in this debate, the Bible must remain the normative foundation. How are we to understand Jerusalem today in the light of biblical teaching?

Jerusalem is undoubtedly sacred in the OT period. Unlike any other city, God endorsed David's choice of Jerusalem and established Solomon's temple as the place where 'his name dwelt' (e.g. 1 Kings 8:29); Mount Zion, the mountain on which the temple was built, became a symbol of God's dwelling among his people.

This was affirmed by Jesus: Jerusalem was 'the city of the Great King' (Matthew 5:35) and the temple was truly God's 'house' (Mark 11:17; John 2:16). Speaking to the Samaritan woman he affirmed Jerusalem's centrality (John 4:22); yet he also said, 'a time is coming when you will worship the Father neither on this mountain nor in Jerusalem' (v. 21). What precisely was the nature of the change he foresaw? Was Jesus simply making a positive point (that God's Spirit would be known everywhere)? Or was he also making a negative point, namely that Jerusalem's previously unique role had now ceased? This chapter argues that the coming of Jesus did indeed significantly change the status of Jerusalem.

From the Old to the New: the Example of the Temple

Any interpretation of the Bible has to discern the relationship between the Old and New Testaments. Those who affirm the Bible's unity and coherence acknowledge that there are certain dramatic shifts between the Testaments. For example, the 'people of God' is no longer defined ethnically but through faith in Jesus, Israel's Messiah, thus opening the door to Gentile believers (Acts 10; Galatians 3:28). Jerusalem needs to be seen in this category: there *is* an element of discontinuity between Old and New Testaments. As a result, OT material on this theme can only be rightly understood when read through the lens of the New.

The clearest example of this is the temple. In Hebrews the temple is only an 'illustration' (9:9) or a 'copy and shadow' (8:5) of the reality now found in Christ and of the access into God's presence now made possible through his sacrificial death (9:28; 10:10, 19–20). Yet this inevitably means that the Jerusalem temple, as an integral part of the 'first covenant' (8:7), has lost its previous status (9:8) and will 'soon disappear' (8:13).

Other NT writers also re-evaluate the temple. John teaches that Jesus is the true 'tabernacle' or 'temple' (John 1:14; 2:21). Paul goes further, identifying Christian believers as God's temple (1 Corinthians 3:17; 6:19). In Revelation the 'New Jerusalem' has no temple 'because the Lord God Almighty and the Lamb are its temple' (Revelation 21:22). The reference to the 'river of the water of life' (Revelation 22:1–2) indicates that the author is reworking the prophecy of Ezekiel (chapter 40ff.) which spoke of a renewed temple, seemingly in Jerusalem. The Seer, however, understands this to be a reference to the New Jerusalem and to the Lamb who is its temple (cf. also John 7:37–9). The NT writers were thus not expecting some 'end-time' temple to be rebuilt in Jerusalem, because Jesus was now that temple.

Jesus claimed to be 'greater than the temple' (Matthew 12:6) and in cleansing the temple was probably signalling its imminent end. He certainly predicts this (e.g. Luke 19:43; Mark 14:58). Thus, although the temple's destruction in AD 70 was a tragic event, Christians were not unduly disturbed by this. They had been prepared by Jesus' teaching.

Whether, then, the temple is thought of as the place which embodied God's presence on earth or as the place of sacrifice, the New Testament affirms that both aspects have been fulfilled in Jesus: his death is the true sacrifice and his person the true *locus* of God's dwelling. By extension, Christian believers too may be seen as a temple. A temple in Jerusalem is therefore no longer necessary, for God's eternal purposes have now been revealed in Christ. Yet if this is the case for the temple, which constituted the central, sacred part of Jerusalem, what about Jerusalem itself (the city considered *apart* from the temple)? Might not that too need to be viewed in a new light?

Jerusalem in the New Testament

The Evidence

'The present city of Jerusalem ... is in slavery with her children' (Galatians 4:25). This startling statement suggests that Paul would have answered the above question in the affirmative. For a Jew of Paul's background to speak thus of Judaism's 'mother city' testifies to a radical shift in perspective. For Christians the focus is now to be upon 'the Jerusalem that is above ... and *she* is our mother' (Galatians 4:26). This proves to be an opening salvo of a re-evaluation of Jerusalem which is found in all the NT writers.

In Mark's gospel (as in Matthew and John) the centrality of Jerusalem is offset by an emphasis on Galilee (including the appearance of the risen Jesus there) which underlines the outgoing nature of the gospel, no longer confined to Jerusalem. In John, Jerusalem is presented as no different from 'the world', the place where Jesus is rejected by 'his own' (cf. 1:10–11). Matthew, with his innate loyalty to Judaism, refers to Jerusalem as the 'holy city' (4:5; 27:53), but this description includes a dose of savage irony. In his version of the wedding banquet, those who murder the king's servants are punished with the burning of 'their city' (22:7). 'O Jerusalem, Jerusalem,' says Jesus, 'you who kill the prophets ...' (23:37ff.). The supposedly 'holy city' has proved itself to be quite the opposite.

Of all the Evangelists, Luke brings the theme of Jerusalem's fate most centrally into his narrative. Indeed, the structure of Luke–Acts is based on Jesus' going up to Jerusalem (Luke), followed by the apostles' going out from Jerusalem 'to the ends of the earth' (Acts). Comparatively early within his gospel, Jesus 'resolutely set out for Jerusalem' (Luke 9:51), 'for surely no prophet can die outside Jerusalem!' (13:33). Jerusalem proves to be the place which 'did not recognise the time of God's coming' and which therefore in the future would experience divine judgement (19:41–4; cf. 21:20–24; 23:28–31).

After the resurrection the disciples witnessed to Christ in Jerusalem, but soon many of them were 'scattered' by persecution (Acts 8:1). Those associated with James who felt called to remain there (signifying that faith in Jesus as Messiah was not marginal to Judaism) found themselves in an increasingly difficult situation (Acts 15:5; 21:20ff.). After his description of Paul's going up (like Jesus) to Jerusalem and experiencing rejection, Luke's narrative turns away from the city. Paul's journey to Rome thus signals a shift in God's purposes away from Jerusalem and into the wider imperial world. Jerusalem has now had its day.

The author of Hebrews similarly reflects on Jesus' being rejected by Jerusalem 'outside the city gate' (13:12) and, like Paul, focuses his readers' attention on the 'heavenly Jerusalem' (12:22). This, not the earthly Jerusalem, is to be central to their identity: 'let us go to him *outside* the camp … For here we do not have an enduring city, but we are looking for the city that is to come' (13:13–14). The book of Revelation sets the seal on this re-evaluation of Jerusalem by seeing the city 'where the Lord was crucified' as no better than the 'great city' of Rome and worthy of being 'called Sodom and Egypt' (11:8). Christians are to focus not on the earthly Jerusalem, but on the 'Holy City, the New Jerusalem, coming down out of heaven from God' (21:2, 10; cf. 3:12).

The above evidence, albeit briefly stated, thus confirms that Jesus' words in John 4 (outlined above) most probably include a negative conclusion concerning Jerusalem. Just as the temple needed to be seen in a new light after the coming of Jesus (John 2), so did the *city* of Jerusalem (John 4).

The Reasons

What caused these predominantly Jewish writers to make such an about-turn on this previously central concept of Jerusalem? Supremely, it was their conviction about Jesus. If Jesus was Israel's Messiah, indeed God's 'Son', then his rejection by Jerusalem, the supposed 'city of God', was no small matter. When Jerusalem then confirmed this negative response to Jesus in its attitude towards his followers, the stage was set for a Christian critique of Jerusalem.

This critique goes back to Jesus himself, who gave a prophetic warning of the city's destiny. Jesus' critique may well, like Jeremiah's (Matthew 16:14), have included an indictment of contemporary practice in the city. Luke indeed suggests that there was an inherent clash between Jesus and Jerusalem. Jerusalem was the place where opposition to Jesus reached its climax, not least because Jesus was claiming to assume the role that previously Jerusalem had thought was distinctively her own – the place of God's presence. Jesus came embodying a counter-system, and people were forced to make a choice. Now that Jesus had come, Jerusalem could never be the same again.

The rapid spread of the gospel message would have contributed further to this playing down of Jerusalem's significance. God's purposes had evidently now broken out from the particular to the universal. If Jewish particularities such as circumcision were no longer essential for Gentile Christians, then the specificity of Jerusalem was likewise undercut. Moreover, the new awareness of spiritual realities would have made it easier for Christians to focus on the spiritual Jerusalem and 'things above' (cf. Colossians 3:1–2). Christian interest in the earthly Jerusalem thus began to wane. Jerusalem's destruction in AD 70 then confirmed this process. Yet the causes of this critique preceded that event. The church had already learnt from its master that it lived in a new age – 'the time of the new order' (Hebrews 9:10).

Conclusions

The New Testament therefore witnesses to a shift in attitude towards Jerusalem. It affirmed the special nature of Jerusalem's past, but it denied its continuing role in the present. The city had now lost its strictly sacred status. This was chiefly because of God's eternal purposes now revealed in Jesus. Yet there was also a sense of God's judgement upon the city – not least because of its response to Jesus.

The fate of Jerusalem thus had a message for all people. First, it demonstrated how God could take away a divine gift. Jeremiah (chapter 7) had foreseen how Jerusalem and its temple could paradoxically become an idol, a bastion against God, leading inexorably to God's judgement (as previously with Shiloh: v. 12). The pattern had now been repeated, but this time there was no promise of restoration. As Augustine said in another context, 'the corruption of the best is the worst'. Jerusalem, for all its divine pedigree, had now been removed.

Second, the fall of Jerusalem gave a foretaste of what awaited the whole world. This link between the fates of Jerusalem and the world at the 'end of the age' is seen most clearly in the Apocalyptic Discourse (Mark 13) where Jesus' prediction of the former becomes entwined with his teaching about the latter. Jerusalem would be judged, but so would the world. Such a consideration would then make Jerusalem's history relevant to all NT readers. It would undercut any incipient pride among Gentiles, gloating over Jerusalem's fall. It would also indicate what lay in store for those who had not taken refuge in Jesus, the one who had already borne in his own body the judgement which he had predicted was awaiting Jerusalem. The resurrection of Jesus was the promise of a way through that judgement. Yet, above all, Jerusalem's fall spelt the end of the city's significance. From that day forward, the divine focus was upon Jesus, not Jerusalem.

Alternative Christian Approaches

Jerusalem, however, exerts a perennial fascination upon the religious spirit. It is very alluring, and easily becomes entwined with people's fundamental convictions and identity. Within the Christian Church this has been justified in two quite distinct ways.

On the one hand, from the time of Constantine onwards (AD 325) Christians emphasized again Jerusalem's holiness through focusing in a sacramental way on the holy places of the Incarnation. This has characterized the approach to Jerusalem of the historic churches ever since. Historical association is powerful, and the belief that the Incarnation occurred in one specific locality a potent belief. Yet few today would wish to give a theological defence of the Crusades – the extreme end-result of such thinking. Instead, John's gospel presents Jesus himself as the ultimate 'holy place' where we encounter God, and access to him is fully possible by the Spirit.[1] There is, therefore, a limit to how much one may legitimately emphasize Jerusalem on this score. We do not deny that the city has a unique place in Christian memory, but we question whether this can become the basis for ascribing to the city an explicitly *theo*logical status, as somehow central within God's purposes today.

On the other hand, in the modern period many Christians have adhered to some form of Zionism – the belief that Zion/Jerusalem and the Land continue to be central in God's purpose and that it is appropriate for them to be in Jewish hands. The above presentation, they would say, emphasizes discontinuity too much at the expense of continuity. Does not the Old Testament plainly indicate that Jerusalem will retain a sacred role in God's purposes for all time (see e.g. Isaiah 2:2–3; 60ff.; Zechariah 12–14)? Are there not NT verses which indicate a distinctive role for Jerusalem, perhaps at the 'end-time' (see Romans 11:26; Luke 21:24; 2 Thessalonians 2:4; Revelation 20:9)? Such questions require some further comment.

Zionism and Jerusalem

Detailed treatment of these last four NT texts can be found in several recent books.[2] Motyer, for example, argues that Paul's (significantly adapted) quotation in Romans 11:26 of Isaiah 59:20 ('the deliverer will come *from* Zion') refers not to Christ's *second* coming from Jerusalem but rather to his *first* – when, as foreseen by Isaiah, the gospel would go out to the 'Gentiles' (v. 25) 'from Zion' (cf. Isaiah 2:3). Paul was not saying anything about the role of Zion in the future, only that the gospel had come 'from Zion'. This one text cannot therefore be used as the basis for constructing an end-times scenario of Israel's conversion in or near Jerusalem. The other three verses similarly offer fragile foundation for the massive construction built upon them. It is too easy for Jesus' plain warnings against end-time speculation (Mark 13:32–7) to be disregarded in the desire for prophetic certainty about the future.

On the former question (concerning OT references to Jerusalem) it is imperative that the Old is read in the light of the New. Some significant points on this are made by Chris Wright. The specific call of Abraham (Genesis 12:2) must be seen as God's remedy for the sin of *all* humankind (Genesis 3–11): 'election involves use of particular means, but for a universal goal'. It is not therefore illegitimate to see a fulfilment in Christ of something which in the Old Testament was cast in a more physical and particular form: for the OT writers necessarily used physical terms which were familiar to their audiences, while at the same time investing those terms with a wider, more spiritual reference. Thus 'Jerusalem' in the later chapters of Isaiah signifies something more than the physical city, becoming a term for God's people in their eschatological fullness. There was an 'awareness that although the future had to be described in concepts drawn from Israel's historic nationhood, it would in fact ultimately transcend them'.

Wright then uses a telling example: a father who in 1890 had promised to give a horse to his infant son on his twenty-first birthday but who then gave him a car instead (because this had been invented in the meantime) might with good reason be annoyed if his son then asked for a horse as well!

> This surely is what literalistic and dispensationalist ... treatments do when they argue that OT prophecies still await a literal fulfilment to match their original predictive form, when the New Testament actually declares such prophecies to have been fulfilled in the coming of Jesus Christ, even though in surprising ways.[3]

Of particular importance is the fact that the New Testament expressly deals with the issue of Israel's prophesied 'restoration'. Even though first-century Jews were in the Land, there was a real sense that the OT prophecies had not been completely fulfilled and that Israel was still in exile (cf. Luke 2:25, 38). Different Jewish groups, such as the Zealots, sought to rectify this anomaly. The New Testament gives its own distinctive answer: Israel's destiny and promised restoration has been fulfilled in the death and resurrection of her Messiah and in the outpouring of the Spirit. Thus in Luke 24 Jesus refers to his rising on the 'third day' as being 'written' in the Scriptures (v. 46). Most probably this refers to Hosea 6:2, which had spoken of *Israel's* being 'revived' and 'restored'. Thus 'the resurrection of Christ *is* the resurrection of Israel of which the prophets spoke'.[4] Meanwhile Jesus' earlier reference to many people coming 'from the east and the west' (Matthew 8:10–12) evokes passages (such as Isaiah 43:5–7; Psalm 107:2–3) which seemingly had referred to a future 'restoration' of Jewish people to the Land.

> Jesus, however, took OT prophecies which had that connotation and applied them instead to the ingathering of the Christian community, even in this case, to the exclusion of some Jews.[5]

This would then explain why a key passage about restoration (Amos 9:11–12) was used by James to justify the gospel's going out to the Gentiles (Acts 15:13–21).

The considered apostolic interpretation of events was that the inclusion of the Gentiles… was the necessary fulfilment of the prophesied
restoration of Israel.[6]

Thus, although they were faced with the same OT passages as we
are today, NT writers did not reach a 'Zionist' conclusion. Instead
they reached a distinctively Christian conclusion which affirmed
the faithfulness of God to his ancient promises and saw these as
now fulfilled, even if in an unexpected way, in the coming of Jesus
and the Spirit. Biblical Christians today need to follow their lead. To
do otherwise (either denying this fulfilment in Jesus, or seeking for a
further, more literalistic fulfilment) belittles and misconstrues the
greatness of what God has done in Jesus and is ultimately deroga-
tory to the person of Jesus and his uniqueness.

Moreover, it runs counter to the teaching of Jesus himself. Despite his natural identification with the aspirations of his own people, Jesus consistently refused to endorse interpretations which led
to an exclusive Jewish nationalism or a belief in God's purposes
being supremely fulfilled in a politically independent Jewish state.
Why was it that Jesus was opposed to the emerging Zealot movement and those who wished for a more politically active Messiah?
Was it just a disagreement over method (pacifism, not armed resistance) or of timing (as some would interpret Acts 1:6–8)? Or was it,
rather, a fundamental critique of the movement's ideology and its
whole hermeneutical framework which did not allow that God was
fulfilling his ancient promises *in Jesus himself*? In his role both as
Messiah and as the one in whom Israel was restored, Jesus was thus
giving a radical new twist to the story of Israel, confounding the
biblical expectations of his contemporaries.

Zionist Christians tend to ignore this NT teaching on restoration
(as well as central claims such as the true 'children of Abraham'
being those who have faith in Jesus: Romans 4; Galatians 3). In part
this is caused by a laudable desire to draw alongside modern
Judaism – especially in the light of the racial anti-Semitism which,
despite the Jewishness of Jesus, has too frequently entered Christian
tradition in disgraceful ways. Yet in seeking to witness to Jesus as
Israel's Messiah and in the name of loving identification, is there not
a real danger that Christians will go too far in endorsing readings of
the Old Testament which ignore the teaching of the New?

With regard to Jerusalem, it is thus hard to see how Christians can share Jewish affection for the city without some major qualifications. Likewise, while some Jewish people might be interested in the rebuilding of the temple, it is quite bizarre that Christians should be supporting them. Does the *Christian* Bible really require a rebuilt temple or give Jewish people a divine charter of ownership over Jerusalem? For ethical and historical reasons, one may have great sympathy with Zionism and the Jewish desire for a homeland at a political level. Yet surely at the *theological* level Christians must be pointing beyond Jerusalem to the reality of Jesus as Israel's Messiah. Despite the temptation to have it both ways, elevating the importance of Jerusalem may serve, albeit unintentionally, to detract from the significance of Jesus. Indeed, if (as suggested above) there is an inherent clash in the gospels between Jesus and Jerusalem, then it may indeed be impossible to promote both claims simultaneously.

Ultimately this is precisely the Christian's responsibility – to emphasize that Jesus is greater than Jerusalem. Moreover, the realization that the political possession of Jerusalem does not provide the longed-for solution to the deep questions of Jewish identity might conceivably be the means by which Jewish people are opened up to him who alone *does* provide that solution. God may indeed still have loving purposes towards the Jewish people, but who is to say that his chosen means of revealing that love must be Zionism's success, rather than its failure? For the Hebrew prophets only ever envisaged a return to the land as an outer sign of the more important return of the people to their God, and in the light of the New Testament that means *to Jesus*. Could not God then be desiring to show the fragility and self-contradiction of a Zionism which has largely been quite secular and which still ignores the Messiah? The twentieth-century return to the Land would then have been within God's providential purposes, but precisely because only so could it be known, not just in theory but in personal experience, that the Land was no longer the answer. As in the first century, so now: Jewish identity can only find its resolution in the Messiah, not in the Land or in Jerusalem.

Practical Implications for Jerusalem

Thus in the light of the New Testament some questions may legitimately be raised about the centrality which is given to Jerusalem by so many people. Precisely because of this over-emphasis, the city today has become a political battleground, fuelled by religious convictions. In such heightened circumstances, has not the time come for the many competing voices which enthuse over Jerusalem to hear again the central message of the New Testament – the uniqueness of Jesus? But with the departure of Jesus from the city, the 'glory has departed' (cf. Ezekiel 11:23 with Luke 24:50–51; 1 Samuel 4:21). How much of Jerusalem's painful history is a desire to possess something of the divine which is no longer there?

Such a stance might seem to encourage a disengagement from concern for Jerusalem; and in a diplomatic context it might appear self-defeating. Yet, rightly understood, it leads to a proper engagement and a way forward for a creative peace. For if, despite its special historical associations, Jerusalem has no *theo*logical status today which sets it apart from any other city, then the normative pattern of God's will as revealed in the Scriptures must apply in Jerusalem just as much as anywhere else. There are, as it were, no special rules for Jerusalem. The value of this insight can be seen in three areas.

Christians in Jerusalem

As in any other place, God's purposes are focused on Jesus and the Spirit. The doctrine of the Holy Trinity and its evangelistic consequences cannot be set aside for the sake of Jerusalem. Yet in practice this is hard. The tiny Christian community is surrounded by two larger communities, both of which for centuries have denied what Christians claim took place in first-century Jerusalem: the Incarnation and the resurrection. Not surprisingly, alternative theologies have been developed, be they of an interfaith variety or of a two-covenant kind (where God has a separate covenant with Judaism, independent of faith in Messiah Jesus). Such theologies, convenient in the short term, subvert the church's obedience to the Great Commission (Matthew 28:19). Jerusalem cannot demand this sacrifice, or be allowed to quell again the testimony of Jesus. Real support and prayerful understanding need therefore to be shown to the city's tiny and struggling Christian community as it seeks to uphold the name of him who once was crucified there.

Second, Jesus' desire that his followers be united (John 17:21) cannot be dismissed as inapplicable in Jerusalem. This speaks not only to the (increasingly healthy) relationships between the many historic churches all represented in the city, but also in a particular way to the divide between Jewish and Arab believers. Though the city's recent history has tended to re-erect it, the 'dividing-wall of hostility' between Jew and Gentile (Ephesians 2:14) was actually broken in Jerusalem at the cross. The number of Palestinian Christians (c.10,000) may sadly be decreasing, but there is an increased number of Messianic Jews in the city (c. 2,000–3,000). This means that in years to come Jerusalem could witness in a unique way to the overcoming of this ancient division, and open up a whole new episode in the church's history in Jerusalem.

Yet, at least till recently, the political division between Jew and Arab has made this virtually impossible. Moreover, given their vulnerability, both sides have tended to make common cause with their respective majority communities (with Arab Christians endorsing Muslim political agendas for Jerusalem, and Jewish believers endorsing Israel's). Not only is this process in itself fraught with danger, but it results in an inevitable collision. Our argument for the theological priority of Jesus over Jerusalem then becomes crucial. To focus on Jerusalem, rather than on Jesus, can only divide the body of Christ.

If reconciliation and unity in Christ (Ephesians 1:10; cf. 2 Corinthians 5:18) still stand as God's purpose for the world and therefore for Jerusalem, it may be that, despite all the continued obstacles, the body of Christ in Jerusalem has a particular calling to act as 'leaven'. Perhaps God has brought back into such close proximity within Jerusalem those who through history have often been bitter enemies for a distinct reason – to reveal that unity which alone can be found in Jesus?

Biblical Ethics in Jerusalem

As in any other place, God intends that people should 'act justly, love mercy and walk humbly with their God' (Micah 6:8). Again, Jerusalem is not so sacred as to be exempt. Yet for many centuries Jerusalem has encouraged in each of the faiths a Crusader spirit, which in the name of holiness leads to its precise opposite. The belief that Jerusalem is 'holy to God' becomes a mandate to possess it 'in his name' and then to be aggressive to any opponents. Paradoxically, treating Jerusalem as specially 'holy' can thus lead instead to its desecration.

This belief in the inherent holiness of the Land (and of Jerusalem) led to Yitzhak Rabin's assassination. Once a person's construction of God's agenda has become merged with their own, then the unethical becomes seemingly legitimate: murder, terrorism, the demonizing of those who oppose a particular nationalism (labelled as 'Zionist' or 'Philistine'), or the appropriation of land. Palestinians, for example, thus have good reason to believe that the same logic is undergirding the current government policy which denies access to Jerusalem for the vast majority of West Bank residents (such that Christians whose families have lived for 600 years in Bethlehem cannot visit Jerusalem, only five miles away).

Similar reasoning is at work among those Christians whose convictions about the holiness of Jerusalem and the Land are based on interpreting OT prophecy without adequate New Testament control. Prophetic interpretation becomes the basis for a political programme, which too easily becomes unethical, ignoring the humanity of those who live there. Our thesis is that a responsible reading of the Bible does not encourage such interpretations. Yet even if, contrary to our argument, there are prophecies which do await a literal fulfilment in Jerusalem, such a prophetic end could never justify unethical means. If it could, then by the same reasoning Judas Iscariot would have to be reinstated as a hero! So too would Rabin's assassin, Yigal Amir.

Those who major on the OT predictive prophecies about Zion should remember that it was precisely the ignoring of ethical considerations under a subterfuge of sanctity which fuelled the prophets' fury: For we will all be judged, not for the rightness of our theology about Jerusalem, but rather for the 'fruit of our lives' (Matthew 7:15–23).

Instead, the true prophetic vision which should fire Christian imagination – in Jerusalem as indeed throughout the world – is that of the 'heavenly, New Jerusalem', causing us to create societies which anticipate the healing and renewal which one day God will bring to pass. 'Yet what better place to do this,' asks Tom Wright, 'than in the old city of peace, Jerusalem?'[7] Whereas the supposed sacredness of Jerusalem may blind people to their ethical responsibilities in the city, this simple acknowledgement (that Jerusalem played a key role in the biblical story) should have the opposite effect. For here, above all, it would be ironic if the biblical message went unheeded, but so appropriate if it was obeyed. 'Righteousness exalts a nation' (Proverbs 14:34).

Jerusalem and the Church

How then can the world-wide church give expression to its indebtedness to Jerusalem without falling into the dangers associated with either the Crusades or extreme Zionism? What is the attitude to Jerusalem which appropriately reflects the priority we should give to Jesus Christ?

First and foremost, we need to express a greater solidarity with the city's indigenous Christian communities (both Palestinian and Jewish). That such communities even exist is a surprise to many in the West – not least because each year myriad Christian tourists are whisked through the country under the auspices of non-Christian guides. Focus on the ancient stones blinds them to the 'living stones' (1 Peter 2:5) – their fellow-believers. God indeed has a temple in Jerusalem today, but it is not a physical one.

Second, while being as sympathetic as possible, we must not too simplistically endorse either Islamic or Jewish theologies and agendas. Some Christian support of the Palestinian cause is no longer distinctively Christian; likewise some manifestations of Christian support for Israel. Why are we left undisturbed by the fact that some Jewish Christians are prevented from becoming Israeli citizens and that the Palestinian Christian community is haemorrhaging into non-existence through emigration? Who do we really think are God's people in the Middle East? The Christian community in Jerusalem (Jew and Gentile) may be tiny and often pressurized to endorse alternative agendas, but the world-wide church with its enormous influence need not be so coerced and could strengthen the indigenous church in its distinctive witness.

In particular, Christian supporters of Israel need to be aware of the consequences of their theology. That which may make them feel better in the comfort of their Western homes (with their particular interpretation of Scripture and their sense of involvement with God's purposes both being affirmed) may lead to suffering on the ground. As one Arab pastor put it, 'it is hard to be told that the return of my Lord Jesus will only take place when I have been expelled from my ancestral home'.

More questions therefore need to be asked in the church about Christian Zionism – at least in its more extreme forms. What are its real, unspoken reasons for supporting Israel? How truly can it claim the high ground of renouncing anti-Semitism, or is it showing a greater interest in the end-times than a genuine, compassionate concern for the Jewish people themselves? Is some such form of Zionism the only way in which Christians can express their eternal debt to Judaism and their special bond of affection for Jewish people? And how does it affect the church's relationship with Islam? Above all, in what ways does Christian Zionist theology serve to promote the gospel, or does Christ's death and resurrection somehow get marginalized in the heady atmosphere of eschatology? Is there not a danger that focusing on Jerusalem and Israel weakens concern for the world-wide church, financially impoverishes its mission, and effectively detracts from the significance of Jesus?

Beyond Jerusalem 3,000: Jesus 2,000!

During the 1990s the Peace Process had some significant effects – though not nearly as many as some would have wished. Nevertheless, it brought into focus for many the fact that the goal of a 'greater Israel' cannot so easily be achieved. As a result, some Jewish rabbis are speaking of 'post-Zionism', the frank acceptance that this dream will not be fulfilled. Meanwhile, the Palestinian dream of a larger homeland has also tacitly been laid aside. Both sides are coming to terms with the collapse of cherished ideals. Will a similar pragmatism prevail whenever – *if* ever – there start to be discussions about the status of Jerusalem? Some have likened this to the heart which is shared by two Siamese twins. Can the city be shared, or will the respective idolizations of Jerusalem prove too strong for any compromise – such that one of the twins has to die?

Yet in this painful situation, where ideals are having to be surrendered, one wonders if the God of surprises might not be mysteriously at work. Might those who have set their heart too intently on Jerusalem now come to see him who is truly at the centre of God's plans? Nearly 2,000 years ago God did something in Jerusalem which affected it for ever: 'See, I lay *in Zion* a stone that causes people to stumble' (Isaiah 28:16 in Romans 9:33). Jerusalem's subsequent history witnesses to the continuation of that stumbling. Yet perhaps the time approaches when people in Jerusalem will at last stumble upon the truth, and find him who, when other alternatives have failed, can alone be the city's true peace (Luke 19:41–4).[8]

1 See W.D. Davies, *The Gospel and the Land* (California University Press, 1974), Chapter 8, and R. Brown, *A Commentary on John's Gospel* (Doubleday, 1970).
2 S. Motyer, *Israel in the Plan of God* (IVP, 1989); C. Chapman, *Whose Promised Land?* (Lion, 1992); C.J.H. Wright, 'A Christian Approach to Old Testament Prophecy Concerning Israel', and N.T. Wright, 'Jerusalem in the New Testament', both in P.W.L. Walker (ed.), *Jerusalem Past and Present in the Purposes of God* (Paternoster/Baker, 1994).
3 C.J.H. Wright, *op. cit.*, p. 5.
4 *Ibid.*
5 C.H. Dodd, *According to the Scriptures* (Nisbet & Co., 1952), p. 103.
6 R.T. France, 'Old Testament Prophecy and the Future of Israel', *Tyndale Bulletin* 26, p. 73 (1975).
7 N.T. Wright, *op cit.*, p. 77.
8 These issues are discussed further in my chapter, 'Jerusalem and the Church's Challenge', in P.W.L. Walker (ed.), *Jerusalem Past and Present in the Purposes of God* (Paternoster/Baker, 1994), and especially in *Jesus and the Holy City: New Testament Perspectives on Jerusalem* (Eerdmans, 1996).

Part VII

POSTMODERNISM
AND CULTURE

Chapter 23

DECONSTRUCTION

Gagging the Speaking God?

MICHAEL OVEY

Summary

This chapter aims to describe how deconstructionism (arising from new literary theories) works, the way it abolishes the idea of a speaking God, and to examine some ideas for rejecting it.

Scholars have been thrilled recently at discovering a hitherto unpublished fragment of Lewis Carroll's work about Alice. It goes like this:

'When I use a word,' said Humpty Dumpty scornfully, 'it means what I want it to mean, neither more nor less.'

'My dear old thing,' said the March Hare, 'there's more to it than that. When you say or write something, you've got to reckon that you can't keep tabs on it. Other people may take what you say quite differently from how you meant it. It's like setting a bird free. Once it's gone, it flies where it wants.'

'I'm afraid he's right, Humpty,' chipped in Alice, passing him his tea. 'If you want to get through to us, you've got to use words in ways that we'll understand.'

'Absolutely,' the March Hare agreed. 'There's no ultimate reason why we shouldn't call that teapot over there by the name "hot water bottle" instead. But if you were the only one who did call it "hot water bottle" you'd be in for a shock come teatime.'

Alice continued, 'Of course, you could start a new fashion, and if you did it frequently enough then at least all your friends could get the hang of it, and we'd know "hot water bottle" meant "teapot".'

The Mad Hatter had been listening to all this with mounting displeasure. 'What tommy rot! You're both talking as though Humpty could use language to communicate something.'

'He's not as thick as that,' objected the March Hare defensively.

'Not just him – anyone,' the Mad Hatter came back, splattering bits of muffin over the tea party in his intensity. 'Language doesn't give me access to what Humpty thinks. How could I know he was using language in the same way I was? When he says, "I'm having a nice time here" he might mean by "nice" what I mean by "nasty". And we could never find that out, because all we have to say is that what we mean by "nice" and "nasty" are other words. It's all just words. It's as though each one of us is inside a little bubble, all on our own, and every now and then we float close to each other, but we never know what's going on in the bubble next door.' He paused for breath and turned to Alice. 'Another cuppa, please, Alice pet, three sugars.'

'Pet, eh?' said Alice from between clenched teeth. 'That sounds like an offensive socially conditioned sexist term.'

'Only to you, Alice dear, just your subjective reaction,' said the Mad Hatter, taking his tea and sipping it. 'Blinking heck, I asked for sugar, didn't I?'

'So sorry,' said Alice sweetly. 'In my language "three sugars" means you don't want any.'

'You know jolly well what I meant …' the Mad Hatter accused as the tea party broke up in disarray.

Introduction

In this 'fragment' the Mad Hatter adopts an approach to interpretation very similar to deconstructionism. Deconstructionism itself is a new and potent player on the interpretative stage, applying to many fields and disciplines. As such it already features in the courses of many of our students, especially the humanities. One Christian student remarked after a year studying deconstructionism that there was simply no point in studying the Bible any more – it could communicate no truth: such were the implications of deconstruction.

This was an understandable reaction. Thus P. Miscall, utilizing deconstructionist approaches, observes that questions of interpretation are insoluble: 'The reader encounters ambiguity, equivocation, opposed meanings and cannot decide for or establish one or the other' (*The Workings of Old Testament Narrative*, Fortress, Philadelphia, 1983,

p. 2). Hence Miscall's reaction to 1 Samuel 17 and David's combat with Goliath: it is impossible to determine what David's character is (*ibid.*, p. 73) and hence what the incident is to teach.

To that extent, deconstructionism tends to eliminate our dependence on the Bible, and indeed the doctrine that God reveals himself. It is, therefore, vitally important to examine it.

The Background

Before plunging into deconstructionism it is as well to set the scene. Several schools of thought have grown up in recent years about how language works and whether words, and literature in particular, can be a vehicle for truth. This is strikingly relevant for the Christian doctrine that God reveals himself in and through the Bible. Whatever else it is, it is also a collection of written words, employing human language.

Some of those schools of thought are represented, albeit in cartoon form, in the literary fragment above. Humpty Dumpty starts with the importance of the author. In the early years of this century, recovering the author's intention was indeed greatly emphasized: what did Isaiah mean in chapter 53? And so on. This emphasis obviously appeals to biblical Christians. If God has inspired human authors, then we long to recover that authorial intent.

However, in the years after the Second World War this 'intentional fallacy', as it was dubbed, came under fire from the so-called New Criticism, which asserted the difficulty/impossibility of recovering authorial intent. Rather, we should accept that a text created by an author becomes, so to speak, independent of the author, as the March Hare's opening remarks suggest. An example of this is the way a legal agreement may be construed in a way the solicitor drafting it never anticipated. So, for this school, we must focus attention on the text, not the author.

Structuralism also concentrates on text. It builds on the work of the great linguist Saussure who pointed out that there is no essential, intrinsic link between the word which signifies and the thing which it signifies. (Alice and the March Hare recognize this conventional, arbitrary aspect of language in their discussion of what to call a teapot.) This means that what a word signifies depends on the place that word has in the overall language system, its structural position. For the structuralist, therefore, it is tremendously important to discover the structure, and accordingly context becomes vital, both the immediate context of a word or phrase in a literary work and also the context of the total language usage of a particular society. In a way this is, of course, a systematic presentation of the old maxim of construction in English law, *Noscitur a sociis* (a thing is known and understood by the company it keeps).

However, other schools would criticize the New Criticism and the type of structuralism described here for implying that meaning in language is objective. That objectivity would be called an illusion. Instead of concentrating on the text, they would suggest a reader-centred approach. Meaning is only what the reader decides the meaning is. The Mad Hatter plays with this when provoking a particular response to Alice by his use of the term 'pet'. Reader response theories are already employed in some feminist and liberation theology readings of certain texts.

The Mad Hatter has another string to his linguistic bow, decon-structionism itself. He takes the line that language is outsideless (a formulation adopted by Don Cupitt, for whom orthodox religious language is non-realist, that is to say, does not refer to anything real). 'Outsideless' refers to the idea that we cannot transcend language and its limits. A crucial claim here is that language is simply self-referring. Thus, any word, any phrase can only be known from other words and phrases. They, in their turn, derive their signifi-cance from their structural position with respect to still more, and so on. As language is essentially self-referring, there is no guaran-teed 'real' meaning. We are in fact in an endless labyrinth. Language therefore deconstructs. Further, as the Mad Hatter continues, it is not even clear whether as individuals we are in the same linguistic labyrinth. I claim to speak 'English', but is this the same 'English' as the man next door? Could I show they are part of the same linguistic system?

This way of putting the deconstructionist case means language disappears as a sure vehicle for transmitting objective meaning between persons – an earth-shaking claim.

What We Gain from Modern Literary Theories

Some modern theories are of great use in reinforcing and expand-ing traditional concerns in interpreting the Bible.

Structuralism, for example, serves both to warn us and to provide incentives for study. By stressing the importance of context it reminds us of the very real danger of 'proof-texting'. It is not a legitimate use of the Bible simply to find a form of words grammatically capable of supporting a particular position. Rather, we are driven to rigorous examination of our texts within the context of the book that contains them and ultimately the canon as a whole. The structuralist view encourages us to beware of an over-atomistic reading of the Bible and to take extremely seriously the principle of looking to the whole counsel of God.

Structuralism pushes us in other directions too. Paul's letters are rooted in the Greek of the Near East of the first century. That puts a value on investigating other uses of the language to rebuild the linguistic context of that particular time. Moreover, it reinforces the usefulness of an informed social history of, say, first-century Corinth.

None of this is strikingly new. But what structuralism does underline for us is the importance of these tasks if we want to arrive at what the text says rather than what we assume it to say.

Text-centred and reader-centred theories can be suggestive in other positive ways. Evangelicals stress the Bible as a living rather than a dead text. It can and does address us in our present-day lives. As we study a passage like Ephesians 4:29 with its instructions about the edifying use of the tongue, we may see it directly applying to us in a current situation. Yet it scarcely seems that Paul could have directly had that in mind. It therefore seems illegitimate to say that the human author 'intended' to address us in that situation (although he might have wanted to had he thought about it). At that point it is clear that *one* way of putting the 'authorial intent' view, far from protecting the Bible, tends to render it a dead letter by restricting it to the particular human author.

This does not, of course, entail accepting extreme reader response views. To say all interpretations are equal distorts our relationship with God (see the theological objections to deconstructionism, below). Rather, the point made here is that text and reader-centred theories can redress certain overemphases in author-centred theories of meaning.

Text and reader-centred theories are also suggestive in approaching another puzzle in our doctrine of revelation: the way that prophecy, for instance, can have a meaning different from the one the original human author had in mind. One example is Matthew

2:15 with its application of Hosea 11:1, 'Out of Egypt have I called my son.' Another is Paul's application of Deuteronomy 30:12 to Jesus in Romans 10:6–7. In neither case does it seem apparent that the human author had Jesus himself in mind. As such, one is conscious that 'authorial intent' defined simply and solely as human authorial intent seems inadequate to draw out the full meaning of Scripture.

Both these instances deal with New Testament applications of Old Testament texts. As such, they may be said to form God's footnotes to his own earlier word, and such use of the Old Testament could be said to be no longer possible (we are not apostles) or at least practised with extreme caution because of the risks of subjectivity. We are nevertheless reminded that human authorial intent does not exhaust the text's meaning. Nor, come to that, do the efforts of generations of interpreters of Hosea before the birth of Jesus.

In this way biblical Christians need not write off all the interpretative theories that have arisen recently as being irrelevant or completely unhelpful. There are congruencies and resonances with traditional doctrines of revelation and they can be useful in helping us to present a properly nuanced account of what inspiration and revelation really involve.

However, the development of deconstructionism has a strong tendency to undermine the doctrine of revelation, with fatal effects elsewhere in our theology. To the consequences of that theory we now turn.

Deconstructionism

At first glance, deconstructionism could appear to be simply an extension, possibly extreme, of some of the approaches outlined above. Is it, in fact, essentially harmful?

The Demolition of Personal Relationship with God

The most serious casualty is what Martin Buber called an I–Thou relationship between humans and God, by which is meant the idea of a relationship between persons in which each encounters the other as a person and communicates with them as a person. This is in contrast to an I–It relationship where I may indeed encounter another person but do not treat them as such nor communicate with them as such.

Deconstructionism tends to destroy an I–Thou relationship with God by denying communication. If language is not a possible vehicle for God to use in revealing himself to us, then the Bible cannot give us direct knowledge of God. Nor can we avoid this by using the notion of 'direct encounter' with God (through prayer, meditation, thought or ecstasy). The results of such encounters ought in principle to be capable of some kind of verbal description. But if verbal description is inherently and totally inadequate, then it is difficult in the extreme to know what kind of relationship there is, what contours it has, what content there is to it. If I cannot say the relationship is pleasant or unpleasant, worthwhile or pointless, then what in fact do I know about it; in what sense is it a genuinely I–Thou relationship?

It may be justly pointed out that the words are not the relationship. Those sympathetic to the deconstructionist view may cite John 5:39 with Christ's warnings about those who scour the Scriptures but do not find Jesus, the person. Yet the thrust of those words (in the context of John) is that the words of Scripture do point to Jesus and that the scribes and others are at fault for not seeing that. C.S. Lewis points out that while Scripture may only be a 'map', and not itself the country that has to be navigated, navigation is nevertheless only possible with a map. This is equally applicable to our relationship with God. If deconstructionism is correct then a certain type of relationship, I–Thou, disappears.

Momentous consequences follow from that.

First, God's personal sovereignty over us necessarily disappears too. God may be the creator and ruler of the universe, but we are capable only of conformity and not of obedience. We may fall in with God's wishes through good fortune, but obedience presupposes knowledge of another's will. That in turn depends on communicating that will, which is just what deconstructionism rules out.

Naturally, with obedience goes disobedience. It is really extremely difficult to say I am answerable to God or responsible to him if his will is unascertainable. Sin becomes meaningless: the concept of rebellion which is central to sin (Romans 1:18ff.) is not applicable in that context. That in turn removes the need for Christ's redeeming death.

Second, God's love becomes problematic. If God cannot express this, how can we know we are loved? We might have a sensation which we think is from God, and which we imagine is produced by his love. But we cannot know this if he cannot tell us.

This in turn throws our entire relationship with him into serious doubt. Logically we can only remain unsure of our status with him and thus insecure. Even if I was right about those feelings (perhaps they were only self-serving delusions?), how can I be sure that they will last for eternity? A very serious casualty of deconstructionism is our assurance of salvation (as well as our assurance that being saved is worthwhile).

The Demolition of Other Personal Relationships

Naturally this demolition of personal relationships extends logically to other relationships with each other as well as with God, although here, of course, we experience strong empirical resistance (see 'The Demolition of the Ego?', below). This leaves us in a kind of linguistic solipsism: we are left only with ourselves because we have no access to others. This may well be attractive to a highly individualistic culture, with its prospect of apparent freedom. Part of its attraction, indeed, may be that it tends to diminish personal responsibility to others.

The Demolition of the Ego?

Yet it is worth questioning whether even this solipsism can be sustained. If even my own language deconstructs by its self-referential nature, can I describe myself, even to myself? And if I cannot describe myself, who is the 'I' of whom I so glibly speak? In that sense the ultimate casualty of deconstruction may be the individual ego.

Given these momentous consequences it is vital to see if deconstructionism is correct.

Objections to Deconstructionism

These can be grouped under three headings.

Theological

Deconstructionism, if it addresses the question of God at all, seems to rest on an implicit doctrine of God. But the God implied by this view is not the God of orthodox Christianity. After all, that orthodox God enjoys the advantages of both omnipotence and omniscience. As such he is surely a competent linguistic performer, able to find apt words to express his meaning even to fallen and finite beings. The 'distance' which exists between the minds of author and reader, the problems created by the difficulty of any individual getting 'outside' his or her own linguistic code, would surely be obviated by these attributes of the orthodox God, who knows the minds of author and reader and can act in the minds of both (although this should not be taken as an endorsement either of a 'dictation' theory of inspiration or a 'dictatorial' theory of reading).

Of course, there are traditional constraints on God's actions: but using his omnipotence to communicate does not seem inherently evil. Nor does it seem self-contradictory (as when one might say that God cannot make both an immovable object and an irresistible force). Rather, it seems that one is simply being faced with the assertion 'Even God cannot use language to communicate.' This assertion seems highly problematic because it involves considerations of the nature of God as well as of the nature of language. Deconstructionism here seems to be saying, indirectly, something about God. But, on deconstructionism's own premises, how can we know that? Is there, in fact, an assumption within deconstructionism that God simply *cannot* be the God of orthodox Christianity? This is why radical employment of the technique of deconstruction is properly termed an 'ism'. It carries an ideological position that takes it beyond being a 'neutral' tool.

In fact, of course, it is just those attributes of omnipotence and omniscience that the biblical God does claim to have.

A second theological objection to a certain kind of deconstructionism (and a certain type of reader response theory) also arises. It could be said that any response by a reader to Scripture is as valid as any other. Thus an interpretation of feeding the five thousand as a sermon on sharing community wealth is as valid as the one that Jesus has miraculous powers. It is said that the Bible is polyvalent (conveys a number of different meanings), and that the *sensus plenior* discussed above ('What We Gain from Modern Literary Theories') recognizes this.

Yet it is one thing to say the Bible is polyvalent, with many meanings, quite another to say it is omnivalent, that it can mean *all* things. This is, however, where these extreme views end up, that the text can 'mean' anything. If it were so, God would indeed be a God of inconsistency (since one could respond to a text with two mutually inconsistent reactions about his character: but both would be true). By saying all things, God would be saying nothing. Moreover, this God would be shaped essentially by us and by our reactions, rather than what he discloses himself to be. Indeed, this is one of the greatest objections to seeing God in I–It terms, that it encourages idolatry.

Theologically, deconstructionism involves us by its assumptions with a 'dark, dumb, idol'. Yet it is precisely that point which remains to be established.

Philosophical

It is extremely hard to rescue deconstructionism from self-refutation. The case is advanced using language and discussed using language. Its proponents write books, apparently expecting to be understood. It seems there is at least one privileged, communicable, objectively true proposition, namely the deconstructionist thesis. But if so, there are two alternatives:

if the proposition is true, then language in at least one instance communicates truth. But the words and concepts used to express this proposition are not severable from the rest of the linguistic structure: they are part of it. In which case, does not the entire system receive some kind of grounding from this proposition? If deconstructionism is true, why does it not apply to the proposition itself? In which case we could ignore it, because it could never be communicated to us.

If the proposition is false then it can be ignored anyway.

Moreover, it is far from clear whether deconstructionism faces us with a correct set of alternatives. It appears to assert that we have a choice between absolute understanding and deconstructionism. But, as has often been observed, there may be other options, such as an understanding which we accept as true but is in principle open to falsification and which we concede is not exhaustive. Thus we understand 'God is love' as indicating that God has a disposition towards us describable as love because it bears an affinity to love in our own lives. We accept that this understanding of the text is *in principle* falsifiable, although falsifying it would involve such a massive shift in our understanding of other texts too that it seems *in practice* inconceivable. We also accept that we have not exhausted what this love means – human love is not a perfect exemplar of it.

However, there is no need to dismiss this knowledge just because it is provisional, and true but not exhaustive. That point could equally be made of my knowledge of the physical world (human senses may be deceptive), but most of us find provisional limited knowledge of the world around us nevertheless useful.

Empirical

Deconstructionism faces a massive difficulty in explaining the successful use of language in the everyday world. True, misconstructions do occur. But the fact that they are occasions for comment or for humour or for irritation reveals how overwhelmingly successful language seems to be. If language is so unreliable, why do we so readily assume it is a viable means of communication?

Part of the answer, no doubt, is the public nature of language. If I use words in an unusual way, others remark on it and correct me. There is a pervasive pressure towards using language uniformly, and with sufficient uniformity comes the possibility of transmitting information. It is doubtful whether the deconstructionist model takes sufficient account of the social pressure created by the public nature of discourse.

This is related to the point that deconstructionism oversimplifies by claiming that language is self-referring. Clearly, language is more than a mere 'nomenclature', but words are often used with respect to physical phenomena ('This knife is sharp'). If I 'misuse' language to convey that, for example, 'This knife is blunt', the fact that words are being used with respect to physical phenomena provides an opportunity for my use of language to be corrected and brought into conformity with others' usage of 'sharp' and 'blunt'. The physical world is a shared world and a public world, and the fact that language is at times used in respect of it suggests that the slogan 'language is self-referring' is not the whole truth. And at that point one is aware that although language may sometimes be a complex maze, it is not quite accurate to say it is simply an endless labyrinth.

Conclusion

Deconstructionism is a curious thesis. In a way it takes the Babel story a stage further. Instead of the multiplicity of languages and the confusion it creates, we are left, as it were, with no language at all, either in which God could speak to us or in which we can address each other. As such it would deprive us of the knowledge of God as well as any rationale for evangelism.

Its influence, however, is pervasive. Since so many academic disciplines employ language, they are all potentially affected by it and our students already have to reckon with it in their courses, sometimes with grave effects for their spiritual lives.

The tragedy is, of course, that there is no compelling (or even ultimately persuasive) reason for adopting the thesis. This should not hide how attractive we may find it in some ways. The serpent now no longer has to say, 'Did God really say ...?' (Genesis 3:1). Instead he may only have to remind us 'God can't really speak anyway ...'

Chapter 24

ENGAGING WITH CINEMA

JOHN COFFEY

I cannot praise a fugitive and cloistered virtue unexercised and un-breathed, that never sallies out and seeks her adversary, but slinks out of the race, where that immortal garland is to be run for, not without dust and heat.

John Milton, *Areopagitica*

I believe there's a spirituality in films, even if it's not one which can supplant faith. I find that over the years many films address themselves to the spiritual side of human nature.

Martin Scorsese

Summary

The relationship between church and cinema has often been one of mutual suspicion. Hollywood has flouted Christian values; Christians have responded with condemnation and censorship. Yet from the earliest days of motion pictures, film-makers have been attracted to religious subjects and spiritual themes. Christians today have much to gain from critical engagement with cinema. At their best, films are works of art that provoke ethical reflection and provide a vital point of contact between believers and unbelievers.

The Church and the Cinema

In the century since its birth, film has established itself as the most popular art form of our age. Each week, millions around the globe flock to their local cinemas or watch films on television and video. Yet the power and popularity of film has caused uneasiness among Christians who have worried that it promotes sexual immorality, violence and impiety.

Throughout the 'golden age' of Hollywood, from the thirties to the sixties, the Catholic Church in the United States policed the movies through its Legion of Decency.[1] Its success was remarkable. Few Hollywood films in this period were released without the Legion's approval, and many were severely cut or rewritten as a result of its censorship. Eventually, however, its campaigns provoked a powerful backlash. By the 1960s, the film industry had become increasingly resentful of the church's interference; the Legion was forced to liberalize its classification system and eventually the production code was abandoned.

Yet as films have become more violent and explicit, concerns about their influence have revived. These concerns are forcefully articulated by the Jewish film critic Michael Medved in *Hollywood versus America* (HarperCollins, 1992). While opposed to censorship, he is scathing in his critique, declaring that 'the dream factory has become the poison factory'. Countless films feature explicit sex, gratuitous violence, obscene behaviour and foul language. Hollywood is guilty of promoting promiscuity, maligning marriage, glorifying violence, trashing heroes, bashing America and attacking religion. In Medved's eyes, the release of Martin Scorsese's controversial film *The Last Temptation of Christ* (1988) was nothing less than Hollywood's 'declaration of war' on Christians.[2]

Medved's judgements are harsh and polemical, but many share comparable misgivings. Films like *Natural Born Killers* (1994) have been linked to copycat murders, and there is now a vigorous debate over the connection between screen violence and real-life killings.[3] The respected British director David Puttnam expresses a widespread feeling: 'Movies now have an underlying nastiness in them. The thing I loathe more than anything has become fashionable – cynicism.'

The irony is that as cinema has become more violent and sexually explicit, Christians have become more relaxed about it. Evangelicals, for example, will happily watch films that would have shocked an earlier generation. As one scholar puts it, contemporary evangelicals are 'comfortable in the world' and 'take for granted many of the cultural norms of middle-class life'.[4] Cinema is lapped up as a form of entertainment, and there is often a lack of critical engagement with the medium or the message. If the danger in the past was cultural separatism, the danger today may be cultural assimilation.

The Need for Distinctive Engagement

To avoid these extremes, Christians need to cultivate a genuinely biblical attitude towards culture. God calls us to be a holy people radically distinct from the world around us. The Old Testament word *qodesh* (translated 'holiness') literally means 'separation' or 'setting apart'. The New Testament contains numerous injunctions to holiness. Jesus taught his followers to be ruthless in maintaining their purity: 'If your right eye causes you to sin,' he said, 'gouge it out and throw it away' (Matthew 5:27–30). One text, in particular, has weighed heavily in Christian thinking about cinema – Philippians 4:8: 'Finally, brothers, whatever is true, whatever is noble, whatever is right, whatever is pure, whatever is lovely, whatever is admirable – if anything is excellent or praiseworthy – think about such things.' Since cinema portrays many things that are false, ignoble, impure, ugly and despicable, many believers have simply avoided it.

However, a passion for holiness needs to be balanced by a commitment to the world around us. Christian lives should be marked by 'holy worldliness'.[5] Christians should live as aliens and strangers, but also as conscientious citizens (1 Peter 2:11–17); as salt amidst the corruption and light in the darkness (Matthew 5:13–16). Salt and light are effective because they are at odds with their environment and present within it. In the same way, we must be involved in a fallen world, resisting the twin temptations to assimilate to it or to insulate ourselves from it. Christ's prayer is not that his disciples are taken 'out of the world', but that they are protected from the evil one and sanctified by God's Word (John 17:13–19).

The Bible gives outstanding examples of this distinctive engagement: Joseph, Esther, Daniel, Paul and Christ himself. Paul was distressed by the Athenians' idolatry and preached against it, but he also engaged with their culture and religion. Fear of contamination did not overwhelm his desire to communicate. He studied their idols, talked with their philosophers, read their poets. When he preached to them, he did not simply denounce; he looked for common ground (Acts 17:16–34). Yet it was Jesus who embodied holy worldliness most daringly. The Pharisees were appalled by Christ's readiness to mix with worldly people in worldly settings. But Jesus taught that evil thoughts, sexual immorality, murder and lewdness came 'from within, out of men's hearts'; isolation from the world did not guarantee holiness (Mark 7:20–3). He broke Jewish taboos with abandon, and mixed freely with 'sinners' (Matthew 9:10–13, Luke 7:36–50). Whilst he called on people to repent, his life was marked by a radical openness to the ungodly (Luke 19:1–10; John 4:4–26; John 8:1–11).

Practising Distinctive Engagement

Few Christians have managed to emulate this balance. Many have settled for the 'safe' option of condemnation and withdrawal from the world and its culture. Yet this strategy has serious drawbacks. The English Puritans often showed real appreciation of music, poetry, painting and even theatre, but if some had had their way, we could well have missed out on Shakespeare. It is a sad irony that a movement founded on the doctrine of grace became a byword for hard-faced moralism. Puritan hostility to theatres, taverns and Christmas alienated contemporaries and gave the impression that Puritanism was a faith for the self-righteous.

Yet in avoiding moralism we should not support a naïve consumption of worldly culture. The quantity of cheap erotica and horror on display in video stores should be disturbing to the Christian. Those who never watch this material should think carefully about viewing 'serious' films that might lead into temptation. Moreover, the worldview of a film can be more insidious than profanity, nudity or violence. But such problems also arise within politics, business, literature or philosophy; each contains its pitfalls, but it is tragic when Christians shun these areas of life. Individuals differ in their capacity to handle challenges to their faith, but each of us in our own way should endeavour to be both distinctive and culturally engaged.

Francis Schaeffer observed that churches often shelter young Christians from 'the world', and then send them out to face it naked and defenceless. However, there are practical things churches can do to assist cultural engagement. Preachers can watch films or read press reviews and incorporate them into their teaching. Parents can use family guides to select appropriate films for watching with their children. Youth groups or house groups can discuss a film from a Christian perspective. *The Truman Show* (1998), for example, would get people thinking about how the mass media manipulates our vision of reality, but it could also prompt deeper questions about God. 'Truman' has been placed in the 'perfect' town of Seahaven by his 'creator', Christof, but this paradise feels oppressive. Is the film simply an exposé of the false creators in the media? Is it an attack on theism? Or does it represent a popular view of God as a distant control freak unconcerned about our welfare?

Asking such questions is the key to *critical* engagement. The danger is that when we watch films, we switch off our Christian minds and soak them up. As the critic Neil Postman suggests, movies that offer spectacle rather than content are particularly problematic. In an age when images overwhelm words, entertainment can become more appealing than truth. Yet cinema and theatre can counteract the trivialization produced by television; they still have the capacity to provoke serious reflection.[6]

If we are to get the most out of films, we need to appreciate three significant dimensions of cinema: the aesthetic, the moral and the religious. While cinema can be aesthetically mediocre, morally offensive and religiously confused, many films have much to offer on each of these levels.

The Aesthetic Dimension

Hans Rookmaaker used to say that 'art needs no justification'. He meant that art is valid even when it serves no obvious utilitarian purpose. God has placed us in the midst of a physical creation, and commanded us to fill the earth and subdue it (Genesis 1:28). When the artist takes a material artefact and fashions it into something delightful, he participates in humanity's vocation to cultivate the earth. Christ died not to replace this created order but to redeem it (see Isaiah 11:1–9; 65:17–25; Romans 8:18–21; Revelation 21:24), so Christians should display a full humanity. As Nicholas Wolterstorff rightly says, 'Life is not meant to be grim.'[7]

There is no need, therefore, to apologize for treasuring the dialogue of *Casablanca* (1942), or admiring the structural brilliance of a Tarantino movie. We must avoid the tunnel vision that focuses exclusively on the problematic aspects of film. The operas of Puccini can be sadistically misogynistic, but there is far more to a Puccini opera than a tawdry plot. Human creativity can be twisted and used to make idols (Exodus 32:1–6; Ezekiel 8; Isaiah 44:6–20), but the aesthetic impulse remains an essential part of God's good creation. To watch the great classics of world cinema is to marvel at the artistry of the directors. Kurosawa's *Seven Samurai* (1954) astonishes with its epic sweep, subtle characterization, gentle humour and cinematic technique. *Citizen Kane* (1941) is just as remarkable, for its 25-year-old director, Orson Welles, displayed an awesome command of the medium, introducing a host of innovations like deep-focus photography, low-angled camera shots and non-linear narrative.

Films can be profoundly rewarding. They can transport us to far corners of the globe and to long-forgotten eras; they can make us laugh and weep and hold our breath; they can introduce us to human cultures in all their colour and diversity, and take us inside the lives of people we have never met. One recalls beautiful films about an Italian postman and a Chilean poet (*Il Postino*, 1995), a simple Chinese peasant woman and her stubborn search for justice (*The Story of Qui Ju*, 1992), and a little Russian boy and his Czech foster-father (*Kolya*, 1996). The world of cinema is packed with hidden jewels, films of compassion and shrewd observation. These works of art entertain, delight and enrich our humanity.

The Moral Dimension

Believers will also want to assess films from an ethical perspective. This should involve more than a concentration on sex, swearing and violence. One American evangelical web site devoted to movie reviews relies entirely on these criteria in its assessment of the ethical value of films, and other moral issues are almost lost from view. Steven Spielberg's powerful Holocaust film, *Schindler's List* (1993), was given a 'Christian rating' of 1 out of 5 (placing it in the category: 'very offensive from a Christian perspective'). The US-based Christian Film and Television Commission also placed an extreme caution warning against *Schindler's List* because of the 'extensive nudity in concentration camp scenes ... graphic sex scenes between unmarried individuals ... [and] 19 obscenities, 8 profanities and several vulgarities'. Faced with one of the great moral evils of our century, these reviewers could do little more than tot up the number of swear words.

By worrying so much about the corrupting influence of cinema, Christians often fail to appreciate its capacity to generate ethical reflection. In our fixation with judging films, we prevent them judging us. Yet many movies have the power to expose our own moral shortcomings. Few works of art dramatize the tension between self-fulfilment and duty more persuasively than Frank Capra's *It's a Wonderful Life* (1946). Recent 'feelgood' films like *Forrest Gump* (1994) and *The Shawshank Redemption* (1995) depict central characters who keep their principles in a demoralized world. The point is not that these films get everything right, but that they put us on the spot, provoking us to think about our own character.

Movies can also deal thoughtfully with specific moral issues. *Platoon* (1986) and *Apocalypse Now* (1979) stand as important contributions to the debate over the Vietnam War. Dark and violent, they remind us of human fallenness in much the same way as the book of Judges. Other films tackle issues like mental illness (*Shine*, 1996), race (*Jungle Fever*, 1991), capitalist speculation (*Wall Street*, 1987), alcoholism (*Leaving Las Vegas*, 1995) and capital punishment (*Dead Man Walking*, 1995). In his ten short films on the Decalogue (1988), the Polish director Krzysztof Kieslowski focuses on the painful moral dilemmas faced by different people living in the same apartment block in Warsaw. At critical junctures, Kieslowski introduces a 'mystery man' who stares intently at the protagonists, as if to imply that God is always watching us and searching our hearts.

The Religious Dimension

Ours may be a 'secular age', but the twentieth century's archetypal art form is shot through with the theological. The obvious religious movies are biblical epics and Christ films, like *The Ten Commandments* (1956), *Ben Hur* (1959), *King of Kings* (1961) and *Prince of Egypt* (1998). Yet the religious dimension of cinema goes far beyond this.

The past decade, in particular, has seen dramatic growth in movies with spiritual themes, though their spirituality is usually highly eclectic. The trend perhaps began with *Star Wars* (1977), and has been reinforced by the fashion for Eastern religion and New Age mysticism. Although 93 per cent of the Hollywood establishment attend no religious services of any kind,[8] the popularity of Buddhism and Scientology is evident in recent films. *Kundun*

(1997) and *Seven Years in Tibet* (1997) present a reverential picture of Buddhism, whilst *Phenomenon* (1996) showcases the Scientologist beliefs of its star, John Travolta. The immense popularity of *Ghost* (1990) has inspired a stream of movies featuring angels, reincarnation, the after-life and other supernatural themes, the latest being *What Dreams May Come* (1998). The New Age spirituality of these movies is deeply problematic, but they provide powerful evidence that, for all its proud boasts, secularism has failed to satisfy twentieth-century people.

Moreover, Christian theology itself continues to be a powerful force in cinema. There is, of course, evidence of secularization; in recent British films, religion plays little or no part in the lives of most of the characters, and in *Four Weddings and a Funeral* (1994) the church is personified by Rowan Atkinson's ludicrously inept young priest. Yet important films continue to provide sympathetic portrayals of Christian believers and theological ideas. *Babette's Feast* (1988) is a minor masterpiece set in an austere Pietist community in nineteenth-century Denmark, and offers a beautiful exploration of the biblical themes of grace, feasting and reconciliation. One thinks too of *Chariots of Fire* (1981), *The Mission* (1986) and of Robert Duvall's extraordinary evocation of Pentecostal culture in the rural American South in *The Apostle* (1998).

Even films that do not feature believers often draw on the Passion narratives and the apocalypse. The director of *Robocop* (1987), Paul Verhoeven – who once had a brief encounter with Pentecostalism but is now a member of the sceptical Jesus Seminar – has described his film as a 'Christian fairytale'.[9] Another science fiction classic, *The Terminator* (1984), centres on a woman of humble status who is chosen to give birth to a deliverer, John Conner (note the initials). *The Terminator*, like King Herod, sets out on a slaughter of innocents in order to destroy this messianic figure, but, in a film heavy with apocalyptic overtones, we know that the woman will give birth and that her child will save humanity from destruction. In many other movies, the hero is a sort of Christ figure; examples include *The Elephant Man* (1980), *E.T.* (1982) and even *Edward Scissorhands* (1990). One of the bleakest thrillers of the nineties, *Seven* (1995), is peppered with references to Aquinas, Dante, Milton's *Paradise Lost* and the seven deadly sins, focusing relentlessly on human corruption and the demand for judgement. Films like this derive their force from the theological discourse they employ.

Secular philosophies cannot carry the same weight, for they have little to say about radical evil or the possibility of redemption. When film-makers grapple with the extremities of human existence, they repeatedly turn to the Christian heritage.

Steve Turner has argued that some of our century's most significant popular music is inspired by the black church, and by the spiritual background and experience of artists like Elvis Presley, Bob Dylan, Marvin Gaye and U2's Bono.[10] Something similar can be said of film directors like Alfred Hitchcock, whose work bears the mark of his Jesuit education;[11] Ingmar Bergman, a Lutheran pastor's son who grappled with 'the silence of God' in films like *The Seventh Seal* (1957);[12] Woody Allen, who has never stopped arguing with Judaism, above all in *Crimes and Mis-demeanors* (1989); and Quentin Tarantino, who was an enthusiastic Christian in his early teens, and who claims that his outrageous *Pulp Fiction* (1994), with its climactic conversion scene, is a movie about redemption.[13]

Religious themes are also of central importance to Paul Schrader and Martin Scorsese, the partnership responsible for *Taxi Driver* (1976), *Raging Bull* (1980) and *The Last Temptation of Christ*. Scorsese once planned to become a Catholic priest, while Schrader was educated at Calvin College under Nicholas Wolterstorff. Although he abandoned the faith, his films develop many Calvinist themes, and feature lonely souls in search of secular redemption.[14] *Raging Bull* takes us through the career of the boxer, Jake La Motta, and is a tale of redemption through suffering. La Motta battles through violence and punishment, but emerges a kinder man. As the film ends we see the words of John 9:24–6 projected on to the screen: '… I was blind and now I can see'. By echoing biblical narrative, film-makers hope to invest secular concepts of redemption with the depth and passion of Christian salvation. For all its faults, their work testifies to the continuing power of the Christian gospel in modern culture, and to the contemporary hunger for transcendence.[15]

Conclusion

Films provide us with a vital point of contact with the world. For preachers and apologists cinema offers a window on to contemporary culture and a source of powerful and accessible illustrations. In the sixties, Francis Schaeffer used the films of Fellini and Antonioni to engage with existentialism; in the nineties, David Lyon began his book *Postmodernity* (1994) with several pages on *Bladerunner* (1982), the classic sci-fi film set in a dismal Los Angeles in AD 2019, where modernity is in ruins, multiculturalism is not working, and reality has been thrown into question. Films are a remarkable resource for anyone who wants to communicate the gospel. Besides having a far greater audience than most books, their vivid images can remain embedded in our memory for years. Film-makers are the storytellers and mythmakers of our culture, and films reflect the contemporary quest for meaning and truth. If we are serious about presenting the Christian gospel in a culturally relevant way, we need to pay attention to these modern-day parables.

Christians still have some way to go to critical engagement. In *The Scandal of the Evangelical Mind* (1994), Mark Noll emphasized how intellectually marginal the American evangelical community has become, despite its size. The scandal of the evangelical imagination is just as worrying. It is relatively easy to find distinguished evangelical academics in the fields of philosophy, science, theology and history. But where are the evangelical artists, novelists, actors, playwrights, composers, critics and film directors? Thankfully, there are some, but our churches need to do much more to encourage a vision for the arts. If we are to act as salt and light in contemporary society, we cannot afford to bypass the darkened theatre and the silver screen.

Books on Religion and Cinema

R. Jewett, *Saint Paul at the Movies* (John Knox Press, 1993) and *Saint Paul Returns to the Movies* (Eerdmanns, 1998); L. Kreitzer, *The New Testament in Fiction and Film* (JSOT Press, 1993) and *The Old Testament in Fiction and Film* (JSOT Press, 1994); I. Maher, *Reel Issues: Engaging Film and Faith* (Bible Society, 1998); C. Marsh and G. Ortiz (eds), *Explorations in Theology and Film* (Blackwell, 1997); J. Martin and C. Ostwalt (eds), *Screening the Sacred: Religion, Myth and Ideology in Popular American Film* (Westview, 1995); M. Miles, *Seeing and Believing: Religion and Values in the Movies* (Beacon Press, 1996); B.B. Scott, *Hollywood Dreams and Biblical Stories* (Fortress Press, 1994).

Internet Sites

www.hollywoodjesus.com/ One of the largest Christian web sites devoted to cinema. Avoids censorious moralism and focuses on the religious dimension of movies. Provides links to other Christian review sites.

www.damaris.org.uk/ A British organization committed to helping Christians assess contemporary culture. Contains a growing number of excellent film study guides, ideal for group discussion.

www.unomaha.edu/~wwwjrf/ An on-line journal containing academic articles on religion and film from a wide variety of theological positions.

1 See F. Walsh, *Sin and Censorship: The Catholic Church and the Motion Picture Industry* (Yale UP, 1996); G. Black, *The Catholic Crusade against the Movie* (Cambridge University Press, 1998).
2 For a helpful discussion of the film and evangelicals' reaction see D. Hilborn, *Picking up the Pieces: Can Evangelicals Adapt to Contemporary Culture?* (Hodder & Stoughton, 1997), pp. 237–45.
3 See K. French (ed.), *Screen Violence* (Bloomsbury, 1996).
4 See M. Shibley, 'Contemporary evangelicals: born-again and world affirming', *Annals of the American Academy of Political and Social Science*, July 1998, pp. 67–87.
5 J. Stott, *Issues Facing Christians Today* (Marshall Pickering, 1984), pp. 24–5.
6 N. Postman, *Amusing Ourselves to Death* (Methuen, 1987).
7 N. Wolterstorff, *Art in Action: Toward a Christian Aesthetic* (Solway, 1997), p. 83. See also Chapter 4 in this volume.
8 M. Medved, *Hollywood versus America* (HarperCollins, 1992), p. 71.
9 R. van Scheers, *Paul Verhoeven* (Faber & Faber, 1998).
10 S. Turner, *Hungry for Heaven: Rock'n Roll and the Search for Redemption* (Hodder & Stoughton, 1995).
11 See N.P. Hurley, *Soul in Suspense: Hitchcock's Fright and Delight* (Scarecrow Press, 1993), p. vii.
12 See M. Bragg, *The Seventh Seal* (British Film Institute, 1993), pp. 9–10.
13 See W. Clarkson, *Quentin Tarantino* (Piatkus, 1995), pp. 40–1.
14 K. Jackson, *Schrader on Schrader* (Faber & Faber, 1990). Recently, Schrader has become a regular attender at an Episcopal church.
15 For more on this theme, see Chapter 24.

Chapter 25

MICHEL FOUCAULT AND POSTMODERN ATHEISM

Life After the Death of God?

JOHN COFFEY

Summary

The French intellectual Michel Foucault (1926–84) was one of the most influential thinkers of the twentieth century. His books on madness, medicine, knowledge, punishment and sexuality have had a major impact across a wide range of disciplines, and become set texts on undergraduate courses throughout Britain and America. His life, moreover, reflected some of the most significant cultural trends of the past thirty years: the rise of the gay subculture, the new openness to the non-rational, the growing experimentation with sex and drugs, the fascination with the body and the self. This chapter suggests that Foucault was driven by an intense desire to find a substitute for communion with God.[1]

Introduction

In 1948 Michel Foucault attempted to commit suicide. He was at the time a student at the élite Parisian university, the École Normale. The resident doctor there had little doubt about the source of the young man's distress. Foucault appeared to be racked with guilt over his frequent nocturnal visits to the illegal gay bars of the French capital. His father, a strict disciplinarian who had previously sent his son to the most regimented Catholic school he could find, arranged for him to be admitted to a psychiatric hospital for evaluation. Yet Foucault remained obsessed with death, joked about hanging himself and made further attempts to end his own life.

This youthful experience of himself as homosexual, suicidal and mentally disturbed proved decisive for Foucault's intellectual development. The subject matter of many of his later books arose from his own experience – *Madness and Civilisation* (1961), *The Birth of the Clinic* (1963), *Discipline and Punish* (1975), and *The History of Sexuality* (3 vols, 1976–84) all dwelt on topics of deep personal concern to their author. Foucault's intellectual career was to be a lifelong crusade on behalf of those whom society labelled, marginalized, incarcerated and suppressed.[2]

Foucault's Critique of Modernity

As a crusader for liberation Foucault stood at the end of a long line of politically engaged French intellectuals – from Voltaire to Émile Zola to Jean-Paul Sartre. Yet Foucault's strategy for resisting oppression was in stark contrast to that employed by previous generations. Thinkers steeped in the assumptions of Christianity and the eighteenth-century Enlightenment had typically appealed to universal categories in order to overthrow tyranny. The French Revolution's Declaration of the Rights of Man and Citizen (1789), for example, had insisted that the aim of every political association was to defend 'the natural, inalienable, and sacred rights of man'.

Postmodern thinkers like Foucault have major problems with this Enlightenment approach. They question the very existence of rights which are natural, inalienable and sacred. If one does not believe in a Creator God, they point out, it is hard to see how all people can be endowed with such natural rights. The nineteenth-century German philosopher, Friedrich Nietzsche – the grandfather of postmodernism – insisted that God was dead and that with him had died all notions of a universal human nature, or of absolute moral laws. These universals and absolutes were now exposed as mere human inventions. 'There are no moral facts whatever,' he declared. 'Moral judgement has this in common with religious judgement – that it believes in realities which do not exist.'[3]

In 1953 Foucault read Nietzsche for the first time, with 'a great passion'. He found Nietzsche's doctrines profoundly liberating, 'a revelation'. It occurred to Foucault that the moral and social 'truths' invoked in order to label him 'deviant' were mere fictions. There was no need to feel guilt over madness, homosexuality or suicidal tendencies. For the rest of his life, he would devote himself to showing how grand slogans and scientific terms were simply tools for legitimizing relationships of power and domination.

In *Madness and Civilisation*, for example, Foucault examined how during the Age of Reason the mad were confined in institutions, whereas previously they had roamed free and been viewed with a certain respect. This 'great confinement', he pointed out, was justified in the name of Reason and Humanity. Those who did not conform to the conventional notion of what was rational were labelled as 'mad', a supposedly value-neutral term, and then marginalized through incarceration. The noble 'truths' trumpeted by the Enlightenment were employed to legitimize the exercise of domination, not to prepare the way to a more humane, rational, benign and liberal society. In *Discipline and Punish* Foucault argued that the decline of torture and public execution and the rise of the prison was far from being a great moral advance. The modern prison, he suggested, does not simply work on people's bodies; it attempts to control their minds. Prisoners are categorized by experts, placed under surveillance, scrutinized and manipulated. Furthermore, he argued, the prison is a microcosm of modern society; we are all under surveillance, labelled and pigeon-holed by bureaucracies, and locked away if we are found to be deviant or abnormal.

The Response to Foucault

Foucault's protests meshed perfectly with the assumptions of a generation shaped by the counter-culture of the late 1960s and early 1970s. Conscious of Vietnam and Watergate, students were highly receptive to conspiracy theories featuring the oppressive power of the Establishment, and Foucault's ideas provided intellectual tools for radical new liberation movements. Most obviously, they were attractive to the burgeoning gay subculture. The universal norm of 'Nature' had been used in both Christian and Enlightenment discourse to brand the homosexual unnatural and perverse. Foucault claimed to unmask the universal norm as nothing more than a tool of oppression being wielded by the powerful. And in doing so he became one of the leading influences upon gay intellectuals and 'Queer Studies'.

Within mainstream intellectual culture, too, Foucault's work inspired extensive commentary. A decade after his death almost one hundred books have been published on his thought. Yet his provocative critique of modernity has not gone unchallenged. His critics argue that he oversimplifies complex developments, bases sweeping generalizations on slender evidence, and underestimates the great achievements of liberal democracies. They also complain that Foucault's work is riddled by internal contradictions. He attacks global norms such as Freedom and Justice, yet his protest against oppression implicitly assumes the very norms that he repudiates. He sets himself the task of unmasking truth-claims, yet he himself appears to be making truth-claims throughout his work. And although much of his thought presents the individual self as a passive victim of structural forces too powerful to resist, he also implies that liberation and self-creation are real possibilities.[4]

This final contradiction in Foucault's thinking seems all the more striking given what we now know about his own life. For as James Miller's recent book *The Passion of Michel Foucault* (1993) demonstrates, Foucault clearly thought of *himself* as an active agent, engaged in a personal project of turning his life into a unique work of art.

Foucault and Self-Creation

The Passion of Michel Foucault caused a storm of protest when it first appeared, for it focused on the most sensational aspects of Foucault's life. To some of Foucault's followers, Miller is a writer with an anti-Foucauldian agenda. Whereas Foucault spoke of the disappearance of the self, Miller places 'a persistent and purposeful self' at the centre of his biography. Whereas Foucault aimed to unmask truth-claims as fronts for power relations, Miller frankly asserts that he has 'tried to tell the whole truth, as best I could'. And whereas Foucault protested against the ways in which modern society categorized and scrutinized people, Miller places Foucault's life under surveillance and tries to make 'sense' of it.

Miller, however, is not so easy to dismiss. He clearly admires Foucault, and his argument is based on a wealth of documentation. His stress on the self and truth-telling, moreover, fits with Foucault's later emphasis on the obligation to tell 'the truth about oneself'. The renowned critic Edward Said spoke for many when he called Miller's book 'an essential companion to a reading of late twentieth-century Western culture'.[5]

What this 'essential companion' reveals is the centrality of the idea of self-creation in contemporary thought. If Nietzsche's iconoclastic attack on universal norms has given birth to postmodernist scepticism, its corollary – that one has to create one's own norms – is becoming almost equally influential. Since individuals have no obligation to conform to a pattern set in heaven, they are free to fashion themselves in whatever way they choose. One's nature and one's values are not given; they are invented. 'Let us,' Nietzsche urged his readers, 'be involved in the creation of our own new tables of values ... we want to be those who give themselves their own law, those who create themselves!' 'One thing is needed,' he declared, 'to give style to one's character – a great and rare art.' And the way to do this, he insisted, was by unlocking the 'Dionysian' element in one's personality – the wild, untamed, animal energy within, one's own personal *daimon*. 'Man needs what is most evil in him for what is best in him.' Only by exercising 'the will to power' could one discover transcendence.

In a 1983 interview, Foucault made it clear that he endorsed Nietzsche's views on self-creation. Sartre and California's New Agers had gone awry, he suggested, because they had introduced the notion of 'authenticity', implying that one had to be faithful to one's *true* self. In fact, there was nothing within or without to which one had to be true – self-creation had no such limits. It was about aesthetics, not morals; one's only concern should be to fashion a self that was 'a work of art'.

Like Nietzsche, Foucault believed that the tools for such self-fashioning were to be found in what he called 'limit experience'– experience of extremes which could release powerful creative forces and produce intense joy. His fascination with madness, death, violence, perversion and suicide was nourished by a conviction that these were not things to be ignored, cured or locked away, but creative phenomena to be released. His books were not simply negative critiques of oppression; they included an implicit challenge to liberate oneself by transgressing boundaries. *Madness and Civilisation*, for example, implied that the irrational side of the human personality should be explored rather than contained.

Foucault's Personal Quest

Foucault himself was committed to doing just this, and Miller calls his entire life 'a great Nietzschean quest'. As a student, his heroes were artists and philosophers fixated on the dark side of life. He decorated his room with Goya's etchings of the grotesque violence of war, and revered the avant-garde actor Antonin Artaud, whose 'theatre of cruelty' was marked by obscenity, glossolalia, rage and incoherent incantations. Foucault also immersed himself in the pornographic writings of the Marquis de Sade, who claimed that through sexual torture one could experience transfiguration.

In his own life, Foucault sought out limit experience. From the late 1960s to the mid-1970s he found them in the disorder produced by the riots of French students and the ultra-left. He maintained that 'the craving, the taste, the capacity, the possibility of an absolute sacrifice' on the part of a crowd led to 'shared rapture'. By the mid-1970s, however, he was becoming disillusioned by political violence, and disturbed by 'the fascism in all of us'. He began to experiment with a very different kind of limit experience. In 1975, on a visit to Death Valley, he took LSD for the first time, just as the sun was setting. The result was a kind of epiphany about which he enthused for years to come. Tears of joy poured down his face. 'The sky has exploded and the stars are raining down on me,' he told a companion. 'I am very happy.'

California in the mid-1970s was also the scene of Foucault's full-scale immersion in consensual sadomasochistic sex (S/M). He was teaching at the University of Berkeley and had easy access to the gay bars and bathhouses of San Francisco. For Foucault, this was the perfect opportunity to put into practice the theories of de Sade. In interviews with gay journalists, Foucault extolled the virtues of S/M. It was, he maintained, 'a kind of creation, a creative enterprise' in which participants invented new selves by exploring 'new possibilities of pleasure'.

If Foucault regarded the pain of S/M as somehow liberating, it is little wonder that he saw death in similar terms. When James Miller interviewed Foucault's lover, Daniel Defert, he was told that the philosopher 'took AIDS very seriously'. Yet Defert also claimed that 'when Foucault went to San Francisco for the last time, he took it as a limit-experience'. Miller concludes from this that 'given the circumstances in San Francisco in the fall of 1983, as best as I could reconstruct them, to have taken AIDS as a limit experience ... would have involved engaging in potentially suicidal acts of passion with consenting partners, most of them likely to be infected already. Deliberately throwing caution to the wind, Foucault and these men were wagering their lives together.'

In the light of Foucault's statements about death and suicide, this reconstruction seems highly plausible. 'To die for the love of boys. What could be more beautiful?' Foucault had once asked. 'One should work on one's suicide throughout one's life,' he stated on another occasion. By throwing himself with reckless abandon into the bathhouse scene when the spectre of AIDS was becoming clear, therefore, Foucault may have been trying to achieve a fitting climax to his life, one which fused his great obsessions: madness, perversion, torture and death. 'The path to one's own heaven,' as Nietzsche had remarked, 'always leads through the voluptuousness of one's own hell.' In June 1984, eight months after his final visit to San Francisco, Foucault died of AIDS.

Learning from Foucault

It would be easy at this point to dismiss Foucault with nothing more than a condemnation of his lifestyle. Christians will recall that Paul in Romans 1 identifies sexual depravity as a sign of human rebellion against God. But we are likely to forget that Paul goes on to assert that we are *all* depraved, every single one of us.[6] We may also forget that Jesus, who denounced sin in the most emphatic terms, befriended 'sinners' and exposed the hypocrisy of those who claimed to be righteous.[7] If we want to be faithful to Scripture, therefore, we must combine the call to repentance with a deep sense that we are sinners saved by grace. Moreover, if we want to understand contemporary culture we should be willing to think hard about Foucault's life and thought.

His *thought*, after all, may have some important things to teach us. His analysis of modern society is often profound and his critique of the Enlightenment's rationalistic hubris is one that Christians should welcome.[8] Moreover, his suspicion that truth-claims act as covers for oppression should alert us to the abuse of power by the church. High-sounding religious claims *can* be used to legitimate self-interest and domination – the theological case made for apartheid in South Africa provides a tragic example. Sensitized by

Foucault's critique, we should be driven back to the scriptural teaching that the church is not meant to conquer by worldly power or wisdom, but by proclaiming the 'foolish' message of a crucified God.[9] This message is certainly the truth, but it is truth that draws people in love and sets them free from a gnawing sense of guilt by enabling them to grow in Christ.[10]

Foucault's *life* may also have a great deal to tell us about contemporary culture. For while it is tempting to dismiss him as an extremist, his popularity suggests otherwise. Foucault has been terribly chic among students and intellectuals over the past two decades precisely because he articulated and personified their sensibilities. Like many others in the counter-culture, he was convinced that a new self could be created through experimentation with drugs and sex, flirtation with the non-rational, exploration of the body and its potentialities. In an age of drug-use, all-night raves, body-piercing and flexible sexuality, Foucault's life takes on considerable relevance. It suggests that there may be something more to this counter-culture than the mere search for a good time.

Idolatry and the Longing for God

Foucault's fascination with limit experience, after all, has an unmistakably theological dimension to it. Even the language of Foucault and his heroes borrows repeatedly from Christianity. One of his mentors, Georges Bataille, maintained that voluptuously painful eroticism made possible 'a negative theology founded on mystical experience'. When Foucault described the sexual experimentation of gay men he did so in frankly sacramental terms; he talked of 'a transubstantiation' of agony into ecstasy, 'an unholy communion' of bodies. He retained a lifelong interest in the demonic, and even talked of writing a book on the subject. He was also attracted to Christians like Saint Anthony, Pascal and Dostoyevsky, who stressed that the route to God lay through suffering and foolishness. He himself was, according to Miller, 'a kind of mystic'.

From a Christian point of view Foucault's atheistic mysticism is unsurprising, for we are fashioned in the divine image, created 'to glorify God and to enjoy him for ever' (Westminster Shorter Catechism). And it is because the human self can only find its true identity in relationship with a Triune God that those estranged from their Creator will continually experience a painful sense of unsatisfied longing.[11] As Augustine put it, God has made us for himself and our hearts are restless till they find their rest in him. Foucault's restlessness, his frenzied quest for transcendence, can be seen as a search for God in the wrong places.

The tragedy of Foucault's life was that he took for granted Nietzsche's brash announcement of the death of God. After reacting against a Catholic upbringing, he never thought of Christianity as a serious option. Nietzsche had once written, 'Have I been understood? Dionysius against the Crucified.' Foucault, unfortunately, understood all too well; when he experienced longing for God, he looked to the Dionysian impulses within, not to Jesus on the cross. Yet as the philosopher Roger Scruton has argued, Foucault was 'a sort of passionate heretic' among modern atheists, 'trying as it were, to use the numinosity of the irrational to plug the supposed gap left by the absent God'. Like the thousands of young people who seek a quasi-sacramental experience by sharing the drug Ecstasy at raves, Foucault was trying to find a substitute for true worship.

Augustine understood this phenomenon. In his *Confessions* he looked back on life before his conversion and realized that all along he had been searching unconsciously for God, even when he had entered a 'dark hell of illicit desire' in Carthage. 'I was looking for you,' Augustine confessed, 'by the sensations of the flesh.' Yet although he felt 'a hunger within' for God, he mistook the 'glittering phantasies' of the world for the Creator and turned to philosophy to justify his own estrangement from the Lord.

The Christian suspects that Foucault was doing something similar. For although he sought to demolish Enlightenment idols, he seems in the end to have slid into a form of self-deification, in which care and devotion were lavished on the self rather than on the Creator. His mentor, Nietzsche, was frank about his own idolatry. 'Let me reveal my heart to you entirely, my friends: if there were gods, how could I endure not to be a god? Hence there are no gods.' For Nietzsche God was a rival, an impediment to his own autonomy. God must be killed if the individual self was to reign.[12] For Foucault the situation was more poignant. His life was devoted not to killing God, but to filling the terrible vacuum left by God's apparent death. His idolatry, like that of the people of Athens in Acts 17, probably arose as much from ignorance and a deep sense of emptiness as from the desire to be autonomous.

Yet like the young Augustine, Foucault was engaged in intellectual self-justification. By portraying the self as a prisoner of society, his writings made it possible to legitimize promiscuity, political violence and sadomasochism as strategies of liberation. For Christians, this is a reminder that our fallenness affects our minds as much as our wills and passions.[13] If appeals to Truth, Justice and Human Nature can mask power bids, then sophisticated intellectual argument can mask rebellion against God. Insofar as Foucault's thought was an attempt to do this, it presents us with a tragic case of self-deception.

Foucault, of course, would have regarded this interpretation of his life as the tool of those determined to condemn and manipulate him, rather than as the truth spoken in love to set him free. But did he begin to feel in his dying days that he had taken the wrong path 'to his own heaven'? James Miller thinks not. He paints an upbeat portrait of Foucault facing death bravely, his life's work successfully completed. Yet the reality may have been much grimmer. Foucault's friend, Hervé Guibert, later wrote a book about how Foucault and a group of gay friends in Paris coped with the coming of AIDS. According to one reviewer,

> Guibert gives a much more painful account of Foucault's mental deterioration and confusion than does Miller, and paints a perfectly horrible picture of the bodily torment of the last few weeks. Worse perhaps, Guibert quotes Foucault saying of his impending death: 'You always think that in a certain kind of situation you'll find something to say about it, and now it turns out there's nothing to say after all.'[14]

1 Foucault's engagement with religion has now been explored in J. Carette, *Foucault and Religion* (Routledge, 1999) and J. Carette (ed.), *Religion and Culture by Michel Foucault* (Manchester University Press, 1999).

2 The best 'way in' to Foucault's thought is through *The Foucault Reader* (Penguin, London, 1991). Quotations are taken from there and from J. Miller, *The Passion of Michel Foucault* (HarperCollins, London, 1993).

3 Nietzsche is quoted from Miller and from *A Nietzsche Reader* (Penguin, 1977).

4 For critiques of Foucault see D. C. Hoy (ed.), *Foucault: A Critical Reader* (Polity Press, 1986); and P. Burke (ed.), *Michel Foucault: Critical Perspectives* (Scolar Press, 1992).

5 For various views on Miller's work see 'A symposium on James Miller's *The Passion of Michel Foucault*', *Salmagundi*, vol. 97, pp. 29–99 (1993). For a critique of Miller see D. Halperin, *Saint Foucault:Towards a Gay Hagiography* (Oxford University Press, New York, 1996).

6 Romans 3:9–20.

7 Matthew 5:27–30; 9:9–13; Luke 18:9–14; John 8:2–11.

8 A brilliant example of Christian interaction with Foucault's work is David Lyon's book, *The Electronic Eye:The Rise of the Surveillance Society* (Polity Press, 1994).

9 2 Corinthians 10:1–4; 1 Corinthians 1:18–31.

10 John 8:32. For further Christian reflections on this see A. Thiselton, *Interpreting God and the Postmodern Self: On Meaning, Manipulation and Promise* (T & T Clark, 1995).

11 See Chapter 1.

12 See B. Ingraffia, *Postmodern Theory and Biblical Theology* (Cambridge University Press, 1995), pp. 96–7.

13 See Romans 1:21; Colossians 1:21.

14 A. Ryan, 'Foucault's life and hard times', *The NewYork Review of Books*, 8 April 1993, p. 17.The English translation of Guibert's novel is entitled *To the FriendWho Did Not Save My Life* (Quartet, 1991).

THE CONTRIBUTORS

Dr Denis Alexander is Chairman of the Molecular Immunology Programme at The Babraham Institute, Cambridge, and Fellow of St Edmund's College. He was previously at the Imperial Cancer Research Fund Laboratories in London and Associate Professor of Biochemistry at the American University of Beirut, Lebanon. Dr Alexander is the author of the book *Beyond Science* and has published numerous papers and reviews. He is the editor of the journal *Science and Christian Belief*, serves on the committee of Christians in Science and lectures widely on the subject of science and faith.

Dr John Coffey trained as an historian at Cambridge University. His research is on Puritanism and religious and political thought in the seventeenth century. He is the author of *Politics, Religion and the British Revolutions: The Mind of Samuel Rutherford* (Cambridge University Press, 1997), and has just completed *Persecution and Toleration in Protestant England, 1558–1689* (Longman, forthcoming). He is a lecturer in history at Leicester University.

Dr Mark E. Dever has his PhD from Cambridge, where he resided from 1988 to 1994. He served there as an elder (1990–94) and associate pastor (1992–94). He has since 1994 been the pastor of the Capitol Hill Baptist Church, Washington DC. He is the author of *Nine Marks of a Healthy Church* (Crossway, 2000), and of the forthcoming book *Richard Sibbes* (Mercer University Press, 2000).

Ranald Macaulay read law at Cambridge. While there he met Francis and Edith Schaeffer who had recently started the L'Abri Fellowship in Switzerland. After working with them for four years, he completed a theology degree at Kings' College, London in 1968. Shortly afterwards he and his family moved to Hampshire to start a L'Abri community and study centre. He co-authored the book *Being Human* (IVP, 1978, republished Solway, 1996). He is still engaged in the work of L'Abri but now lives in Cambridge.

Dr Paul Mills graduated in economics at Cambridge University and worked as a researcher at the Jubilee Centre for a year before returning to the University. Having completing his PhD in economics, he now works as an economist at the newly created Debt Management Office, an agency of the Treasury. He has co-authored *Islamic Finance: Theory and Practice* (Macmillan, 1999).

Michael Ovey qualified as a lawyer and worked in Whitehall drafting government legislation. After training at Ridley Hall, Cambridge, he served as a curate at All Saints' Church, Crowborough. Having taught Christian doctrine and philosophy at Moore College, Sydney, while also doing research on John's Gospel, he is currently the Kingham Hill Research Fellow at Oak Hill Theological College.

Julian Rivers studied law at the Universities of Cambridge and Göttingen and now lectures in law at Bristol University. He specializes in constitutional law and legal philosophy, but also has interests in comparative, international and ecclesiastical law. He has written several articles and contributed chapters to *Christian Perspectives on Law Reform* (Paternoster, 1998), *Law and Religion* (Ashgate, 2000) and *Christian Perspectives on the Limits of Law* (Paternoster, 2000).

Dr Michael Schluter is the founder and director of the Jubilee Centre, a Christian research group based in Cambridge. He is also director of the Keep Sunday Special Campaign and the Relationships Foundation. He has a PhD in agricultural economics from Cornell University and worked in East Africa for six years as a consultant for the World Bank. Dr Schluter co-authored *The R Factor* (Hodder & Stoughton, 1993) and contributed chapters to *Relational Justice* (Waterside Press, 1994), *Building a Relational Society*

(Ashgate, 1996) and *Christian Perspectives on Relationism and Law* (Paternoster, 2000).

Christopher Townsend read economics at Cambridge University and now works as a solicitor, specializing in corporate tax law. He has previously spent four years at the Jubilee Centre, assisting the Keep Sunday Special Campaign, and examining biblical and theological issues underlying the Centre's work. He co-authored *Political Christians in a Plural Society* (Jubilee Centre, 1994) and contributed to *Relational Justice* (Waterside Press, 1994).

Dr Peter Walker read Classics at Cambridge and then pursued doctoral studies on Constantinian Jerusalem. He was in pastoral ministry for four years before returning to Cambridge as a Research Fellow at Tyndale House. He now teaches New Testament at Wycliffe Hall, Oxford. Since 1981 he has made frequent visits to Jerusalem, which have led to the writing and editing of various books, including *Holy City, Holy Places?* (Oxford, 1990), *Jesus and the Holy City: NT Perspectives on Jerusalem* (Eerdmans, 1996) and *The Weekend that Changed the World* (HarperCollins, 1999).

CAMBRIDGE PAPERS
How to become a subscriber

The aim of *Cambridge Papers* is to make clear the relevance of biblical teaching to a range of contemporary issues. Written from a Christian perspective, each Paper presents a concise and carefully argued case relating to an important topic, assisting reflection on the implications of a Christian worldview and intended to prompt further discussion. A wide range of issues is addressed, including controversial and neglected topics, as the contents of *Christianity in a Changing World* illustrates.

Papers are produced once a quarter, each about 4000 (or occasionally 6000) words in length, a format designed with the needs of busy Christians in mind. The Writing Group includes academics and professionals with diverse backgrounds and areas of specialist knowledge who collaborate in the preparation of each Paper by subjecting successive drafts to critical scrutiny. The ambition of *Cambridge Papers* is to make a strategic contribution to debate in Christian circles and in the public square at a time of rapid social and cultural change.

Cambridge Papers is a non-profit making, quarterly publication. Income from subscriptions is used for production, administration and distribution costs. Any surplus income is used to extend the readership to as wide an audience as possible.

If you would like to subscribe to *Cambridge Papers* you can obtain a subscription form:

- by visiting the *Cambridge Papers* website at http://www.campublic.co.uk/cpapers
- by requesting one:
  by e-mail on cpapers@campublic.co.uk
  by telephone/fax on +44(0) 1223 501631
  by writing to Cambridge Papers, PO Box 27, Cambridge CB8 1TR, UK